The Provincial Fiction of Mitford, Gaskell and Eliot

Nineteenth-Century and Neo-Victorian Cultures
Series editors: Ruth Heholt and Joanne Ella Parsons

Recent books in the series
Domestic Architecture, Literature and the Sexual Imaginary in Europe, 1850–1930
Aina Martí-Balcells

Assessing Intelligence: The Bildungsroman and the Politics of Human Potential in England, 1860–1910
Sara Lyons

The Idler's Club: Humour and Mass Readership from Jerome K. Jerome to P. G. Wodehouse
Laura Fiss

Michael Field's Revisionary Poetics
Jill Ehnenn

The Provincial Fiction of Mitford, Gaskell and Eliot
Kevin A. Morrison

Forthcoming
Lost and Revenant Children 1850–1940
Tatiana Kontou

Olive Schreiner and the Politics of Print Culture, 1883–1920
Clare Gill

Literary Illusions: Performance Magic and Victorian Literature
Christopher Pittard

Pastoral in Early-Victorian Fiction: Environment and Modernity
Mark Frost

Spectral Embodiments of Child Death in the Long Nineteenth Century
Jen Baker

Women's Activism in the Transatlantic Consumers' Leagues, 1885–1920
Flore Janssen

Life Writing and the Nineteenth-Century Market
Sean Grass

British Writers, Popular Literature and New Media Innovation, 1820–45
Alexis Easley

Oscar Wilde's Aesthetic Plagiarisms
Sandra Leonard

Reading Victorian Sculpture
Angela Dunstan

Mind and Embodiment in Late Victorian Literature
Marion Thain and Atti Viragh

Drunkenness in Eighteenth and Nineteenth-Century Irish Literature
Lucy Cogan

Philanthropy in Children's Periodicals, 1840–1930: The Charitable Child
Kristine Moruzi

Narrative, Affect and Victorian Sensation: Wilful Bodies
Tara MacDonald

Violence and the Brontës: Language, Reception, Afterlives
Sophie Franklin

The British Public and the British Museum: Shaping and Sharing Knowledge in the Nineteenth-Century
Jordan Kistler

The Provincial Fiction of Mitford, Gaskell and Eliot

Kevin A. Morrison

EDINBURGH
University Press

Edinburgh University Press is one of the leading university presses in the UK. We publish academic books and journals in our selected subject areas across the humanities and social sciences, combining cutting-edge scholarship with high editorial and production values to produce academic works of lasting importance. For more information visit our website: edinburghuniversitypress.com

© Kevin A. Morrison 2023

Edinburgh University Press Ltd
The Tun – Holyrood Road
12(2f) Jackson's Entry
Edinburgh EH8 8PJ

Typeset in 11/13pt Sabon
by Cheshire Typesetting Ltd, Cuddington, Cheshire, and
printed and bound in Great Britain

A CIP record for this book is available from the British Library

ISBN 978 1 3995 1608 2 (hardback)
ISBN 978 1 3995 1610 5 (webready PDF)
ISBN 978 1 3995 1611 2 (epub)

The right of Kevin A. Morrison to be identified as the author of this work has been asserted in accordance with the Copyright, Designs and Patents Act 1988, and the Copyright and Related Rights Regulations 2003 (SI No. 2498).

Contents

	List of Illustrations	vi
	Acknowledgements	viii
	Series Preface	xi
	Introduction: The Politics of Provincial Fiction	1
1.	Sketches of Rural Character: Mary Russell Mitford's 'Fugitive Pieces'	30
2.	Sketches of Rural Scenery: Mitford's Country Rambles	76
3.	From Sketches to Papers: Gaskell's Country Village	122
4.	Landscape-Shaped Subjectivity: George Eliot's 'Mother Tongue'	171
5.	A Wider Horizon: Portable Interiority and Provincial Life	223
	Conclusion	272
	Bibliography	277
	Index	300

Illustrations

Figures

I.1	'Country Pictures'. Illustration by Hugh Thomson	21
I.2	Mary Russell Mitford watering her flowers. Illustration by Hugh Thomson	22
1.1	Mitford's cottage at Three Mile Cross, Berkshire. Unknown artist	32
1.2	Mary Russell Mitford. Illustration from a portrait by A. Burt	68
1.3	Fashion plate from the *Lady's Magazine* (January 1831)	69
1.4	Fashion plate from the *Lady's Magazine* (August 1831)	70
2.1	Mary Russell Mitford with Mayflower. Illustration by Hugh Thomson	77
2.2	'Bean-setting'. Illustration by Hugh Thomson	99
2.3	Mary Russell Mitford among her violets. Illustration by Hugh Thomson	100
2.4	'Grazing under the tall elms'. Illustration by Hugh Thomson	113
3.1	Miss Matty in her tea shop. Illustration by Hugh Thomson	132
3.2	Heading to Chapter One of *Cranford*. Illustration by Hugh Thomson	133
3.3	Miss Matty in a state of surprise. Illustration by Hugh Thomson	134
3.4	Elizabeth Gaskell. Chalk portrait by George Richmond	135

3.5	Miss Matty's brother, Peter, and their father. Illustration by Hugh Thomson	136
3.6	Signor Brunoni. Illustration by Hugh Thomson	137
3.7	Landscape scene. Illustration by Hugh Thomson	138
3.8	Cover page of the 1853 edition of *Cranford*	145
4.1	Cover of the third stereotyped edition of *The Mill on the Floss* (1867) featuring Dorlcote Mill. Illustration by E.M.W. Engraved by James Cooper	174
4.2	'It was one of their happy mornings'. Illustration by W. J. Allen. Engraved by James Cooper	197
5.1	Cover of *Middlemarch* (1871–72 parts publication). Illustration by Myles Birket Foster. Engraved by C. Jeens	241
5.2	Cover vignette of *Middlemarch*, cheap edition, 1874. Illustration by Myles Birket Foster	242
5.3	Illustration of Casaubon and Dorothea by an unknown artist, 1888	243
6.1	George Eliot. Chalk portrait by Sir Frederic William Burton, 1865	275

Table

2.1	A selection of articles published in *Lady's Magazine*, 1823–24	82

Acknowledgements

It is a pleasure to recognise the friends, colleagues, acquaintances and institutions whose various forms of assistance have made this book possible. Jill Delsigne, Victoria Ford Smith, Jeffrey E. Jackson, Kara Marler-Kennedy, Jennifer McDonell, Frederick Burwick, Alvin Snider, Lisa Surridge, Mary Elizabeth Leighton, Judith Mitchell, and various reviewers for the journals in which portions of this study originally appeared commented on individual chapters. Linda H. Peterson, Donald E. Hall, Dennis Denisoff and Christopher Keep offered early encouragement to further develop the ideas contained in Chapter Four. Logan Browning, Robert L. Patten, Colene Bentley, Helena Michie and Elizabeth K. Helsinger read multiple versions of several chapters and provided exacting and stimulating feedback. As I neared the finish line, Andrew Daily read a complete draft of the manuscript and helped me to see the forest through the trees. I am very grateful to them all.

I had the good fortune to complete the bulk of the manuscript while serving as the Lynn Wood Neag Distinguished Visiting Professor of British Literature at the University of Connecticut's Department of English during the spring 2020 semester. I am grateful to the department for their invitation to spend a semester in residence and to Bob Hasenfratz, Fred Biggs, Clare Costley King'oo, Gregory Semenza, Victoria Ford Smith and Dwight Codr for extending such a warm welcome. While I was in Storrs, a coronavirus pandemic (COVID-19) was declared, and worldwide travel bans made a return to China, where I currently live and work, impossible. UConn permitted me and my family to stay in a campus residence for a year and very generously ensured that I had uninterrupted access to electronic resources and – when mitigation efforts permitted – the stacks at Homer Babbidge Library. Without this assistance, the book simply could not have been written in a timely way.

The Armstrong Browning Library at Baylor University, Waco, Texas, invited me to spend a month as a visiting scholar to work on an entirely different project. Owing to the pandemic, I took up the fellowship a year later. When I discovered that the ABL had in its possession many of the materials I needed to finish this manuscript, the director, Jennifer Borderud, very graciously allowed me to shift my focus in order to bring this project to completion. Great thanks to Jennifer Borderud, Laura French and Christi Klempnauer for providing all manner of support and to Joshua King and Jennifer Hargrave for intellectual camaraderie.

Librarians and archivists at the British Library, London; Babbidge Library, the University of Connecticut; the Zimmerman Library, University of New Mexico; Central Library, the National University of Singapore; Houghton Library, Harvard University; the John Rylands Research Institute and Library, Manchester; Reading Central Library, Reading; the Huntington Library, San Marino; the Portico Library, Manchester; the Shakespeare Birthplace Trust; Keele University Library, Keele; Wedgwood Museum, Stoke-on-Trent facilitated access to needed materials.

I returned to Edinburgh University Press for this project because of the professionalism, diligence and dedication of its editorial staff. In particular, I thank Michelle Houston for securing such wonderful readers of the proposal and manuscript, and Emily Sharp for shepherding the project to completion. I am grateful to the reviewers for their engagement and many helpful suggestions.

I have been thinking and writing about the provincial fiction of Mitford, Gaskell and Eliot for more than twenty years. Throughout the past two decades, my mom, Gayle Morrison, has been an indispensable interlocutor and editor. My dad, Gary L. Morrison, continues to take an avid interest in everything I write or teach. Other family members, including Jennifer, Justin and Kieron Chapa; Jean, Michael and Cole Thompson; and Betty Fisher and Jack Bowers have all aided my efforts to complete this project – from offering us a place to stay to providing childcare to shipping us gifts to keep the kids entertained on long-haul trips. Audrey, Camden and Dorothea would have probably preferred a settled life in a village to the departure lounges in Shanghai

Pudong and Heathrow Terminal 5; nondescript hotel rooms in cities we never have time to properly visit; and overpriced takeaways. Nevertheless, as this project has taken me to London (too many times to count), Storrs, Waco, Los Angeles, Shanghai and Cambridge, Massachusetts, we have managed to always find a way to be together. Owing to the pandemic, Franklin and Wylie have enjoyed a more settled existence! This book is dedicated to Audrey, whose support, inspiration and love makes all things possible.

Portions of this book draw on previously published material. I am grateful to the following journals for permission to reproduce these essays in different form: 'Modulating Narrative Voice: Mary Russell Mitford's Sketches of Rural Character', *Women's Writing*, 22.4 (2015): 505–524; 'Foregrounding Nationalism: Mary Russell Mitford's *Our Village* and the Effects of Publication Context', *European Romantic Review* 19.3 (2008): 275–87; '"The Mother Tongue of Our Imagination": George Eliot, Landscape-Shaped Subjectivity, and the Possibility of Social Inclusion', *Victorian Review: An Interdisciplinary Journal of Victorian Studies* 34.1 (2008): 83–100; and 'Cultural Embeddedness, Gendered Exclusions: The Symbolic Landscapes of *Middlemarch*', *Victorians Institute Journal* 39 (2011): 317–35.

Series Editors' Preface

This interdisciplinary series provides space for full and detailed scholarly discussions on nineteenth-century and Neo-Victorian cultures. Drawing on radical and cutting-edge research, volumes explore and challenge existing discourses, as well as providing an engaging reassessment of the time period. The series encourages debates about decolonising nineteenth-century cultures, histories, and scholarship, as well as raising questions about diversities. Encompassing art, literature, history, performance, theatre studies, film and TV studies, medical and the wider humanities, *Nineteenth Century and Neo-Victorian Cultures* is dedicated to publishing pioneering research that focuses on the Victorian era in its broadest and most diverse sense.

Ruth Heholt and Joanne Ella Parsons

Introduction: The Politics of Provincial Fiction

Although Mary Russell Mitford, Elizabeth Gaskell and George Eliot were near contemporaries, spanning two generations, and were celebrated for their representations of rural life, the three authors have never been extensively studied together.[1] Readers often considered that the authors' glimpses of rural life were based on their individual experiences, and their works were marketed accordingly. Yet when Elizabeth Gaskell undertook in 1851 to write the literary sketches for *Household Words: A Weekly Journal Conducted by Charles Dickens* that would later appear as *Cranford* (1853), she looked to Mitford. In *Our Village* (1824–32) Mitford established the prototype of a new genre to which many writers throughout the century attributed aspects of their craft. In turn, when Mary Ann (or, alternatively, Marian) Evans – who had been a journalist, translator and editor – tried her hand at fiction, the future George Eliot drew inspiration from *Cranford* and from the thematic and formal techniques of both Gaskell and Mitford.

Tracing this chain of influence, *The Provincial Fiction of Mitford, Gaskell and Eliot* shows how, for all three writers, a sense place drives cultural, social and political thought. It also demonstrates that Mitford, Gaskell and Eliot, whose representations of place have often been employed in service to projects of restorative nostalgia that seek to reconstruct the present in the image of the past, worked within a reflective strain that accepted the pastness of the past and embraced, however reluctantly and wistfully, change.[2] I consider the challenges the three authors encountered in achieving distinction as writers of provincial fiction within the literary sphere, including the various pressures exerted on them by publishers, reviewers and editors. I also analyse the

I

possibilities afforded by different modes of publication – including periodicals, anthologies, the one-volume novel, the three-volume novel, and monthly and bimonthly instalments – as well as their concomitant limitations. In so doing, the book offers a reassessment of Mitford's and Gaskell's provincial fiction, which has been frequently derided as a 'minor literature'. It also demonstrates the importance of their work to the development of Eliot's liberalism in the age of high realism. Indeed, Eliot's fictional villages, so often associated with traditionalism or pastoralism, were, in fact, a central element of her liberalism. In the provincial village, Eliot found a means of thinking through one's reciprocal responsibilities and obligations as a member of a liberal polity; and in the countryside, she found an alternative to either the proprietary or the rational, dialogic models of citizenship promulgated by many of her contemporaries.

Provincial writing from Mitford to Eliot

The question of one writer's influence on another is always vexed. In 1973 Harold Bloom put forth his thesis that new poems are derived from older poems. The young emerging writer of poetry attempts to escape the anxiety of influence and 'clear imaginative space' for oneself by creatively misreading or significantly reworking earlier poems (Bloom 1997: 1). In Bloom's terms, only those poets who surpass or undo the work of writers who precede them achieve greatness. Although many scholars have subsequently engaged, not uncritically, with this notion of influence, others have questioned the value of such a concept. Certainly, proving one writer's direct impact on another, supported by indisputable biographical evidence, is often difficult, if not impossible. But insofar as influence is 'an author-centered and evaluative concept', interest in its study waned as the notion of 'author as agent' was displaced in the 1980s (Clayton and Rothstein 1991: 5, 11). Discussing connections between Emmanuel Levinas and Ludwig Feuerbach in *Writing and Difference*, first published in 1978, Jacques Derrida proposes the term 'convergences' rather than 'influences' because, in his estimation, 'the latter is a notion whose philosophical meaning is not clear' (Derrida 2021: 111). By the 1990s, the study of literary influence had given way to the analysis of intertextual connections: similarities, resemblances and correspondences between works.[3]

Because this book is a contribution to the nineteenth-century history of authorship, it is informed by biographical considerations and deploys a notion of influence. As Susan Stanford Friedman has noted, '[b]iography has traditionally been an important methodological tool in the study of influence, often essential to the documentation of the author's intention and knowledge of a precursor or preexisting source' (Friedman 1991: 151). Although I work with the concept of influence and the biographical material on which it rests, I am as interested in the determinative material conditions of the literary marketplace, the constraints and possibilities of the genre of provincial fiction, and the circumstances of the literary field into which Mitford, Gaskell and Eliot respectively entered as I am in simple biographical explanation.

Of the three writers considered in this book, George Eliot has been extensively studied in relationship to contemporary as well as historical writers and intellectuals. Most of these analyses avoid the question of influence.[4] Indeed, although Gaskell was influenced by Mitford and Eliot was influenced by Gaskell, only a small number of scholars who work on the subgenre of the novel known as provincialism have considered the affinities and resemblances among all three writers. By distinguishing the categories of regional and provincial fiction and suggesting that the two are dialectically interrelated, Ian Duncan has offered the most influential definition of the genre. For Duncan, provincial fiction is the conservative counterpart to the more forward-looking regional novel. He writes: 'Regional fiction specifies its setting by invoking a combination of geographical, natural-historical, antiquarian, ethnographic, and/or sociological features that *differentiate it from any other region*' (Duncan 2002: 322; emphasis his). The places depicted in regional fiction are 'tied to a real historical geography, locatable on the map' (2002: 323). With their own identities and meanings, the settings for Romantic-era Irish and Scottish fiction are qualitatively distinct from the nation against which they are defined. By contrast, Duncan continues, the locales of provincial fiction are wholly within the nation, rather than on its periphery, and are defined in opposition to urban centres. They are 'not London (or, secondarily, not Edinburgh or Manchester)'. The sense of distance from metropolitan environments is archetypal. It is a measurement of 'alterity' rather than geography. In these works, moreover, provincial life 'assumes the burden of national representation' (2002: 322). Because they possess fictional names, these provincial locales have only 'tenuous associations' to real places, which 'are sustained by biography and tourism, rather than by the fiction itself' (2002: 323). Thus, the villages and towns of provincial fiction are generic and, therefore, interchangeable.

In Duncan's account of provincial fiction, the genre is static and nostalgic. It originates as a 'minor literature', he argues, in *Our Village* (2002: 329). Mitford's work establishes many of the tropes on which provincialism depends, including the presentation of the village – modelled on Three Mile Cross, Berkshire, where she spent much of her adult life – as secluded ('a little world of our own'), compact ('I like a confined locality'), traversable ('will you walk with me'), easily apprehended ('where we know every one, and are known to every one') and unchanging ('a trick of standing still'). Focusing on Mitford's presentation of her semi-fictional village as a site of remarkable seclusion, Duncan argues that provincial writing resists change by denying its own historicity. Mitford can, therefore, present her village as 'disconnected from a global historical economy and its transforming pressures'. It exists 'outside history, out of the world' (2002: 329).

By the middle of the nineteenth century, Duncan acknowledges, provincial fiction no longer denied historical change. Combining 'an earlier, minor and idyllic provincialism with the critical ambition of national representation', these works, including Gaskell's *Cranford* and Eliot's *Middlemarch*, aim 'to domesticate history as a manageable, orderly, morally accountable process' (2002: 331). Although the provincial locale remains defined in its opposition to the city, its generic status allows it to be read as the 'typical setting of a traditional England, responsive to the pressures of modernity (politics, debt, fashion, crime) that have overwhelmed metropolitan life, but resisting or absorbing them' (2002: 323). By incorporating change, the provincial locale restores and revivifies rather than abandons its traditional characteristics.

For Franco Moretti and John Plotz, the provincial novel's indifference to wider geography is displaced by its keen attention to the spatial distribution of each element in its fictional world – for example, the distance of the village to town or the proximity of the manor house to the labourer's cottage. Moretti, whose cartographic project to map the nineteenth-century literary novel was stymied by provincial fiction, concludes that the disavowal of historical geography underscores the essential lack of the sites represented. The provinces, he argues, 'are "negative" entities, defined by what is not there'. This explains 'why one cannot map provincial novels – you cannot map what is not there' (Moretti 2005: 53). If provincial fiction eludes geographic knowability, Moretti continues, the locations it represents are nevertheless diagrammable in terms of their distance from each other.

Plotz acknowledges that the logic of the diagram is a distinguishing characteristic of provincial fiction. In fact, the genre's refusal of geographic specificity and its embrace of a compact world amenable to diagramming is precisely what rendered it commercially successful. Provincial fiction was one of the items carried by itinerants, settlers, sojourners and migrants as they move from one location to another (Plotz 2008: 1–23). Its depictions of 'a readily generalizable English setting' aided in the process of relocation by suggesting that place itself is moveable (2008: 75). Although individual villages and towns in provincial fiction may have some distinctive qualities, these are 'never presented as an impediment to the act of metonymy' that enables its fictional world to stand 'in for English country living as a whole' (2008: 75). Thus, the provincial novel does not seek to assert the 'triumph of the local over the cosmopolitan' but instead 'to locate its inhabitants at once in a trivial (but chartable) Nowheresville and in a universal (but strangely ephemeral) everywhere' (2018: 102). The significance of diagrammatic logic to the genre calls attention to another, just as vital, facet that cannot be managed diagrammatically: 'even the most seemingly sedentary provincial worlds always contain linkages to a greater world beyond' (2018: 105).

In a series of compelling essays, Josephine McDonagh has likewise shown that since its inception in *Our Village*, provincial fiction is far more engaged with modernity than Duncan's account admits. For her, the province is represented 'less as an outpost than as a miniaturized version of the nation' (McDonagh 2012: 370). In addition to serving as a means to imagine the nation, it is also a symbolic reminder of a displaced past (2016). Unfolding coevally with my own earlier reassessments of Mitford's and Eliot's villages,[5] McDonagh has demonstrated that provincial writing consistently evinces its awareness of the wider developments of which it is a part. Yet, it simultaneously depicts the province as self-sufficient.

McDonagh's essays complicate understandings of provincial fiction in two additional ways. First, she asserts that provincial writing emerged from periodical print culture. By contrast,

Duncan – whose publication dates for *Our Village* and *Cranford* occludes their origins in magazines and annuals – accords primacy of place to books. Second, McDonagh contends, provincial fiction is 'closely and specifically aligned to women's writing' (2016: 401). At the heart of her argument is an understanding of provincial fiction as a mechanism that enabled women to reimagine their socially marginal positions. The village story that Mary Russell Mitford inaugurates, therefore, held 'special currency for women writers' as a mode that draws its 'pace and rhythm from social life outside the capital, where women typically flourish' (2018: 126). This mode, as it evolved from the village tale to episodic novel and then to the weighty and intricately plotted realist novel, connects Mitford, Gaskell and Eliot. Or as Plotz, who also shares this view, puts it: provincial writing 'is built around the significantly insignificant life, a life worth remarking on because it is invisible' (Plotz 2018: 111).

Yet what eludes many of these studies is a rigorous engagement with form and context. Duncan ignores the distinctions among different types of provincial fiction entirely. Although McDonagh indicates that magazines, newspapers and other periodicals were significant in producing provincial fiction, she has little to say about the genre's emergence in the literary sketch. Indeed, she tends to use the terms *tale* and *sketch* interchangeably. But to the extent that the tale is plotted and emphasises continuous temporal movement, this is an inapt descriptor of Mitford's writings – on which I will shortly elaborate. Plotz is perhaps the most attentive to the proliferation of fictional forms at the genre's inception, including the sketch, tale, short story and, of course, the novel (2018: 19–47). However, he does not ask why, on its emergence, provincial fiction assumed the form of the sketch or, for that matter, how they were conditioned by the medium of the periodical in which they first appeared.

Although publishing was an industry dominated by men for much of the nineteenth century, periodicals served as an important site for the emergence of women as professional writers. As Linda H. Peterson has shown, the burgeoning periodicals of the early nineteenth century both greatly expanded the type of material available to women as readers as well as enabled them to pursue careers. 'Most studies of professional authorship have omitted women from consideration, especially at its inception [in the 1820s and 1830s]', she writes, 'assuming that women ... were largely excluded from periodical writing because of their sex, or that they did not seek (or publicly acknowledge) professional status as it would undermine social respectability' (Peterson 2009: 13–14). Whereas Peterson focuses broadly on models of female authorship in the nineteenth century, others, including Alexis Easley (2004) and Katherine D. Harris (2015), have concentrated on specific modes of authorship and particular venues of publication. Easley examines the relationship between unsigned periodical journalism and signed book authorship in order to show how women writers exploited various publishing conventions to carve out professional paths for themselves. In her account of the literary annual, Harris has shown how crucial the genre was in elevating women's position in the profession. 'Initially published in duodecimo or octavo sizes, the decoratively bound volumes', she notes of the miscellanies, which entered the literary marketplace in 1822 and lasted through to 1860, 'exuded a feminine delicacy that attracted a primarily female readership that participated in the production and evolution of the Poetess Tradition' (Harris 2015: 1–2). But although poetry was a crucial feature of literary annuals, they offered much else besides, including short stories, dramatic scenes and travel writing – and, therefore, a range of opportunities for aspiring writers (Harris 2015: 20).[6] To the extent that provincial fiction is 'closely and specifically aligned to women's writing', monthlies and quarterlies, literary annuals, as well as Christmas books and gift books, were all crucial sites for its emergence.

These new (or increasingly accessible) venues for publication provided women writers with opportunities for remuneration and, in some cases, to achieve fame. Nancy Henry has recently argued that attending to the financial histories of women, as she does with several notable writers of fiction, enables one to recast 'the trajectories of women's lives as a set of financial events, conditions, and decisions, which are at least as important as the parallel domestic landmarks of marriage and childbirth' (Henry 2018: 4). For her part, Henry focuses on women writers who were also investors in the nineteenth-century British economy. Through their investments in publicly traded companies, Gaskell and Eliot, among others, 'could participate in local, parochial, national, and global economies' (2018: 6). Their participation in cultures of investing had important implications for their fiction, where aspects of these economies appear explicitly or implicitly throughout their *oeuvres*. While I do not examine this aspect of Mitford, Gaskell or

Eliot's careers, I do consider how, especially in the case of Mitford, financial considerations determined, to a considerable extent, the genres in which one worked and the modes of publication for which one advocated.

Sketch, papers, novel

Mitford's rise to fame as the pre-eminent writer of sketches about village life was in no way inevitable. She started out as a poet before attempting to establish herself as a playwright and literary critic. Encountering a series of obstacles present for many women who aspired to be writers, Mitford ultimately found unanticipated success by drawing on established precedents in writing the village sketch. These irregularly published, largely descriptive pieces are something of a hybrid. In considering the local customs, characteristics and setting of a rural hamlet, the sketches appropriate aspects of the novel of manners as well as contemporaneous works of natural history, but they also resemble the informal and unceremonious style of the periodical essay that Charles Lamb and William Hazlitt were refining at the same moment (Morrison 2012).

Reflecting Mitford's interest in non-narrative forms, such as the essay and the letter, most of *Our Village* is plotless. It largely consists of narratorial judgements, asides and digressive descriptions of people and place. Thus, the chief appeal of her sketches is their distinctive narratorial voice, which assumes an easy familiarity with the reader. Besides an exhaustively described shared locality, this voice provides the non-narrative interconnectedness among Mitford's sketches.

Beginning in 1822, Mitford published her sketches anonymously or pseudo-anonymously. Within two years, however, she developed a practice of writing village sketches for periodicals and literary annuals before subsequently collecting her pieces and publishing them in anthologies. The five biennial volumes entitled *Our Village* – with the subtitles *Sketches of Rural Character and Scenery* (1824, 1826, 1830, 1832) and *Country Stories, Scenes and Characters* (1828) – appeared between 1824 and 1832. They were commercially successful as well as influential in literary circles.

In fact, many authors found her freely discursive style, which combines direct address, detailed commentary and exhaustive description, congenial. Charles Dickens, Frances Trollope, Harriet Martineau and Walter Savage Landor, among many others, made explicit references to, or implicitly invoked, her work. On the occasion of Mitford's death in 1855, Landor wrote a poem attesting to her influence over him:

> The hay is carried; and the Hours
> Snatch, as they pass, the linden flow'rs;
> And children leap to pluck a spray
> Bent earthward, and then run away.
> . . .
>   I never view such scenes as these
> In grassy meadow girt with trees,
> But comes a thought of her . . .
> . . .
> Nor . . . could any tell
> The country's purer charms so well
> As Mary Mitford. (1876: 301)

Martineau spoke for many of her generation when she declared in her autobiography, written mid-century, that Mitford pioneered 'a new style of "graphic description" to which literature owes a great deal' (Chapman 1877: 418). By the 1830s, even writers such as Dickens, more interested in urban life than rural settings, were quick to appropriate Mitford's descriptive literary sketch (Butt and Tillotson 2013: 41).

Sketch writing was highly popular from the 1820s to the 1840s, yet it has not been accorded the same critical attention as other literary forms. In the past two decades, work by Alison Byerly, Richard Sha, Amanpal Garcha and Martina Lauster has begun to address this omission. For Byerley and Sha, the literary sketch must be understood as part of a broader category that encompasses visual and verbal artifacts including drawings, watercolours and short prose works. Whereas Byerley argues that the nineteenth-century sketch 'sacrifices aesthetic finish for a sense of spontaneity' (1999: 349), by examining its eighteenth-century antecedents Sha demonstrates how provisionality came to be highly vaunted. Although sketching was once considered a private activity, undertaken by writers or artists as a step towards a more complete whole, a growing appreciation for artlessness in the eighteenth century provided the conditions for it to flourish in the Romantic era. Sketches were increasingly seen as evidence of genius and originality and accorded equal or even greater value than finished works.

Lauster and Garcha consider both written and illustrative sketches. However, the significance of their studies lies in demonstrating how, as prose works, sketches supplanted the tale – with its focus on the supernatural and the exceptional – by according primacy of place to the ordinary and the quotidian. With the realist novel emerging in the Victorian period as the pre-eminent literary form, sketches were not, therefore, simply displaced. 'The fictional sketch of the early nineteenth century', Garcha writes, 'constitutes one origin of the Victorian novel' (2009: 8). In other words, descriptive realism, the signature characteristic of prose sketching from the 1820s through to the 1840s, became a defining feature of the Victorian novel.

Elizabeth Gaskell was one of Mitford's early readers. Only eight years Martineau's junior, Gaskell was part of the generation that recognised Mitford for her innovativeness. As a pupil at the all-girls Avonbank School, where she studied the leading women writers of the day, Gaskell recognised the formal qualities and textual content of *Our Village* as worthy of emulation. One of Gaskell's earliest known non-fictional prose works, 'Clopton Hall', likely written while she was a student, evinces her inchoate capacity for first-person description. William Howitt, to whom she sent 'Clopton Hall', selected it for inclusion in his descriptive anthology, *Visits to Remarkable Places: Old Halls, Battle Fields, and Scenes Illustrative of Striking Passages in English History and Poetry* (1840). Like his spouse Mary, William was one of Mitford's foremost admirers and therefore partial to her approach.

While popular titles by the Howitts, including the *The Book of the Seasons* (1831), *Sketches of Natural History* (1834), *The Rural Life of England* (1838), *The Boy's Country Book* (1839), *Homes and Haunts of English Authors* (1847) and *The Tear-Book of the Country* (1850) were descriptive works focused on the countryside, Gaskell would trace a more varied career. While Gaskell's social-problem novels, for which she was widely lauded by her contemporaries, contain numerous passages that reflect a more fully developed and greatly honed capacity for descriptive representation, *Cranford* has struck critics, then and now, as bearing the most obvious resemblance to *Our Village*. Yet, because *Cranford* contains few descriptive passages of place, the specific forms of its indebtedness have gone largely unanalysed. Connections between the texts are often discussed in diffuse terms: *Cranford* has been cast as a 'rewriting' of *Our Village*, Mitford's sketches deemed 'an obvious forebear' to Gaskell's Cranford papers, as she called them (Moretti 2005: 62; Easson 2016: 98). In fact, even nineteenth-century readers intuitively knew that the two works were connected, even if the precise nature of that relationship was not clearly established. *Our Village*, wrote one commentator, is a 'precursor, in some sort' to Gaskell's later work (Kemble 1875: 445).

Instead of outlining a direct line of descent from *Our Village* to *Cranford* in terms of descriptive writing, my principal contention is that at the level of narration the two works resemble each other. Mitford's use of direct address influenced Gaskell's development of a textual 'I' that traverses the diegetic boundaries between the real and fictional worlds in *Mary Barton: A Tale of Manchester Life* (1848) and *Ruth* (1853). By contrast, Gaskell utilises a character-narrator in *Cranford*, Mary Smith, who is limited in her ability to see beyond the events she experiences or to provide any real insight into the interiority of other characters. Nevertheless, all three of her narrators possess certain commonalities. They also share significant affinities with Mitford's narrator, including specific appeals to the reader's sympathy and identification. This resemblance may be seen as Gaskell's response to her predecessor's stylistic experiments.

Although *The Provincial Fiction of Mitford, Gaskell and Eliot* is not a work of narratology, it does employ certain tools of narratological analysis as well as book-historical study in order to link content and form. I am interested in both how the texts under consideration attempt to communicate as well as what they have to say, and the extent to which their meanings have been apprehended or misapprehended according to their format of publication and the historical contexts of their reception. The work of Gérard Genette and Robyn R. Warhol, who have analysed instances in which the fourth wall is broken, has been particularly useful. For Genette, who refers to these narrative interventions as *metalepsis*, the result is most often 'comical' or 'fantastic' (1980: 235–236). In his view, the effect of metalepsis is to distance the reader from the narrator by calling one's attention to the fictionality of the text. In her further elaboration of this narrative strategy, Warhol argues for a plurality of metaleptic forms. Some fictional works contain third-person references to 'the reader', a narratee with whom the actual reader has trouble identifying. The effect of such references is to distance the actual reader from the work being read. Other works may combine approaches that distance and engage readers by referencing 'specific narratees who are meant to represent large segments of the intended audience' (Warhol 1989: 110). Finally, there are narrators whom the reader is encouraged to view as the actual author, a textual 'I', and a narratee, a textual 'you', with whom the reader self-identifies (Warhol 1986: 11).

Because the three authors I examine experimented with narrative voice, particularly in utilising direct-address structures to draw the reader and narrator closer together, I will briefly elaborate on this last form, which Warhol terms *engaging narration*. Whereas distancing narration is masculine, often used to engender 'laughter, or even annoyance, from the actual reader' (Warhol 1982: 32), engaging narration is feminine and, typically, used by women writers to elicit the feelings of those who encounter the text. Engaged narrators speak earnestly to the reader. They interrupt the unfolding of a story in an attempt to guide the reader to a political position or moral stance on a given issue. The primary purposes of engaging narration are to efface the differences between the inscribed narratee and the actual reader as well as to elide the fictionality of the text itself (Warhol 1989: ix–x). In so doing, the engaged narrator encourages the reader to redirect whatever emotional lessons have been apprehended in one's encounter with the fictional work to the non-fictional world in which one lives.

For Warhol, only heterodiegetic narrators – those occupying a position outside of the story world – are, strictly speaking, engaging. Homodiegetic narrators, that is to say character-narrators, participate in the story. As a result, the reader never confuses the narrative persona with the author. Thus, Warhol argues, although *Cranford*, which Gaskell wrote between *Mary Barton* and *Ruth*, is replete with examples of direct address, these do not constitute instances of engaging narration. In Warhol's view, Gaskell invents the engaging narrator in *Mary Barton* as a strategy to elicit sympathy for working people. Eliot, discovering this precedent, improves on it in her works of fiction that eschew homodiegetic narrators (Warhol 1989: 10).

If Gaskell invented this narrative technique, she found the resources for it in *Our Village*. Although Warhol does not consider *Our Village* in her analysis, her definition of engaging narration certainly would exclude Mitford. Even if one accepted, as Gaskell did, that *Our Village* was more closely aligned to the fiction that it invokes, particularly the novel of manners, than to non-fiction, the narrator goes on lengthy walks through her hamlet as well as excursions to neighbouring villages, and frequently interacts with those around her. Nevertheless, neither are fully developed characters. The reader of *Our Village* gleans few personal details about the narrator. Mary Smith, the narrator of *Cranford*, who undertakes repeated visits to the eponymous village from her home in Drumble, an industrial town modelled on Manchester, discloses little about herself.

In fact, both the narrators of *Our Village* and *Cranford* present themselves as somewhat removed from the worlds they describe. They serve as intermediaries between the provincial communities depicted and the urban readership presupposed by the texts. The narrator of *Our Village*, for example, can celebrate 'the peculiar and characteristic beauty' of 'country fog' precisely because she knows and has experienced 'London fog', which '[o]f all detestable things ... is the most detestable' (Mitford 1828: 255). The basis for comparison equips the narrator with heightened capacity for responding to the natural world around her. The 'genuine feeling for nature', she avers, in implicitly aligning herself with an urban readership rather than the rural inhabitants who are her neighbours and friends, is a 'faculty, oftener perhaps claimed than possessed' (1828: 255). Similarly, Mary Smith, who 'as a well-to-do ... young woman' differentiates herself from the older, and financially precarious residents of Cranford, occasionally utilises their modes of expression – such as 'elegant economies', which transforms stringent financial circumstances into a genteel practice that repudiates the spending of money – only to note how easy it is to slip into their peculiar 'phraseology'. Like Mitford's narrator, Mary Smith, who has 'vibrated' all her 'life between Drumble and Cranford', aligns her views and perspectives with urban readers as well (Gaskell 2008: 154). This alignment, Kate Flint has argued, leads Mary Smith to maintain an 'ironic distance' throughout *Cranford* (Flint 1995: 31). Gaskell found the origins of this technique in *Our Village*.

Nevertheless, although they are somewhat removed, both narrators have far more in common with other engaged narrators than with distancing narrators. Addressing themselves to the narratee – whom the reader is encouraged to see as oneself – as a correspondent or friend, they may occasionally find humour in the situations they encounter or experience. The narrator of *Our Village*, on occasion, will ask the reader a question or anticipate one's thought. In recounting a village resident, for example, the narrator notes in an aside: 'You might guess a mile off that he was a schoolmaster, from the swelling pomposity of gait, the solemn decorum of manner, the affectation of age and wisdom, which contrast so oddly with his young unmeaning face' (Mitford 1824a: 65). After describing 'three or four ladies' of the town gathering one spring evening on a doorstep in 'calashes', Mary Smith asks whether the reader is familiar with the silk hood ('Do you know what a calash is?'), before providing a description. Ultimately, however, whatever amusement they derive from local customs or characteristics is subsidiary to the sympathetic identification they attempt to engender in the reader. Working with a less rigid definition, one can recognise *Our Village* and *Cranford* as experiments in engaged narration. Not only do their homodiegetic narrators attempt to engage readers, but their tone – ironic and humorous, but ultimately earnest and sympathetic – differs from distanced narration.

The narrative techniques of *Our Village* and *Cranford* have frequently been read as eliciting the reader's nostalgia, understood in a narrowly restrictive sense of longing to return to a past that has either disappeared or is in danger of doing so. Yet the texts themselves frequently suggest that such a possibility is either illusory or futile. Take, for example, the narrator's insistence in the initial sketch of the second volume of *Our Village* (1826) that her small locale never changes. In reacquainting the reader with her village, she claims that it possesses 'a trick of standing still, of remaining stationary, unchanged and unimproved in this most changeable and improving world'. In order to underscore this point, she continues: 'except that it is two years older, I cannot point out a single alteration which has occurred in our street' (Mitford 1826a: 1). Yet if the street, which scholars often read as a metonym for the town and its residents, has not been altered in any way, the volume itself documents many different changes, including rising and falling fortunes, especially the financial dissolution of an 'ancient and distinguished family' who are plunged into 'actual poverty' (1826a: 244); death and loss, with the passing of a beloved cricketer and the presumed drowning of the much-liked husband of a vicar's maid (1826a, 80); and signs of increasing modernisation, such as the construction of a Macadamised turnpike just a few miles away (1826a: 2). Similarly, although Franco Moretti has argued that *Cranford* is 'Madame Tussaud's idea of a village story' (2005: 63), the text itself engages, as many scholars now agree, with a variety of contemporaneous social and economic issues, from the coming of the railways to the precariousness of life – with the collapse of the Town and Country Bank – under capitalism to colonialism and the global trade in commodities.

In making this argument, I draw on Svetlana Boym's distinction between restorative and reflective nostalgia. Whereas the former is concerned with reconstructing what has been lost, the latter accepts the pastness of the past and embraces, however reluctantly and wistfully, change. In Boym's terms, 'restorative nostalgia does not think of itself as nostalgia, but rather as truth and tradition'. Thus, restorative nostalgics recognise in their longing an outcome to be realised: the eradication of the pain that comes with change and loss. By contrast, reflective nostalgia critically examines 'the ambivalences of human longing and belonging'. 'Restorative nostalgia protects the absolute truth', Boym continues, 'while reflective nostalgia calls it into doubt' (2001: xviii). All three writers – as I will elaborate in the next section of this introduction – have often been employed in service to projects of restorative nostalgia. Yet it is the reflective quality of their nostalgia that has largely gone unnoticed.

An essential insight George Eliot gleaned from her reading of Gaskell is that one could both long for rural community and be aware of that longing. This recognition enables an individual to maintain a distance from the longing one feels, subjecting it to critical reflection. Yet, as I show, this is precisely the lesson Gaskell drew from Mitford as well. By the time that Eliot began to write her first work of fiction, *Our Village* was, for reasons that I document, typically considered autobiographical. It was also developing the reputation, which it continues to maintain today, as a source of rural nostalgia. Thus, although Eliot was familiar with both writers, she found herself more heavily influenced by Gaskell. She began by experimenting with different styles of narration in *Scenes of Clerical Life* (1857) and *Adam Bede* (1859), which were modelled on *Mary Barton* and *Cranford*, the two novels she was reading while writing. She ultimately settled on a mode of direct address that furthered one aim of her liberalism: the cultivation of a political feeling, attached to the English landscape, which binds intimates and strangers. In Eliot's *The Mill on the Floss* (1860) and *Middlemarch* (1871–72), direct address and excessive description represent more than simple pauses in the narrative progress of her novels. What may be perceived as narratively static passages are, in fact, intrinsic to textual meaning.

The village and restorative nostalgia

While Garcha considers how authors who began their careers as sketch writers, including William Thackeray, Dickens and Gaskell, harnessed the descriptive and essayistic analytical elements of this popular short form for novelistic storytelling, I am interested in teasing out a more indirect genealogy. Mitford's sketches laid the foundations for Gaskell's village story. Although *Cranford* sold few copies and was scantly reviewed when it first appeared as a slim novel in 1853, a new edition published two years later proved more successful. Among its many readers was George Eliot. Familiar with Mitford's *Our Village* and the many imitations it spawned, Eliot recognised the village story 'as a successful and lucrative genre well suited to women writers' (McDonagh 2016: 363). At the same time, she also saw an opportunity to establish herself as the foremost novelist of provincial life, displacing Mitford whose stories had come to be seen, at mid-century, as a literary salve for a nostalgic urban readership.

Yet the fate that befell *Our Village* by mid-century is one that encompassed works by Gaskell and Eliot as well. Because this book focuses on the influence of Mitford's sketches on Gaskell, and the effect, in turn, of Gaskell's sketches on Eliot, I want to briefly underscore this point by surveying the publication history of *Our Village* in the years after its author's death in order to demonstrate how critical perceptions of Mitford's work were shaped and how aspects of her reception inevitably inhibited her reappraisal. As I will consider more fully in Chapters One and Two, Mitford's discontinuous sketches, which appeared in a variety of periodicals and annuals, as well as the first five biennial volumes of *Our Village* were unillustrated. Mitford played a role in selecting the scenes that would be included as woodcut illustrations in a new three-volume edition of *Our Village* in 1835, when her publisher, George B. Whittaker, sought to capitalise on the emergent trend of illustrated books.[7] This publication laid the groundwork for a proliferation of illustrated editions of *Our Village* throughout the nineteenth century.

In 1893, Anne Thackeray Ritchie selected fifteen sketches from the first four biennial volumes of *Our Village* for inclusion in a volume with more than 100 illustrations by Hugh Thomson. This edition of *Our Village* was included in the twenty-four-volume series of classic reprints by Macmillan. Begun in 1875 with the publication of Washington Irving's *Old Christmas*, the series overwhelmingly privileged works of rural writing that were amenable to illustration. The fashion for illustrating books had, by this point, changed dramatically. The etchings and wood-engravings made on steel printing plates were supplanted by photo-mechanical processes of reproduction, which made it possible to produce illustrations in books at a substantially lower cost (Felmingham 1988: 1). The development of these processes led to a 'boom in illustrated books' that far surpassed the surge that occurred after the patenting of steel printing plates in 1819. In the last quarter of the nineteenth century, editors and publishers took advantage of the emerging market for amply illustrated books among members of the middle class who, as Lorraine Janzen Kooistra points out in a different context, were 'eager for objects that would confirm for themselves and display to their visitors their own sophisticated status' (2002: 2). Heavily illustrated editions made it possible for publishers to market to two very distinct audiences simultaneously: the middle-class adult and the middle-class child.

Of all the books she might have selected, Ritchie had good reason to single out *Our Village*. By the end of the century, Mitford's rural sketches were celebrated for their cheerful optimism and warm compassion. 'Few authors have a better right to genial appreciation', declared the preface to one edition, 'than Mary Russell Mitford, who has produced much that the world will not willingly let die. She has written in a beautifully correct and pleasing way regarding country life and English country scenes, and has woven into dainty and pleasing forms many a romance of country life' (Anon. 1885: 5). Framed as the embodiment of respectable morality, *Our Village* was increasingly marketed to children, a segment of the population with no disposable income of their own.

Soon after Parliament passed the Forster's Education Act (1870), several publishers tapped into the burgeoning children's market with illustrated editions of *Our Village*. In order to sell books to children, publishers needed to appeal simultaneously to adults. Parents, but especially teachers and librarians, often sought reassurance about the moral and pedagogical value of literature they sought to buy for children.[8] In the 1870s, Ward, Lock and Company launched a Lily Series, in which Mitford's sketches figured prominently. Taking its name from an established repertoire of literary tropes used to describe femininity, the Lily Series primarily targeted women and young girls. The publisher's preface to its edition of *Our Village: Tales* reads:

> The design of this New Series is to include no books except such as are peculiarly adapted by their high tone, pure taste, and thorough principle, to be read by those persons, young and old, who look upon books as upon their friends – only worthy to be received into the Family Circle for their good qualities and excellent characters. (Anon. 1873: n.p.)

Additional anthologies and editions continued to frame her work as propagating stable family life and its values. George Routledge and Sons, whose Toy Books had made children's literature 'big business' in the 1860s (McLean 1972: 62), excerpted a number of her sketches and in 1880 published them as a separate series under the title *Children of the Village*.

William Blackwood and Sons marketed *Our Village: Country Pictures and Tales* as part of its Educational Series in 1884. The preface to the volume notes: 'It will be seen that, in the arrangement of the book, a Story and a Descriptive Scene have been alternated [i.e., changed] – the purpose being to give attractive views of English life in English scenery' (1884: n.p.). The altered sketch happens to be one of Mitford's most politically ambivalent, 'Violeting', which I discuss at greater length in Chapter Two. The publisher excised the narrator's ruminations about encountering a workhouse and the poverty and deprivation visible to her, thereby allowing the sketch to be read as a celebration of the happiness generated by rural retreat. The conception of 'childhood as a protected space of pure happiness on which no shadows ought to fall' frequently structured texts for the juvenile and children's market (Kooistra 2002: 214). By linking such innocence with the rural landscape, the altered sketch constructs nature itself as a place where such innocence is still possible and, by naturalising myths about nature before the child has the capacity for critical reflection, as Roland Barthes would argue in his essay about toys, it instils such a conception in its child readers (Barthes 1972: 53).

Mitford's sketches, therefore, were increasingly marketed as a way to return, imaginatively and, indeed, nostalgically, to that space of childlike innocence. According to Deidre Lynch, many of these 'newly kitschified' editions emphasised the text's outdated 'evocation ... of home' (Lynch 2000: 1106). Nostalgia, as Nicholas Dames argues, plays a significant role in a society 'for whom mobility and the possibility of rapid change is increasingly likely'. He continues: 'The past in its particularity gradually vanishes; the pleasure of recollecting that vague, disconnected past becomes more keen ... [and the] consequentiality of the past dwindles into its capacity to provide pleasure, security, self definition' (Dames 2001: 14). For late-nineteenth-century readers, displaced from the countryside to industrial cities or the colonies, Mitford's repackaged sketches offered the kinds of pleasure and comfort that Dames identifies. They continue to pay such dividends today because the historical geography about which Mitford wrote, now understood to be lost, evokes that 'ideal of a valued childhood ... which, while lost or betrayed' which, as Patrick Wright puts it, describes the 'deep psychological investment and compensatory meaning' generated by narratives of a national past that 'still gleams through occasionally' (Wright 1986: 168). By the early twentieth century, publishers across the Atlantic altered the subtitle of *Our Village* that was used for the 1824, 1826, 1830 and 1832 editions from *Sketches of Rural Character and Scenery* to *Sketches of English Character and Scenery* and marketed a selection of her pieces under that name (Mitford 1909; Mitford 1928). More recently, the back cover of an illustrated gift-book edition of 1986 promotes its 'new selection of Miss Mitford's sketches of village life' as a cultural artifact from a 'long-vanished rural England', while the back cover of a 1987 edition promises that the text contains 'stories and reflections of an English lady's life ... [from] a now forgotten era' (Mitford 1986; Mitford 1987). However, the nationalism that critics have identified in *Our Village* is itself partly the product of publishing and republishing these pliant and multivocal sketches in ways that foreground their nationalist implications.

Because each sketch was self-contained, Mitford's work may have been the most amenable to such alterations. Those sketches that Ritchie selected for the volume emphasise the aspects that she found most compelling and that would arouse for readers lost rural origins. She argues that Mitford's descriptive capacity evident in her correspondence – a 'pleasant unconscious art ... describes what is not there' to her correspondents 'and brings in her banks of violets to perfume the dull rooms' (Ritchie 1893: xli) – fed an equally lively evocative power. 'I cannot help thinking that what is admirable in her book', Ritchie writes, 'are not her actual descriptions and pictures of intelligent villagers and greyhounds, but the more imaginative things; the sense of space and nature and progress which she knows how to convey; the sweet and emotional chord she strikes with so true a touch' (1893: xxv–xxvi).

The strength of Mitford's writing, in other words, is presented in terms of its ability to call to mind images of rural simplicity and to generate longing in the reader, rather than in its fidelity to place. To draw out the evocative nature of Mitford's writing, Ritchie retitled some of Mitford's sketches; the opening piece, 'Our Village', is renamed 'Country Pictures' for an audience whose relationship to the rural was primarily representational (Figure I.1). Thomson's illustrations work in tandem to further tease out this aspect of the text.

Mitford was not alone. *Our Village* would sit alongside George Eliot's *Scenes of Clerical Life* and *Silas Marner* as well as *Cranford*, which, soon after its publication in 1891, gave the series its name. All of the titles in the series were published in dark green cloth binding with gilt edges. They were also copiously illustrated. Although he was not the only illustrator on the series, Thomson, who had been a 'pioneer' of the first photochemical method of reproduction known as process line block in the 1880s (Balston 1934: 167),[9] happened to work on the novels by all three authors. His illustrations reflect a move away from the texts themselves and towards visual images that offer themselves as faithful interpretations. Mitford's sketches of a semifictional village became indubitably associated with Three Mile Cross. The frontispiece to the volume depicts Mitford tending to her garden. The quotation ('watering my flowers') ostensibly by her cues the reader to perceive the text in solely autobiographical terms (Figure I.2). Gaskell's *Cranford* was seen as a slightly veiled version of Knutsford, the village in Cheshire where she spent her childhood and youth, and which she continued to visit once she took up residence in Manchester. Eliot's provincial communities have long been likened to Nuneaton, the Warwickshire village in which she was born.

All three authors were also routinely marketed to children and youth. Just as Mitford's sketches were extracted and anthologised, chapters from Eliot's fiction, especially *The Mill on the Floss* and *Middlemarch*, neither of which appeared in Macmillan's

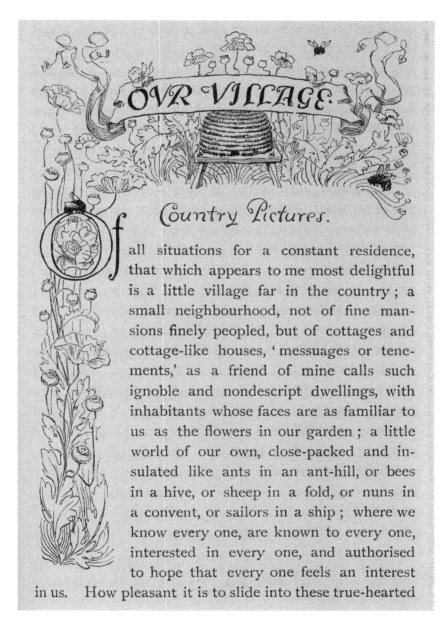

Of Country Pictures.

all situations for a constant residence, that which appears to me most delightful is a little village far in the country; a small neighbourhood, not of fine mansions finely peopled, but of cottages and cottage-like houses, 'messuages or tenements,' as a friend of mine calls such ignoble and nondescript dwellings, with inhabitants whose faces are as familiar to us as the flowers in our garden; a little world of our own, close-packed and insulated like ants in an ant-hill, or bees in a hive, or sheep in a fold, or nuns in a convent, or sailors in a ship; where we know every one, are known to every one, interested in every one, and authorised to hope that every one feels an interest in us. How pleasant it is to slide into these true-hearted

Figure I.1 'Country Pictures'. Illustration by Hugh Thomson. Mary Russell Mitford, *Our Village*. With an introduction by Anne Thackeray Ritchie and One Hundred Illustrations by Hugh Thomson. London and New York: Macmillan and Co., 1893. Author's copy.

Cranford series, were mined for this purpose. Following Eliot's death, a spate of anthologies that included chapters evocative of childhood and rural origins and accompanied by copious illustrations were published under such titles as *Child-Sketches from George Eliot: Glimpses at the Boys and Girls in the Romances of the Great Novelist* (Magruder 1895); *Tom and Maggie Tulliver* (Eliot 1909); and, further cementing the relationship between the author's fiction and the places of her birth and childhood, *Scenes from the 'George Eliot' Country* (Parkinson 1888). Precisely because it is short and its content has always been highly malleable, *Cranford* has had little need to be anthologised. *A Mother's List of Books for Children*, published in 1909, proclaimed that it offered 'a picture of life in a small English town during the first half of the nineteenth century' and assured readers that 'girls fourteen years and up are quite able

Figure I.2 Mary Russell Mitford watering her flowers. Illustration by Hugh Thomson. Mary Russell Mitford, *Our Village*. With an introduction by Anne Thackeray Ritchie and One Hundred Illustrations by Hugh Thomson. London and New York: Macmillan and Co., 1893. Courtesy of the Armstrong Browning Library, Baylor University.

to appreciate the book's charm' (Arnold 1912: 226). A Carnegie Library catalogue for illustrated editions of children's books, published in 1915, recommended *Cranford* to readers. Macmillan's edition, it declared, offered '[a] delightful picture of English village life when ladies went about in poke-bonnets and pattens' (Anon. 1915: 18). Through much of the twentieth century, few critics would have disagreed. Yvonne French, to take one example, flatly declares that '*Cranford*'s real importance lies in the fact that it is thoroughly representative of Mrs. Gaskell's ... Englishness' (1953: 140). By the 1890s, then, the reputations of Mitford, Gaskell and Eliot would be cemented as chroniclers of England's past and their work sentimentalised as nostalgia.

While the writings of Mitford, Gaskell and Eliot have, at various points, been subsumed into projects of restorative nostalgia, such as Macmillan's Cranford series, I insist that their work always resisted the impulse to deny change or to reconstruct lost worlds, even as it refused indifference to economic globalism and its pressures. One aim of this book is to recover the responsiveness of provincial fiction to contemporaneous economic, social and political transformations. This assertion runs counter to Ian Duncan's claim that provincial fiction is, at its outset, 'disconnected from a global historical economy and its transforming pressures' (Duncan 2002: 329). Yet, as I will demonstrate, Mitford presented her village as a full participant in the wider social, economic and political changes commonly associated solely with urban settings. From its inception, therefore, provincial fiction does not, as Duncan insists, signify 'a negative difference, based on a binary opposition' to metropolitan centres (2002: 322). What provincialism does do, however, as it expanded in the hands of Gaskell and Mitford, is to present the village as Janus-faced: a model social formation that looks backward – the characteristic so often ascribed to it – as well as forward. As Ruth Livesey remarks in her study of novels concerned with 'the "just" past', Eliot's novels do not 'retreat backwards from the face of the dislocations of modernity', but instead serve as 'an insistent reminder that the recent past is still moving alongside us, shaping our route' (Livesey 2016: 2).

Liberalism and the emotions

Offering a reassessment of Mitford's and Gaskell's provincial fiction, too often dismissed or ignored, the book further demonstrates their importance to the development of Eliot's liberalism in the age of high realism. Suggesting that earnestly engaged narrators are a distinguishing characteristic of provincial fiction, this book therefore contends that the ephemeral and largely plotless village sketch, the episodic novel and the weighty and intricately plotted realist novel are part of a shared tradition of women's writing. This tradition includes – in the case of Mitford and Gaskell – fiction with a liberal accentuation as well as – in the case of Eliot – novels about liberalism. Thus, a reconsideration of provincial fiction is also a contribution to the ongoing re-evaluation of liberalism by scholars in literature and history. In *Victorian Liberalism and Material Culture: Synergies of Thought and Place*, I considered how epiphanic thought – and its corresponding emotional states such as surprise, wonder or excitement – differs from more widely practiced and vaunted modes of liberal cognition, including objectivisation, distantiation, impersonality and disinterestedness (Morrison 2018a). In *The Provincial Fiction of Mitford, Gaskell and Eliot*, I continue this line of inquiry by considering how intense feelings for place might be integrated into the Victorianist literary study of liberalism.

As a political philosophy, nineteenth-century liberalism has roots in multiple and, at times, conflicting sources. These include the Scottish Enlightenment, Benthamite utilitarianism, German Romanticism and Evangelicalism. Because liberalism has been, since its very inception, fraught with internal tensions and contradictions, the political theorist Wendy Brown has cautioned it must be approached as a 'contingent, malleable, and protean set of beliefs and practices' (2009: 23). Similarly, Mark Bevir (2001) has suggested that one's individual liberal outlook might be shaped by any one of its individual strands or even by a mixture of different traditions.

Nevertheless, most Victorianists have approached liberalism as a principally cognitive or ethical practice. Amanda Anderson has argued that Victorian liberals conceived of the self as rationally governed and informed by self-reflective and self-critical practices, including critical scrutiny of one's own values and beliefs through careful thought and vigorous dialogue with others. Similarly, David Wayne Thomas has contended that liberalism in this period promoted the 'aspiration to many-sidedness' through its conception of regulative agency, 'a reflective locus of purposeful self-understanding and action' (Thomas 2004: 26, 158).

For Elaine Hadley, formalised mental attitudes, such as objectivity, disinterestedness, reticence, impersonality, conviction and sincerity, function alongside distinctive modes of thought production that include logical reasoning, internal deliberation, abstraction, reflection and free thought (Hadley 2010: 10). These cognitive practices, Hadley argues, were encouraged as a means of replacing 'situated and habituated bodies', especially 'gendered and classed bodies', with 'abstracted bodies thinking disinterested thoughts in an abstracted time and place of serene meditation' (2010: 13).

By focusing solely on the rational dimensions of liberalism, however, one may overlook the significant role emotion played as a foundational attribute of liberal culture in the nineteenth century. When Matthew Arnold championed culture and conduct as an antidote to 'anarchy', he did so in emotional registers. Proclaiming himself to be 'a believer in culture' and encouraging others to embrace the pursuit of 'sweetness', 'light' and 'perfection' (Arnold 1965: 88, 99, 91), Arnold sought to restore reverence for 'the best that has been known and said in the world, and thus with the history of the human spirit' (1968a: 151). In becoming one's impersonal 'best self', which he believed could be educed only by culture (1965: 162), the 'instinct' for life is 'truly served and the desire [for happiness] truly satisfied' (1972: 42). One who, after strenuous effort, is able to achieve a 'higher and impersonal life', Arnold avers, is 'thus no longer living to himself, but *living*, as St. Paul says, *to God*' (1972: 62). For Arnold, who by the age of twenty-two had come to reject Christ's divinity as proven by prophecy and miracle seriously questioned the immortality of the soul, God was simply 'a deeply moved way of saying *conduct* or *righteousness*' (1968b: 193). Even John Stuart Mill, who often holds a privileged place in these studies as a champion of ratiocination, recognised in the aftermath of his well-known mental crisis the necessity of cultivating the emotions to guard against a thoroughly ratiocinated outlook. He valued strongly the private self, constituted by both 'liberty of thought and feeling' (Mill 1977c: 225) and the public self who participated in civic debate.

In the case of Eliot, emotional response to the landscape was – for reasons that I discuss in Chapters Four and Five – a key element in her liberalism. By restoring this dimension to Eliot's work, and thereby distinguishing her novels from the traditionalism and pastoralism with which they are often confused, I attempt to forge closer relations between literature, liberalism and the emotions. As Jock Macleod and Peter Denney have recently argued, although there has been a significant increase in scholarship on the history of the emotions over the past decade and a concomitantly robust investigation of the history and literature of liberalism, there has been almost a complete absence of 'dialogue between what have been two largely separate fields of study' (2018: 4). For Eliot, emotional responses to the village landscape – informed by the tradition of writing inaugurated by Mitford and extended by Gaskell – do not suspend or supersede liberal thought. Rather, they make liberal thought possible.

The book's arc

This book begins by re-establishing the origins of provincial fiction in the periodical culture of the 1820s. Chapter One focuses on the challenges Mitford encountered in attempting to achieve professional status and a consistent income in the literary sphere. It shows how Mitford's sketches of village life originate as a response to the demands of reviewers, the contingencies of the literary profession and the realities of the market. Focusing particularly on Mitford's character sketches and examining them synchronically with surrounding copy in the periodicals where they first appeared, I argue that voice – combining direct address, detailed commentary and exhaustive description – is an intrinsic element of provincial fiction since its inception.

In Chapter Two, I turn from Mitford's sketches about village inhabitants to those concerned with the location's rural setting. For a number of critics, including Elizabeth Helsinger, Franco Moretti and Ian Duncan, these sketches evidence Mitford's portrayal of a provincial village that exists outside of history. Yet, as I show through both a synchronic examination of the sketches within their original publication contexts, and a diachronic analysis of various editions throughout the latter half of the nineteenth century, these critiques are wide of the mark. They focus on what Mitford's narrator occasionally says – such as her village having a remarkable ability of 'standing still, of remaining stationary, unchanged, and unimproved' – rather than on what the sketches actually show. Attending to Mitford's subtle depiction of historical change, this chapter excavates the lessons Elizabeth Gaskell would have derived from *Our Village* on the basis of the formats and editions available to her, including ironically inflected narration and descriptive detail.

Chapter Three recovers Elizabeth Gaskell's engagement with *Our Village* at the level of narration. It shows how Mitford's use of direct address influenced Gaskell's development of a textual 'I' that crosses the diegetic boundaries between real and fictional worlds in her social-problem novels, as well as her employment of a character-narrator who, like Mitford's narrator, acts as an intermediary between the provincial community depicted in *Cranford* and the urban readership predisposed by it. The chapter proceeds to document how, as George Eliot was attempting to become a writer of fiction, she was influenced by the narrative discourse of *Cranford* rather than its descriptive detail.

In Chapter Four, I argue that George Eliot's *The Mill on the Floss* (1860) intervenes in debates about the affective dimension of citizenship in a liberalising polity. Whereas her contemporary and associate John Stuart Mill was arguing that a vast expansion of the franchise would elicit the 'feelings' of citizenship, Eliot was less inclined to see the vote as a vehicle for cultivating a sense of national belonging. Drawing on thematic and formal techniques from Mary Russell Mitford and Elizabeth Gaskell, Eliot counters the emerging abstraction *nation* with the everyday knowledge derived from the English provincial village. Yet Eliot is less interested in opposing the abstract and the concrete than infusing the former with the latter by suggesting that affectionate ties to the nation as home-scene can serve as the basis for a more inclusive definition of citizenship. For Eliot the provincial village functions, at its best, as an inclusive social formation in which mutual support, cooperation and shared sensory experiences of topography and milieu can form the basis of wider attachments.

George Eliot's *Middlemarch: A Study of Provincial Life* (1871–72), the quintessential example of a nineteenth-century realist novel, announces a seriousness of purpose in its subtitle that *Our Village* and *Cranford* – more indebted to the novel of manners – would seem to lack. Yet *Middlemarch* is the final link in a chain of influence that this book intends to trace. Revisiting the question of the novel's political depth, my final chapter argues that *Middlemarch* is interested in how the feeling of citizenship that the movement towards representative government engenders shapes imagination, thought and action. In the novel, Eliot returns to her notion of the 'home-scene', which, as I argue in Chapter

Four, is used by the narrator as an umbrella term to encompass the landscape, physical buildings and set of relations located in the circumscribed geographic setting of one's birth. Instead of serving to limit the individual, however, as it does in *The Mill on the Floss*, the dynamic of exchange between mind and landscape paradoxically generates what we might call a *portable interiority* that does not require physical attachment to the local, and raises the possibility of a national interiority of affectionate ties to the nation as home-scene.

Notes

1 Shelagh Hunter has considered Mitford's *Our Village*, Gaskell's *Cranford* (as well as other fictional work by her) and Eliot's *Adam Bede* as 'idylls', 'a distinctively Victorian transformation of the pastoral genre'. These idylls are 'realistic', but such realism is 'grafted on to a meditative poetic structural pattern of great antiquity, which may be rephrased and repossessed whenever circumstances [require]' (1984: 3, 225). In differentiating his study from hers, P. D. Edwards has contended that *Our Village*, *Cranford* (as well as *Wives and Daughters*) and Eliot's 'Amos Barton' as well as *Silas Marner* are *realistic idylls*. Edwards is particularly interested in how these idylls – a term that is, for him, 'roughly synonymous with happy' (1988: 153n7) – navigate 'subjects which tend to pose the most obvious threat to the idyllic mood as well as the most obvious challenge to the author's power of sustaining it without surrendering his or her claims to realism' (1988: 3).
2 Born Mary Anne Evans, she began using Mary Ann Evans in the late 1830s, Marian Evans in 1851 and Marian Lewes in 1854. She was known in the last year of her life as Mary Ann Cross, having assumed on marriage the surname of the banker who had worked for her and George Henry Lewes for a number of years.
3 In order to more clearly distinguish studies of intertextuality from analyses of influence or, more reductively, source studies, Julia Kristeva, who coined the neologism, increasingly preferred the term *transpositions* (1986: 111).
4 K. M. Newton argues that an analysis of George Eliot's engagements with other writers should go 'beyond influence from or allusion to her literary predecessors' and instead be seen as 'interacting' with such work 'in an almost dialectal spirit' (2005: 241–42). Deborah Guth contends that Eliot's works are best seen as 'opening' themselves 'towards other texts' in a kind of dialogic fashion (2003: 3). Similarly,

John Rignall argues that Eliot's fictional writings 'took the form of a creative dialogue in which she took comparable material [on which other writers had drawn] and gave it her own distinctive inflection' (2011: 3).

5 For previous articulations of the ideas contained in this study, see Morrison 2015, 2011, 2008a, 2008b.

6 The published content of literary annuals offered a delimited range of subjects: 'Religion (Christianity), married life, mild social concerns, moral lessons, and medieval romance were acceptable' (Ledbetter 1996: 236).

7 As Richard Maxwell has remarked, 'an unprecedented range of extraordinary illustrated books' were produced throughout the nineteenth century. The first great wave of such publications, he argues, occurs in the 1830s and the 1840s with illustrators working 'in a mode predominantly satirical or grotesque'. Although Maxwell has in mind here the collaborations of Charles Dickens and his several illustrators, including George Cruikshank and Hablot Browne, his claim is somewhat skewed towards the novel rather than the many giftbooks, annuals and keepsakes whose illustrations were neither satirical nor grotesque. Nevertheless, as Maxwell rightly notes, 'by the mid-1840s, illustrated books ... were successfully produced for almost every level of Victorian Society' (2002: xxi).

8 As Lorraine Janzen Kooistra notes, libraries and schools 'became the principal consumers of children's books, with 70–90 percent of the contemporary market for juvenile publications going direct to libraries' (2002: 192).

9 The process line block technique involved photographing the original artwork, reducing or enlarging its size, and then transferring it to a zinc printing plate. The illustration would be etched on the plate with acid to create a relief devoid of white elements. The resulting block would be used to print the illustration alongside text. Thomson would accrue additional fame in 1893 by quickly adapting to the new half-tone process (Balston 1934: 167).

1

Sketches of Rural Character: Mary Russell Mitford's 'Fugitive Pieces'

In *Figures of Literary Discourse,* Gérard Genette appears to attack plot's stranglehold on criticism: literary texts, he argues, comprise many elements that compete with the forward movement of plot. Narratorial asides that express subjective opinions or observations are 'alien' to narrative. Yet Genette quickly backs away from the full implications of this observation because he cannot, finally, imagine any text in which description and narration would be opposed. Plot must take precedence over minutiae, excessive literary word painting and digressive authorial chatter because, he insists, 'description might be conceived independently of narration, but in fact it is never found in a so to speak free state' (Genette 1982: 134). Plot, therefore, makes a sequential narrative possible. As Peter Brooks has argued, it 'moves us forward as readers of the narrative text' (Brooks 1985: 35).

It is thus to plot that critics have turned in their attempts to account for the interpellative power of literature. Precisely because it generates, as Brooks puts it, 'the play of desire . . . that makes us turn pages and strive toward narrative ends' (Brooks 1985: xiii), plot produces readers as ideological subjects. Through its boundedness, plot orders the psyche and demarcates the limits of desire. This theory of plot relies, however, on an ahistorical conception of reading. As Linda K. Hughes and Michael Lund have pointed out about serialisation, narratological and reader-reception studies 'have traditionally discounted the extended time frame and periodic structure it imposed on narrative' (Hughes and Lund 1995: 143). For the Victorians, who 'read their literature piecemeal' (Patten 2006: 11), it was almost impossible to read for plot. Novels were published in separate volumes; they were released in parts spanning the course of several months, a year or longer; and they appeared episodically, whether weekly or monthly, in the pages of periodicals.[1]

To the theories of reading concerned with serialised novels in the Victorian period, several critics have recently argued, Richard Sha and Amanpal Garcha in particular, that we should add a model that accounts for the pleasures readers in the Romantic era derived from the sketch. A pre-eminent genre of the early nineteenth century in which, *pace* Genette, description does not serve an auxiliary function, the sketch requires a different model of reading precisely because it has no rhythm. The sketch, which purports to represent a 'slice of life' or a moment in time rather than a sequential narrative of successive events,[2] might appear as a stand-alone piece or as part of a series that treats different aspects of, say, scenery, social setting or human character.

In 1822, Mary Russell Mitford began publishing loosely related prose sketches of provincial life and topography. Drawing on her experiences of Three Mile Cross, Mitford alternated between sketching the Berkshire village, south of Reading, where she would reside for much of her life, the people who inhabited or visited it, and the areas that surrounded it (Figure 1.1). The motivation behind these sketches of village inhabitants and topography was 'to know and to love the people about us, with all their peculiarities, just as we learn to know and to love the nooks and turns of the shady lanes and sunny commons that we pass every day' (Mitford 1822d: 645 . Their focus ranges from quotidian experiences – May Day, a cricket match, a shopping excursion – to occurrences of greater significance, such as processes of modernisation, as they affect the quaint hamlet. Although the sketches lack plot, the pieces, individually and collectively, convey a strong sense of place.

Mitford wrote more than one hundred of these sketches over a ten-year period. They appeared, often anonymously, in several different periodicals, including the *New Monthly Magazine*, the fledgling *Museum* and the long-running *Lady's Magazine*, as well as in a variety of literary annuals. Between 1824 and 1832, Mitford reprinted the pieces in five biennial volumes under the titles *Our Village: Sketches of Rural Character and Scenery* (1824, 1826, 1830, 1832) and *Our Village: Country Stories, Scenes and Characters* (1828).

Published by George B. Whittaker, the volumes were highly successful: the first went to fourteen editions in eleven years, including

Figure 1.1 Mitford's cottage at Three Mile Cross, Berkshire. Unknown artist. Elizabeth Lee, ed. Mary Russell Mitford Correspondence with Charles Boner & John Ruskin. With 8 Illustrations. London: T. Fisher Unwin, 1914. Courtesy of the Armstrong Browning Library, Baylor University.

three before 1825, while the first edition of the fifth volume sold out in just one day (Garrett 2004; see also Mitford 1870b: 137). In 1835, Whittaker produced a three-volume anthology compiling most of the sketches along with woodcut illustrations. In 1848, the publisher Henry G. Bohn released a two-volume anthology, which reordered and clustered the sketches according to theme, substantially altering the reader's experience. These would appear in different editions through the next decade. Finally, near the end of the nineteenth century, one-volume, heavily illustrated anthologies that predominantly gathered the topographical sketches, began to appear.

What, then, we might ask, is *Our Village*? Is it the original sketches published in magazine and annuals? The first or all five of the biennial volumes? The first two-volume edition? The second two-volume anthology with its thematic reorganisation? The later one-volume edited selections? These questions are crucial, if not also rhetorical – in a sense, *Our Village* is all of these – because the material aspects of publication and modes of circulation generate both different textual meanings and different audience relationships to those texts. Roger Chartier has pointed out the importance of reconstructing 'the "actualization" of texts in . . . [their] historical dimensions'. Such an approach, Chartier argues, 'requires that we accept the notion that their meanings are dependent upon the forms through which they are received and appropriated by their readers . . . a text, stable in its letter, is invested with new meaning and status when the mechanisms that make it available to interpretation change' (Chartier 1994: 3). By focusing solely on the two-volume anthologies or one-volume selections published in the late nineteenth century, as most critics have done, one neglects the role of periodical publication, perhaps revealing the social conditioning that accustoms us to prioritise the book over the periodical. As a result, our understanding of the kinds of cultural work that *Our Village* performed at different historical moments – and the distinct versions read by Elizabeth Gaskell and George Eliot – remains limited.

Insofar as they were all about some aspect of life in and around a Berkshire village, Mitford's sketches appear to have struck a chord with an increasingly urban readership eager for icons of constancy during a period of destabilising change.[3] As I will discuss at greater length in Chapter Two, literary critics overwhelmingly have tended to account for the popularity of her sketches in terms of their conveyance of comforting ideology: the existence of an idyllic English hamlet untouched by the forces of industrial capitalism and the quickened pace of modernity. Yet, as Amanpal Garcha has recently reminded us, early nineteenth-century sketches – and subsequently those episodic and essayistic Victorian novels that contain the vestigial traces of shorter literary forms – were lauded by readers precisely because they were stylistically distinctive (Garcha 2009: 16–23).

This was certainly the case with Mitford's discontinuously published and plotless sketches. Even after the first volume of *Our Village* was released under her name in 1824, and Mitford's subsequent decision to capitalise on its success by publishing further sketches and volumes credited to her, the chief appeal of the sketches was derived from their narrative voice, which also provides much of the non-narrative interconnectedness among the sketches. Repeatedly referred to as 'charming' and 'fresh', for many of her contemporaries it seemed as if Mitford was talking directly to the reader in her sketches (Anon. 1850: 3, 4). Yet the 'casual offhandedness' of the sketch form (Sha 1998: 105), with its qualities of digressiveness and excessive description, has held little appeal for scholars trained to recognise the aesthetic and ideological significance of plot. Mitford's sketches have alternately been described as 'decorative' and written as if rural life 'were already a picture, poem, or story' (Moretti 2005: 39; Helsinger 1997: 121). But admirers and detractors alike have focused solely on her style or tone as it is reflected in the later published bound volumes.

While recounting Mitford's pursuit of a literary career, including the financial exigencies that shaped much of her output, this chapter builds on the insights of Laurel Brake and Maura Ives, who have argued that analyses of the original periodical context of much nineteenth-century writing can generate variant readings of 'official' publications in bound volumes. The transposition of Mitford's understudied character sketches from magazine to various book forms tells us about the modulation of narrative voice in different print venues (Ives 1995; Brake 1995). As such, I isolate Mitford's character sketches from the pieces on rural scenery that will be my focus in Chapter Two in order to examine them synchronically within the surrounding copy of *Lady's Magazine*. I do so in order to show how, in the periodical context, different inflections in Mitford's authorial voice can be discerned that differ from the voice found in those bound volumes. These periodical sketches are often acerbic, ironic and ambivalent about the emerging domestic ideology that the magazine intended to reinforce. Because Gaskell – unlike Eliot, who was nine years her junior – may first have encountered the sketches in periodical form, but certainly read them in the original biennial volumes, I consider the extent to which paratextual framing and other editorial decisions soften, but do not greatly alter, the experience of the sketches in this later format. I conclude by showing how the Bohn edition, which Eliot likely read, varies considerably.

Writing for money

Mitford was in the vanguard of early nineteenth-century sketch writers. She was also a writer out of necessity in an era that looked on professional writing with disdain. Born in 1787 to the wealthy, educated heiress Mary Russell and the profligate surgeon George

Mitford, she was their only surviving child. Owing to her father's financial recklessness, Mitford had a tumultuous childhood. Except for a few prosperous and steady years in Alresford, Hampshire, Mitford's family was forced to repeatedly relocate as their fortunes ebbed and flowed: from Alresford to Lyme Regis, then to London, Reading, Grasley and, ultimately, Three Mile Cross.

During a period in which the family's fortunes flowered, George Mitford sent his daughter to St Quentin's boarding school at 22 Hans Place in Chelsea. The educational institution, which Caroline Lamb attended and where Letitia Elizabeth Landon would study, boasted a curriculum that included Latin, history and geography, drawing and Romance languages and literatures. Under the tutelage of poet Frances Rowden, Mitford cultivated an early interest in verse, which was encouraged by her parents. She also accompanied Rowden to see plays at Drury Lane (L'Estrange 1870a: 11–12). This was an interest that the headmaster of Reading School, Richard Valpy, who she befriended after moving back to the area in 1802 at the age of fifteen, continued to stoke. Four years later, the family relocated to nearby Grasley, where they would live for the next fourteen years in a grand residence that George Mitford built for them, utilising most of the £20,000 his daughter had won in a lottery. He named it Bertram House in order to evoke vague associations with the Mitfords of Bertram Castle, Northumberland (Astin 1930: 26).

All authors, male and female, confronted challenges entering the literary field. The obstacles for women, however, were substantial and varied. Up to the eighteenth century, as Catherine Gallagher has argued, women writers were largely delimited to drama and fiction, as was the case for the five authors she studies: Aphra Behn (1640–1689), Delarivier Manley (1663–1724), Charlotte Lennox (1729–1804), Frances Burney (1752–1840) and Maria Edgeworth (1768–1849). This constraint was true even if one worked across a greater variety of genres (Gallagher 1995: xiii–xxiv).[4] Thus, when Mitford entered the literary marketplace with a book of poems privately published in 1810 by Abraham John Valpy, Richard's son,[5] she experienced the kind of reception that tended to fortify poetry as a predominantly male domain. The *Literary Panorama* declared, 'If they are not of the first rate, there is a respectability about them which secures them from contempt' (Anon. 1811). However, the venerable *Quarterly Review* was scathing:

the poems themselves signify that they were composed with the applause of many friends; and that the author's chief motive in their publication was to shew how skilfully the lyre might be swept by a lady's hand. The subjects on which her talents are exercised are of a very miscellaneous nature, and such as we should not have supposed peculiarly attractive to a female mind . . . . It must be apparent, we think, to every one, that Miss Mitford's taste and judgment are not yet matured; that her poems ought to have been kept back much longer, and revised much oftener, before they were submitted to the public; and, above all, that she wanted some friend who, without wounding her feelings, or damping the fire of her genius, would have led her to correcter models of taste, and taught her more cautious habits of composition. (Mitford and Gifford 1810: 514, 517)

Such a pronouncement might have caused another author to blanch, however Mitford was sanguine. 'I have little reason to complain', she wrote to her father who, at the time, was struggling to find work in London in a letter dated 7 January 1811. Believing William Gifford, the editor of the *Quarterly Review*, to have written it, she thought the piece – by associating her with a poet and playwright whom she admired – worked to her advantage: 'If he attacked Joanna Baillie, even to be *abused* with her is an honour' (L'Estrange 1870a: 113).[6]

Mitford's poems varied in subject, but several touch lightly on politics. A Whig, Mitford's father was friends with leading political figures, including several Radicals who found their way into the pages of *Poems* (1810). In 'To G. L. Wardle, Esq. on the Death of His Child', Mitford contrasts public celebration with private grief. The first two stanzas depict Gwyllym Lloyd Wardle – the Welsh politician who, in 1809, protested against the government's use of libel laws against the press to suppress stories about the Duke of York's corruption in his capacity as the army's commander-in-chief – as a bulwark against tyranny: 'To chase Corruption from Britannia's strand, / To call back Freedom to her native land, / The Patriot rose' (1810: 94). But whereas the nation celebrates, Wardle is unable to hear 'The shout of triumph, or the song of praise' as he grieves the loss of his infant son (1810: 95). The poem concludes by urging Wardle to translate his private pain into public service: 'By patriot deeds exalt thy deathless name, / And add fresh blossoms to thy wreath of fame' (1810: 96).

Two other poems provide some indication of Mitford's own political sensibilities. In 'On a Bust of Fox', Mitford reflects on the incapacity of sculpture to capture the humanity or living dynamism of the sitter. Of Charles James Fox, who distinguished himself in the House of Commons through his powerful oration on such topics as individual freedom and religious tolerance, she writes:

> IN this cold Bust, a faint attempt we see,
> A vain attempt, great Fox! to picture thee.
> For say, can bronze, or marble e'er impart
> That magic charm, warm breathing from the heart?
> That fire, which darting from th' expressive eye,
> Wings with redoubled force the keen reply!
> Or, when thy eloquence, with milder flow,
> In Freedom's cause, bids wond'ring senates glow? (1810: 117)

The poem emphasises the disjuncture between the three-dimensional representation of Fox and the person himself in order to argue that the 'nobler monument' is his own fame: 'Fix'd on the firmest base – a nation's love: / To distant ages shall thy name descend, / And grateful Britons hail Britannia's friend' (1810: 118).

In contrast to these two poems, 'On Maria's Winning the Cup' has no overt political content. It is a poem on greyhound coursing. Nevertheless, it is inscribed to William Cobbett, the pamphleteer and combative editor of the partisan *Political Register*. By the time Mitford published her poem, Cobbett had established the *Register* as a leading venue of Radicalism.

As far as politics go, of course, this is all very tame. Mitford had apparently intended to include several additional poems that were more explicitly political, but the publisher excised them.[7] Yet to the *Quarterly Review*, even those that appeared in print were beyond the pale: '[W]e should not have supposed [the topic of politics] peculiarly attractive to a female mind' (Anon. 1810: 514–15). Rebuking her for leaving the drawing room and entering the political realm, the reviewer writes: 'we must take the liberty of hinting to Miss Mitford, that in selecting the objects of her admiration, she has manifested as little female delicacy as judgment' (Anon. 1810: 516). There was, however, one aspect of her poetry that the review singles out as laudable. Her 'description of natural scenery, or the delineation of humbler and calmer feelings' was generally quite fine (Anon. 1810: 517). However, the review warned, unless Mitford forever abandoned 'the thorny and barren field of politics', her muse would 'sing unheard or unattended' (Anon. 1810: 518). In order to be fairly judged on her abilities as a writer, Mitford certainly concluded, she would have to be more circumspect going forward.

Between 1810 and 1814, the family finances were once again precarious. In 1811, Mitford's father was, in her own words, 'a ruined man', with the family contemplating various measures to stay in their house including selling most of their belongings (L'Estrange 1870a: 140). Yet, during this period, there remained sufficient resources and continuous reassurance from her father that all would be well so that Mitford could have less need of money and impatience for fame. She was certainly 'shocked' by the printer's bill for *Poems*, which she found 'exorbitant' (L'Estrange 1870a: 91). As she explained in a letter dated 30 June 1811 to William Elford, the Tory politician and amateur landscape painter who was one of her most intimate correspondents, 'I believe I fare the worse for employing an old friend – or, rather the young son of an old friend, who, having dandled me as an infant, romped with me as a child, and danced with me as a young woman, finds it quite impossible to treat me or my works with the respect due to authorship' (L'Estrange 1870a: 135). But the emphasis here is much more on her status – as an author to whom respect is due – than on finances.

Despite *Poems* having been panned by some critics, Mitford was able to parlay it and her subsequent narrative poem into further opportunities to publish. In 1811, she released *Christina, The Maid of the South Seas* (1811c). As with *Poems*, Abraham John Valpy published this multi-canto romance in tetrameter couplets. Taking as its focus the mutiny on the HMS *Bounty* in April 1789, the poem contains strong thematic links with the Pacific islands romance written by Byron.[8] Prior to publication, Mitford's father had asked Samuel Taylor Coleridge, an acquaintance, to review it. According to Mitford, in a letter to her father dated 3 March 1811, Coleridge had 'taken out what could well be spared' and added 'his own beautiful lines' (L'Estrange 1870a: 119). After Coleridge corrected her proofs for *Christina*, she wrote to her father on 7 June 1811 to express 'how delighted' she was 'with Mr. Coleridge's approbation'. She continues: 'To be, some time or other, the best English poetess ... is the height of my ambition' (L'Estrange 1870a: 133). In a preface to her *Dramatic Works*,

Mitford writes of Felicia Hemans – who, at the time of Mitford's emergence as a writer, was fixing her reputation as the pre-eminent poetess of home and nation – that the two would have been 'rivals if we had not determined to be friends' (1854: xxix).

Over the next several years Mitford maintained a steady output. In 1811 she also published two poems in the venerable *Lady's Magazine*, founded in August 1770 by the bookseller John Coote and first published by John Wheble, with attribution: 'Beauty: An Ode', which appeared in the June issue accompanied by an editorial note that read 'intended for the second Edition of Miss Mitford's Miscellaneous Poems now in the Press', and 'Blanch'.[9] A year later, she put out *Watlington Hill* (1812c), a long 'descriptive' poem on hunting, which seems to have heeded the *Quarterly Review*'s advice to focus on country scenery. *Narrative Poems on the Female Character* (1813) followed a year later.[10] In addition to these major works, she continued to publish periodical poetry, including two in the *Poetical Register* and several in the *Lady's Magazine*, including 'Love-Sick Maid' (1812b), 'Another – The Storm' (1812a), 'Solitude' (1814), 'Coursing' (1815) and 'The Hermit' (1815b). Several of these had already been previously published, including 'Another – The Storm', which appears in *Christina, Maid of the South Seas*. Her new poems included prefatory remarks that encouraged readers to seek out forthcoming publications as well.

By the early 1820s, any concerns about Mitford's respectability as a poet had been allayed. Indeed, Alexander Dyce selected her for inclusion in his *Specimens of British Poetesses*, a publication that sought 'to exhibit the growth and progress of the genius of our country-women in the department of poetry' (1825: iii). Throughout much of the nineteenth century, to be recognised publicly for one's poetry as a woman was to have the title of poetess conferred on oneself, regardless of how one felt about the attribution. The term could be used, as Dyce clearly intended it to be, as a way of lauding the accomplishments of a woman writer. Although their individual styles were distinct, poetesses were recognisable as a group for poetry that 'tended to be narrative in nature, direct in expression, musical in appeal, and affective or sentimental in content, dilating on losses familiar to all: the disappearance of rural and other Edenic states of bliss and innocence, such as childhood; the death of family members, friends, and lovers; and the erosion of time and hope' (Kooistra 2011: 131). The term *poetess* could also be used to disparage a woman writer and the tradition in which she worked precisely for these qualities.

Given Mitford's 'ambition' to be recognised as 'the best English poetess', her inclusion in Dyce's pantheon of literary worthies – with her 'specimen' being an excerpt from 'Blanch', first published in the *Lady's Magazine* – was cause for celebration. But her poetry throughout this period is deceptive. Take *Christina*: stung by the criticism that she had waded into a domain unbefitting a woman, Mitford maintains clearly demarcated spheres for women and men in the poem (Bolton 2016: 143). Nevertheless, a careful reading of *Christina*, Elisa E. Beshero-Bondar has compellingly argued, shows the poem 'actively engaged with issues of identity and sexuality raised by global intercultural encounters' (2009: 279). This is perhaps indicative of Mitford's interest in having her poetical work situated in what Tricia Lootens calls the 'history of Poetess performance' (2017: 117). A trope into which one could step, the poetess stakes her moral authority on womanhood in poems that quicken domestic feeling for hearth and home to address contemporaneous social and political issues. Poetess performance, therefore, 'by definition, [is] a political mode' (Lootens 2017: 15, 65, 64).

The *Lady's Magazine*, to which Mitford contributed a number of other poems in this period, catered to a largely upper-middle-class readership from its founding in 1770 up through 1832.[11] The magazine 'defined public issues for women' throughout this period (Copeland 1995: 119). Despite its title and reputation as being published for ladies by ladies, the magazine always commanded a mixed-gender readership (Batchelor 2011). Nevertheless, as Jacqueline Pearson has pointed out, the editors of the eighteenth-century original series 'maintained the fiction that it addressed women specifically' (Pearson 1996: 5). For much of the magazine's run, women were encouraged to send in copy. The editor might include a few works deemed publishable. Although they were not remunerated, aspiring writers hoped that inclusion in the magazine would help to launch their careers. It was far more routine, however, for the magazine to publish the work of established or emerging professional writers. As a result of *Poems*, Mitford fell into this latter category.

The *Lady's Magazine* was priced toward the lower end of periodicals. In the early 1800s, it cost a shilling, which compares favourably with the leading reviews at two shillings and more general publications at one shilling and sixpence. Nevertheless, few people could afford to own individual copies. Those members of the upper-middle class who could spare the expense displayed copies in their drawing rooms, while many middle-class readers turned instead to subscription reading rooms (Altick 1998: 319). Schools also routinely subscribed (Fergus 2007: 197–236).

As Mitford's stature grew, the family's financial situation was becoming increasingly dire. On 19 January 1814, Mitford wrote to her father to explain that he had just been served legal papers, which she accepted at the house in his absence. The legal documents stated that 'if the mortgage and interest be not paid before next Monday, a foreclosure and ejectment will immediately take place; indeed I am not sure whether this paper of jargon is not a sort of ejectment' (L'Estrange 1870a: 255). They managed to stave off immediate foreclosure and eviction, and over the next several years, George Mitford engaged in an extended Chancery suit with the prospective buyer of the property. In the end, Mitford lost. The family relocated to a cottage at Three Mile Cross in March 1820.

With the full implications of her father's repeated speculations and large gambling debts apparent to her, Mitford assumed the burden of supporting her parents as a writer. Although many authors wrote out of need, early nineteenth-century culture continued to propagate the myth of the writer unfettered by economic or other financial considerations. Robert L. Patten explains the prevailing view:

> Sir Walter Scott noted approvingly Thomas Campbell's toast to Napoleon because he had once hanged a bookseller. Samuel Rogers grumbled that to make literature the business of life was to make it a drudgery, Coleridge advised 'never pursue literature as a trade', and Lamb urged Bernard Barton not to give up his bank job and try to live by his writings alone. (Patten 1978: 10–11)

Yet with a father unwilling to take on any form of employment and a mother increasingly ill, Mitford, as a woman, had limited options. Consequently, she was prolific and throughout the 1820s and 1830s worked across genres to maximise financial gain.

'[T]he plague of authorship'

For Mitford, the emergence of a robust periodical market in the first two decades of the nineteenth century made it possible to pursue authorship as a profession. As Alexis Easley has argued, any study of women's authorship in the period necessarily 'begins with an exploration of the periodical medium itself' (Easley 2004: 2). Whereas women who sought remuneration for their work throughout much of the eighteenth century had been largely confined to two genres, the expansion in 'generic range' toward the end of the 1700s contributed to the professionalisation of the woman writer (Schellenberg 2005: 12). The growth and development of the periodical market offered a plethora of new opportunities – including literary reviews, biographical vignettes, travelogues, serialised tales, essays and historical anecdotes and reflections – for women to receive professional payment for their work (Peterson 2009: 4).

In 1821, Mitford began to write frequently for the periodicals. Her well-connected friend Thomas Noon Talfourd acted in an informal capacity as her literary agent at a time when that profession did not yet exist. To the painter Benjamin Robert Haydon, Mitford writes, on 7 January 1821, that Talfourd 'gives me that which is most precious, time, and advice and criticism' (Mitford 1870b: 124). Talfourd read drafts of her 'portraits in verse' and 'dramatic sketches', and undertook negotiations with editors on her behalf. On 9 March 1821, she beseeched Talfourd to assist her in placing several sonnets in the *New Monthly Magazine*: 'My Dear Sir, I avail myself of your kindness to trouble you with some poetry, which if you think it has any chance of admission you will have the goodness to transmit to [the publisher] Mr. [Henry] Colburn' (Mitford 1821b: n.p.). Encouraged by Colburn's response to his request on Mitford's behalf, Talfourd approached the *London Magazine*, which accepted a couple of dramatic sketches as well.

With Mitford's work in these genres receiving positive affirmation, Talfourd suggested that she also consider writing prose. Mitford, however, was reticent. In a letter dated 16 March 1821, she explains that, unlike poetry or drama, she felt out of her depth:

> The real truth is I believe that I have been for many years a most egregious letter writer, & have accustomed myself to an incorrect & gossiping rapidity which does very well in writing to indulgent friends but will by no means suit that tremendous Correspondent the Public – so that in addressing that high personage I am frightened out of my wits – ponder over every phrase, disjoint every sentence, & finish producing such

marvellous lumps of awkwardness as those which I have the honour to send you. Will they be accepted do you think? I promise to improve, for that I am resolved, cost what it may. (Mitford, 1821c: n.p.)

Mitford enclosed two essays for Talfourd to review. They ranged in style and approach from the analytical ('On the Comedies of Thomas May') to the descriptive ('Field Flowers'). Regardless of any doubts about her own ability, Talfourd immediately recognised Mitford's potential. He forwarded the essays to Colburn, who accepted them for publication in the *New Monthly Magazine*, which he had acquired in 1820.

Writing for periodicals could lead to a steady income. It was not, however, particularly lucrative. Having heard anecdotes about what Colburn would be willing to pay writers, Mitford overestimated the amount she might earn publishing in these venues. On 12 December 1820, she wrote to William Elford to express her astonishment at Colburn's 'magnificent offers'. He had, Mitford averred, paid the poet Horace Smith 'twenty guineas a sheet (five more than Hazlitt gets for the "Table Talk" in the "London") ... for any contribution, prose or verse'. Moreover, when Thomas Campbell assumed the editorial reigns at the *New Monthly Magazine* and launched a new series, Colburn pledged to Talfourd, who wrote the periodical's dramatic reviews, 'his weight in gold rather than part with him' (Mitford 1870b: 119). Mitford also concluded from hearing these accounts that the more sheets she could produce, the greater her pay. Prose sketches – despite any lingering doubts about her ability to work in the genre – seemed the most profitable route forward.

As soon as Mitford began to contemplate sketches of rural life and scenery, she imagined her readership to be predominantly urban. In a wide-ranging letter to Talfourd dated 9 June 1821, she enclosed 'more bad prose': a sketch of Three Mile Cross about which, she confessed, to 'have great qualms of conscience' because it was 'true almost to the letter'. Although she urges him to return the sketch if he thinks 'it at all improper, or liable ever by possibility to hurt any one's feelings', she undercuts any professed misgivings by remarking that no one in her village 'knows what a magazine looks like' (Mitford, 1821e: n.p.). Talfourd was enthusiastic. With 'Our Village' and two other sketches in hand, he represented Mitford in negotiations with several journal editors.

Talfourd first approached Thomas Campbell at the *New Monthly Magazine*. Although Vera Watson (1949: 141–143) and William A. Coles (1957: 40) have argued that Campbell failed to recognise the merit of these sketches, the sticking point was remuneration. Mitford wanted more than Campbell was willing to pay. In his memoir, Cyrus Redding, who was the magazine's deputy editor, recalls the experience of working with Mitford. 'She wrote the most graphic and minute descriptions of country life and manners', he notes affirmatively. 'She was in prose what [John] Clare was in the poetry of the country'. Yet Redding felt that her own estimation of the 'value' of her work was rather 'extravagant'. He includes the text of a letter written to him by Mitford that reads in part as follows:

> I am quite astonished that there can be the slightest misunderstanding respecting the price of my articles. I stated that I had no objection to contribute to so respectable a publication, but that I considered it right to state that I never received less than six guineas an article, prose or verse, short or long. A respectable magazine is continually craving for my papers at that price, and the remuneration I receive from the annuals is much higher. I received a letter to say that the price of six guineas is not objectionable, and that the copyright (for which I had also stipulated) was with the author. This letter I have kept, and you shall see it when my father goes to London, as I expect he will, in about a fortnight, and then the matter will be cleared up. In the meanwhile, the scene you have (unless you decide on continuing the price at six guineas) had better remain unprinted. (1858: 215)

In this stressful attempt to negotiate terms for the publication of her work, Mitford pits one magazine against another. She implies not simply that she will pull her piece if her requirements are not met, but also suggests that she will place it with another equally 'respectable' periodical – that is to say, a rival, comparable in stature. As if she had not made herself clear, Mitford appends to the letter a postscript: 'To imagine for a moment that I should write at six guineas per sheet (or twelve?) is ridiculous. I left off writing for the magazines generally because sixteen was not enough ... six guineas an article, long or short'. Redding thought she was 'extortionate' (1858: 215). After publishing several of her poems and prose pieces in 1821, the magazine did not deal with her further until 1824.

Sketches of Rural Character: Mitford's 'Fugitive Pieces' 45

Frustrated in part by the limited income she received from writing for periodicals, Mitford decided to try her hand at playwriting. Her interest in theatre stemmed from her youth when, as a pupil, she made regular outings to the theatre and opera in London with Frances Rowden. After her return to Reading in 1802 she attended local productions. Unlike periodicals, which offered her steady but modestly compensated work, a well-received theatrical production could yield hundreds of pounds. After seeing William Charles Macready perform the lead role in C. E. Walker's *Wallace* at the Covent Garden Theatre on 6 December 1820, she set about writing a play especially for him.

Helping to nourish her aspiration to become a historical dramatist, Talfourd agreed to act as her emissary to Macready. After reading a draft of *Fiesco*, about the nobleman who conspired against the powerful Doria family at the political, economic and military centre of twelfth-century Genoa, the actor indicated a willingness to approach his managers. He was not, however, particularly optimistic about the outcome. Although he found elements of the play compelling and was intrigued by her capacity to write dialogue, Macready was concerned by the play's 'want of force & of situations' (Mitford, 1821e, n.p.). In a letter dated 24 March 1821, Mitford confessed to Talfourd that she was persuaded to his view:

> I am quite prepared for rejection – which Mr. Macready, though he has caught some of your infectious goodwill, seems himself to anticipate. Nevertheless I shall go on. You have inspired me with the hope that I may sometime or other produce something worthy even of his powers & I have set before my eyes the example of Mr. [John] Tobin who after eleven rejected Dramas wrote the Honeymoon. I will write a good Tragedy, even if I first write eleven bad ones. On this I am determined. (Mitford, 1821d: n.p.)[12]

A few weeks later, in a letter dated 4 April 1821, she reported to William Elford that the actor had concluded that *Fiesco* possessed 'too little of striking incident, and too little fluctuation to be successfully staged (Mitford 1870b: 129). But Macready was willing to read and consider performing in her future plays In a letter dated 9 June 1821, Mitford thanks Talfourd for his assistance in negotiations among playwright, actor and managers: 'I am delighted to hear that there is a chance of my little dramas finding a place in the London [Royal Theatres] – even if the profit were out of the question it is such an honour to be there' (Mitford, 1821e: n.p.). Mitford immediately began work on *Foscari*, a play about the famous Venetian doge Francesco Foscari.

If Mitford hoped that writing for the stage would lead to immediate financial success, she was mistaken. Macready proved exceedingly difficult in the subsequent negotiations over *Foscari*. He insisted that the script be rewritten multiple times; struck up a feud with fellow actor Charles Kemble over who should play the lead role; and ultimately suggested during rehearsals that unless his rival were dropped from the production, he would refuse to play his own part. As a result of the backstage turmoil, *Foscari* would not be staged until 1826.[13]

Despite the temptation, therefore, Mitford could not avoid publishing in periodicals. She needed the regular, if limited, income. As she explained to William Elford in a letter dated 22 March 1821 while working on *Fiesco*: 'I am also writing for the magazines – poetry, criticism, and dramatic sketches. I work as hard as a lawyer's clerk' (Mitford 1870b: 126). Besides misapprehending how much she could gain from periodical writing, Mitford was also frequently asked by friends to aid them in their efforts to break into the very competitive marketplace. She reluctantly wrote for the *Museum*, after being approached by its proprietor and her former printer, Abraham John Valpy. To Talfourd, she wrote on 31 March 1822: 'those papers which nobody else will take he shall have' (Mitford 1822a: n.p.). She was poorly remunerated. Owing to the family connection, Valpy may have assumed she would accept lower terms than other authors of comparable standing. But other writers for the publication recounted similar experiences. Of his contributions to the publication, the noted bibliographer Thomas Frognall Dibdin recounts: 'I never knew the extent of the sale, nor the amount of the profits – including even my own. Nor indeed do I remember upon what terms I was engaged; but I was true to my post, and tolerably abundant as well as regular in my contributions' (1836: 702). A monthly that never gained a footing after its launch in January 1822, the *Museum* folded three years later.

Sketching and prattling

By the end of 1821, Talfourd had still not found an editor willing to accept 'Our Village'. He advised Mitford not to 'write any more fugitive pieces' of country life and scenery until he was able to place the sketches in his possession (1821: n.p.). In the spring of 1822, with 'Our Village' still under consideration by another publication, Talfourd approached the relatively new editor of the *Lady's Magazine*, with whom he had an ongoing association after it launched as a new series in 1819. Talfourd offered Samuel Hamilton, Jr, the son of its long-time printer, the opportunity to review other work by Mitford. In an undated letter to Talfourd, likely written in the summer of 1822, Mitford expresses her gratitude for the opportunity: 'I will go about the articles for Mr. Hamilton immediately ... god bless you my dear friend!' (1822b: n.p.). Although she had previously published in the magazine, she was unfamiliar with Hamilton and had not submitted her work for consideration in a number of years. Hamilton accepted the dramatic sketch, 'Claudia's Dream', and a character sketch, 'Lucy', both of which appeared in the September 1822 issue.

More encouragingly, Hamilton indicated an eagerness to publish further pieces by Mitford. After accepting 'Boarding School Recollections. No. I. The French Teacher' and 'Boarding School Recollections. No. II. My School Fellows', which appeared in the October and November 1822 issues respectively, Hamilton commissioned her to write 'Boarding School Sketches. No III. The English Teacher' as well as another character sketch, 'The Talking Lady'. In an undated letter from November 1822, Mitford dispatched one of the sketches to Talfourd: 'I enclose you, my dear sir, the first of the two articles Mr. Hamilton desired & I will take care to send the other in time. If he won't wish me to furnish him with any more papers you will have the goodness to let me know' (1822e: n.p.). With both sketches in hand, Talfourd took the liberty of also submitting 'Our Village', which other editors had passed over.

What unfolded was an arrangement that was to the mutual benefit of editor and author. Mitford needed reliable work and Hamilton, as for most editors, needed a steady stream of reliable copy. Although Mitford had not yet conceived of an 'Our Village' series, her boarding school recollections already formed loosely connected vignettes. Hamilton recognised this potential. To Mitford's delight, he accepted all three sketches. In a letter to Talfourd dated 20 November 1822, Mitford expresses her satisfaction with the amount Hamilton was willing to pay for 'Our Village' (1822d: n.p.). He may not have offered what she had hoped to gain from Campbell and Redding, but it was 'higher than I expected & quite as much as I deserve' In fact, despite claiming otherwise in her letter to Redding, Mitford did not receive six guineas for each poem or prose work. The deputy editor had dismissed this assertion out of hand: 'the magazines generally paid no such price' (1858: 216). Mark Parker confirms that periodicals in the 1820s generally paid the same rate with only slight variation: twelve to sixteen guineas per sheet (2000: 12–13). Mitford was frequently paid ten to twelve guineas a sheet.[14] The *Lady's Magazine* paid her roughly four guineas a piece.[15] More than satisfactory remuneration, however, Hamilton offered Mitford the possibility of a steady income. Up until she severed her connection with the magazine, Mitford published at least one piece in every monthly issue. Compared with the hassles and inconveniences of other periodicals, the *Lady's Magazine* provided Mitford with a reliable income and considerable latitude.

Publishing largely self-contained sketches without attribution worked to the advantage of both the writer and the periodical. Many issues contained at least one, and sometimes as many as three, pieces by Mitford. For Mitford, this meant a greater income than if she were to publish serial fiction in which each instalment were to appear sequentially. Barbara Onslow has inaptly characterised Mitford's pieces as a 'series'. 'Like the tale', she argues, the descriptive rural sketch 'was short and self-contained; presented within a "series" it tempted readers with the promise of "more to come" rather as the serialised novel would do later, yet was more flexible since it could appear sporadically' (2000: 91). Given that Mitford worked across a number of periodicals of which the *Lady's Magazine* was only one, to say nothing of the fact that the sketches published in periodicals and included in *Our Village* were not solely topographical, the characterisation of them as constituting a series is wide of the mark. Nevertheless, her fundamental point holds: 'If a new series proved popular the writer would be encouraged to continue, if it failed the experiment could be cut off abruptly' (91). Mitford's descriptive rural sketches proved remarkably successful, and she began to produce ever greater numbers as a consequence.

Enabling those in unstable financial positions to make a living without stigma, anonymity was a significant component of periodical publication during the early and middle years of the nineteenth century. It protected authors who wrote for multiple periodicals to avoid being perceived as hacks (Brake 1994: 21–22). Periodicals were especially instrumental in enabling women to write and many achieved literary careers through anonymous periodical writing. As Alexis Easley contends, anonymous periodical publication was beneficial to women for several different reasons. First, it enabled women 'to evade essentialised notions of "feminine" voice and identity' (Easley 2004: 1). Second, it allowed them to write on subjects that were otherwise considered inappropriate, including 'slavery, women's emancipation, parliamentary reform, and industrialism' (Easley 2004: 2). Certainly, as Mitford discovered on the publication of her *Poems*, touching on topics deemed unsuitable could result in considerable rebuke.

The *Lady's Magazine* generally eschewed politics or, in fact, any topics of the moment. During much of Mitford's tenure as a contributor, the magazine was published by Robinson and Roberts, Chapter House Passage, Paternoster Row, London. By the time Mitford began to contribute sketches to the magazine, it was being printed as a small-format miscellany, with a heavy emphasis on its engravings, and later etchings, on fashion. Much of the magazine's content reflects the ideal – but certainly not, as a number of scholars have now established, the reality – of separate spheres, which was gaining purchase in the years leading up to Victoria's accession to the throne. The domestic woman was, therefore, most often the implicitly addressed reader. An essay might lament the loss of manners in the modern world, insisting that for the housewife 'highly-finished manners are superior to every other attainment' (Anon. 1823a: 150), while a fictional piece would present saccharine images of courtship:

> When a lover is on the eve of returning to a mistress, from whom he has [for] months been separated, how quickening and inflammable his sensibility [. . .]. Each lengthening day is to me a lover's mile-stone and tells me that I am a day nearer heaven. (Anon. 1823e: 41)

In January 1823, just a few months after Mitford's first piece appeared in print, the editor, Hamilton, stated his intention to adapt the magazine, 'with the exception of the monthly detail of fashions, to the perusal of both sexes' (Hamilton 1823: 2). But the journal rarely covered domestic and foreign news or the issues of broad social concern more characteristic of male-orientated periodicals.

This suited Mitford. Still smarting from the criticism of her *Poems* and frustrated by her failed attempts to become a successful playwright, Mitford was eager to provide copy to magazine editors that – in closely aligning with their own priorities – had the greatest odds of being accepted. As Vera Watson notes of this period, Mitford 'does not appear to have considered her magazine articles as anything more than a side-line, a means to obtain much needed money' (1994: 144). While Mitford had followed the lead of the *Quarterly Review* in writing pieces that were predominantly natural description, her early submissions to Hamilton indicate an interest in character sketches as well.

One way to understand how Mitford's periodical sketches worked with and against the *Lady's Magazine* is to consider the copy that surrounded her sketches in each issue as a type of paratext. We enter a text, Genette has suggested, through any number of thresholds: the title, the cover design, the dedication, the foreword, the author's preface, the introduction, the date of publication, in short, any device or industry norm that frames and mediates the reader's experience of a text. These paratexts profoundly shape the reading experience.[16] Prefatory remarks may attempt to provide guidance about how the rest of the text should be read; the cover design may evoke generic expectations by calling attention to the factuality or fictionality of the contents; a date of publication provides chronology, which is especially important if one is looking for a third – rather than, say, a first – edition or a particular reprint. While Genette's theories might, at first glance, seem most applicable to the original volume of *Our Village*, given that his study is focused on the material book, in his conclusion to *Paratexts: Thresholds of Interpretation*, Genette notes that the 'paratextual relevance' of serial publication and illustration 'seems to me undeniable' (1987: 405). He declines to elaborate, however, because properly examining each would require an extensive and detailed historical analysis. Moreover, he expresses a methodological concern that by not restricting the definition of paratext, under a principle of economy, one runs the risk of proclaiming that everything aside from the main body of a work functions as a threshold.

Yet for nineteenth-century readers who encountered fiction and literary non-fiction (including the discontinuous sketch) in periodicals, Genette's theories seem essential. His somewhat circumscribed understanding of seriality as a mode of publication in which 'cuts and deletions' are 'performed on texts', largely against the author's knowledge or will and according to the exigencies of form, perhaps accounts for some of his hesitation.[17] Certainly, Genette's description of serial publication is true. But it is also true that serial and discontinuous publication, whether in periodicals or in separate parts, was dynamic. Authors responded to reader feedback, utilised the form to craft the text and story in particular ways, and often conformed their stories to the editorial mission and scope of a periodical, complementing or competing with other writers and stories. We might think usefully, therefore, of different kinds of paratexts according to different forms of publication.

More recently, Linda K. Hughes has argued for a similar kind of approach to analysing periodicals. Although she does not use the term *paratexts*, Hughes is nevertheless interested in how 'interactive convergence[s]' among different elements of a periodical may be discerned when read horizontally within a specific issue and across a given volume (2014: 20). She refers to this mode of reading as 'sideways': moving through 'successive pages of a single periodical title over several issues constructs an ad hoc horizon of expectations that makes legible an array of temporal and material cruxes in print culture, from changes in formatting to interruptions of serial features by news events or by popular demand' (2014: 21). Although Hughes is arguing for a specific approach that, in enabling the researcher to 'understand how print organizes itself locally, materially, and temporally' (2014: 20), complements data science methods, I share her explicit – and Genette's implicit – assumption that reading in this way more closely approximates the experiences of an original reader.

In the case of Mitford's periodical sketches, her contributions to the *Lady's Magazine*, like the other solicited or reprinted content, were often melded into a house style. In this process, 'the polyphonic "miscellany"' of the magazine – with its emphasis on fine arts, music, drama and fashions – becomes unified into a 'material whole' (Patten 1996: 42). 'Magazines aim to develop their own distinctive personality', Robert L. Patten has argued, and 'editors, designers, writers, and artists all direct their efforts toward that end' (1996: 36). As Charles Dickens put it to the biographer and critic John Forster, as he laboured to launch *Household Words* later in the century, the editor needed to 'bind' the 'original matter' such as 'essays, reviews, letters, theatrical criticisms, &c, &c' in order to 'get a character established as it were' (1981: 622).

How an author might write about subjects was highly circumscribed according to the stated mission of the periodical and the generic modes that editors expected authors to utilise. 'The nature of [any] magazine', Richard Pearson has pointed out, 'is to fragment; it is a miscellaneous collection of disparate elements from salaried staff and external contributors, which is assembled as a whole rather than is naturally homogenous'. Pearson continues: 'The editorial function in any magazine is thus to hold together this collection [. . .] by fostering a corporate identity for the magazine which encompasses and even extends beyond any individual contribution' (2000: 183). Whatever work appears in the pages of a periodical, therefore, may be read in terms of how it fulfils the stated editorial vision.

Yet, within this circumscribed framework, Mitford ambivalently engaged with the textual culture of the *Lady's Magazine* as often as she helped to affirm it. This ambivalence is discernible in 'Lucy', one of the first sketches Mitford published in the magazine, in which the quality of her informality and the complex irony, rather than the one-dimensionality, of her sketches become apparent immediately. The sketch, which appeared in the September 1822 issue, begins:

> About a twelvemonth ago we had the misfortune to lose a very faithful and favorite female servant; one who has spoiled us for all others. Nobody can expect to meet with two Lucies. We all loved Lucy – poor Lucy! She did not die – only married. (1822c: 478)

On its surface, 'Lucy' would appear to be concerned with lauding women's responsibilities in the domestic realm, as did many of the essays and fictional pieces in the magazine. 'What a pleasure it is to see Lucy presiding in that parlour', the narrating self exclaims on visiting her former servant's new home, 'in all the glory of her honest affection and her warm hospitality, making tea [. . .] vaunting with courteous pride her home-made bread and her fresh butter' (1822c: 482). This apparent celebration of hearth and home is quickly undermined, however. While ostensibly rejoicing in Lucy's 'remarkably pretty' appearance and her 'pleasant and amusing qualities', Mitford's sketch repeatedly deploys apophasis, or backhanded compliments: 'Her face was round and dimpled, with [. . .] a complexion that entirely took away the look of vulgarity which the breadth and flatness of her face might otherwise have given' (1822c: 478). Lucy is described as the perfect servant yet, as the story progresses, she appears to have been known largely for her tittle-tattle – 'Lucy liked talking, and every body liked to hear her talk'; 'she was an incomparable gossip' (1822c: 478, 479) – and her village flirtations, rather than her work. Scathing humour hides behind a mask of benevolent maternalism. 'Scattered amongst her great merits Lucy had a few small faults, as all persons should have', the narrator notes with a seeming generosity of spirit, before continuing with a lengthy list of imperfections that point to Lucy's unstable temperament:

> She had occasionally an aptness to take offence where none was intended, and then the whole house bore audible testimony to her displeasure: she used to scour through half a dozen doors in a minute for the mere purpose of banging them after her [. . .] Oh! her door-clapping was nothing to her singing! it rang through one's head like the screams of a peacock. (1822c: 479)

Structurally, Mitford's sketch differed little from the many other biographical sketches that dominated the pages of the magazine, but its tone, however, was strikingly different. Rejecting the domestic sphere, Mitford's narrator exclaims: 'Lucy's pleasure is in her house; mine is in its situation' (1822c: 482). She then proceeds to provide an account of the village landscape, its topographical characteristics and its historical character. What is emphasised at least in this sketch, is that the countryside works as an enabling mechanism for the narrator's escape from the confines of the home, a realm so privileged in the *Lady's Magazine*.

Literary sketching was seen as a particularly appropriate genre for women writers because it was considered a less ambitious literary form. Women were often encouraged, as Richard Sha points out, to take up verbal and visual sketching in order to become ladies through the 'passive copying of nature' – which was certainly what the *Quarterly Review* suggested Mitford do – or in crafting sentimental biographical portraits. 'Lucy' undermines many of the generic and gender expectations of the sketch form (Sha 1998: 105). The distinctive rhetorical style Mitford appears to have been cultivating in her periodical publications was a kind of nattering to readers in witty, ironic and often cutting ways.

For Mitford, sketching became a mode of writing for an intimate public. As Clifford Siskin points out in his discussion of the rise of the novel, writers in the late eighteenth and early nineteenth centuries 'vied generically to produce the kind of writing most suitable to the demands of conversation' (1998: 165). '[T]he "distance" of print does dislocate', Siskin notes, 'however, that dislocation is precisely what recuperates both the private – in enabling one-to-one speech acts – and a new kind of public – in the reproducibility and dispersal of those acts' (1998: 164). Mitford was not alone in recognising the power of a conversational tone. 'We are free and easy in these days', she wrote to Elford on 23 June 1824, 'and talk to the public as a friend' (Mitford 1870b: 25).

In essence, Mitford took what she believed to be the greatest deficiency in her capacity for prose writing and turned it into a significant strength. As a letter writer, she delighted in sharing gossip with her correspondents. To William Elford, for example, Mitford conveys the following assessment of Jane Austen, whom Mitford's mother had known in her younger years: 'she herself is an old maid (I beg her pardon – I mean a young lady) [. . .] Mamma says that she was then the prettiest, silliest, most affected husband-hunting butterfly she ever remembers; and a friend of mine, who visits her now, says that she has stiffened into the most perpendicular, precise, taciturn, piece of "single blessedness" that ever existed [. . .] she is [. . .] a poker of whom everyone is afraid' (L'Estrange 1870a: 306). With Elizabeth Barrett Browning, Mitford shared a love of titbits about others, perhaps only surpassed by their mutual interest in the antics of Flush, a cocker spaniel gifted by the latter to the former (Morrison 2021a). Of William Cowper, she once remarked to Barrett Browning in a letter dated 4 May 1842, 'I never doubted his insanity, knowing as I did his kinswoman, whose melancholy tale I must have told you . . . whose madness was always said to be hereditary. There could be no question of the taint in the blood' (1842: 85). As she laments in her letter to Talfourd dated 16 March 1821, she had habituated herself to 'an incorrect & gossiping rapidity' (1821c). By sketching, Mitford could engage in a kind of discursive play that she termed 'prattle' (1821a).[18] In the true spirit of prattle, Mitford's sketches – much like her letters – were opinionated, conveying the impressions she had formed of an individual based on a short acquaintance or, conversely, rendering judgements based on a very long acquaintance but inspired by a chance encounter or reflection.

The *Lady's Magazine* encouraged contributors, if only implicitly, to employ a casual tone in their submissions. It also regularly

Sketches of Rural Character: Mitford's 'Fugitive Pieces'

published articles on the pleasures correspondents could derive from letter reading and writing. One article, titled 'Paris Chit-Chat', with the author writing under the pseudonym Marmaduke Tattle, for example, begins:

> *Me voila*! Ladies! – I have had reproaches, remonstrances on your account; and I fear I have deserved them. What has become of me? After so kind a reception, to neglect my fair friends – 'tis really ungrateful, discourteous, altogether unlike me. (Tattle 1823: 13)

This is certainly relaxed and conversational. It is also vapid.

In her sketches, Mitford repeatedly uses forms of direct address as well. In 'Our Village', which appeared in the 31 December 1822 issue of the *Lady's Magazine*, the narrative 'I' is personal and addresses a distinct 'you': 'Will you walk with me through our village, courteous reader? The journey is not long'. Of course, the question presupposes the reader's assent and it is immediately followed by specific instructions: 'We will begin at the lower end, and proceed up the hill' (1822d: 645). Sometimes the rhetorical questions are so idiosyncratic that no reader would be able to furnish the correct answer. In 'A Country Cricket Match', which ran in the July 1823 issue, the somewhat disjointed prose, interrupted by a series of dashes and interrogatives, recounts a game between neighbouring parishes: '*They* began the warfare – these boastful men of B. And what think you, gentle reader, was the amount of their innings? These challengers – the famous eleven – how many did they get? Think! imagine! guess! – You cannot? –Well! –they got twenty-two, or rather they got twenty; for two of theirs were short notches, and would never have been allowed, only that, seeing what they were made of, we and our umpire were not particular' (1823k: 390).

At other times, the narrative 'I' does not ask a question but makes a confidential statement. In 'Ellen', which opened the September 1823 issue, the narrator relays an experience of accompanying her eponymous acquaintance to the residence of a neighbour – whom she had not previously met – for dinner. The narrator declares: 'He was, as Ellen truly described him, tall and graceful, and well-bred almost to a fault; reminding her of that beau-ideal of courtly elegance George the Fourth, and me, (pray, reader, do not tell!) me, a little, a very little, the least in the world, of Sir Charles Grandison' (1823j: 492). Although by the time this sketch was published the editor had stated his intention of broadening the readership beyond women, the narrator's intimate aside – remarking on the slight resemblance of Captain Falkner to Samuel Richardson's chivalrous nobleman – suggests that the periodical remained female-orientated.

What made Mitford's mode of discursivity and engagement more distinctive than the magazine's standard fare was that she also modelled herself on some of the leading prose writers of the day. Before she had started the sketches for the *Lady's Magazine*, she had been trying her hand at literary and dramatic criticism. She quickly grew to admire William Hazlitt, whose lectures at the Surrey Institution in 1818 she attended. On 3 March, she wrote to her parents and expressed delight with his lecture, 'On the Modern Poets', in which 'most charmingly he trimmed the whole set of them'. She recounted the incident to Elford a few days later, proclaiming that Hazlitt was 'amusing past all description to everybody but the parties concerned – them to be sure he spared as little as a mower spares the flowers in a hayfield' (qtd. in Jones 1989: 284).

In addition to hearing Hazlitt speak, Mitford also studied his writings. In a letter to Elford dated 28 December 1818, she avers that '[s]o much of Hazlitt is rather dangerous to one's taste – rather like dining on sweetmeats and supping on pickles'. 'So poignant is he, and so rich', she continues, 'everything seems insipid after him' (Mitford 1870b: 47). She took such pleasure in his satirical skills that she recommended in a letter to her conservative friend the following year, dated 28 December 1819, that he put aside his political biases to read *Characters of Shakespeare's Plays* (1817), *Lectures on the English Poets* (1818) and *Lectures on the English Comic Writers* (1819):

> I am sure you would like them; they are so exquisitely entertaining, so original, so free from every sort of critical shackle; the style is so delightfully *piquant*, so sparkling, so glittering, so tasteful, so condensed; the images and illustrations come in such rich and graceful profusion that one seems like Aladdin in the magic garden, where the leaves were emeralds, the flowers Sapphires, and the fruit topazes and rubies. Do read some of the lectures. (Mitford 1870b: 79)

Certainly, Mitford did not recommend Hazlitt's political writings to Elford. But, even in these literary works, his politically motivated aesthetic judgments are often clear. Nevertheless, Mitford assures her correspondent that one need not accept Hazlitt's views to enjoy his bravura prose.

If Mitford drew inspiration from Hazlitt, she also saw in Charles Lamb's idiosyncratic personal essays a way to render her sketches more distinctive than what often appeared in the *Lady's Magazine*. Abjuring formality and ceremony, Hazlitt's and Lamb's works are sinewy, pointed and – the term she uses to define both – piquant. Lamb 'write[s] so delightfully', she exclaims to Haydon in a letter dated 7 January 1821 (Mitford 1870b: 123). To Elford on 28 April 1822, she declares that

> Charles Lamb's articles, signed 'Elia', are incomparably the finest specimens of English prose in the language. The humour is as delicate as Addison's, and far more piquant. Oh how you would enjoy it! Do borrow or hire all the numbers of Taylor and Hessey's 'London Magazine', and read all Elia's articles ... and tell me how you like Charles Lamb. (Mitford 1870b: 151)

On 9 February 1824 she pronounced Hazlitt's essays written under the pseudonym 'Table Talk' 'delightful' (Mitford 1870b: 175). She particularly appreciated his 'genius for contempt'. This may be a surprising admission coming from a writer who, by the time the fifth volume of *Our Village* was published in 1834, was lauded as a 'kind-hearted writer, who never looks upon human nature but when the sun shines upon it' (Reedpen 1834: 52) and whose posthumous reputation approached sainthood. Even before Mitford's death, as Constance Hill declares, Mitford's 'sunny nature ... spread such a halo about the scenes' in Three Mile Cross that were the basis for *Our Village* that 'pilgrims' flocked to the area (1920: ix).

While adopting some of the conventions of the *Lady's Magazine*, particularly first-person address, Mitford also adapted them by engaging with and learning from the work of her contemporaries. Her appreciation for Hazlitt's contemptuousness is evident in a number of sketches, such as 'The Talking Lady'. In this piece, which appeared in the January 1823 issue, Mitford recounts four days spent with an 'old maid': 'four days hard listening; ... four days chained by "sad civility" to that fire-side, once so quiet, and again – cheering thought! – again, I trust to be so, when the echo of that visitor's incessant tongue shall have died away' (1823c: 16).

'The Talking Lady' opens by paying tongue-in-cheek homage to the biographical sketch form preferred by the editors of the *Lady's Magazine*:

> The visitor in question is a very excellent and respectable elderly lady, upright in mind and body, with a figure that does honor to her dancing-master, a face exceedingly well preserved, wrinkled and freckled, but still fair, and an air of gentility over her whole person, which is not the least affected by her out-of-fashion garb. (1823c: 16)

With her 'air of gentility' and 'out-of-fashion garb', the talking lady anticipates Elizabeth Gaskell's *Cranford*. Governed by a strict code of gentility and dressing 'very independent of fashion', the Cranfordian women – whom I discuss in Chapter Three – conclude that it does not 'signify how we dress . . . where everybody knows us', and outside of Cranford, 'where nobody knows us', it does not matter either.

Such moments do not evince kind-heartedness. Rather, they suggest that Mitford revelled in 'contempt', the application of which she learned from Hazlitt. 'I am afraid, very much afraid, that I like him the better for it', she approvingly notes of his capacity 'to turn the grandest compliment into the bitterest sarcasm' (qtd. in Jones 1989: 285). As the sketch continues, the narrator observes the many activities that the lady passes over in favour of talking. 'Walking exhausts the breath that might be better employed', she amusingly recounts. 'She will talk you sixteen hours a day for twenty days together, and not deduct one poor five minutes for halts and baiting time', the narrator continues. 'Talking, sheer talking is meat and drink and sleep to her. She likes nothing else. Eating is a sad interruption' (1823c: 17).

Thus, the lady's capacity to speak on any topic becomes a means of accounting for her many flaws. The narrator notes:

> Allude to some anecdote of the neighbourhood, and she forthwith treats you with as many parallel passages as are to be found in an air with variations. Take up a new publication, and she is equally at home there; for though she knows little of books, she has, in the course of an up-and-down life, met with a good many authors, and teazes and provokes you by telling of them precisely what you do not care to hear, the maiden names of their wives, and the Christian names of their daughters. (1823c: 17–18)

Sketches of Rural Character: Mitford's 'Fugitive Pieces'

As the sketch continues, the narrator outlines the substance of their conversations:

> All the news and scandal of a large county forty years ago, and a hundred years before, and ever since, all the marriages, deaths, births, elopements, lawsuits, and casualties of her own times, her father's, grandfather's, great-grandfather's, nephew's, and grandnephew's, has she detailed with a minuteness, an accuracy, a prodigality of learning, a profuseness of proper names, a pedantry of locality, which would excite the envy of a county historian, a king at arms, or even a Scotch novelist. (1823c: 17)

The narrator concludes by noting what she has learned about the lady's family during the course of the visit:

> Father, mother, uncle, sister, brother, two nephews, and one niece, all these have successively passed away, though a healthy race, and with no visible disorder – except – but we must not be uncharitable. They might have died, though she had been born dumb. (1823c: 18)

This hilariously contemptuous piece lampoons both the conventions of the biographical sketch and the domestic concerns such as hosting and entertaining guests, with which many other pieces in the *Lady's Magazine* are concerned.

Although offering a variety of material to the reader, including divergent points of view, the overall editorial framework of the *Lady's Magazine* tended to reflect and reinforce domestic ideology. Mitford's ambivalence toward the periodical's textual culture is precisely what makes her sketches distinctive. Other pieces reflect an outright disdain for anything associated with the feminine. In 'A Great Farm-House', which I will revisit in the next chapter, Mitford's narrator recalls encountering one of her neighbours – a farmer – with a group of puppies that he adores. '[T]o my thinking, these pretty creatures were fitter for the parlour than the field', she observes to the reader.

> They were strong, certainly, excellently loined, cat-footed, and chested like a war-horse; but there was a want of length about them – a want of room, as the coursers say; something a little, a very little inclining to the clumsy; a dumpiness, a pointer-look. (1823d: 103)

Scrutinising the features of each of the dogs, from their feet and loins to their overall demeanour, Mitford dismisses them as too effeminate for hunting, thereby suggesting that she is a better judge of the animals' potential than their male owner.[19] The narrator in several of these sketches repeatedly identifies not with the drawing room but rather with the countryside – once the province of the wandering (male) poet or, in the tradition of Washington Irving, the sketch artist, but increasingly the domain of women writers.[20]

Not all of Mitford's sketches were equally sharp-edged. 'Hannah', which appears in the same issue as 'The Talking Lady', relates the story of a working-class mother, Dame Wilson (the use of the honorific intended to be both affectionate and humorous), left to raise two children on her own and of the romance that sweeps one of the daughters off her feet. The titular character is described by the narrator as 'the sweetest flower of the garden' and the 'prettiest' and 'best' girl in the village. She is lauded for her 'modesty', which elevates her in the narrator's eyes above the 'common country rosebud'; 'generosity'; many domestic talents ('accomplished in all the arts of the needle'); and faithful devotion to her mother. Hannah is rewarded in this story by marrying a wealthy suitor (1823b: 26). The sketch is not without its own ambivalence: Hannah has difficulty in adjusting to her new life. On the whole, however, it is a celebration of domesticity.

Mitford's more challenging sketches suggest that she was interested in exploiting both the periodical medium and the generic form in order to develop a distinctive rhetorical mode and to fashion some semblance of authorial agency. Her frustrated ambitions as a novelist led her to invent the sketch form of writing that Harriet Martineau termed 'graphic description' (Chapman 1877: 418). 'I began a novel myself once', Mitford wrote to Elford on 30 January 1820, 'and got on very prosperously for about a hundred pages of character and description .... I came to a dead stop for want of invention. A lack of incident killed the poor thing' (Mitford 1870b: 84). Mitford's sketches – all character and description – do indeed have a recognisable authorial voice. But in the context of their periodical publication, this voice is, to a great extent, at odds with the way critics have tended to characterise it. Even Garcha, who is fully alert to the significance of narrative style, argues that the biographical subjects in Mitford's sketches uniformly possess a 'sunny contentment and boundless, naïve energy', while the narrator herself has a 'light-hearted, idyllic nature' (2009: 9).

Sketches of Rural Character: Mitford's 'Fugitive Pieces'

'[F]rom the *pen* of a Lady'

While Mitford was constructing a literary career as a prose sketch writer, she was also continuing to make progress on becoming an historical dramatist. In 1823, Mitford won over Macready with her script for *Julian*. The lead role in the political tragedy, set in medieval Sicily but based on Greek tragedy, was written with him in mind. There was no part for Kemble to play. After a number of back-and-forths over the script, Macready signed off. To William Elford, she wrote on 28 February, 'After a degree of contention and torment and suspense such as I cannot describe, one of my plays – my last and favourite play – is, I do really believe, on the point of representation, with my favourite actor for the hero. He (Mr. Macready) read it in the green-room on Wednesday, and I suppose it will be out in ten days or a fortnight' (Mitford 1870o: 157). *Julian* opened on 21 March and played to full houses during its run. Mitford published the script contemporaneously.

After eight nights, the play was closed, ostensibly to accommodate another production. If it had continued to a ninth night, however, the theatre would have been forced to pay Mitford another £100 (Coles 1957: 36). But there were also the reviews – overwhelmingly, although not exclusively, scathing – with which to contend. If the audiences were satisfied with the performances and dialogue, the theatre critics were not. The Saturday 22 March edition of the *London Literary Gazette* was perhaps the kindest: '*Julian* ... acts better than it reads' (Anon. 1823b: 178). The following day, the *Examiner* rendered its judgement: 'Julian is too sensitive and lacrymose [sic] for us, – a hero of the feminine gender, – a victim rather to sentiment than situation – netted by cobwebs, and as helpless in his difficulties as a fine lady'. The chief complaint of this theatrical reviewer is her 'sex of mind'. 'Miss Mitford is known as the Authoress of some pleasing poems', he notes, 'although not of an order of merit which suggests an idea of tragic capability' (Anon. 1823c). A review in the 24 March issue of *John Bull* was particularly harsh:

> Covent Garden, last Saturday, put forth one of those Melo-dramas, which, in these degenerate days, are called *Tragedies* – under the title of JULIAN.
>
> It is from the *pen* of a Lady, of the name of MITFORD known to her publisher and her particular friends as the Authoress of some

poems; and the very mention of this fact, would have induced us to have overlooked the sundry absurdities with which the performance is sprinkled, had she not, with a rashness, wholly unaccountable, *published it*. (1823d: 94)

All three reviewers, as well as other critics, including those whose assessments were more positive, highlighted the playwright's gender as significant. In a vein similar to the evaluation of Mitford's poems in the *Quarterly Review*, these critics chastised her for entering a predominantly male domain. Macready thought that Mitford's 'sex was, in great part, the occasion of the intolerable malignity with which "Julian" was attacked' (Mitford 1870b: 167).

In the early nineteenth century, women faced particular obstacles in their attempts to break into the theatrical world as dramatists. Those who did write or produce plays took advantage of personal or familial connections to make it possible (Donkin 1995: 31). Mitford was able to become a dramatist largely without such aid. The critical reception of her first dramatic work, however, indicates the extent to which the theatre remained a male-dominated and controlled industry.

In staging *Julian*, Mitford also entered the political arena. Portraying regicide and the overthrow of ancestral rule, the play tackles themes that remained, more than a decade after the appearance of *Poems*, unfeminine. Although *Julian* largely focuses on the past, whereas Mitford's more politically orientated poems had focused on the present, the play nevertheless directly alludes to contemporary geopolitical concerns. By drawing implicit parallels between its medieval setting and the concerns of modern-day Sicilians, who failed in their uprising against Bourbon rule in 1820, it is critical of state corruption but simultaneously wary of movements promising change. On balance, however, the play aligns itself – in a prototypically liberal move – with resistance to tyranny. Had the play treated political events differently, articulating views at variance from, rather than identified with, Whigs and Radicals, the reception of her play among these reviewers may well have been very different.

Nevertheless, even if *Julian* had been well received critically, the hassles surrounding its production were almost too much for her to bear. In addition to the difficulties of writing for Macready, Mitford repeatedly haggled over remuneration. As she explained to Elford on 25 April 1823, she was 'not paid ... for the third and sixth nights'. She remarks that, by this point somewhat wistfully, 'to undergo all this misery, and not get my money, would be terrible indeed!' (Mitford 1870b: 162). Eventually, Mitford earned £200 from the play.

It is true that Mitford needed money and the proceeds from *Julian* provided a much-needed infusion of cash. But she had also long sought acclaim and celebrity and this goal seemed increasingly realisable after *Julian*. Soon after the production ended, Mitford began to think about ways to capitalise on its success. In April 1823, she contemplated approaching Hamilton with a proposal to publish a collection of her best sketches from the *Lady's Magazine*. In an undated letter written that month, she asks Talfourd, 'Would a Volume of Dramatic Scenes & sonnets... answer do you think? Or a Vol. of prose – some of the best things in Mr. Hamiltons – I mean of my best – & others of the same sort with as much Dutch picture finishing as possible? I think that would – but then Mr. Hamilton having bought the Articles I suppose the right to them is in him now' (1823f: n.p.). Twelve days later, however, she wrote to Elford to share, among other matters, rather shocking news: Hamilton had gone bankrupt and 'absconded above forty pounds in my debt'. Many other contributors were similarly affected. Lamenting the situation, Mitford continues: 'Oh! who would be an authoress! The only comfort is, that the Magazine can't go on without me' (Mitford 1870b: 162).

This, perhaps, overestimates her significance to the *Lady's Magazine*. Although the magazine's prominence had begun to wane by the 1820s, it remained a significant force in publishing. But Hamilton had certainly relied on her to produce regular content. Mitford once claimed to Elford in a letter dated 13 May 1823 that the periodical's success was 'chiefly' her own doing: 'the sale of the magazine [increased] from two hundred and fifty to two thousand' (Mitford 1870b: 163). Most critics have repeated this assertion as fact. To take one (because prominent) example: in his entry on Mitford in the *Oxford Dictionary of National Biography*, Martin Garrett asserts that 'sales of the magazine' increased 'dramatically as a result' of her sketches. What Garrett does not explore are other factors that likely affected the increase in subscriptions, including improved distribution systems and expanding literacy rates.[21]

In any case, it initially seemed likely to Mitford that the *Lady's Magazine* would fold under the weight of Hamilton's improprieties.

Although her work occasionally appeared in other periodicals as well, none of these outlets provided Mitford the same frequent opportunities to publish. Between 1822 and April 1823 she published more than fourteen pieces in the magazine (Coles 1959: 222–223). Lamenting this turn of events, Mitford tells Talfourd in a letter dated 24 April 1823 that although she hoped to receive some kind of settlement from Charles Heath, Hamilton's brother-in-law who had taken over as editor, her 'prime wish' was that it continue publication: 'I should like constant employment there or else where – for I begin not to dislike that sort of writing, & as to the stage I am heartsick at the very thought'. Fearing a return to the unpredictability and financial precarity of irregular publication, Mitford declares herself more 'vexed at this affair' than 'Julian'. 'That Magazine did seem something certain', she laments, 'but there is nothing sure in this world but disappointment' (1824g: n.p.).

Heath and Mitford, however, were able to come to an agreement that would enable the magazine to continue to publish her as a contributor and to lay the groundwork for the first volume of sketches in bound form. Insisting that he would be unable to pay off Hamilton's debts, Heath offered Mitford a deal: he would continue to include her work and pay her accordingly, but he would not reimburse her for her losses. In lieu of payment for the sketches that had already appeared, he would give her the copyright and, with it, the opportunity for republication.[22] In a letter to Talfourd dated 17 May 1823, Mitford seeks his advice: 'Do you think the permission to print the papers worth any thing?' She goes on to outline the possible contents of a collection of sketches: 'Certainly Lucy, Hannah, Our Village & one or two more would with some new Articles make a pretty Volume – & if that could be done I might go on quietly under the new arrangement' (1823i: n.p.).

Recognising the strain of her labours and the particular blow of Hamilton absconding to France with her payment, Mitford's father paid lip service to the idea of seeking employment, which she took as sincere. On 13 May 1823, she wrote to Elford:

> My father has at last resolved – partly, I believe, instigated by the effect which the terrible feeling of responsibility and want of power has had on my health and spirits – to try if he can himself obtain any employment that may lighten the burthen. He is, as you know, active, healthy, and intelligent, and with a strong sense of duty and of right. I am sure

Sketches of Rural Character: Mitford's 'Fugitive Pieces'

that he would fulfil to the utmost any charge that might be confided to him; and if it were one in which my mother or I could assist, you may be assured that he would have zealous and faithful coadjutors. For the management of estates or any country affairs he is particularly well qualified; or any work of superintendence which requires integrity and attention. The addition of two or even one hundred a year to our little income, joined to what I am, in a manner, sure of gaining by mere industry, would take a load from my heart of which I can scarcely give you an idea. It would be everything to me; for it would give me what, for many months, I have not had – the full command of my own powers. Even 'Julian' was written under a pressure of anxiety which left me not a moment's rest. I am, however, at present, quite recovered from the physical effects of this tormenting affair, and have regained my flesh and colour, and almost my power of writing prose articles; and if I could but recover my old hopefulness and elasticity, should be again such as I used to be in happier days. Could I but see my dear father settled in any employment, I know I should. (Mitford 1870b: 163–164)

Mitford was gravely disheartened by the situation at the *Lady's Magazine* but encouraged by the prospect of her father taking up work. This possibility alleviated at least some of the vexatiousness she felt at not being paid by Heath for pieces already written. But her father did not make good on his word. On 21 August 1823, she reports to Elford that her father had not even begun to look for work. 'I do not press the matter, though I anxiously wish it', she says with resignation (Mitford 1870b: 166).

Although Mitford was able to support her family on the income she derived from writing, the threat of poverty was always present. This acted as a spur to continued production (Morrison 2012: 865–869). Mitford had already told Elford – in her letter dated 25 April 1823, in which she writes about not being paid for the third and sixth nights of *Julian* and Hamilton's £40 debt to her – that she was increasingly despairing of writing at all. 'I would rather serve in a shop – rather scour floors – rather nurse children', she exclaims, 'than undergo these tremendous and interminable disputes' (Mitford 1870b: 162). In a subsequent letter dated 21 August, she contends that she writes solely from necessity:

> If I could but get the assurance of earning for my dear father and mother a humble competence I should be the happiest creature in the world. But for these dear ties I should never write another line, but

go out in some situation as other destitute women do. It seems to me, however, my duty to try a little longer; the more especially as I am sure separation would be felt by all of us to be the greatest of all evils. (Mitford 1870b: 166)

Yet, although Mitford frequently professed herself open to any form of employment that might keep her and her parents afloat, one suspects disingenuousness. She disdained writing for an income as she averred to Talfourd in an undated letter of 1822 or 1823: 'What a dreadful debasing thing it is to want money!' (undated: n.p.). But as I discuss more fully in the next chapter, Mitford was not at all averse to fame.

Because of her father's unwillingness to work, a new source of potential income was essential. By 3 July 1823, she had arranged for Whittaker to publish a collection of her sketches from the *Lady's Magazine*. By April 1824, the volume was in press. 'It will be a pretty little book', she writes to Talfourd, in a letter stamped 12 April 1824, 'about the size & type of a Vol of the Scotch novels. I wonder whether it will gain me employment which has been my object in the bringing it out – Really I see worse writing in the great Magazines – Many articles much better of course – but still some that are worse' (1824c, n.p.). In this letter, Mitford indicates clearly her aims in publishing the volume. She reiterates this goal several months later in a letter to Talfourd, dated January 1824, expressing the hope that 'it might be the means of procuring for me some employment in that line [of prose sketching]' (qtd in Coles 1957: 43). In other words, periodical publication had led to the production of a book, which in turn could be leveraged for further opportunities in the periodicals.

With this goal in mind, Mitford accepted Whittaker's terms, although they were far from favourable, and organised her discontinuous sketches into a loosely cohesive narrative of rural life. In a letter to Talfourd dated 23 September 1824, she indicates that her royalties were a mere £20. Although Whittaker approached her about the possibility of a second volume, she wondered if '[i]t would be better to go on with the magazines' (1824f: n.p.). In an undated letter from the autumn of that year, she confesses that part of her motivation in contemplating a second volume is to call attention to the first (1824g). Yet although her royalties were initially lacklustre, Mitford continued to profit. The first volume ultimately went through three editions in its first twelve months of

Sketches of Rural Character: Mitford's 'Fugitive Pieces' 67

publication. It soon became clear that the most advantageous path forward would be to publish in both formats – individual sketches in magazines and collections of sketches in bound volumes – rather than choosing between them.

Becoming Mary Russell Mitford

At the time of the publication of *Our Village*, Mitford had not yet achieved financial security. She had, however, obtained a level of fame as indicated by, among other developments, the wide circulation of her likeness in print culture. One portrait (Figure 1.2), for which Mitford likely sat in the late 1820s or early 1830s, was published in 1836 at the height of her career. The engraved print, which – before the emergence of the medium of photography – enabled interested persons to view and buy portraits of artists and intellectuals, shows Mitford in the exuberant fashion of this time. Throughout the decade known as the Romantic period in dress, women of the middle classes often appeared in bold, richly coloured silk or velvet garments. Their figures were often an exaggerated hourglass, with bell-shaped skirts, wide shoulders and puffed gigot sleeves. This was often offset by artificially curled hair, frequently a wig or fake locks. Massive, opulent headwear – as evidenced by two representative fashion plates from the *Lady's Magazine* (Figures 1.3 and 1.4) published around the time that Mitford would have sat for the portrait – was de rigueur. Although Mitford's headpiece dominates, the style itself is matronly, a white frilled and beribboned day cap, which middle-class ladies in their forties and fifties preferred.

Mitford's letters indicate that beyond immediate financial concerns, fashioning a literary career and an identity as an author was a conscious project (in which, in fact, her letters themselves – as well as the engraving – participate). Just before the first volume of *Our Village* appeared, Mitford wrote to Elford in a letter dated 18 January 1824: 'It . . . will be published with or without my name, as it shall please my worshipful bibliopole. At all events, the author has no wish to be *incognita*; so I tell it you as a secret to be told' (Mitford 1870b: 172). After some negotiation with Whittaker, the volume appeared under her authorial signature, accompanied by the phrase 'Author of Julian, a Tragedy'.

The transformation of Mitford's sketches from anonymously published pieces to signed collections reflected a significant

Figure 1.2 Mary Russell Mitford. Illustration from a portrait by A. Burt. Constance Hill, *Mary Russell Mitford and Her Surroundings. With Illustrations by Ellen G. Hill and Reproductions of Portraits.* London: John Lane, The Bodley Head; New York: John Lane Company, 1920. Courtesy of the Armstrong Browning Library, Baylor University.

historical change. By the late eighteenth century, the older patronage system in publishing had given way to a variety of relationships among authors, editors and publishers, and for the first time the cultivation of a mass readership was possible. At the very moment when opportunities for anonymous periodical writing became available, there was also an increasing demand for authenticity and attribution. Authorial self-fashioning was a way of calling attention to oneself in a competitive market.

When they finally began to appear in print, reviews of *Our Village* were almost uniformly positive.[23] Even the *Quarterly Review*, which had skewered her poetry, pronounced the volume a success. Heath, however, was apoplectic. He demanded that those sketches which she had not included in the volume be reprinted

Sketches of Rural Character: Mitford's 'Fugitive Pieces' 69

Figure 1.3 Fashion plate from the *Lady's Magazine* (January 1831). Reproduced by kind permission of the Syndics of Cambridge University Library.

by him and he insisted on retaining the copyright for any further pieces. In a letter dated 6 June 1824, she wrote to Talfourd:

> I have now to ask your advice what I should do with regard to writing for them in future. Their terms are six guineas a sheet, of very small print in double columns – little enough God knows – yet if I might reserve the right of copy for this I should not so much care – but it is clear that whilst offending & neglecting & beating me down they yet think well enough of the articles to desire to publish them in a Volume on their own account – Now this I should particularly dislike – I have selected the best for my own Volume – & of those that remain there are several that I should dislike exceedingly to be printed with my name – because there is a mixture of pungency, which in an obscure magazine where the author is unknown can hurt no one, but which when the writer is avowed would assume quite a different character, & probably be assigned to people whom I never dreamt of – Nevertheless

Figure 1.4 Fashion plate from the *Lady's Magazine* (August 1831). Reproduced by kind permission of the Syndics of Cambridge University Library.

> it is throwing myself out of all employment to give them up & that I hardly dare do. What would you advise? (1824e: n.p.)

Her use of the term *obscure* here, one she would repeat in *Recollections of a Literary Life*, appears to be a jab that contrasts the limited reach of a magazine – in which she published her sketches anonymously – to the wider circulation and sustained presence of a book bearing attribution. Talfourd advised her not to accept Heath's terms and she duly severed her association with the magazine.

Mitford's letter to Talfourd reveals just how conscious she was of authorial self-construction. Having been searingly reviewed for her *Poems* and *Julian*, but praised for her prose sketches of village life, Mitford settled on working primarily in a remunerative genre that would be perceived as appropriate for women writers. Her reticence to republish some of her more pungent sketches indicates

Sketches of Rural Character: Mitford's 'Fugitive Pieces'

a clear awareness that, unlike Lamb, her maliciousness had to be masked by anonymity and, even in the anonymous sketches, obscured by maternal beneficence. Her remark also suggests a keen awareness that assessments of *Our Village* would be based on narrative voice rather than – since there would be none – the forward movement of plot.

Despite occasional direct or indirect cross-references from one sketch to another, the real consistency is Mitford's engaged narrator. Although Mitford uses forms of direct address in these sketches, speaking informally to the reader who is figured as the 'you', it was initially impossible for anyone to associate the textual 'I' with a specific author. Without the veil of anonymity, many of the topics Mitford explored, as well as the occasional tenor of her voice, would have been deemed improper. Once her authorship became known, however, the reader was encouraged – initially by Mitford herself and then by a variety of publishers – to conflate the narrator with the author and to view the sketches as reflections of her own experiences in Three Mile Cross.

Mitford initiated a process, beginning with the first volume of *Our Village* in 1824, of paratextually reframing her sketches as offering 'some of the sweetest glimpses' of rural life.[24] 'The following pages contain an attempt to delineate country scenery and country manners', the preface to that first volume begins, 'as they exist in a small village in the south of England'. The author, according to Mitford, who writes in the third person,

> has painted, as they appeared to her, their [the village residents] little frailties and their many virtues, under an intense and thankful conviction, that in every condition of life, goodness and happiness may be found by those who seek them, and never more surely than in the fresh air, the shade, and the sunshine of nature. (1824a: v–vi)

Mitford pledges her fidelity not to the subjects about which she writes, but rather to her artistic rendering of them, evoked by the adjective *paint*: 'If she be accused of having given a brighter aspect to her villagers than is usually met with in books, she cannot help it, and would not if she could'. Mitford presents herself as a model of moral sensibility, able to look past the 'little frailties' of others and toward 'their many virtues' (1824a: v). The wicked irony of her anonymously published sketches, such as 'Lucy' and 'The Talking Lady', and the provocative nature of 'A Great Farm-House', arrest the reader's attention because these sketches differ so strikingly from the other essays in the same periodical. These aspects become less noticeable, however, when plucked from the textual environment in which they initially appeared. The bound-volume formats encouraged readers to take delight less in the discursivity of the sketches than in the authorial personage behind them. Now identified as quasi-autobiographical, Mitford's sketches cued the reader to see the text as flowing from the pen of a loving and virtuous mistress, one who provides the reader with a decidedly sentimental and charmingly (rather than acerbically) funny glimpse into English rural life.

The preface, therefore, calls attention to the book's distinctiveness as a commodity: it is an embodiment of the respectability and compassionate vision of its author. This is certainly how Mitford's later readers would evaluate *Our Village*. Thus, as Constance Hill averred in 1920, 'The more we study the life and character of Mary Russell Mitford the more we become attached to her, for we come under the influence of a nature that seems to radiate peace and good-will upon all who surround her' (1920: v). In the periodical context, the anonymous sketches have no obvious didactic purpose. The prefaces to the bound volumes, by contrast, frame the readerly experience as fundamentally pedagogic: through the collected sketches, readers can come to see, like Mitford, 'that in every condition of life, goodness and happiness may be found by those who seek them'. *Our Village*, in other words, is intended to function as a modelling mechanism, designed to teach urban readers how to view the world through different eyes.

By the time George Eliot encountered *Our Village*, this transformation – set in motion by Mitford and, as I will discuss in Chapter Two, greatly extended by later publishers – was complete. But Gaskell would have read a series of volumes that carried fundamental tensions between paratext and text that had not yet been smoothed over. While the pleasures of Mitford's sketches are principally discursive, their stylistic effects are not simply the result of distinctive sentences and paragraphs laboriously constructed by the author. They were, and are, the result of the publication context. Mitford's sketches of rural character have been subject to a variety of bibliographic modulations (paratext, illustrations and typography) because the author herself utilised, as have her many subsequent editors and publishers, the distinctively pliable nature of the sketch form to serve distinct ends.

Notes

1. Hughes and Lund have proposed a gendered model of textual pleasure based on two different narrative structures: a 'male' pattern characterised by ascending tension, climax and release – that is to say, plot – and a 'female' pattern concerned with expectation, the prolongation of desire and a cyclic periodicity that resembles the pattern of menstruation.
2. In his discussion of non-narrative elements within a narrative text, Genette inadvertently provides a description of the sketch: 'it lingers on objects and beings considered in their simultaneity, and because it considers the processes themselves [that is, actions or events] as spectacles, seems to suspend the course of time and to contribute to spreading the narrative in space' (Genette 1987: 136).
3. On the social transformation of English countrysides and the corresponding emergence of cultural-aesthetic ideals of rural life, which I will discuss in greater detail in Chapter Two, see Bermingham (1989) and Helsinger (1987).
4. As Susan Staves notes, historical writings, travelogues, biography and prose reviews were all dominated by men (2006: 244). Women did write in these genres but were rarely compensated. Periodicals opened the door (Staves 2006: 436).
5. She published a new edition the following year containing more than twenty additional poems.
6. In fact, it was the work of John Mitford (a cousin), heavily edited and rewritten by Gifford. See Cutmore 2008: 117.
7. In a letter to her father dated 19 February 1810, she expresses her disappointment: 'From seeing none of the Political Poems printed, I take it for granted they are to be omitted'. The result, she thought, was a volume characterised by 'insipidity' (L'Estrange 1870a: 91).
8. For analyses, see Addison 1988 and Beshero-Bondar 2009.
9. See Mitford 1811a, 277 and 1811b, 334. The latter was a fragment of a then-unfinished poem.
10. In context with *Christina*, see Saglia, 213–225.
11. The *Lady's Magazine* and the *Lady's Museum* merged in 1832 and continued publication through 1837 as the *Lady's Magazine and the Museum of the Belles Lettres*. Another merger with the *Court Magazine and Monthly Critic* in 1837 led to the formation of the impossibly named *Court Magazine and Monthly Critic and Ladies Magazine and Museum of the Belles Lettres*.

12 During his lifetime, Tobin was an unsuccessful dramatist. In his final year, *The Honey Moon* was picked up by Drury Lane, but staged posthumously. It was widely acclaimed and routinely performed for more than twenty years.

13 Mitford would follow with *Rienzi* (1828), which dramatises fourteenth-century Rome. It ran for thirty-four nights at Drury Lane Theatre. Her controversial play, *Charles I*, which had been refused a licence, was staged in 1831. Inspired by the librettist Pietro Metastasio, Mitford also wrote *Sadak and Kalasrade* (1835), which was performed at the Lyceum Theatre in April 1835. Critics were merciless and the blank verse opera libretto was shuttered after one night. Three other plays, *Gaston de Blondeville* (1826), *Inez de Castro* (1827) and *Otto of Wittlesbach* (1829), were never produced.

14 As she mentions to Talfourd in an undated letter of 1823, Colburn had offered her twelve guineas a sheet (1823a: n.p.). She was receiving ten guineas a sheet from the *Monthly Magazine* in 1826 (Chorley 1870a: 133). Ten guineas was also the amount she was paid by *Blackwood's*, although this was particularly bad for authors because, as Mitford notes, the magazine appeared in double columns (L'Estrange 1870b: 220).

15 Mitford was not entirely clear on this matter. Coles, however, arrives at this figure by examining various references in her letters to the number of pieces she published in the *Lady's Magazine* with amounts paid and owed to her by its publisher (1956: 266).

16 Genette subdivides paratexts into two broad categories: the peritext and the epitext. The peritext refers to a threshold within a book; the epitext concerns paratexts outside of the book – from advertisements to reviews.

17 Genette 1987: 405. His comments about serial publication as a system of 'disadvantages' that 'often ended up presenting the public first with a disfigured text pending publication in book form' indicate a certain fetishisation of the book (406).

18 Alison Booth helpfully refers to Mitford's 'digressive', 'sprightly conversational style' as *sprezzatura* (2016: 107).

19 Mitford, like many women of her time, took an active interest in coursing – as her 1815 poem on greyhound coursing suggests. Donna Landry has pointed out that 'Mitford neither blushed at canine anatomy nor failed to notice that sex made a difference to a dog'. In Landy's estimation, 'For her to dismiss distinctly feminine characteristics as inferior to masculine ones, as if she could choose her side of the anatomical line, and then follow, as enthusiastically

Sketches of Rural Character: Mitford's 'Fugitive Pieces'   75

as any sportsman, coursing dogs seeking to kill hares, was positively offensive' (2001: 101–102).

20 Sha has pointed out that women writers in the Romantic period who utilised the sketch form often probed 'the limits of domestic ideology even as they paid lip service to it to gain the confidence of readers' (1998: 144). Certainly, middle-class women writers could be subversive. But they were also just as likely to be ambivalent – recognising the limits of domestic ideology while also embracing many of its aspects.

21 Between 1700 and 1830, in Michael Suarez's estimation, adult literacy rates had increased by some 238.4 per cent (2009: 11).

22 As explained by Mitford to Talfourd in an undated letter from the spring of 1823 (1823a: n.p.).

23 At the time that the first volume entered a second printing in September 1824, Mitford laments to Talfourd, in an undated letter, that 'not one of the great reviews or magazines have honoured it by any notice' (1824g: n.p.).

24 As claimed by a contemporaneous assessment of her prose works. See Anon. 1854: 301.

2

Sketches of Rural Scenery: Mitford's Country Rambles

When Mary Russell Mitford began publishing her sketches of provincial life in the *Lady's Magazine* beginning in September 1822, she did so anonymously. Mitford appended a single initial at the end, 'M', or, inexplicably and misleadingly, 'K'.[1] Others included no attribution at all.[2] As I noted in Chapter One, anonymity facilitated Mitford's ability to write for multiple periodicals without accruing a reputation for being a hack. While she aspired to be a historical dramatist, staging her plays was fraught with difficulties. By contrast, the *Lady's Magazine* and, to a lesser extent, other periodicals and annuals, offered her comparatively steady remuneration. 'Many writers began their careers in this way', Adrian Room has argued of anonymity, 'believing that if what they wrote was worth reading, the public would buy it for its own sake, irrespective of whoever the author might be'. 'But there is a snag', Room continues. 'If your work has no name to it, how can the public obtain more if they want it?' (Room 1988: 26). In Mitford's case, she developed an easily recognisable narrative voice: acerbic, ironic, ambivalent.

She also developed a signature topos. Almost all her topographical sketches, distinguished from the studies of character examined in the preceding chapter, include some version of a country walk.[3] In the early years, Mitford's narrator was often accompanied on these local expeditions by a young neighbour who is frequently at her side, as well as her dog, Mayflower (Figure 2.1). While wandering through the village with her companions, the narrator encounters neighbours, registers architectural differences among houses, remembers anecdotes, and delights in fall foliage or gets caught in spring showers. The very features of Mitford's sketches

Sketches of Rural Scenery: Mitford's Country Rambles

Figure 2.1 Mary Russell Mitford with Mayflower. Illustration by Hugh Thomson. Mary Russell Mitford, *Our Village*. With an introduction by Anne Thackeray Ritchie and One Hundred Illustrations by Hugh Thomson. London and New York: Macmillan and Co., 1893. Author's copy.

that have struck literary critics as 'slightly simpering' or 'anodyne' (Aslet 2010: 200; Gifford 2020: 134) registered very differently for her contemporaries. For, as Harriet Martineau insisted at midcentury, while looking back on her own childhood in the first decade of the nineteenth century, Mitford had invented – as I have noted earlier – 'a new style of "graphic description" to which literature owes a great deal'. Before Mitford took up her pen, Martineau avers, 'there was no such thing known . . . as "graphic description"'. Thus, Martineau continues, she and her generation delighted in 'gorgeous or luscious generalities . . . because we had no conception of detail like . . . Miss Mitford's in scenery' (Chapman 1877: 418). In Mitford's hands, the village sketch became an 'extremely influential' genre that 'later women writers found congenial' (Donovan 1983: 23).

Among the few extant studies of *Our Village*, most critics agree on two points: for all of its attention to detail and the illusion of realism this generates, Mitford's text represents only a partial view of its subject matter, and it participated in what can be understood retrospectively as a project of cultural nationalism.[4] Several Mitford scholars have faulted *Our Village* for representing a stable and tranquil English countryside at the expense of a realistic assessment of 1820s rural life, thereby effacing the profound social disturbances taking place in the years leading up to the Great Reform Act of 1832. In W. J. Keith's influential estimation, *Our Village* offered its original readers a 'sheltered cosiness' (1974: 130), while Terry Gifford has contended that Mitford was 'interest[ed] in offering . . . "a pretty picture", [which] tended to narrow to a fine account of wild flowers' (2020: 73). As Elizabeth K. Helsinger argues in one of the most significant and persuasive readings of *Our Village*, Mitford 'develops strategies for creating a stable, metaphorically English space by inviting us to forget how it is embedded in a national geography' (Helsinger 1997: 128). In Helsinger's account, Mitford's local rural scene, geographically and temporally severed from the rest of the nation, obscures the ways in which it is already tied to the nation politically, culturally and economically. *Our Village*, she continues, 'practice[s] simple metaphoric substitution' of the local for the national and forecloses on questions of '*how* rural locality and nation are connected'. Mitford's representation thus serves a stabilising function by largely evading the 'relations of power that tie local, rural places to national politics, economics, and culture' (Helsinger 1997: 121, 132).

In *Graphs, Maps, Trees: Abstract Models for a Literary History*, Franco Moretti seeks to show how diagrammatic representations of fictional texts help us to grasp the ideological work that British village stories, such as Mitford's, accomplish. In using the term *literary maps*, Moretti refers to a kind of visualisation of a text's verbal descriptions of rural geography. Mapping the first volume of *Our Village*, Moretti suggests that Mitford labours to create a circular system of geography that can reverse 'the direction of history' and make 'her urban readers . . . look at the world according to the older, "centered" viewpoint of an unenclosed village' (Moretti 2005: 38–39). She accomplishes this shift in perspective through her many country walk sketches. Like spokes radiating from the centre of a wheel, Mitford's walks wander through various topographies, but she always finds her way back to the 'undisputed centre of the surrounding countryside': her village (Moretti 2005: 57).

According to Moretti, Mitford's circular, rather than linear, perspective is established through the sketches that detail her walks in her village for which she had become known. He writes: 'out of the free movements of *Our Village*'s narrator, spread evenly all around like the petals of a daisy, a circular pattern crystallizes' (2005: 39). The country walk sketches thus help to establish the bound volumes as a quintessential 'centric composition' (Arnheim 1988: 4). Such a circular geography, writes Moretti, enables the village to be read as a 'space of *leisure* rather than work':

> Slow easy strolls, thoughtless, happy, in the company of a greyhound called May; all around, a countryside full of picturesque natural views, but where very few people are actually doing anything. Decorative: for each page devoted to agricultural labour, there must be twenty on flowers and trees, described with meticulous precision. If urban readers are made to share the village's perception of space, then, it's also true that this space has been thoroughly *gentrified*; as if Mitford had travelled forward in time, and discovered what city-dwellers will want to find in the countryside during a brief week-end visit. (2005: 39–40)

Yet what enables Moretti to make this argument are not the sketches themselves; rather, it is 'the five volumes of *Our Village* [which] offer a splendid test case' (2005: 57). In other words, Moretti privileges the material form of the book.

As I argue in Chapter One, at an early stage Mitford herself set in motion her evolution from anonymous to signed pieces and from discontinuous periodical pieces to collections in bound volumes. In so doing, she created the conditions for the emergence of 'amply illustrated, newly kitschified editions' of *Our Village* in the last quarter of the nineteenth century and well after her death (Lynch 2000: 1106).[5] These were marketed as implicitly leading all readers back to childhood. Raised on these educational and amply illustrated books for children, more recent editors have continued to laud *Our Village* for enabling one to see the world, if only for a moment, through more innocent eyes. 'Many of Miss Mitford's experiences were exactly my own', Anne Scott-James, the editor of the 1987 Penguin edition, remarks, 'picking baskets of violets, driving in a trap, making friends with the village boys, searching the fields and the woods inch by inch for unusual flowers' (1987: xii). According to a promotional statement on its back cover, this edition of *Our Village* offers 'the memories and reflections of a warm and resilient woman' who endured a variety of difficulties and yet continued to look on the world and her fellow citizens with warmth and compassion. To those living in the supposedly more brutish world of the 1980s, *Our Village* is framed in nostalgic rather than pedagogic terms, harkening back to an earlier era, whether Mitford's or the editor's own, of social stability and rural values (respectability, compassion, simple pleasures, unyielding optimism).

This is not simply tangential information. I am suggesting that the reassessment of Mitford that began in the 1970s, with such studies as W. J. Keith's *The Rural Tradition: A Study of the Non-Fiction Prose Writers of the English Countryside* and continued through the 1980s with P. D. Edwards's *Idyllic Realism from Mary Russell Mitford to Hardy*, took place against the backdrop of these kinds of understandings of Mitford and her work. Certainly, the forceful arguments about Mitford's rural scenes call attention to some of their ideological implications. However, because these critics each relate to *Our Village* as a static literary text, their arguments have their problems. In particular, most studies have been based on the various two-volume anthologies or one-volume selections published in the mid- to late nineteenth century.

My contention in this chapter is that the nationalistic dimensions of *Our Village* do not inhere solely in the sketches themselves but result, at least in part, from their context of publication. In my first two sections, I analyse Mitford's sketches in their original periodical contexts to argue that, when examined synchronically with their surrounding copy, these sketches appear far less concerned than later instantiations with discursively constructing notions of Englishness. They are ambivalently torn between the idyll and the real world and conflicted about how best to respond to the social turmoil affecting the English countryside in the 1820s. In my third section, I turn to a diachronic analysis and consider how the sketches, published in various editions since the mid-nineteenth century, have been increasingly framed in ways that minimise their ambivalence and thus interpreted as effective instruments of cultural nationalism. Also at stake in these observations, I want to suggest, are the lessons Elizabeth Gaskell derived from Mitford, and that George Eliot, in turn, learned from Gaskell.

Sketches of Rural Scenery: Mitford's Country Rambles

The village tour

By the time that Mitford published 'Lucy', her first sketch of provincial life in the September 1822 edition of the *Lady's Magazine*, the periodical had a well-established reputation for encouraging travel among its readers. Many of the voyages that readers were encouraged to undertake, however, were *in situ*: following the writers as they travelled from place to place (Pearson 1996: 7). When the new series of *Lady's Magazine* was launched in 1820, Samuel Hamilton, Jr, who had just assumed the editorial reins, continued to publish a substantial number of fictional and non-fictional accounts of life abroad as well essays on the literature and culture of other countries. The following table (Table 2.1) does not provide a comprehensive account of all such content, but instead offers a sense of the range of foreign topics the magazine covered between January 1823 and January 1824.

When Thomas Pringle, the editor of *Friendship's Offering*, sought to generate interest in his newly established literary annual, he naturally turned to the *Lady's Magazine*. With Rudolph Ackermann's publication of *Forget Me Not* in November 1822, literary annuals quickly became prized as an attractive gift for predominantly, but not exclusively, middle-class women – family members, friends and lovers – at year's end. They were sold in the late autumn and imprinted with the upcoming year. As Katherine D. Harris explains, typically 'eighty to one hundred entries of prose and poetry were compiled for each annual, with over fifty different authors included in any one volume' (2015: 2–3). In addition to a mixture of poetry and prose on largely sentimental, amusing topics and moral, prescriptive and religious themes, literary annuals contained superb steel cut engravings. Moderately to expensively priced, annuals appeared in duodecimo, octavo or, in later years, quarto forms, and were generally bound in silk with gilded pages.

In what amounted to an advertisement for the annual, in the November 1823 issue Pringle published several descriptive paragraphs of Lausanne excerpted from a forthcoming essay in *Friendship's Offering*. As exemplified in these passages, he avers, the 'contents [of the periodical] are various and interesting, namely, new descriptions of remarkable towns upon the continent, an original tale by Mrs. [Amelia] Opie, some poetical pieces by the same lady and other ingenious writers, an account of a late ascent to the summit of the Peak of Teneriffe, a canzonet in score

Table 2.1 A selection of articles published in *Lady's Magazine*, 1823–24

Title	Issue	Author
'German Popular Stories'	January 1823	Translated from the *Kinder-und-Haus Marchen*, collected by M. M. Grimm
'Paris Chit-Chat'	January 1823	Marmaduke Tattle
'The Son of Erin, or the Cause of the Greeks by George Burges, a Native of Bengal'	April 1823	None listed
'Narrative of a Journey from the Shores of Hudson's Bay to the Mouth of the Copper-Mine River, and Thence, in Canoes, Along the Coast of the Polar Sea'	May 1823	John Franklin
'Travels in Scandinavia'	June 1823	Edward Daniel Clarke
'Account of the Colonisation, and the Manners and Customs of the Colonists, of New Russia'[1]	August 1823	None listed
'Statements and Observations Connected with Natural History' [includes discussion of North American wolves, West Indian rats and Jamaican crows in their habitats]	September 1823	None listed
[Description of Lausanne]	November 1823	[Thomas Pringle]
'Denmark Delineated, or, Sketches of the Present State of that Country'	January 1824	None listed
'Letters from the Caucasus and Georgia, with an Account of a Journey into Persia'	January 1824	None listed
'Description of a Hindoo Festival by an Officer'	January 1824	None listed
'A Ride of Eight Hundred Miles in France'	January 1824	None listed

[1] Review of *Journey from Riga to the Crimea*, an eight-volume work by Mary Holderness.

and two quadrilles, &c.' 'The engravings are neat and elegant', he continues, 'more particularly the views of Madrid, Florence, and Dresden' (Pringle 1823: 655). To readers of the *Lady's Magazine*, already predisposed to appreciate accounts of foreign life and scenery, Pringle's teaser was surely compelling.

Mitford lacked the financial resources for foreign exploration and, unlike many of the other female contributors to the *Lady's Magazine* who travelled to the Continent or beyond with their husbands, she remained unmarried throughout her life. The stories Mitford could tell were drawn from the village of Three Mile Cross, Berkshire. Her accounts of country life were often the only pieces in the magazine that were substantially and specifically concerned with England.

During the Napoleonic Wars, English tourists set out to discover their own country. Improved roads designed to facilitate long-distance rather than local traffic and enhanced communications systems made travelling easier and more enjoyable. As Ian Ousby points out, these developments opened 'people's eyes to how much remained to be seen and explored' in their own country (1990: 10). Following the Battle of Waterloo, however, English tourists once again flocked to the Continent.

Given Mitford's abiding interest in Italy as a focus for her historical dramas, one can conclude that her decision to write on England was calculatedly pragmatic. As I noted in Chapter One, she spoke incessantly in her correspondence about the financial pressures under which she laboured. In a letter to the painter Benjamin Robert Haydon, dated 7 January 1821, Mitford makes the link between her literary output and her need for an income explicitly, if abruptly: 'I have been very busy – audaciously busy – writing.... We are poor, you know' (Mitford 1870b: 123). She explained to another correspondent, William Harness, in a letter dated 29 July 1824: 'to get money, if I can, is so much my duty, that that consciousness takes away at once all the mock modesty of authorship, for the display of which the rich have leisure'. She continues: 'I write merely for remuneration; and I would rather scrub floors, if I could get as much by that healthier, more respectable, and more feminine employment' (Mitford 1870b: 185). This statement is, of course, entirely disingenuous. It does suggest, however, that once Mitford found a remunerative genre in which to work, she was reluctant to give it up, even if her interests and aspirations tended towards theatre.

Mitford thus carved out a niche for herself within a magazine dominated by literary accounts of foreign tourism. Her stories reminded readers how much rural England still had to offer the tourist. In 'Our Village', which appeared in the 31 December 1822 issue, Mitford provides a synoptic view of her hamlet. The sketch begins by noting that the most 'delightful' of all 'situations for a constant residence' is 'a little village far in the country' where the faces of the inhabitants 'are as familiar to us as the flowers in our garden; a little world of our own, close-packed and insulated ... where we know every one, are known to every one, interested in every one, and authorised to hope that every one feels an interest in us'. She continues:

> Nothing is so tiresome as to be whirled half over Europe at the chariot-wheels of a hero, to go to sleep at Vienna, and awaken at Madrid; it produces a real fatigue, a weariness of spirit. On the other hand, nothing is so delightful as to sit down in a country village in one of Miss Austen's delicious novels, quite sure before we leave it to become intimate with every spot and every person it contains; or to ramble with Mr. White over his own parish of Selborne, and form a friendship with the fields and coppices, as well as with the birds, mice, and squirrels, who inhabit them; or to sail with Robinson Crusoe to his island, and live there with him and his goats and his man Friday; – how much we dread any new comers, any fresh importation of savage or sailor! We never sympathise for a moment in our hero's want of company, and are quite grieved when he gets away .... And, a small neighbourhood is as good in sober waking reality as in poetry or prose; a village neighbourhood, such as this Berkshire hamlet in which I write. (1822d: 646)

In this crucial passage reflecting on her own practice, Mitford makes two related claims. First, she dismisses elaborate novelistic expeditions and wearisome travelogues as tiresome, including those that regularly appeared in the *Lady's Magazine*, so to assert the pleasures of the local. If 'Lucy', which I analysed in Chapter One, established Mitford's distinctive authorial voice, 'Our Village' initiates the country walk as the series' signature topos. Collapsing the distinctions among the narratee, the addressee and the factual recipient, Mitford invites the reader to identify as the text's 'you'. In this sketch, Mitford asks the reader to join her in an exploration of her village: 'Will you walk with me through our village, courteous reader? The journey is not long' (1822d: 646).

Sketches of Rural Scenery: Mitford's Country Rambles

The insistence that this is a minimally taxing expedition reinforces Mitford's preference for confined localities even as it describes the experience of reading a sketch. In highlighting the fatigue produced by some works, and the invigorating joys by others, Mitford links the country outing with the act of sketch reading.

Second, she suggests that the village sketch draws its resources from fictional as well as non-fictional prose. She appreciates the novelists Jane Austen and Daniel Defoe for the same reasons that she values Gilbert White, the Oxford graduate and English clergyman who wrote a phenomenally successful late eighteenth-century work, *The Natural History and Antiquities of Selbourne*. Yet while invoking Defoe in this passage, it was Austen and White who were particularly influential for her. Both were highly attentive observers of their circumscribed social and natural worlds. Mitford would have thus concurred with George Henry Lewes who, writing later in the century, esteemed Austen in these terms: 'her world is a perfect orb and vital', he claimed. 'To read one of her books', he continued, 'is like an actual experience of life' (1852: 134). Where Austen's novels of manners might have provided Mitford with one source for the social elements of her sketches, White's *Natural History* supplied a topographical model in his minute study of flora and fauna.[6]

In 'Our Village', Mitford directs the reader's vision to features of her Berkshire hamlet that account for its charm. The walk 'begin[s] at the lower end' of the village with descriptions of various residences and their occupants, then 'comes the village shop', then more residences. Fluid prose and exacting description – 'next to his house', 'the tidy square red cottage on the right hand', 'divided from the shop by a narrow yard' (1822d: 646) – engender the sense that the reader is present. She encourages the reader to note certain details ('Look at the fine-flowered window blinds') and ensures no divergence from the prescribed path: 'We must now cross the lane into the shady rope-walk', before 'proceed[ing] up the hill' (1822d: 646). Subsequent sketches written in this vein were entitled 'Walks in the Country', to which various subtitles were appended such as 'Frost and Thaw', 'The First Primrose' and 'Walks in the Country: Violeting'. Others introduce the reader either to particular residents or guests ('Ellen', 'Lucy', 'Tom Cordery') or aspects of the village only glossed in the walks ('A Great Farm-House', 'Bramley Maying').

In writing her sketches, Mitford fashioned herself as a kind of tour guide for a national and distinctly urban readership. As Ousby notes, the concept of the *guidebook* originated in the eighteenth century, while the term itself was coined in the early 1800s. Books and sketches about travel in the early nineteenth century, although 'usually presented as personal narratives, including the various accidents and encounters of the journey ... are clearly written more and more with an eye to helping subsequent travellers along the same road' (Ousby 1990: 12). While Mitford's periodical sketches do not present the village as an actual site one could visit, they nevertheless capitalise on the growing demand for printed material about different localities. Even if they are about a non-specific locality, the sketches fuelled the English cultural imagination: there were rural places like Mitford's village waiting to be discovered by the traveller. Readers were enthusiastic about the sketches, and the journal's editor encouraged a steady stream of submissions.

In the May 1823 issue, Mitford published 'Bramley Maying', in which she positions her narrator as more knowledgeable of local practices than either her readers or, in an intertextual engagement with Washington Irving's *Sketch Book*, the observant Geoffrey Crayon. She begins the sketch by referring to Crayon's explorations of English culture from an American perspective:

> Mr. Geoffrey Crayon has, in some of his delightful but somewhat fanciful writings, brought into general view many old sports and customs, some of which, indeed, still linger about the remote counties, familiar as local peculiarities to their inhabitants, whilst the greater part lie buried in books of the Elizabethan age, known only to the curious in English literature. One rural custom which would have enchanted him, and which prevails in the north of Hampshire, he has not noticed, and probably does not know. (Mitford 1823h: 280)

Mitford explicitly invites a comparison between her own understanding of rural culture and Irving's travelogue. She goes on to note that, unlike Irving, whom she admired, her awareness of rural customs derives from her embeddedness in rural geography. While residing in Britain during the composition of the *Sketch Book*, Irving, she implies, drew his understanding of local customs and practices from a careful study of books and not from a long, lived acquaintance with them. His, then, are 'somewhat fanciful writings'. Hers are presented as realist.

Sketches of Rural Scenery: Mitford's Country Rambles

Through direct address, Mitford's engaging narrator gently but imperiously guides the reader to a specific conclusion. The passage continues:

> Did any of my readers ever hear of a Maying? Let not any notions of chimney-sweeps soil the imagination of the gay Londoner A country affair is altogether a different affair from the [London] street exhibitions. . . . A country Maying is a meeting of the lads and lasses of two or three parishes, who assemble in certain erections of green boughs called May-houses, to dance. (1823h: 280)

Instead of being addressed to a singular reader, the rhetorical question inquires into the experiences of all readers who are presumed, at least here, to be urban. To make an inquiry, of course, even a rhetorical one, is to imagine a conversation. Thus, the narrator must immediately thwart any association that metropolitan readers might have between the term *Maying*, as a description of an activity occurring in her rural locality, and the celebratory rituals with which chimney-sweeps engaged on May Day, when they would – as William S. Walsh put it somewhat derisively later in the century – 'parade the streets togged out in tawdry finery, ribbons, and green boughs' (1898: 686).

The realism of Mitford's sketch is intensified by her suggestion of having an on-the-ground experience that those who reside in cities cannot share. Because the season of 'Maying' is nearing its end, Mitford's narrator must travel to the neighbouring village of Bramley to partake in the festivities. Although geographically proximal, Bramley is presented as far removed from the great towns and landed estates. It is, seemingly, a world away: 'a country of peculiar wilderness and beauty', she avers, wanting in 'decent roads', which render it 'a sort of modern Arcadia' (1823h: 281).

Conforming to the house style of the *Lady's Magazine*, the content and form of the sketch work in tandem to emphasise the 'foreignness' of the English countryside. In a piece titled 'Bramley Maying', one would expect Mitford's narrator to recount her visit to the village and the activities that took place within its confines. Yet much of the sketch is devoted instead to her trip to the neighbouring village by gig. The directions themselves, which she relays to the reader, underscore Bramley's uneasy accessibility: 'first to the right, then to the left, then round Farmer Jennings's close, then across the Holy Brook, then to the right again'. Here the horizontal journey to the village is cast in vertical terms as downward movement: 'On we went, twisting and turning ... getting deeper and deeper every moment'. Instead of a maze, which would suggest cul-de-sacs from which no exit is possible, the trip is presented as labyrinthine: 'Not a soul was in the fields; not a passenger in the road; not a cottage by the roadside: so on we went – I am afraid to say how far (for when people have lost their way, they are not the most accurate measurers of distance) – till we came suddenly on a small farm-house, and saw at once that the road we had trodden led to that farm, and thither only' (1823h: 281). At one point they stop to ask for directions: 'Only two miles the nearest way across the fields ... we would soon be there, only over that stile and then across that field, and then turn to the right, and then take the next turning – no! the next but one to the left'. Eventually, the narrator draws a parallel between the act of travelling from one place to another and the process of chronicling it: 'But I am losing my way here, too; I must loiter on the road no longer. Our other delays of a broken bridge – a bog – another wrong turning – and a meeting with a loaded waggon, in a lane too narrow to pass – all this must remain untold' (1823h: 281).

The final stage of the journey is by foot. Once out of her two-wheeled carriage, Mitford and her companion must walk to the green where the Maying festivities take place. To get there, they must pass a 'small, simple, decaying, almost ruinous' church, its Gothic details – an arch, a large window, an accompanying sculpture – 'alone ... worth losing our way for'. Speaking of the church window, the narrator likens it to one of the apertures 'in the Arabian tales': the sun projecting 'the monumental figures with an effect almost magical' (1823h: 282). When they reach the 'turfy little spot' itself, the narrator delights in what she sees: children 'laughing, eating, trying to cheat, and being cheated, round an ancient and practiced vender of oranges and gingerbread; ... a few decent matronly looking women, too, sitting in a cluster; and young mothers strolling about with infants in their arms; and ragged boys peeping through the boughs at the dancers; and the bright sun shining gloriously on all this innocent happiness' (1823h: 283). Only a single paragraph is devoted to the Maying itself.

We can read this invocation of Arcadia as evoking lost English rural origins. Yet the references to the village's remoteness, its Arcadian status, its 'gay crowds of rustics', and its forgotten and neglected activities, all specifically evoke its exoticness. In other sketches, she presents her village as far more remote than it, in fact, was: Three Mile Cross, just a few miles south of Reading, was located on a major turnpike. Yet Mitford refers to her 'little village' as 'far in the country' and as 'close-packed and insulated'. By shading these finer details, Mitford could present the Berkshire hamlet, with its inhabitants, activities and surrounds, as comparable in exoticism to the subjects of the travelogues regularly printed in the *Lady's Magazine* that acquainted readers with foreign cultures and practices. Mitford draws on a number of rhetorical tropes, including Arcadian imagery, to give expression to this foreignness.

Mitford's reflective nostalgia

At the same time, however, in making Three Mile Cross the object of empirical inquiry, Mitford's sketches often bring to the fore what the *Lady's Magazine* as a whole sought to efface: rural England was entering the darkest phase of the agrarian depression. Because sketches foreground their own provisionality and fluidity, the reader is 'invited', as Richard Sha suggests, 'to participate in the act of meaning' (1998: 165). Mitford's cacophonous sketches often present a range of observations about rural life and refrain from leading the reader to any one conclusion. In playing off of surrounding copy in the *Lady's Magazine*, Mitford's sketches were just as likely to have been read for their incipient social critique as their celebrations of English rurality.

In the February 1823 issue, one of the main features is an extended article entitled 'The Village Bells'. Its unnamed author begins with this observation: 'There is no music on earth that for the softness and sweetness of expression, or the power of exciting the feelings, can compare with the simple harmony of village bells' – the ringing chimes from a central location that accompany births, deaths and other significant occasions. The author returns to his country home after an absence of twenty years:

> Seated in the same beautiful little cottage, which formerly my father's presence enlivened, I once more hear their pensive chimes, as, stealing with a softened swell across the Severn, they 'breathe the language of days that are past, pleasant, yet mournful for the soul'. What a host of melancholy reflections they excite! What a throng of spectral remembrances, whose substance has been long buried in the grave of dead ages, does their voice awaken from the sepulcher! (Anon. 1823g: 81)

In this account, the village bells – 'whose music was for years to be denied to me' – are transportive. They carry the writer back to childhood: 'Life was then gay and glittering with sunshine [and] hope threw her rainbow hues athwart the cloudless horizon of the future'. The village bells, like literature, have the power to evoke for this writer 'melancholy and grateful associations' of a tranquil rural childhood: 'In its power of thus awakening the feelings through the simple medium of music, poetry, or any other such excitement, the past has to me more reality and life than the present' (Anon. 1823g: 81). To the implicitly urban reader, beleaguered by the hurried tempo of modern life, this piece offers the imaginative pleasures of escape. Unlike the acoustic phenomena intrinsic to city life, the sound of ringing bells is a singular auditory sensation. Its rhythm and pace are slow and steady and, supposedly, closely connected to the rhythm and pace of life itself. The chiming bells signify the continuity of experience characteristic of traditional, collectivist societies.

In contrast to the soothing tranquillity offered by 'The Village Bells', Mitford's sketch in the same issue begins and ends in economic disruption and social dislocation. 'These are bad times for farmers', the narrator states at the outset of 'A Great Farm-House'. She continues:

> I am sorry for it. Independently of all questions of policy, as a mere matter of taste and of old association, it was a fine thing to witness the hearty hospitality, and to think of the social happiness of a great farm-house. No situation in life seemed so richly privileged; none had so much power for good and so little for evil; it seemed a place where pride could not live, and poverty could not enter. (1823d: 102)

In her use of the past participle *seemed*, the narrator acknowledges as chimerical her perception that the great farmhouse, as a social institution, could remain untouched by the transformations wrought by modernity.

Much of the sketch is devoted to the narrator's nostalgic recollections of a particular farmhouse in the village with which she is familiar. It was here, 'ten or twelve years ago', she avers, where 'I used to spend so many pleasant days'. The owner, 'a thick, stout man, of middle height, and middle age, with a healthy, ruddy, square face, all alive with intelligence and good-humour', and his wife – 'like him in voice and phrase, only not so – loud; like him

Sketches of Rural Scenery: Mitford's Country Rambles

in merriment and good-humour; like him in her talent of welcoming and making happy, and being kind; like him in cherishing an abundance of pets, and in getting through with marvellous facility an astounding quantity of business and pleasure' – were models of 'good fellowship'. In drawing an implicit analogy with the industrial-capitalist forms of farm production that would supplant traditional methods, the business of growing crops and rearing animals, she notes, 'seemed to go on like machinery, always regular, prosperous, and unfailing'. Its success secured the farmer's place in the community: 'he was a sort of standing overseer and church-warden', 'who took a prime minister's share in the government of the large parish to which it was attached' (1823d: 103). He also oversaw the estates of the borough's member of parliament. His wife managed the poultry and cultivated a flower garden. 'She was a real genuine florist', the narrator recalls who 'valued pinks, tulips, and auriculas, for certain qualities of shape and colour, with which beauty has nothing to do; preferred black ranunculuses, and gave into all those obliquities of a triple refined taste by which the professed florist contrives to keep pace with the vagaries of the Bibliomaniac' (1823d: 104).

And yet, at the close of the sketch, the farmhouse – the supposed symbol of stasis and continuity within the village – is shown to be subject to the ruptures and impermanence of modernity. After recounting at length the virtues of the great farmhouse and its inhabitants in times past, the narrator laments:

> The walls were covered with portraits ... [including] the master and mistress of the house in half-length. She as unlike as possible, prim, mincing, delicate, in lace and satin; he so staringly and ridiculously like, that when the picture fixed its good-humoured eyes upon you as you entered the room, you were almost tempted to say – How d'ye do? Alas! the portraits are now gone, and the originals. Death and distance have despoiled that pleasant home. The garden has lost its smiling mistress; the greyhounds their kind master; and new people, new manners, and new cares, have taken possession of the old abode of peace and plenty – the great farm-house. (1823d: 104–105)

In other words, unlike 'The Village Bells', the present – with its widespread suffering and profound social disturbances afflicting the English countryside in the 1820s – serves as bookends to the narrator's recollection. Whereas the rural home in the story of the village bells is presented in terms of bucolic simplicity, as a place in which the urban writer can seek refuge, Mitford's sketch provides a more complicated image of a village caught up in larger social and economic forces.[7]

Mitford, therefore, denies the reader the compensatory comforts that restorative nostalgia, to borrow a term from Svetlana Boym, generates. In her study, Boym differentiates between two different forms of nostalgia: 'not actual types, but rather tendencies, ways of giving shape and meaning to longing' (2001: 41). Restorative nostalgia is a response to the pervasive sense of longing opened up by modernity. The sense that something has been lost leads to the invention of compensatory customs and traditions that seek to rally people around a particular way of life: 'the stronger the rhetoric of continuity with the historical past and emphasis on traditional values, the more selectively the past is presented' (2001: 42). Reflective nostalgia is 'concerned with historical and individual time, with the irrevocability of the past and human finitude ... It reveals that longing and critical thinking are not opposed to one another' (2001: 49–50). Whereas the past for the writer of 'The Village Bells' is 'more reality and life than the present', for Mitford in this sketch the past is presented in terms of its irrecoverability. To the extent that Mitford's sketches in periodical format elicit the urban reader's nostalgia for country life, they might be seen less as restorative than as reflective. According to Boym, reflective nostalgia recognises loss, yet contains within it a 'utopian dimension consisting in the exploration of other potentialities and unfulfilled promises of modern happiness' (2001: 342). Like the sketch form itself, reflective nostalgia is 'ironic, inconclusive, and fragmentary' (2001: 50). To draw out this point more fully, I want to turn briefly to another sketch, 'Walks in the Country: Violeting', as it appeared in its original publication context.

The countryside in politically progressive literature of the 1820s was often troped as a grave in order to give expression to the widespread sense that English rurality, as it had become known, was entering its death struggle. Historically, a thematic of death was often present in the *Lady's Magazine*, which had established itself as a primary venue for serialised Gothic romances. In the early 1820s, while occasionally grappling in oblique ways with issues of the moment, social loss was often converted into individual loss and, occasionally, displaced into humour. One essay in the April 1823 issue, entitled 'On the Folly and Wickedness of Having a

Long Nose', explores the anonymous author's 'distressing' nasal pedigree: 'I am he whose nose hath taken centuries to grow, and now bears upon its blushing front the honours of countless ancestors'. The writer continues:

> As I walk the streets, I monopolise all public astonishment. I look like a caricature by Cruikshanks, that has suddenly stepped from its print-shop under the influence of galvanism. The schoolboy avoids me as a monster, the old woman as a conjuror, and even the bailiff himself, instead of running after, runs away from me. To petrify a bailiff! ([Anon.] 1823f: 227)

After exploring the various implications and consequences of possessing such a nose, the writer questions the meaning of his existence. He concludes with a fervent plea that his nose be 'melted down to orthodox dimensions' but concludes that 'such happiness is too visionary for realization; and in the grave – in the cold grave alone – can my nose and myself find peace' (1823f: 229).

In this same issue, Mitford published 'Walks in the Country: Violeting', a sketch in which the narrator, newly returned from the capital, sets out on a walk to collect violets for her mother in the hope of 'regain[ing] the repose of mind, the calmness of heart, which has been lost in that great Babel' (Mitford 1823d: 229). As with 'The Village Bells', Mitford's sketch contrasts the countryside – here, on a cool, crisp, 'dull grey morning, with a dewy feeling in the air' – with 'the heat, the glare, the noise, and the fever of London' (1823d: 229). To recover her 'serenity of feeling', she eschews the companionship of Lizzy as well as Mayflower. 'I shall go quite alone, with my little basket, twisted like a bee-hive, which I love so well, because *she* gave it to me', the narrator recounts of her mother, 'and keep sacred to violets and to those whom I love; and I shall get out of the high road the moment I can' (1823d: 229). Because she wishes to avoid company, the narrator chooses a less trodden path. While traversing it, Mitford once again presents facts about her village that would have appeared foreign to an urban readership. She notes, for example, that she has 'the good fortune to live in an unenclosed parish' (1823d: 229). By 1823 this was highly unusual as more than 2,000 Parliamentary enclosure acts had been passed between 1793 and 1815. After 1815, as G. E. Mingay notes, 'the number of enclosures dropped away, mainly because there were by then relatively few parishes left to enclose'

(1998: 5). The process of enclosure, which restricted access to common land, dispossessed large segments of the labouring class. Newly wage-dependent, these labourers were particularly susceptible to fluctuations in crop and farm production.

The sketch would seem, at first, to be uninterested in registering these changes. No sooner has the narrator set out on her walk across the common ('the lea, as it is called') than she passes 'by a most picturesque confusion of meadows, cottages, farms, and orchards; with a great pond in one corner, unusually bright and clear, giving a delightful cheerfulness and day light to the picture'. Delighting in the scene, she further observes:

> The swallows haunt that pond; so do the children. There is a merry group round it now; I have seldom seen it without one. Children love water, clear, bright, sparkling water; it excites and feeds their curiosity; it is motion and life. (Mitford 1823d: 229)

This is a moment in which one might conclude that Mitford, who refers to this spot as 'picturesque' and a 'picture', is inviting the reader to metaphorically substitute *rural locality* for *nation*. In Elizabeth K. Helsinger's terms, such occasions – and there are many throughout Mitford's series – seem to offer 'a relation to the local and the rural that can be contained in acts of cultural consumption – buying, reading, looking at what are already, within the narratives of production or discovery offered by the writer, framed as cultural artifacts: sketches, little pictures, songs, stories' (1997: 122).

Yet as the narrator continues her walk, the sketch upends any readerly expectation that the unenclosed parish remains untouched by the forces of industrial capitalism. In an extended passage, she notes the following:

> The path that I am treading leads to a less lively spot, to that large heavy building on one side of the common, whose solid wings, jutting out far beyond the main body, occupy three sides of a square, and give a cold shadowy look to the court. On one side is a gloomy garden, with an old man digging in it, laid out in straight dark beds of vegetables, potatoes, cabbages, onions, beans; all earthy and mouldy as a newly dug grave. Not a flower or a flowering shrub! Not a rose-tree or a currant-bush! Nothing but for sober melancholy use. Oh how different from the long irregular slips of the cottage-gardens, with their

gay bunches of polyanthuses and crocuses, their wall flowers, sending sweet odours through the narrow casement, and their gooseberry-trees, bursting into a brilliancy of leaf, whose vivid greenness has the effect of a blossom on the eye! Oh how different! On the other side of this gloomy abode is a meadow of that deep intense emerald hue, which denotes the presence of stagnant water, surrounded by willows at regular distances, and, like the garden, separated from the common by a wide, moat-like ditch. That is the parish workhouse. All about it is solid, substantial, useful; – but so dreary! so cold! so dark! There are children in the court, and yet all is silent. I always hurry past that place as if it were a prison. Restraint, sickness, age, extreme poverty, misery, which, I have no power to remove or alleviate, – these are the ideas, the feelings, which the sight of those walls excites; yet, perhaps, if not certainly, they contain less of that extreme desolation than the morbid fancy is apt to paint. There will be found order, cleanliness, food, clothing, warmth, refuge for the homeless, medicine and attendance for the sick, rest and sufficiency for old age, and sympathy, the true and active sympathy which the poor show to the poor, for the unhappy. There may be worse places than a parish workhouse – and yet I hurry past it. The feeling, the prejudice will not be controlled. (Mitford 1823d: 229–230)

Although her steps may accelerate, the sketch itself slows down as the narrator passes these scenes of poverty. Witnessing the old man tilling the soil on unenclosed land, Mitford mobilises nouns and adjectives with which long-time readers of the magazine, accustomed to a steady stream of serialised Gothic narratives, would have been familiar ('gloomy', 'dark', 'grave'). Under straightened economic circumstances, a garden cannot offer the supplementary visual joys ('bursting into a brilliancy') or olfactory pleasures ('sweet odours') of flowers and blossoming shrubbery when basic needs must be met. Among the fetid smell of fungal growth, however, the man, who is himself decaying, cannot adequately cultivate and maintain the staples – leafy greens, starch and protein – of rural consumption.

If the old man's garden is supposed to be practical rather than attractive, the workhouse itself is run on serviceable principles. While the imposing building meets its purpose by housing the destitute, the narrator experiences it in passing as depressing, inhospitable and, in a play on the term *dark*, both unilluminated and, given the purpose of the institution, grim. Unlike the merry children gathered around the pond, whom she encountered earlier in her walk, the youngsters who occupy the court of the workhouse congregate in distinctive, because unnatural, silence. The narrator comforts herself by insisting that 'the ideas, the feelings, which the sight of those walls excites' may be more 'morbid' than the actual state of things (Mitford 1823d: 230). This is not, however, wilful blindness. The odd phraseology *yet, perhaps, if not certainly* expresses a desire for the latter but the likelihood of the former, which is itself tentative rather than definitive. In addition, the phrase modifies an adjective that means 'very great' or 'highest degree'. Even if the workhouse *certainly* contains less of that extreme desolation that the morbid fancy is apt to engender, desolation it nonetheless contains.

As she continues, the narrator walks along another field of arable land. Here she notices 'troops of stooping bean-setters, women and children, in all varieties of costume and colour; and ploughs and harrows, with their whistling boys and steady carters, going through, with a slow and plodding industry, the main business of this busy season'. She exclaims:

> What work bean-setting is! What a reverse of the position assigned to man to distinguish him from the beasts of the field! Only think of stooping for six, eight, ten hours a day, drilling holes in the earth with a little stick, and then dropping in the beams one by one. They are paid according to the quantity they plant; and some of the poor women used to be accused of clumping them – that is to say, of dropping more than one bean into a hole. It seems to me, considering the temptation, that not to clump is to be at the very pinnacle of human virtue. (Mitford 1823d: 230)

The myth of the agrarian idyll, which Mitford is often said to be complicit in propagating, is certainly not evident here. Instead of functioning as a nurturing or even a safe place, the farm requires women and children to perform strenuous and taxing repetitive labour. Although Mitford does not give the ages of the children, those as young as seven were employed as casual field workers during the spring, summer and early autumn in most rural counties through mid-century.[8]

The scene eschews pathos (a quality of writing Mitford deplored), but it nevertheless seeks to evoke sympathy. While the narrator does not fully draw out the physical consequences of this

Sketches of Rural Scenery: Mitford's Country Rambles

task on the labourer's body, she does ask the reader to reflect on it. The direct injunction *only think* calls on the reader to imagine spending one's days 'stooping', 'drilling' and 'dropping'. Spurred to engage in the sort of critical reflection that restorative nostalgia would seem to deny, the reader must imagine the physical pain of the labourer. This mental activity realigns one's perspective from the farmer, who is said at times to be cheated, to the worker. The purpose of Mitford's intervention is to engender cognitive and emotional sympathetic connections in the reader. For example, if one is to only think of children performing this job, one might consider the impairment of musculoskeletal development as a result. One might argue, however, that Mitford ends this passage by celebrating the virtuous worker who, although paid by the bushel, has not yielded to the temptation to set more than one bean in any given hole. But in characterising the refusal to clump as 'the very pinnacle of human virtue', she offers an incipient critique of the practice of bean-setting. Asking the reader to recognise the humanity and physicality of these women and children, she suggests that their positions and postures, likened to beasts, are entirely unnatural.

Before reaching her destination, Mitford must pass one more site: a ruined farmhouse. She writes: 'It is a long, low, irregular building, with one room, at an angle from the house, covered with ivy, fine white-veined ivy; the first floor of the main building projecting and supported by oaken beams, and one of the windows below, with its old casement and long narrow panes, forming the half of a shallow hexagon.' For reasons she cannot explain, the farmhouse reminds her of Shakespeare's era, an association that evokes for the reader the continuity that modernity breaks: the farmhouse, she laments, is 'crumbling to decay under a careless landlord and a ruined tenant' (1823d: 230).

After recounting the variety of hardships and sufferings that she witnessed, the narrator reaches her beloved violets, which she intends to pick for her invalid mother: 'What happiness to sit on this tufty knoll, and fill my basket with the blossoms! What a renewal of heart and mind!' (1823d: 231). While the sketch provides the reader of the *Lady's Magazine* with what would have been an expected conclusion – what Helsinger calls the seemingly 'happy displacement' in which 'the private replaces the public as an arena where troubles are more easily resolved' (1997: 129) – the rhetorical linkages between the 'The Village Bells' and 'Violeting', and their mutual references to the grave, call attention to Mitford's complicated use of such imagery to evoke images of social death. For what the sketch seeks is less an evasion than a double reprieve: first, from the immediate recollection of the sensory dimension of urban experience, and then, as her walk unfolds, from the signs everywhere around her that the village is not immune to disruptive socio-economic change. After all, once she has collected her violets, the narrator must traverse the same distressing path to return home to her mother's bedside.

One can only push this point so far. Mitford was no William Cobbett, who documented the pernicious impact of Malthusian national policies on the lives of English agricultural workers and the land they tilled in the series of essays published in *Political Register* throughout the 1820s. Nevertheless, shorn from its original periodical context, Mitford's embedded critique becomes difficult to discern. Although Hugh Thomson illustrated bean-setting in Anne Thackeray Ritchie's edition of 1893, there is little in his depiction that captures the physical toll on the labourer's body (Figure 2.2). The sketch closes with a rather dreamy portrayal of Mitford herself stretched out among her violets (Figure 2.3). Yet throughout the 1820s and 1830s the condition of agricultural labourers was much on her mind. She complained to William Harness in a letter dated 2 May 1834 that 'our wise legislators never think of the rural districts – *never*' (L'Estrange 1870: 11). As a consequence, she believed, the House of Commons repeatedly passed legislation that exacerbated poverty rather than alleviated it.

Although the reader may well be aware that Mitford must take the same path home, she does not recount that journey. But she does admit that such scenes with her violets are 'fleeting': 'Oh that my whole life could pass so, floating on blissful innocent sensation, enjoying in peace and gratitude the common blessings of Nature'. 'Alas', she concludes, 'who may dare expect a life of such happiness?' (1823d: 231). The sketch registers both a yearning for utopia (the renewal of heart and mind that comes with a carefree walk among flora) and a deep awareness of economic hardship that renders such happiness momentary. In other words, it takes up a politically charged topic – the economic hardships of the labouring poor – but does so in a manner that would have been considered appropriate for a woman author. Mitford thereby avoids the censure and rebuke she experienced after the

Sketches of Rural Scenery: Mitford's Country Rambles

Figure 2.2 'Bean-setting'. Illustration by Hugh Thomson. Mary Russell Mitford, *Our Village*. With an introduction by Anne Thackeray Ritchie and One Hundred Illustrations by Hugh Thomson. London and New York: Macmillan and Co., 1893. Author's copy.

publication of her first volume of poetry, which might have had implications for the future income to be derived from her sketches.

From periodicals to literary annuals

As I argued in the last chapter, Mitford played a role in reshaping the perception of her sketches as undeviatingly cheerful and of herself as maternal and beneficent. In a letter to Talfourd dated 6 June 1824, she expresses anxiety about reprinting some of her anonymous sketches with her name appended to them: 'because there is a mixture of pungency, which in an obscure magazine where the author is unknown can hurt no one, but which when the writer is avowed would assume quite a different character' (1824e: n.p.). Instead of rewriting the sketches, she reframed them in ways that diluted their caustic character. By the time of her

Figure 2.3 Mary Russell Mitford among her violets. Illustration by Hugh Thomson. Mary Russell Mitford, *Our Village*. With an introduction by Anne Thackeray Ritchie and One Hundred Illustrations by Hugh Thomson. London and New York: Macmillan and Co., 1893. Author's copy.

death, Mitford's sketches were read as providing cheerful moral lessons. She was, in John Ruskin's words, 'merry Miss Mitford' (1885: 17), with a sensibility, according to the preface of a late nineteenth-century edition, 'so happy, so lighthearted' and 'bright' (Rhys 1891: xvi).

But the eight-year period between the publication of the first and last volumes of *Our Village* was dynamic. Even as she was assembling previously published sketches into individual volumes, Mitford was also writing new pieces that appeared in a number of periodicals and literary annuals. The precarity of her family's finances necessitated that she pursue all available opportunities. When the first biennial volume of *Our Village* was at the press, Mitford encouraged Elford, in a letter dated 5 March 1824, to market her work: 'it will be an obligation if you will cause it to

Sketches of Rural Scenery: Mitford's Country Rambles

be asked for at circulating libraries, etc.' (Mitford 1870b: 23). In a follow up letter of 23 June 1824, she thanks him 'for promoting the sale', telling him that 'it sells well, and has been received by the literary world, and reviewed in all the literary papers, etc., better than I, for modesty, dare to say' (Mitford 1870b: 26–27). Her increased visibility in the literary world thus translated into a wider variety of opportunities for writing and, she hoped, a stabilisation of the family's precarious finances. The first volume went to fourteen editions in eleven years, including three before 1825.

Yet a new crisis soon emerged. By the time that Mitford ended her association with the *Lady's Magazine* in 1824 after failing to reach an agreement with its editor, Charles Heath, over republication rights to her sketches, the opportunities to write – owing to her increasing fame – had multiplied. But she continually haggled with editors and publishers over the timing and amount of payment for her work. In the summer of 1826, Whittaker, worried about the market, decided that it would be best to hold back the release of a second volume of *Our Village*. At roughly the same time, John Thelwall's short-lived *Panoramic Miscellany*, appearing monthly between January and June 1826, folded. Mitford had just submitted three short stories. On 20 September 1826, she wrote to Barbara Holfland, who, like Talfourd, had occasionally served as an intermediary with editors, to express her frustration:

> ... Mr. Thelwall's magazine has stopped, and he has not paid me a farthing. He says, indeed, that he has no doubt but that Mr. Friend (their treasurer), when he recovers, will pay me; but that he has advanced 700*l.* for the concern, and cannot lose more. Now I have nothing at all to do with his losses. He applied to me, and I shall always consider him as bound in honour to pay me. Don't you? You know the fuss he made to get me .... I don't want any fuss made about it, because there's no good comes of making enemies, and because Mr. Friend may pay me; but if he does not in the course of a month or two, I shall certainly apply again to Mr. Thelwall, considering him as personally bound, so far as honour and honesty go, to remunerate my labours, which were undertaken for him at his request, and on his responsibility ... I am very sorry for the ill success of his speculation; but I can't help it. I am sure my papers were not the cause of his failure .... Now, don't you think I have claim on Mr. Thelwall? The money is between seven and eight pounds – nothing in his 700*l.*, but a great deal to me ... all that I earn comes in small sums. (Mitford 1870d: 132)

If she intended to secure a 'magnificent' income in setting out to write for serials in 1820, she acknowledges here, six years later, that it provided only very modest returns. Moreover, Thelwall had been 'the most fidgety and troublesome' of the editors with whom she had worked. According to her, 'he found fault, sent back my articles (a thing which never happened to me in my life before), and worried me to death'. She continues:

> Moreover, he kept an article of mine to which I was writing a continuation, so long, that as it was about wheat hoeing, and was dated, I shall be forced to keep that, and the subsequent one, till next year, before they can be inserted in Mr. Baylis's magazine, because one can't expect to put in a paper dated May, in October, or one dated June, in November; and altogether Mr. Thelwall has worried me more than anybody I ever had to do with before. (Mitford 1870d: 132)

As she exclaimed to Talfourd, in an undated letter written in 1824, 'I am sick to death of the plagues of authorship – to be pestered by every body to write for them & then not be paid' (1824h: n.p.). Even as the number of periodicals available to her expanded, financial security remained elusive.

Thus, the literary annual, a new and sensationally popular genre that dominated the end-of-the-year holiday market, proved particularly attractive. For writers, annuals were an economic boon. Remuneration was – as she mentions in her letter to Cyrus Redding quoted in Chapter One – significantly higher than for periodicals. Mitford could gain 'twenty or thirty' from a single published piece in these volumes devoted to a mix of poetry, fiction and sentimentally evocative illustrations (Mitford 1870b: 220). As a result, she frequently overcommitted. In 1824, she was penning, as she says, with her usual hyperbole, 'a thousand and one articles for annuals, of which a new one seems to start every week for my torment' (Mitford 1870d: 127–128). The following year, she contributed to at least six, including *Friendship's Offering*, the *Amulet*, and *Forget Me Not*. But after the failure of Thelwall's magazine, her contributions to annuals increased markedly. In a letter to William Harness dated 16 October 1827, she writes: 'I have been torn to pieces by the annuals, who will have at least twenty articles of mine amongst them' (Mitford 1870b: 244). Perhaps not a thousand and one pieces, but certainly a significant output.[9]

The annuals were a new venue for her village sketches. Just as she had with the *Lady's Magazine*, Mitford carefully negotiated the textual cultures of these publications. Additionally, unlike periodical publication, the sketches in literary annuals appeared with attribution. Because annuals were intended to be given as presents at the holiday season, they generally eschewed political themes or contentious social issues. As Kathryn Ledbetter points out, 'Taste, gentility, and high moral sentiments were the standard for annual contributors'. Editors were particularly vigilant because 'if the books did not sell' publishers assigned responsibility to them for selected contributors with 'bad taste'. As a result, many topics were considered unacceptable, including 'politics, current events, radical social opinions, hints at sexuality (although the engravings were sometimes overtly sensual), crude or hard language, and extreme negative emotions (grief and sorrow were the noble exceptions)' (Ledbetter 1996: 236). Yet even these sketches, when restored to their original publication context, can be plausibly read to contain oblique social and political commentary.

To understand why Mitford raises political and social issues indirectly, I find it helpful to consider Robyn Warhol's analysis of narrative gaps. Warhol distinguishes among four categories of the unnarratable: the subnarratable, the supranarratable, the antinarratable and the paranarratable. The *subnarratable* is information that an author must excise owing to the spatial constraints of any given work. It is whatever is deemed 'not worth narrating' (Warhol 2005: 222). By contrast, the *supranarratable* is the inexpressible, which calls attention to the 'inadequacy of language or of visual image to achieve full representation, even of fictitious events' (2005: 223). The *antinarratable* is whatever an author cannot directly discuss or describe because of social taboos. Her least developed category, and the one most useful for my purposes, is the *paranarratable*: information that must be excluded because of formal or generic conventions. 'Laws of literary generic convention are more inflexible', Warhol argues, 'than laws of social convention, and have led throughout literary history to more instances of unnaratability than even taboo has led' (2005: 226). In the context of literary annuals primarily given to middle- and upper-class women at Christmas, the grievances of farm labourers – such as, I will shortly consider, the introduction of threshing machines that resulted in the loss of their livelihoods – is inadmissible information. To illustrate this point, I turn to a consideration of a few sketches that appeared in separate annuals over a number of years.

In the autumn of 1826, Mitford published 'The Chalk-Pit' in the *Amulet; or Christian and Literary Remembrancer*, which bore the following year's date. (She included the sketch in the third biennial volume of *Our Village* published in 1828.) This annual was familiar to her. Its founder and editor, Samuel Carter Hall, had enlisted her help with its launch a year earlier, to which she had contributed 'The Vicar's Maid: A Village Story'. In his preface to the first volume, Hall asserted that the *Amulet* had staked out a unique position for itself in an increasingly crowded holiday market by offering a blend of 'religious instruction with literary amusement' (1826: v). However, instead of adhering to a specific Christian dogma, its poetry and prose works reflected a range of religious denominations. The editor selected pieces according to demonstrable 'literary merits' and the extent to which they 'impress[ed] some moral lesson', and offered the volume to readers in the hope that it would – consistent with 'the class of works to which the present publication belongs' – 'sweeten social intercourse, and enhance domestic enjoyment' (1826: v). To varying degrees, individual pieces all contributed to this editorial mission. 'The Vicar's Maid' appeared alongside poems on religious themes, including two by Felicia Hemans ('The Hebrew Mother', 'The Trumpet') and one by Letitia Elizabeth Landon, as well as fictional and non-fictional stories of Christianity ('What is the World' by the evangelical writer Mary Martha Sherwood and 'Some Account of the Chaldaean Christians' by the chaplain of the British Embassy at Constantinople).

There is nothing particularly religious or moral about the 'The Vicar's Maid'. The story introduces Mr Mansfield as the vicar of the neighbouring village of Aberleigh, newly arrived with his family from the coast of Sussex. It outlines his sterling character as well as the many virtues of his wife and children and describes, at some length, the country parsonage where they reside. But the Mansfields serve largely as a pretence for a character sketch about Mary, their female servant, who has difficulty adjusting to her new environment. According to Mitford, Mary 'languished under the reverse disease, of a calenture, pined for the water, and was literally, and in a new sense of the word, sea-sick' (1826b: 135). It becomes clear, however, after one young village man after the next tries to win her heart, that Mary yearns less for the sea than the seaman Thomas Clere, a suitor from the South Downs, whom she introduces as her half-brother when he relocates to the area, 'although Mary was so little used to telling fibs, that her blushes and down cast looks and smiles between, in short, the whole pervading consciousness would have betrayed her' (1826b: 138).

Mitford does not directly address the reader in 'The Vicar's Maid'. However, in various asides, she positions herself in perfect accord with the perspective of an urban English reader. For example, Mitford enumerates the 'professional qualifications' of Thomas, who takes a job at a respectable country inn: 'Besides his good humour, his liberality, and his sea jokes, next to Irish jokes, always the most delightful to rustic ears, perhaps because next to Irish the least intelligible, your country bumpkin loves a conundrum, and laughs heartiest at what he does not understand.' Thomas, moreover, is described as 'eminently obliging and tolerably handy', only for this statement to be quickly qualified: he does 'less harm than most amateur helpers' (1826b: 138). Mitford then recounts several incidents of his help, such as when he knocks down a line of clothes he had been assisting Mary to hang, thereby requiring that the garments all be rewashed, or when they, apparently distracted by each other, 'overheated the oven', which resulted in 'a whole batch of bread and three apple-pies .. [being] scorched to a cinder' (1826b: 139). Although the sketch is ostensibly religious, the reader may experience more joy from the laughter one derives from the narrator's snarkiness – evincing Mitford's indebtedness to Charles Lamb – than from any exemplary Christian virtues displayed by the vicar and his family.

If the first half of the story engenders humour, the latter half generates anxiety as the pace quickens. A series of heart-rending tragedies accumulate. The preoccupied couple soon wed and, after a brief honeymoon, Mary re-enters the vicar's service. Thomas sets out on a final voyage, a six-month trip to Canada aboard a merchant ship.[10] Thereafter, Mitford narrates a series of incidents, including Mary losing her ring finger as well as the symbol of her love in a mishap, and Thomas being thought lost at sea. Mary's beloved survives the shipwreck but, by the time he returns to her, the grief and agony take their toll. After a joyful embrace, Mary faints and the couple collapse 'on the snowy ground; and when loosened from his long embrace, the happy wife was dead! The shock of joy had been fatal!' (1826b: 146). For the reader expecting a blissful reunion or the pathos of a death scene, the startling abruptness of the sketch's end is an appalling surprise.

'The Chalk-Pit (A True Story)', which appeared in the *Amulet* a year later, functions somewhat as a companion story insofar as it uses the vicar's wife and daughters as the pretence to tell another equally gloomy story, but one lacking in malice. The sketch is formally innovative with a contrastive structure – the first half focuses on ladies in the parlour while the second half addresses agricultural labourers, especially young men and a boy, in the field – and a distinct form of narration. The narrating self relates a series of earlier life events: social calls with her 'friend Mrs. Mansfield, the wife of the good vicar of Aberleigh', and her daughters, who 'are just what might be expected from girls trained under such a mother' (Mitford 1827a: 145, 146). Midway through the sketch, however, Mitford narrates a story, as told to her by Mrs Mansfield, as if she experienced the event herself. This peculiarity would seem to be the source of the sketch's inherent appeal as well as its affecting intensity.

The first several pages of 'The Chalk-Pit' suggest that it will be a character sketch along the lines outlined in Chapter One. The narrator reflects on the eldest daughter Ellen's personality – she possesses 'those invaluable every-day spirits which require no artificial stimuli, no public amusements, no company, no flattery, no praise' (Mitford 1827a: 146) – and appearance ('One forgets to make up one's mind as to her prettiness; but it is quite certain that she is charming' [1827a: 146]). She singles out Ellen's preferred pastime of drawing flowers for commendation, and recommends this form of leisure to readers as a safe and pleasant way to engage with the natural world:

> It is a most quiet, unpretending, womanly employment; a great amusement within doors, and a constant pleasure without. The enjoyment of a country walk is much enhanced when the chequered fritillary or the tinted wood anemone are to be sought, and found, and gathered, and made our own; and the dear domestic spots, haunted by
> 'Retired leisure,
> Who in trim gardens takes his pleasure',
> are doubly gardens when the dahlias and china-asters, after flourishing there for their little day, are to reblossom on paper. (Mitford 1827a: 147–148)

Mitford's choice of adjective, *haunting*, which precedes the lines quoted from John Milton, is peculiar. Although retired leisure is said to frequent these cherished locales, the passage also evokes, in a Wordsworthian vein, the notion of the landscape as the haunted ground of prior poets.

But if the flowers one procures in this field re-blossom in the pages of a keepsake, they also come to life through Emily's extraordinary skill in drawing. Introducing the concept of realism in portraiture, the narrator explains:

> I have never seen any portraits so exactly resembling the originals, as her carnations and geraniums. If they could see themselves in her paintings, they might think that it was their own pretty selves in their looking-glass, the water. One reason for this wonderful verisimilitude is, that our fair artist never flatters the flowers that sit to her; never puts leaves that ought to be there, but are not there, never makes them hold up their heads unreasonably, or places them in an attitude, or forces them into a groupe. Just as they are, she sets them down . . . (Mitford 1827a: 147)

Like much of the first few pages of the sketch, these remarks are seemingly pointless because their focus shortly turns to another topic entirely: an incident at the Lanton parish chalk-pit. From another perspective, however, introducing the concept of verisimilitude is crucial. Just as Mitford insists on the verisimilar quality of Emily's drawings, she will also insist on the realism of the dark story she is about to tell.

The sketch is Mrs Mansfield's, who relays to the narrator the details of a terrible tragedy at a quarry in one of the parishes where the family had resided. Yet this occurrence is communicated to the reader neither through dialogue nor through a recognisable technique of focalisation (along the lines of 'Mrs. Mansfield saw . . '), but instead through the narrator's abrupt seizure of the narrative herself: 'I shall try to tell it as shortly and simply as it was told to me; but it will want the charm of Mrs. Mansfield's touching voice, and of Ellen's glistening eyes' (1827a: 149). In other words, Mitford's stated intention is to provide the reader with a sketch – which is to say a rough delineation or brief account – of the incident. To do so, Mitford adopts an innovative narrative technique in which she relays second-hand information as if it were based on first-hand knowledge:

> Toward the bottom of one of the green hills of the parish of Lanton, was a large deserted chalk-pit; a solemn and ghastly-looking place,

blackened in one part by an old lime-kiln, whose ruinous fragments still remained, and in others mossy and weather-stained, and tinted with every variety of colour – green, yellow, and brown . . . . The road that led by the pit was little frequented. The place had an evil name; none cared to pass it even in the glare of the noon-day sun; and the villagers would rather go a mile about, than catch a glimpse of it when the pale moonlight brought into full relief those cavernous white walls, and the dark briars and ivy waved fitfully in the night wind. It was a vague and shuddering feeling. (1827a: 149–150)

While the first half of 'The Chalk-Pit' focuses on Emily's faithful portraits of her flowers, the second half insists on the accuracy of its transmission of Mrs. Mansfield's story. In so doing, it invites an explicit comparison between visual and verbal forms of sketching and underscores the realism of both.

The sense of foreboding that this paragraph generates is followed by heightened suspense – increasing the reader's anxiety – as the narrator moves from the general ('a vague and shuddering feeling') to the specific ('One October day'). The indeterminate sense of dread that the residents feel about the chalk-pit is confirmed one late-morning when a group of agricultural workers close to the site, engaged in 'the lively work of ploughing, and wheat-sowing, and harrowing', are caught in a thunderstorm. While the 'seeds-men, ploughmen, and carters, hastened home with their teams', a group of boys are left behind to fend for themselves:

The storm increased apace; and it was evident that their thin jackets and old smock-frocks would be drenched through and through long before they could reach Lanton Great Farm.

In this dilemma, James Goddard, a stout lad of fifteen, the biggest and boldest of the party, proposed to take shelter in the chalk-pit. Boys are naturally thoughtless and fearless; the real inconvenience was more than enough to counterbalance the imaginary danger, and they all willingly adopted the plan, except one timid child, eight years old, who shrunk and hung back. (1827a: 150–151)

Reluctant to make the journey back to the farm alone, the boy – one Harry Lee – is equally apprehensive about entering the chalk-pit. The narrator suggests that his constitutionally timorous and hesitating spirit is partially attributable to a defining childhood event: his father, a fisherman, drowned at sea only a few months after he was born. Thus, whereas the other boys are undaunted, Harry experiences fear: a particularly strong emotion caused by the anticipation of risk or peril.

Although the vagaries of weather largely determined each day's work, the sketch suggests that the sense of social support among this young cohort of agricultural labourers is constant. With meagre resources, Harry's mother raised him until, incapacitated by illness, she agreed to let him enter the service of a farmer. Under the watchful eye of James Goddard, the radiant and gentle boy and the most promising pupil in Mrs Mansfield's Sunday school, where he excelled at reading, has been learning to till the land. Thus, when James, who functions as a kind of older brother, assures Harry that the pit is safe, the young lad takes shelter with the other boys:

> At last James Goddard thought that he heard a strange and unaccustomed sound, as of bursting or cracking – an awful and indescribable sound – low, and yet distinctly audible, although the wind and rain were raging, and the boys loud in mirth and laughter. He seemed to feel the sound, as he said afterwards; and was just about to question his companions if they too heard that unearthly noise; when a horseman passed along the road, making signs to them and shouting. His words were drowned in the tempest; James rushed out to enquire his meaning, and in that moment the side of the chalk-pit fell in. He heard a crash and a scream – the death scream – felt his back grazed by the descending mass; and, turning round, saw the hill rent, as by an earthquake, and the excavation which had sheltered them, filled, piled, heaped up, by the still quivering and gigantic fragments – no vestige left to tell where it was, or where his wretched companions lay buried. (1827a: 152)

The narrator then recounts the frenzied scene in which would-be rescuers, including fathers, brothers, kinsmen and friends gather onsite to sift through the rubble while mothers and sisters stand by in anguish and grief. Of James Goddard, she notes: 'A thousand and a thousand times did he crave pardon of that distracted mother, for the peril – the death of her son; for James felt that there could be no hope for the helpless child, and tears, such as no personal calamity could have drawn from the strong hearted lad, fell fast for his fate' (1827a: 153). By dusk, James's belief that Harry could not have survived the collapse of the pit is confirmed. As the narrator concludes the story, 'Alas! only by his raiment could that fond mother know her child! His death must have been instantaneous. She did not linger long. The three boys were interred together in Lanton churchyard on the succeeding Sabbath; and before the end of the year, the widow Lee was laid by her son' (1827a: 153).

I have lingered over this story because 'The Chalk-Pit' does much to counter the notion that Mitford presented rural life as uniformly charming and upbeat. Sven Halse, for example, has argued that 'Mitford presents a light, positive picture of rural life that seems completely unthreatened by industrial development or other dangers. The greatest danger for the narrator would seem to be unforeseen rain and a dog that does not obey her commands' (2008: 402). Yet in this sketch, rain is more than an unforeseen inconvenience. It precipitates multiple deaths. To be sure, 'The Chalk-Pit' does not tackle rural poverty directly. But it repeatedly touches on the precariousness of life for those who labour under material scarcity: the fisherman; the frequently ill widow, who '[n]ight and day had . . . laboured for her poor Harry' (Mitford 1827a: 151); young Harry himself, who, at eight, is below the average age at which boys enter farm service; and James Goddard and his companions, who experience agricultural work as part of their life cycles. While the first half of the sketch raises the romantic notion of poets haunting the landscape, the second half concludes with the burial of young agricultural workers in the land they once tilled.

Written in 1831, 'The Incendiary: A Country Tale', which appeared in *Friendship's Offering* for the following year and in the final volume of the *Our Village* series, engaged with an issue of the moment. It recalls the armed uprising of rural workers in the south and east of England during the autumn of 1830 over stagnant wages and the introduction of threshing machines. Philip Owen, a poor resident of the village with otherwise sterling qualities, is tried for rick-burning before a special commission. Just before he is due to be sentenced, his love interest, Lucy, confesses to having inadvertently started the conflagration. Because Lucy's yeoman father disapproved of their relationship, the pair hide notes to each other in a hayrick. One evening, while attempting to retrieve her expected note Lucy is startled by her father and flees without her candle, which sets the hay on fire. The village rejoices to learn that Philip remains the person they thought they knew, and with the blessings of all, the couple enter into 'one of the best and happiest' unions in the kingdom.

Positing *Our Village* as a pre-eminent form of idyllic realism, P. D. Edwards asserts that 'The Incendiary' is representative of the work as a whole. For although the sketch alludes to the Captain Swing riots – so-called because labourers often left threatening letters for landowners signed by the mythical figure (whose name evokes swinging from the gallows) – as threatening the village's social fabric, 'love and reconciliation assert themselves' (Mitford 1832b: 25). In her later reading, Elizabeth Helsinger notes that, precisely because it is allusive, the sketch 'is neither accurate nor complete'. Mitford's most significant omission, she continues, 'is any indication of what the labourer's grievances were – or even that they had any' (1997: 130). Instead of identifying and discussing the structural causes of the labourers' unrest, Mitford redirects the reader's attention from 'public social histories' to individual dramas. In so doing, she can maintain 'an illusion that the rural scene exists apart from history, as the stage for a private quest for identity and security' (1997: 131–132).

These appraisals have been so persuasive that it has been hard for critics to render any other judgement. To the extent that social issues are raised, Sven Halse declares, they 'do not seriously blight the harmonious, happy picture Mitford presents' (2008: 402). While critics have focused on the ways that Mitford converts public social issues into private histories, where solutions can be rendered more easily, they have devoted insufficient attention to how she uses private histories to illuminate public social issues.

Without the *Lady's Magazine* apolitical contents or the literary annuals against which the sketches were originally set, the first set of *Our Village* volumes loses some, but not all, of its edge. When Mitford organised her pieces in bound form and added paratextual material to each volume, the topographical sketches assumed increased prominence. Although 'Lucy' was the first sketch of provincial life to appear in the *Lady's Magazine*, Mitford places 'Our Village', which provides an overview of the locale's human and physical topography, at the outset of the 1824 volume. The country walk sketches, which appear sporadically throughout the book, serve as extensions that enable the reader to gain some semblance of bearings. This is reinforced by the concluding sketch, 'A Parting Glance at Our Village'. If one employs what Robert L. Patten has called a 'hermeneutics of literary geography' to analyse the spaces created in and by *Our Village*, one can discern how essential the country walk sketches are to the volumes as a whole

(2003: 192). They introduce the reader to the constructed environment contained within the text (the village shop, the tidy square red cottage) and structure the textual environment by linking together the sketches across several years of periodical publication and bound volumes. They also organise the manufactured environment of reading by figuring readerly activity as a country walk. In other words, when encountering the sketches in periodical form, one has no real sense of organised space because they were discontinuously published and appeared across a variety of publications. As a result, individual sketches – which, unlike the later serialised novel, were largely self-contained – generated meanings independent of each other. By contrast, in bound volumes, the somewhat insular and circular geography of the village, latent in the periodical sketches, is increasingly realised.

As a result, Mitford, despite political views that leaned towards the Radical end of the political spectrum, could be seen as propagating an ideal of the old agrarian communal order and as, therefore, essentially a conservative. Various editions, with their bucolic illustrations of rural scenes – such as Thomson's depiction of cows grazing in the field (Figure 2.4) against the backdrop of tall elms – have contributed greatly to this perception. But Mitford recognised that her own contradictory stances could lead to confusing or inaccurate understandings of her work. In a letter dated 4 April 1842 to her long-time correspondent Elizabeth Barrett Browning, a self-proclaimed democrat, Mitford acknowledged a persistent tension in her political views: 'I am an inconsistent politician, I confess it, with my aristocratic prejudices and my radical opinions' (L'Estrange 1870c: 143).[11] Unlike her father, a proud Whig, Mitford insisted, as early as 2 February 1810, that she was not 'partisan'. Instead, she proclaimed in a letter to William Elford, 'One thing is certain, if not a Reformer I am nothing' (L'Estrange 1870a: 198). This placed her, as she freely acknowledged, at odds with both Tories and Whigs. Writing to Elford on 11 April 1813, when the Tories were in government, Mitford declared: 'I have as pretty a contempt for the ministers as my whiggish papa; and as comfortable a dislike to the Whigs as my ministerial uncle' (L'Estrange 1870a: 229). Precisely because her political views aligned more closely with the Whigs, she frequently singled out party luminaries for contempt. She thought Richard Brinsley Sheridan, whose reputation as a womanising drunk preceded him, a 'vile degenerate Whig!' (L'Estrange 1870a: 71). On reading in the

Sketches of Rural Scenery: Mitford's Country Rambles 113

Figure 2.4 'Grazing under the tall elms'. Illustration by Hugh Thomson. Mary Russell Mitford, *Our Village*. With an introduction by Anne Thackeray Ritchie and One Hundred Illustrations by Hugh Thomson. London and New York: Macmillan and Co., 1893. Author's copy.

26 April 1809 edition of the *Statesman* that Earl Grey had dined with the Duke of York, who was caught up in a scandal involving the sale of army commissions by his ex-mistress, Mitford wrote to her father the following day to playfully declare: 'you must now give up your Whigs, at least the late ministers and their adherents. That man (Lord Grey) must have an innate propensity to corruption, as some people are said to have for thieving; for in point of rank and fortune he is far above temptation' (L'Estrange 1870a: 73). On 2 February 1810, in a letter to her father, she again refers to party figures derisively as 'Your Whigs' (L'Estrange 187a: 90)

Because Mitford considered herself a reformer, she supported efforts to transform the British electoral system. In the lead up to the Reform Act of 1832, she explained to William Elford in a letter dated 31 March 1831 that she saw change as pragmatic. Although Radicals were divided over the bill's efficacy, Mitford does not take a position on whether universal suffrage and vote by ballot might constitute a better way forward than disenfranchising proprietorial constituencies. Instead, she expresses anxiety about what might occur if no electoral changes were implemented: 'I can not help thinking but a House of Commons, chosen according to the new plan, will be a much better thing than the mob' (Mitford 1870b: 126). The comment about mob rule grates. But it might also substantiate the view of Mitford as a writer who held consistent beliefs but adapted her expression of those beliefs to suit an audience. Elford was, after all, not only a long-standing friend but also a Tory politician. Only a few years later, in a letter to Henrietta Harrison dated 31 July 1837, daughter of an independent clergyman and a future poet and novelist, Mitford expressed her satisfaction with the results of the general election. 'Reading has done itself honour by electing two Reformers', she enthusiastically declares (Mitford 1870d: 269). The two members were Charles Fyshe Palmer, an advanced Whig, and her friend of many years, Thomas Noon Talfourd, who stood as a Radical.

In its assessment of the 1825 volume, the *Quarterly Review*, which had been so scathing in its evaluation of her poems, offered a somewhat backhanded compliment that called attention to a democratic strain in her writings. 'The sketches of country scenery', the review begins, 'have such a convincing air of locality; the human figures, interspersed among them, are touched in such a laughter-loving, good humoured spirit of caricature, innocent, and yet often pungent withal, that we scarcely know a more agreeable portfolio of trifles for the amusement of an idle hour' (Anon. 1825: 166–167). Although the author clearly discerned the sardonic wit of the character sketches, he laments that she failed to grasp that it is possible,

> to seize, and to record with fidelity, the peculiarities of uneducated society, without identifying herself too closely with them; to describe the manners, the occupations, and even the pastimes of her rustic neighbours, without adopting their vulgarisms of language, or descending to clothe her ideas in the phraseology of the dog-kennel and the kitchen. (Anon. 1825: 167)

For this reviewer Mitford identifies too closely with the rustic. Rather than merely quoting the terminology of labourers, she uses them as part of her own descriptive passages: 'such low and provincial corruptions of language as . . . "betweenity", "dumpiness", "rolypoly", "kickshaws", "hurry-scurry", "scrap-dinners", "pot-luck", and similar flowers of diction scarcely worth of Lady Morgan' – a reference to the novelist, whose publications had vexed the *Quarterly Review* for a decade (Anon. 1825: 167).

Although the reviewer does not quite put it this way, Mitford depicts the village as a space of sociability in which old maids and young maidens, rat-catchers and lords of the manor, butchers and high sheriffs, and gamekeepers and lord-lieutenants all intermingle. To be sure, stratification remains and inequality persists. As Mitford notes in the last volume of *Our Village*, 'country society . . . is, for the most part, quite as exclusive as that of London' (1832a: 62). Thus, whatever exchanges between the classes that do exist are selective and transitory. But in Mitford's village residents come together as people rather than as abstractions.

Throughout the publication of the first five volumes, reviewers and the general public tended to appreciate Mitford's biographical vignettes as much as they did her topographical sketches. Indeed, the *Quarterly Review* commends to the reader's attention such sketches as 'The Talking Lady', which I analysed in the preceding chapter, as one of many pieces 'abounding in arch and amusing touches of character, which prove that Miss Mitford has observation and tact, and playful *badinage*, to catch higher follies as they fly, than the whims and eccentricities of village life'. He concludes: 'we part from her in her own good-humoured mood, and with no disinclination to be her debtors for another smile' (Anon. 1825: 174). Although some of the sharp edges of Mitford's character sketches are dulled in bound volumes published under her own name, her witticisms were recognisable and celebrated.

Whittaker, who appears to have been fairly flexible in contractual and copyright negotiations for the first volume, was reluctant to make many significant alterations to the pieces.[12] After its success and his initial hesitation about the timing of a second volume, he asked Mitford to write more volumes, and he began to take an active role in *Our Village*'s publication. He grew increasingly interested in marketing the collected volumes of *Our Village* precisely as representations of an actually existing idyllic countryside and reflecting the virtuous character of its residents. He insisted on a hurried production schedule and encouraged successive sketches well after Mitford's enthusiasm for the volumes had subsided. Mitford was interested in using her newfound fame for other purposes, including completing a novel long in the making and advancing her career as an historical dramatist, which seemed all the more promising after the successes of *Rienzi* and *Charles I: An Historical Tragedy in Five Acts*. In the opening of the fifth volume she notes that it has been 'ten long years', 'ten weary years', of writing sketches, producing 'five tedious volumes' of a 'history, half real, and half imaginary, of a half imaginary and half real little spot on the sunny side of Berkshire'. Gesturing to her emerging reputation as a dramatist, she quips: 'The longest tragedy has only five acts' (1832a: 3).

As her reference to the village as half real and half imaginary indicates, Mitford was unwilling to completely collapse fantasy and reality, even as she relished her newfound fame and the interest readers took in her life at Three Mile Cross. In her prefaces to these volumes, Mitford does not purport to offer actual representations of the English countryside but rather her unique vision of it. The preface to the first volume of 1824 begins by suggesting that Mitford will in fact offer a faithful representation of the village in which she lives: 'The following pages contain an attempt to delineate country scenery and country manners as they exist in a small village in the south of England'. Throughout the sketches, Mitford's engaging narrator repeatedly describes the village and its residents in ways that are intended to reinforce the notion that this location and the people who inhabit it are real. In the first volume, the narrator observes of her companions, her dog, Mayflower, and the young girl named Lizzy: 'What a pretty picture they would make; what a pretty foreground they do make to the real landscape' (1824a: 14). Of the experience of getting caught in the rain, she enthuses: 'how cheerful I am now! Nothing like a shower-bath – a real shower bath, such as Lizzy and May and I have undergone, to cure low spirits. Try it, my dear readers, if ever ye be nervous – I will answer for its success' (1824a: 145). This passage suggests that Lizzy and Mayflower are as real as the narrator and the narratee, who are acknowledged to be the actual writer and readers of the work.

At the same time, the preface's claim to mimeticism is quickly qualified. Speaking of herself in the third person, Mitford continues: 'She has painted, as they appeared to her', the village residents' 'little frailties and their many virtues'. On the one hand, then, *Our Village* is paratextually framed as real. On the other hand, the reality of the village becomes filtered through the author's moral

Sketches of Rural Scenery: Mitford's Country Rambles

sensibilities: her desire to look past 'little frailties' and towards the 'many virtues' of the residents she describes. This claim flattens many of the distinctive literary qualities of the character sketches, such as their acerbic wit, to produce a different authorial voice.

Mitford may have tired of *Our Village*. Yet Whittaker continued to see untapped potential in the series. After the original five unillustrated volumes were completed, he recognised the emerging market in amply illustrated books for members of the middle class. In early February of 1835, Mitford received an 'unexpected visitor, in the shape of an artist, sent by George Whittaker, to take views for an edition of "Our Village" with eighteen plates' (Mitford 1870b: 157). Whittaker and the artist contrived to focus on sketches of the countryside, and Mitford participated by pointing out 'the most desirable scenes'. She was, however, largely ignorant of illustration processes and relied on the guidance of the illustrator, George Baxter. Writing to her father, Mitford notes that Whittaker and the artist envisaged the illustrations not as 'great pictures, filling the page, but [as] beautifully finished vignettes, printed on the same page either with the title or the beginnings of the articles'. This, she goes on to comment, 'is the present fashion for illustrating books' (Mitford 1870b: 158). Baxter, who developed a special technique for producing 'coloured impressions of a high degree of perfection, and far superior to those which are coloured by hand', had established himself a year earlier as the pre-eminent book illustrator (qtd. in Ray 1976: 63).

In 1835, *Our Village* was reissued in a handsome three-volume format, books which call attention to themselves as objects for display. They are uniform in external appearance: pale red board covers with quarter green leather bindings. The spines contain a gold embossed flower-and-leaf design as well as gold embossed lettering including the title (*Our Village*), author (Miss Mitford) and respective volume number in Roman numerals. The gold page trim and eighteen woodcut illustrations are, in Mitford's words, of 'admirable softness and beauty' (Mitford 1870b: 160). These vignettes, which appear at the beginning of some sketches, reinforce the autobiographical elements of the text. The illustrated title page of the first sketch, 'Our Village', depicts Mitford engaged in an act of on-the-spot composition, modestly turning her face away from a passing male agricultural worker.

The 1835 edition initiated a process of selling the work in increasingly consolidated form. But in this version, comprised of three rather than five volumes, the sketches still follow the same order in which they originally appeared. The reading experience can thus, at times, be rather jarring: 'A Parting Glance at Our Village', which concludes the first volume of 1824, appears here as the twenty-fourth sketch in the first volume. But in this edition, the sketch does not serve as a conclusion: the first nine sketches of the 1826 volume follow it. Beginning in 1843, *Our Village* was published as an illustrated two-volume anthology, about which I will have more to say in chapter five. Most of the sketches were reordered and clustered according to theme, thus substantially altering the reader's experience.

As Vera Watson notes in her biography of Mitford, the illustrations for *Our Village*, beginning with the three-volume anthology of 1835, tend to skew readings of the text. They shift the focus away from the character sketches and de-emphasise some of Mitford's 'more subtle and worldly characterizations' (1949: 164). These 'worldly' aspects of the text, as Watson concludes, may simply be more difficult to illustrate. But illustrations also provide visual cues to the reader on how to interpret the meaning of a text, so what one chooses to include and exclude is ideologically significant. The foci of these illustrations are landscape scenes that highlight rural labourers engaged in honest work and children in innocent play rather than calling attention to the agrarian hardships of the period, such as ruined farmhouses and mechanistic, seemingly futile, labour.

These illustrations become invitations to nostalgia – not the reflective nostalgia evident in the original sketches (which sought to resist the effacement of rural hardships in the *Lady's Magazine* or national-historic events, such as the Swing riots, in literary annuals), but the restorative nostalgia that becomes crucial to shaping a national consciousness through shared images of rural England. Whittaker began to exploit growing interest in portable icons of Englishness around the time of the first Reform Act. These verbal and visual icons offered the middle-class reader 'possession of an England', understood to be rural, whose images and literary descriptions 'have been placed in circulation' – therefore reflecting a new conception of property ownership in which the nation was no longer seen solely as an aggregate of landed properties or social authority vested exclusively in the landed class (Helsinger 1994a: 105). These icons of Englishness, as Helsinger points out, 'become the portable possessions that can sanctify the new places of urban and colonial Britain, icons of a movable English home' (1997: 59).

By the time that George Eliot picked up her pen to write fiction, *Our Village* was widely perceived as offering its urban and colonial readers such compensatory pleasures. But the young Elizabeth Gaskell, who was honing her compositional skills as Mitford was making a name for herself, drew entirely different conclusions. It is to Mitford's influence on Gaskell that I now turn.

Notes

1 At an earlier stage, I thought perhaps the initial had been used in honour of Mitford's lady's maid Kerenhappuch Taylor, who was known as 'K'. However, she was not employed by Mitford until the 1830s.
2 For several years, the identity of the author who was contributing sketches of rural character and scenery to the *Lady's Magazine* would have been unknown to readers. But once the first volume of *Our Village* was published, it would have been apparent – at least to crossover readers. Mitford also began to publish sequels to earlier sketches (see, for example, 1824b).
3 Focusing on novels between 1840 and 1870, Charlotte Mathieson has argued that the journey – a more capacious category than travel – promoted national consciousness: 'It is through bodies on the move that the place of the nation is produced, both internally and in confluence with global networks; like the mobile bodies themselves, this production is fluid and ongoing, a "placing" that is always in process' (2015: 16). As Mathieson helpfully notes, a walk of limited duration no less than an arduous sea voyage could engender a sense of national identity.
4 On Mitford and cultural nationalism, see Helsinger (1997) and Lynch (2000). W. J. Keith (1974) and Peter David Edwards (1988) are somewhat less focused on national implications, although they both see Mitford as an important figure in cultural representations of the English countryside.
5 Deidre Lynch notes that they served as 'props for rituals of homesickness, vehicles securing the continuity of everyday Englishness across cultural divides' (2000: 1106). As the reach of England's empire grew, so too did nostalgia for its countryside.
6 It is, I think, important to keep both influences in mind. Nevertheless, in a wonderfully stimulating reading that focuses on Mitford's

topographical sketches, Amy King argues that *Our Village* should not be seen solely 'as a social history of village life, but as an unacknowledged natural history' (2019: 9). As Alison Booth points out, although readers of Gilbert White 'would recognize the country-village and seasonal setting in Mitford', the latter's 'digressive personal essays' and 'spritely conversational style' differ 'from White's minutely observed letters to naturalists' (2016: 107).

7 Mitford's letters suggest that 'A Great Farm-House' was not originally intended for the *Lady's Magazine*. Abraham John Valpy, editor of the *Museum*, had requested a prose sketch from her. While working on 'A Great Farm-House', Mitford expresses some frustration, in a letter to Talfourd dated 18 April 1822, with not knowing 'what kind of things he [Valpy] wishes'. It is unclear whether Valpy rejected the piece (Coles 1856: 541–545, 544).

8 On children's employment as field labourers, see Horn 1980: 138; see also Verdon 2009. Given Mitford's use of the term *boys* in this and other sketches in reference to teenagers, she is no doubt referring to those roughly between the ages of seven and twelve.

9 Katherine Harris has identified 102 poems and prose works by Mitford that appeared between 1826 and 1845 in the leading annuals of the day, including some that were printed in more than one publication. These include seventeen in *Forget Me Not*; thirteen in *Friendship's Offering*; twelve in *Literary Souvenir*; thirteen in the *Amulet*; six in *Pledge of Friendship*; two that appeared in both *Bijou* and *Cameo*; two in *Winter's Wreath*; one in *Anniversary*; four in *Gem*; one in *Remembrance*; two in *Comic Offering*; and twenty-one in *Finden's Tableaux*, of which Mitford was editor during the entirety of its run between 1837 and 1844 (Harris 2015: 306–309).

10 In the version of the story that appears in the *Amulet*, Thomas is mistakenly referred to twice as William. It seems unlikely that the printer mistook a *Thomas* for a *William* and slipped the typographical errors in himself. Mitford was working on a number of stories that season. She corrected the error when including 'The Vicar's Maid' in the third volume of *Our Village* (1828).

11 Mitford died a decade before the appellation 'Liberal' was first used to designate a political party and four years before representatives of varied interests gathered on 6 June 1859 at Willis's Rooms in St James's Street, London, and agreed to rally around Lord Palmerston in their bid to oust the Conservative minority Derby administration from power. This anti-Conservative coalition, which included Radicals, who advocated for parliamentary reform; Peelites

Sketches of Rural Scenery: Mitford's Country Rambles 121

    (those Tories who believed in free trade and, following Robert Peel, split with their party over its protectionist policies); and Whigs (who, on one end of the spectrum, were amenable to forming a government with Conservatives and those, on the other end, who insisted on maintain their oppositional status) would eventually call themselves Liberals. Successful in toppling the Derby administration, this coalition simply crystallised the relationship among anti-Conservatives that had been taking shape for two decades (Parry 1993: 1).

12 Mitford appears to have retained the copyright on the first volume until late April or early May of 1826, nearly two years later, when her father negotiated on her behalf the sale of the second volume. Whittaker paid £150 for the rights to the first and second volumes at the same time (L'Estrange 1870b: 58). She sold the third and fourth volumes to Whittaker for the same amount (Watson 1949: 193).

3

From Sketches to Papers: Gaskell's Country Village

George Eliot was a toddler when Mary Russell Mitford first made her mark on the literary world, and she was just beginning to consider writing fiction when Mitford passed away in 1855. By contrast, Elizabeth Gaskell, who was ten years older than Eliot, encountered Mitford at the height of her popularity. The question is not, therefore, 'Did Elizabeth Gaskell read *Our Village*' but 'When did she first encounter it?' At the time that she set out to write the eight literary sketches for *Household Words: A Weekly Journal Conducted by Charles Dickens* that would later appear as *Cranford* (1853), Gaskell modelled not only her distinctive mode of publication on Mitford's work but also its content and form. She knew that Dickens would be particularly receptive to this approach. His own pieces that used walks as an armature formed the basis for the 'Sketches of London' series published in the *Evening Chronicle* between January and August 1835. They provided an urban counterpart to Mitford's country strolls. The last four in the series of fourteen appeared with the subtitle 'Our Parish', while the final sketch carried the phrase as its title. These irregularly published, but clearly related, sketches 'form a kind of serial' (Butt and Tillotson 2013: 41). As Mitford had done, Dickens subsequently collected these works, as well as others that had first appeared in newspapers and periodicals, and published them in bound form as *Sketches by Boz*.[1]

When Dickens established *Household Words* he viewed the sketch form as a particularly appropriate genre of writing to fulfil his editorial aims. 'To show to all, that in all familiar things, even in those which are repellent on the surface', he writes in the first number, 'there is Romance enough, if we will find it out'

(Dickens 1850: 2). As he put it to the biographer and critic John Forster in a letter dated 7 October 1849, Dickens sought submissions that were 'as amusing as possible, but all distinctly and boldly going to what in one's own view ought to be the spirit of the people and the time' (1981: 622).[2] 'Odd, unsubstantial, whimsical' – these were the particular qualities of individual submissions that Dickens thought would be 'just mysterious and quaint enough to have a sort of charm for . . . [the reader's] imagination, while it will represent common-sense and humanity' (1981: 623). Common sense and humanity, it would seem, emerge from the charm of the peculiar.

Soon after Dickens decided to establish *Household Words* he began to look for contributors whose views and literary approach aligned with his. He contacted Gaskell, whose social-problem novel, *Mary Barton*, he had admired since first reading it while on a Brighton holiday in 1848.[3] As with Mitford, Gaskell began her career as a contributor to periodicals, including a poem co-written with her husband, which appeared in *Blackwood's Magazine* in 1837, and, under the pseudonym Cotton Mather Mills, Esq., several short stories in *Howitt's Journal*. She contemplated publishing *Mary Barton* under a pseudonym as well. 'Shall you have any objection to the name of "Stephen Berwick" as that of the author of "Mary Barton"', she asked one correspondent in a letter dated 19 October 1848 (Chapple and Pollard 1966: 59). Ultimately, however, she opted to publish it anonymously. As Alexis Easley has pointed out, 'Anonymous publication meant that neither the novel's narrative voice nor its audience was immediately classifiable in terms of conventionally masculine or feminine reading material' (2004: 91). Nevertheless, on its publication, reviewers speculated that the novel had been written by a woman. Towards the end of the year Gaskell relented in responding to direct inquiries from friends. 'I cannot tell you what a surprise your letter was to me last night', she proclaimed to one correspondent in an undated letter written in late 1848, 'but I will throw myself on your honour and confess that the surprise was simply occasioned by the intelligence that "Mary Barton" was so much read, and that you had guessed (*I cannot imagine how?*) that I had written it' (Chapple and Pollard 1966: 67). Gaskell's name was added to subsequent editions within a few months.

After providing Dickens with a few pieces of original fiction for his two-penny weekly magazine, Gaskell sent him a sketch modelled on *Our Village* but also resonating with 'Our Parish'

Dickens was so 'delighted with it' that he suggested its name, 'Our Society at Cranford', and, as he explained to Gaskell in a letter from December 1851, placed it first in the issue dated 13 December – a sign of his conviction that Gaskell would help sell copies of the journal (1988: 549). The first of what would be eight sketches, 'Our Society at Cranford' immediately 'strengthen[ed] the moral purpose' that Dickens had 'announced in the opening number' (Collin 1986: 59). Finding romance in all 'familiar things' is, of course, a way of invoking the *everyday*, which is the focus of her sketches: the daily routines of 'the Amazons'; a group of spinsters and widows enduring financial hardship; the social community they establish for themselves; and the wider network of friendships they cultivate.[4] As someone who had utilised the sketch form himself, Dickens recognised its capacity – through provisionality, tangentiality and digression – to charm. He also believed that the genre's conditionality and comparative formlessness enabled authors to play with new ideas in a reflective rather than assertive way.

Since its publication in 1853 as a single volume by Chapman and Hall, Gaskell's *Cranford* has been compared to Mary Russell Mitford's earlier work. Both followed a similar trajectory. Gaskell's discontinuous, non-narrative sketches first appeared at irregular intervals in *Household Words*. They were also published anonymously.[5] Instead of country walks, Gaskell organised the sketches according to a series of visits, but both feature a narrator who is more metropolitan than provincial. Mitford's lived in the village, but her sensibility is considerably more urbane than the residents whose lives she chronicles. She thus acts as a kind of intermediary between rustics and urbanites ('Did any of my readers ever hear of a Maying?'). Where readers are invited to associate the narrative persona of *Our Village* with Mitford herself, the narrator of *Cranford* is a fictional character. But Mary Smith (unnamed throughout most of the sketches) has 'vibrated all ... [her] life between Drumble and Cranford', the former an industrial town and the latter a village, and thus occupies a similarly privileged position (Gaskell 2008: 154). She is able to interpret and translate the peculiarities of village customs, mores and values for a reader presumed to be a city dweller: 'Do you ever see cows dressed in grey flannel in London', Mary Smith asks in the epistolary voice of a traveller (Gaskell 2008: 5).[6]

Whereas Mitford's informal, improvisatory and conversational sketches of rural life alternate between topography and character in their subject matter, Gaskell's episodic 'papers' focus almost entirely on friendship and community. As an early reader remarked:

> Very unlike Miss Mitford's pictures of country-town life, owing nothing to description, limiting itself to a small circle in a small place, omitting even antiquarian associations, not hinting at religious differences, nor even romancing about pretty maidens and country swains, it is wonderful how the interest is sustained throughout. (Anon. 1853: 494)

Although this anonymous review suggests that the differences were substantive, owing in part to Mitford's greater interest in providing descriptions of country scenery, it nevertheless acknowledges that certain resemblances – not least of which is the sketch form both authors employed – are undeniable. Most nineteenth-century readers certainly perceived *Our Village* as a 'precursor, in some sort' to Gaskell's later work (Kemble 1875: 445).

Likewise, twentieth- and twenty-first-century critics have noted the close associations between *Our Village* and *Cranford*. Perhaps the most vociferous in his insistence on the links between the two is Franco Moretti, who has labelled *Cranford* a 'rewriting' of *Our Village* (2005: 62). While discerning clear parallels, others adopt more cautious terminology. Robin B. Colby contends that Gaskell's sketches are 'reminiscent' of Mitford's earlier work (1995: 66). Coral Lansbury similarly argues that Gaskell herself invited 'comparisons to be made' between her novel and the 'direct tradition of Mary Mitford and the visionary *Our Village*' (1984: 72). Angus Easson flatly observes that *Our Village* is an 'obvious forebear' to *Cranford* (2016, 98). One of the problems in determining the extent of Gaskell's indebtedness to Mitford is that no one knows precisely when she first read *Our Village*. The lending ledgers of the Portico Library, Manchester's premier subscription library, give some indication of at least one occasion when she re-read it. As chairman of the library from 1849 to 1884, Gaskell's husband, William, frequently borrowed books for his wife to read or consult. On 27 September 1858, he checked out the first two volumes of *Our Village*. He returned the following day to collect the third and fourth volumes. A few days later, on 4 October, he returned for the fifth volume.

In the absence of any letters or journal entries that provide a reason for borrowing *Our Village* from the Portico at this time, one can only hazard a few guesses. Anyone who has engaged in some form of biographical inquiry into Gaskell has confronted the problem of archival gaps and silences. Vocally opposed to research into her own life, she pleaded with correspondents to destroy her letters. To her eldest daughter Marianne, she wrote in (possibly early March) 1854: 'Pray burn any letters'. 'I am always afraid of writing much to you', she continues, 'you are so careless about letters' (Chapple and Pollard 1966: 274). Following the death of her second eldest daughter, Margaret Emily (Meta), much of Gaskell's remaining correspondence was indeed burned.

Perhaps Gaskell asked her husband to obtain *Our Village* for her because she wanted to revisit, as I will soon discuss, a formative work she encountered earlier in life. Or maybe she wished to share it with her two youngest daughters, Florence and Julia, aged sixteen and twelve. With the publication of Bohn's 'perfected' two-volume edition of *Our Village* between 1843 and 1856 – the version George Eliot would have read – Gaskell may have been interested in comparing it to the original five biennial volumes.

In any event, Gaskell's extant letters do not contain any reference to when she first encountered *Our Village*, which appeared in print when she was a teenager. Although many of her surviving letters are seemingly thorough, on closer analysis they are surprisingly reticent about key details of her life. Deirdre D'Albertis summarises the problem of Gaskell's inclination to privacy and discretion:

> [W]e know very little about what Gaskell thought of her childhood adoption into her mother's family, the disappearance of a beloved brother, John Stevenson [on a voyage overseas], the death of her father, or her marriage in 1832 to the Reverend William Gaskell. As a chronicler of her own life, in other words, Gaskell practiced self-censorship to a surprising degree. (2007: 11).

This self-censorship extends to less significant events in her life, including to those writers we might expect Gaskell to mention as influences.

Throughout *Cranford* there are obvious allusions and less apparent citations of her predecessor's work. As this chapter will explain, there is every reason to believe that Gaskell read the original biennial volumes of *Our Village*. There is also circumstantial evidence to suggest that she first encountered the sketches in the *Lady's Magazine*. Even if Gaskell only read Mitford's sketches in bound volumes, however, the editions available to her in the 1820s and early 1830s differ substantially from those published in later decades, including in 1856.

As I sought to show in the preceding chapters, the material aspects of publication and their modes of circulation engender different textual meanings and different audience relationships. If Gaskell read *Our Village* after 1835, she would have encountered – often gold-embossed and amply illustrated – editions that were marketed as transportable representations of Englishness for the middle classes displaced from the countryside to the city. If Gaskell read Mitford's work as discontinuous, non-illustrated volumes in the 1820s, she would have been more alert to the play of irony, acerbity and ambivalence that the illustration and design of later editions tend to mute. If she read the sketches in the *Lady's Magazine*, she would almost certainly have understood them as more akin to William Hazlitt's essays than as their cheerful counterparts. Thus, establishing which version or versions Gaskell read has significant implications for understanding how *Our Village* informs *Cranford*. Because *Cranford* has been subject to some of the very same modulations as *Our Village*, this chapter will also consider which editions of both texts Marian Evans, as she was becoming George Eliot, would have read and how this informed her views of Gaskell and Mitford.

Editions matter/the matter of editions

As with later instantiations of *Our Village*, various editions of *Cranford* have fixed certain meanings and obscured others. The age of the novel's principal characters is a case in point. Critics generally agree that Gaskell depicts a community of 'elderly' women. Thus, as Olivia Malfait observes of the small fictional village based on Knutsford in Cheshire where Gaskell grew up, '*Cranford* is populated with frail, elderly women, whose everyday concerns are very much domestic' (2010: 72). Anna Koustinoudi concurs in her assessment of the 'community of unmarried, elderly ladies, and childless widows in the margins of a Britain rapidly transforming from a rural to an industrial economy' (2012: 43). In Talia Schaffer's reading of the novel's mimicry of craft practice, 'its plot compiled from carefully preserved fragments', she notes that the village's 'elderly spinsters live in rooms full of faded, fragile remnants' (2011: 61). Yet the ladies of the novel are, in fact, middle-aged or only slightly older. How have so many critics come to conclude otherwise?

Take Miss Matty. Over the course of *Cranford*, she ages from her mid-forties in chapter two (part of the first 'paper' published in *Household Words*), to her late forties in chapter three, to fifty-one in chapter four, to fifty-eight in chapter fourteen. As Kay Heath (2009) has suggested, Victorian women were generally considered to be middle aged when they were in their thirties and forties. As they moved into their fifties, they would be considered old. By this definition, Miss Matty would be elderly at the end of *Cranford*, but not before.

Yet the distinction in this period between middle and old age was by no means fixed. As Karen Chase (2009) has argued, until the nineteenth century there were only limited and haphazard attempts to define old age in terms of years. As a result, within the nineteenth century, the definition of *old age* was often in flux. In Heath's view, Gaskell perpetuates rather than interrogates a Victorian understanding of the divisions between middle and old age. Yet because Miss Matty could expect to live into her eighties,[7] the novel seems instead to undermine eager classifications along these lines.

There are, it seems to me, three primary reasons why so many critics have concluded that Miss Matty is, along with her relatives and friends, elderly. The first is that Mary Smith is considerably younger than the women she visits. The daughter of a Drumble businessman, Mary regularly visits her close friends and likely distant relations, Deborah and Mathilda Jenkyns, which brings her into contact with a wide array of Cranfordians. Once Deborah passes away, Mary continues to stay with Miss Matty, as she is called by those closest to her, and, on one occasion, with the town gossip Miss Pole. Because the novel is told from the point of view of a young woman in her teens through her early twenties, Mary's perception of the women is deliberately skewed. Although she does not attribute it to the narrator's age, Kate Flint has remarked that 'a somewhat ironic distance is maintained' throughout the text (1995: 31). This is certainly true of the early chapters when Mary is still in her teens, but it is less the case as the narrator grows older.

In her depictions of the women themselves, Gaskell suggests that perceptions of ageing are not static. Thus, the second reason is that the women of Cranford engage in anachronism as a performative mode. Of course, as spinsters and so-called old maids they are inherently anachronistic insofar as they have remained single beyond the age at which they were expected by their families and expected by social mores to marry. They are 'a mistake in a normative systemization of time', to borrow a phrase from a different study focused on ageing women in Western culture (Russo 1999: 21). Because Victorian women's lives were symbolically confined to the developmental trajectory of daughter, wife and mother, any conscious or unintentional deviation from this path could result in what Mary Russo calls a 'scandal'. 'Not acting one's age', Russo contends, 'is not only inappropriate but dangerous, exposing the female subject, especially, to ridicule, contempt, pity, and scorn – the scandal of anachronism' (1999: 21).

In 'The Great Cranford Panic', Mary Smith returns to the village for the magician Signor Brunoni's performance. She arrives bearing a gift for the genial Miss Matty: 'a pretty, neat, middle-aged cap' that, she believes, will complement the latter's 'small gentle mousey face'. Miss Matty, hoping for a 'great Saracen's-head turban', immediately experiences disappointment. 'I am sure you did your best, my dear', she tells Mary. 'It is just like the caps all the ladies in Cranford are wearing', she continues, '[and] I should have liked something newer' (2008: 81). What is newer to Miss Matty is precisely what is considered older by the norms of the wider community of which the Amazons are a part: the turban style had faded by the 1840s in England, though it was becoming newly fashionable in France, and the actual type of turban Miss Matty desires is modelled on the headgear of Crusader-era Muslims. Her desire, as revealed here, is to use anachronism as a mode of self-stylisation in order not to appear like the other 'ladies in Cranford', each of whom wears a 'pretty, neat, middle-aged cap' – moving backward by English standards or forward by French standards in order to be distinct.

Refusing to dress the part, the Cranfordian women consequently do not act their age. It is not just a critic as astute as Talia Schaffer who characterises Miss Matty as 'an elderly woman' (2008: 52). Even Miss Matty's housekeeper, Martha, makes the mistake of assuming that her employer is older than she in fact is:

> 'Eh! dear ma'am, to think of your going out in an evening in such a thin shawl! It's no better than muslin. At your age, ma'am, you should be careful.'

'My age!' said Miss Matty, almost speaking crossly, for her, for she was usually gentle – 'My age! Why, how old do you think I am, that you talk about my age?'

'Well, ma'am, I should say you were not far short of sixty; but folks' looks is often against them – and I'm sure I meant no harm.'

'Martha, I'm not yet fifty-two!' said Miss Matty, with grave emphasis; for probably the remembrance of her youth had come very vividly before her this day, and she was annoyed at finding that golden time so far away in the past. (2008: 36)

In her late teens or early twenties, Martha's perception of her employer's age differs from Miss Matty's own. Mary Smith, slightly younger than Martha, shares a similar view of the housekeeper, believing that Miss Matty's annoyance likely stems from having been reminded of her youth on encountering a former suitor earlier in the day. Another moment later in the novel underscores Gaskell's interest in perceptions of ageing. After the passage of a few years, Mary observes that 'Miss Matty had a few little peculiarities which Martha was apt to regard as whims below her attention, and appeared to consider as childish fancies of which an old lady of fifty-eight should try and cure herself' (2008: 132). The term *old* is used here to underscore that one's attitude about elders is in part shaped by the perceiver's stage of life. In other words, the humour of the scene between Miss Matty and Martha is generated by uncertainty over when midlife ends and old age begins.

The widows, in rejecting a life of mourning, act out in ways that are anachronistic as well. Sometimes they behave younger than they are, but in so doing reinforce the reader's impression that they are elderly. Initially an outsider, the eccentric Lady Glenmire, who arrives in Cranford midway through the novel, is described as 'a bright little woman of middle age, who had been very pretty in the days of her youth, and who was even yet very pleasant-looking' (2008: 76). Although she is aristocratic, Lady Glenmire flouts protocol, much to the dismay of the Cranfordian women. Nevertheless, having 'evidently taken very kindly to Cranford', that is, become one of its own, she falls in love with and marries the village doctor, Mr Hoggins – a decision that is met with universal consternation: 'Mrs Hoggins! Had she absolutely dropped her title, and so, in a spirit of bravado, cut the aristocracy to become a Hoggins! She, who might have been called Lady Glenmire to her dying day!' (2008: 95, 143). Lady Glenmire's anachronistic act, in its seemingly youthful impetuosity, goes against the grain of community norms even as it empowers her to achieve her own desires – signified by those 'becoming blushes of hers' that the women notice after her marriage (2008: 143).[8] Anachronistic behaviour, therefore, is both part of the Amazon ethos that these women establish for themselves and an individual mode of empowerment that can sometimes conflict with the social expectations of their community.

However, a third reason why so many critics have assumed that the women of Cranford are elderly has nothing to do with the text itself. In 1891, Macmillan published an edition with a preface by Anne Thackeray Ritchie and lavish illustrations by Hugh Thomson. The frontispiece depicts Miss Matty in her tea shop, which she establishes with the help of Mary Smith at the end of the novel (Figure 3.1). Although Gérard Genette refers to frontispieces only in passing, they are part of the paratextual apparatus and shape the reading experience.[9] Thomson's frontispiece performs two different kinds of work. On the one hand, it plays a role in transforming a collection of sporadically published papers into a novel with some semblance of plot. After the failure of the joint-stock bank in which Miss Matty had – on the advice of her overbearing sister, Deborah – invested all of her funds, she must sell off the majority of her belongings, rent out rooms in her house and engage in some form of economic activity to survive. Because Miss Matty loathes the idea of becoming a tradeswoman and thereby yielding her genteel status to the 'degrading characteristics' of shop ownership (2008: 142), Mary oversees the conversion of her parlour into a discreet commercial space. In Thomson's image, she appears somewhat cosy, not at all unhappy with her fate, surrounded by the appurtenances of tea selling – a ledger, shipped boxes and canisters into which their contents are placed, a scale – and sitting at the small table that has been repurposed to serve as a counter.

Yet although Miss Matty is certainly a leading character, the novel, owing to the circumstances of its composition, does not unfold her story in a linear fashion. Indeed, in the first two Cranford papers, Deborah – whom, Mary Smith later tells us, fittingly relished her role as a decisive leader of and stern judge over the Cranfordians, in keeping with her 'Hebrew' namesake (2008: 12) – is the dominant character. Gaskell had planned to end the papers with the publication of the second sketch in which Deborah, having grown 'old and feeble, and had lost something of

Figure 3.1 Miss Matty in her tea shop. Illustration by Hugh Thomson. Elizabeth Cleghorn Gaskell, *Cranford*. With a preface by Anne Thackeray Ritchie and illustrations by Hugh Thomson. New York and London: Frederick A. Stokes Company, [1900?]. Courtesy of the Armstrong Browning Library, Baylor University.

her strong mind', nears death (2008: 22), but Dickens – noting the praise Gaskell's papers had received – persuaded her (as Whittaker had persuaded Mitford) to carry on. Although Gaskell would write an additional fourteen papers, Miss Matty's near-financial ruin and subsequent salvation only occur in the last two papers. Nevertheless, the illustration directs the reader to understand the text to be about Miss Matty and thus to construct in the reader's mind a narrative while reading what is otherwise, at best, inchoate.

Not only does the frontispiece introduce the text to the reader, but it also establishes the foundation for all subsequent illustrations. The very next illustration, which appears above the first chapter's title, would at first seem to undercut the assertion that visual images play a role in fixing an understanding of the women as elderly (Figure 3.2). Four Cranfordians sit at a table playing

From Sketches to Papers: Gaskell's Country Village   133

Figure 3.2 Heading to Chapter One of *Cranford*. Illustration by Hugh Thomson. Lebrecht Music & Arts/ Alamy Stock Photo.

cards and only the identity of Deborah, positioned at the head of the table in a stiff upright posture, is discernible. The other two women are all far younger than the text itself implies. By depicting the women in this way, Thomson is able to immediately frame Deborah as an imperious figure who has assumed an almost parental role to those around her. At the same time, their dress, which lacks historical specificity, does less to locate them in time than in an entirely different genre: the fairy tale. The so-called colourised edition of 1898 only accentuates this element.

Most of the other illustrations, however, portray the women of Cranford as Martha (and to a lesser extent Mary Smith) perceives them. In Chapter Seven Miss Matty is depicted in a state of surprise at receiving an unexpected guest (Figure 3.3). Betty Barker, preoccupied with an errand – and, Mary Smith hastens to add, 'not so young as she had been' – calls on Miss Matty outside the hours of twelve to three, the window established by the Cranfordians for visiting (2008: 60). In her hurry to get ready, Miss Matty, who has forgotten that she is already wearing a cap, adds another to her

Figure 3.3 Miss Matty in a state of surprise. Illustration by Hugh Thomson. Elizabeth Cleghorn Gaskell, *Cranford*. With a preface by Anne Thackeray Ritchie and illustrations by Hugh Thomson. New York and London: Frederick A. Stokes Company, [1900?]. Courtesy of the Armstrong Browning Library, Baylor University.

head, before quickly taking a seat. Having neglected to put on her spectacles, however, Miss Matty is unable to see her guest clearly. Instead of capturing the ridiculousness of the moment that results from Betty Barker's violation of etiquette, Thomson's illustration renders it as a product of age. Miss Matty, seated in her chair, looks out at Betty Barker with an almost vacant stare. Wearing two caps on her head and without her spectacles, Miss Matty appears somewhat confused and overwhelmed at the moment, which she does her best to suppress by appearing polite but nevertheless uncomfortable.

Thomson's illustrations, therefore, single out certain strands of the text – in this case the perceptions of Martha and Mary Smith of Miss Matty's elderliness – and prompt one to read *Cranford* in specific ways. In Thomson's hands, the years in which Miss Matty ages in the novel mark out a cognitive and physical decline, whereas the text contests such perceptions of middle age. After all, Gaskell was roughly the age of Miss Matty in the novel's first two chapters. When she sat for George Richmond's widely circulated chalk drawing, she was forty-one (Figure 3.4). Thus, although Annette B. Hopkins insists in her biographical study that if Gaskell had seen 'these inimitable sketches' she would have been delighted because they appear 'so utterly right that they seem like an integral part of the text' (1952: 103), Thomson's illustrations are more appropriately viewed as a form of comic deprecation that serves up saccharine images of aged women who seemingly exist out of time.

Although he is unconcerned with Thomson's depictions of age, Thomas Recchio has provided the finest study to date of the illustrated editions of *Cranford*. In Recchio's estimation, Thomson is able to capture in compelling ways some of the novel's narrative tensions, particularly the fraught relationship between Miss Matty's

Figure 3.4 Elizabeth Gaskell. Chalk portrait by George Richmond.
© National Portrait Gallery, London.

brother, Peter, and their father, which culminates in the son presumed dead after leaving for battle in India (Figure 3.5).

Ultimately, however, Recchio concludes, Thomson's images frame, in order to reduce, the possible meanings of Gaskell's work. The 'illustrations seem less engaged in interpreting *Cranford* as a novel', he observes, 'than in projecting images out of *Cranford* that connect the novel to an idea of a visually recognizable, quintessential English nation' (2009: 113). By drawing out nebulous orientalist elements of the text, such as the appearance of the supposedly Italian Signor Brunoni who wears a turban 'like a Turk', and whose magical performance in the village's assembly rooms causes much anxiety among the ladies, Thomson's illustrations reinforce notions of racial otherness on which nineteenth-century

Figure 3.5 Miss Matty's brother, Peter, and their father. Illustration by Hugh Thomson. Elizabeth Cleghorn Gaskell, *Cranford*. With a preface by Anne Thackeray Ritchie and illustrations by Hugh Thomson. New York and London: Frederick A. Stokes Company, [1900?]. Courtesy of the Armstrong Browning Library, Baylor University.

From Sketches to Papers: Gaskell's Country Village   137

Figure 3.6 Signor Brunoni. Illustration by Hugh Thomson. Elizabeth Cleghorn Gaskell, *Cranford*. With a preface by Anne Thackeray Ritchie and illustrations by Hugh Thomson. New York and London: Frederick A. Stokes Company, [1900?]. Courtesy of the Armstrong Browning Library, Baylor University.

constructions of Englishness depended (Figure 3.6).[10] By contrast, Gaskell's own treatment of race is more subtle.[11]

One of the other ways in which Thomson shapes *Cranford* into a chronicle of national characteristics, Recchio contends, is through his depiction of landscape scenes. Although Recchio does not mention it, there are few descriptive passages of scenery in *Cranford*. This was not lost on Gaskell's contemporaries, one of whom remarked, in a review quoted at the outset of this chapter, that such an absence strongly differentiated her work from Mitford's. By foregrounding the village landscape, however, Thomson could subsume it into the larger project that editions of *Our Village* at mid-century and beyond were seen to represent. In 'Riding Over', Thomson relies on a different kind of visual stereotype (Figure 3.7). Although ostensibly depicting the Cheshire landscape of Gaskell's youth, Thomson never travelled there and instead relied on the far more accessible Wimbledon Common, the former interchangeable with the latter 'because both are simply recognizably English' (Recchio 2009: 118). Because Thomson's illustrations were remarkably successful, these stereotypes were

Figure 3.7 Landscape scene. Illustration by Hugh Thomson. Elizabeth Cleghorn Gaskell, *Cranford*. With a preface by Anne Thackeray Ritchie and illustrations by Hugh Thomson. New York and London: Frederick A. Stokes Company, [1900?]. Courtesy of the Armstrong Browning Library, Baylor University.

clearly 'shared by the book buying public', Recchio observes, 'and the shared world of those stereotypes is based upon a useable nostalgia in which rural, village life functions ideologically as a normative image for the nation' (2009: 113). Subsequent adaptations across media as well as illustrated editions have followed Thomson's lead.[12]

Eliot's *Cranford*

It is perhaps inevitable, therefore, that twenty- and twenty-first century critics have viewed Gaskell's text, even unwittingly, through Thomson's lens. Hilary Schor has contended that the novel 'registers panic about change' (1992: 85), while Franco Moretti claims that it is 'Madame Tussaud's idea of a village story' (2005: 63). To see *Cranford* through George Eliot's eyes, however, requires putting aside any impressions established by

From Sketches to Papers: Gaskell's Country Village 139

these, or in fact any, illustrations. The earliest illustrated edition of *Cranford* appeared five years after Eliot first read it, in 1864 – published by Smith, Elder & Co., with artwork by George Du Maurier. Eliot and her partner, George Henry Lewes, purchased the 'cheap edition' of 1855, but she did not read it until 1857, as she explained to Gaskell (Baker 1981: 72).

In the late spring of 1859, Gaskell, who had been suspected of writing *Adam Bede*, sent a letter to Eliot through the latter's publisher, William Blackwood. The first novel to be written by George Eliot, *Adam Bede*, had appeared earlier in the year. Gaskell had also read Eliot's three short stories published under the title *Scenes of Clerical Life* in 1857 and admired both works. Although aware that they were published under a pseudonym, Gaskell did not know on 3 June 1859, the day she sent the letter, who had composed them:

> Since I came from Manchester to London I have had the greatest compliment paid me I ever had in my life. I have been suspected of having written 'Adam Bede'. I have hitherto denied it; but I really think, that as you want to keep your name a secret, it would be very pleasant for me to blush acquiescence. Will you give me leave?
>
> Well! if I had written Amos Barton, Janet's Repentance [two of the vignettes in *Scenes of Clerical Life*] and Adam Bede I should neither be to have nor to hold with pride and delight in myself . . . . [I]t is a pity so much heart admiration should go unappropriated through the world. (1955a: 74)

Gaskell could not have known that her letter would be well received. In a letter to Blackwood dated 6 June, George Eliot characterised the letter as 'pleasant' (1955a: 76). For her part, she had long appreciated Gaskell's fiction. In 1856, Eliot published an unsigned essay in the *Westminster Review*, entitled 'Silly Novels by Lady Novelists', in which she exempted Gaskell's work – along with Harriet Martineau's and Currer Bell's, the pseudonym used by Charlotte Brontë – from a general condemnation of women's writing. Criticising much literary production by women as unrealistic and hopelessly clichéd, Eliot claims that these authors mistake 'vagueness for depth, bombast for eloquence, and affectation for originality' (1856b: 455). To Eliot, Gaskell's fiction was remarkably different.

This was borne out by contemporary assessments of Gaskell's work as well. Through what Eliot calls a 'peculiar thermometric adjustment', praise for women writers reaches its 'boiling point' when they possess 'zero' talent, whereas, if they obtain 'excellence, critical enthusiasm drops to the freezing point' (1856b: 460). As Eliot notes in 'Silly Novels by Lady Novelists', Gaskell has been treated as 'cavalierly' by reviewers as if she had been a man (1856b: 460). In contrast to what Eliot perceived to be the critical admiration of fatuous writing, this approach to Gaskell's work was perhaps worth lauding if for no other reason than it meant that reviewers were assessing its literary quality on its own merits.

'Silly Novels by Lady Novelists' has often been read as an indictment of women writers who wrote out of financial necessity. Wendy S. Williams is not alone in claiming that the essay takes aim at women 'writers who forfeited quality for monetary gain' (2014: 69n5). Eliot's point, however, is rather the obverse. 'We had imagined that destitute women turned novelists, as they turned governesses', Eliot notes, 'because they had no other "lady-like" means of getting their bread'. 'Empty writing was excused by an empty stomach', she quips (1856b: 443). Much literary production by women is 'written under totally different circumstances' (1856b: 444). Instead of pressing economic concerns, many women were motivated to take up a 'ruby pen' in their 'elegant boudoirs' and write 'with equal unfaithfulness' about 'what they *have* seen and heard, and what they have *not* seen and heard' by feelings of superiority or ennui (1856b: 444). These women are, Eliot insists, 'inexperienced in every form of poverty except poverty of brains', and yet 'betray no closer acquaintance with any other form of life' (1856b: 444). In her attempt at verisimilitude, Gaskell differentiated herself.

In 1853, Gaskell published her third novel. Far more akin to her first work of fiction, *Mary Barton* (1848) – which concerns the plight of the working class in Manchester – than to *Cranford*, *Ruth* focuses on the social ostracisation of a fallen woman and the stigma of having a child out of wedlock. When Eliot undertook to write *Adam Bede* later in the decade, she had *Ruth* in mind as a novel by a woman writer that had successfully grappled with social concerns. Soon after reading Gaskell's novel, in a letter to the women's rights activist Clementia Taylor dated 1 February 1853, she described its 'style' as 'a great refreshment to me, from its finish and fulness' (1954b: 86). 'How women have the courage to write and publishers the spirit to buy at a high price the false and feeble representations of life and character that most feminine novels give', she continues, 'is a constant marvel to me' (1954b: 86). She expresses regret, however, that Gaskell does not convey 'the half tints of real life', which are to Eliot the basis of sympathy. Instead, she is 'misled by a love of sharp contrasts' that fails to 'secure one's lasting sympathy' (1954b: 86). This may in part reflect their different aims. In writing *Ruth*, Gaskell wanted to spur social and legal change. In taking up the trope of the working woman who is seduced, impregnated and discarded by an aristocrat in *Adam Bede*, Eliot wanted to expand the reader's sympathies.

Nevertheless, Eliot expressed high regard for other elements of *Ruth*. She found Gaskell's descriptive abilities, her skill in rendering 'pretty' and – in a nod to the mode of writing inaugurated by Mitford – 'graphic' scenes, awe-inspiring. 'That little attic in the minister's house, for example, which, with its pure white dimity bed-curtains, its bright-green walls, and the rich brown of its stained floor, remind one of a snowdrop springing out of the soil', she exclaims (1954b: 86). 'Then the rich humour of Sally [a housekeeper]', Eliot goes on to note, 'and the sly satire in the description of Mr Bradshaw [the titular character's employer]'. 'Mrs. Gaskell has certainly a charming mind', she concludes, 'and one cannot help loving her as one reads her books' (1954b: 86). Because Eliot had not yet read *Cranford*, she clearly means to refer to Gaskell's first novel in using the plural *books*.

Although there is no extant record of Eliot's initial impression of *Mary Barton*, an exchange between her and Gaskell reveals her sense of obligation to it. Having learned several years later that Eliot was the likely author of *Scenes of Clerical Life* and *Adam Bede*, Gaskell reread them and then offered, in a letter dated 10 November 1859, fulsome praise: 'I must, once more, tell you earnestly fully, and humbly I admire them. I never read anything so complete, and beautiful in fiction, in my whole life before' (1954b: 197). Eliot reciprocated by remarking, in a letter dated 11 November 1859, on the formative influence on her craft of the early pages of *Mary Barton* and *Cranford*:

My dear Madam
   Only yesterday I was wondering that artists, knowing each other's pains so well, did not help each other more, and, as usual, when I have been talking complainingly or suspiciously, something has come which serves me as reproof.

That 'something' is your letter, which has brought me the only sort of help I care to have – an assurance of fellow feeling, of thorough truthful recognition from one of the minds which are capable of judging as well as of being moved . . . .

I had indulged the idea that if my books turned out to be worth much, you would be among my willing readers; for I was conscious, while the question of my power was still undecided for me, that my feeling towards Life and Art had some affinity with the feeling which had inspired 'Cranford' and the earlier chapters of 'Mary Barton'. That idea was brought the nearer to me, because I had the pleasure of reading Cranford for the first time in 1857, when I was writing 'Scenes of Clerical Life', and going up the Rhine one dim wet day in the spring of the next year, when I was writing 'Adam Bede', I satisfied myself for the lack of a prospect by reading over again those earlier chapters of 'Mary Barton'. I like to tell you these slight details because they will prove to you that your letter must have a peculiar value for me, and that I am not expressing vague gratitude towards a writer whom I only remember as one who charmed me in the past. (Eliot 1955a: 198–99)

There are several noteworthy aspects of this letter. First, it shows Eliot conscious of herself as a relatively new entrant in the literary marketplace for fiction. Gaskell's affirming words are received as a form of warm encouragement from someone who had obtained the kind of professional status that Eliot had not fully realised as a novelist. Second, the letter suggests that *Cranford* and *Mary Barton* provided Eliot with two quite different forms of inspiration.

Although Eliot does not say it, the early chapters of Gaskell's first novel, which depict a working-class tea party and holiday in the countryside as a welcome respite from industrial labour, contain lengthy passages of natural description. The novel opens in Green Heys Fields, a rural area less than two miles from Manchester:

Here and there an old black and white farm-house, with its rambling outbuildings, speaks of other times and other occupations than those which now absorb the population of the neighbourhood. Here in their seasons may be seen the country business of hay-making, ploughing, &c., which are such pleasant mysteries for townspeople to watch; and here the artisan, deafened with noise of tongues and engines, may come to listen awhile to the delicious sounds of rural life: the lowing of cattle, the milk-maids' call, the clatter and cackle of poultry in the old farm-yards.

You cannot wonder, then, that these fields are popular places of resort at every holiday time; and you would not wonder, if you could see, or I properly describe, the charm of one particular stile, that it should be, on such occasions, a crowded halting-place. Close by it is a deep, clear pond, reflecting in its dark green depths the shadowy trees that bend over it to exclude the sun. The only place where its banks are shelving is on the side next to a rambling farm-yard, belonging to one of those old-world, gabled, black and white houses I named above, overlooking the field through which the public footpath leads. The porch of this farm-house is covered by a rose-tree; and the little garden surrounding it is crowded with a medley of old-fashioned herbs and flowers, planted long ago, when the garden was the only druggist's shop within reach, and allowed to grow in scrambling and wild luxuriance – roses, lavender, sage, balm (for tea), rosemary, pinks and wallflowers, onions and jessamine, in most republican and indiscriminate order. (Gaskell 2006: 5–6)

Highly evocative in its appeal to various senses, including the visual ('Here in their seasons may be seen'), the aural ('the delicious sounds of rural life') and the olfactory ('a medley of old-fashioned herbs and flowers'), the passage is comparable, as I will discuss in subsequent chapters, to Eliot's descriptive practices; hence, the suspicion that Gaskell was the author of *Adam Bede*. It is, perhaps, particularly telling that Eliot consoles herself 'for the lack of a prospect', or a wide view of the landscape while sailing up the Rhine on a rainy and overcast day, by rereading the first few chapters of *Mary Barton*.

Cranford, however, contains few detailed observations of flowers, trees or plants. Its focus is on the social rather than the natural world. The 'pleasure' Eliot derived from reading the novel was different. Yet, given that *Scenes of Clerical Life* deals with social issues including rural poverty and alcoholism, Eliot's indebtedness to *Cranford*, with its seeming pastoralism and social comedy, may not be obvious. But in a journal entry of 18 March 1857, Eliot describes *Cranford* as 'pretty' (1998c: 67), the same adjective she uses in praising the descriptive amplitude of *Ruth*. As Eliot acknowledged, despite the deficiencies of *Ruth*, Gaskell's conveyance of quotidian details – through her attentiveness to decorative interiors and characterological traits – created a more faithful representation of life and people than those 'false and feeble' visions proffered by lady novelists.

As Eliot admits in her letter to Gaskell, she read *Cranford* during a period in which she was struggling with her first work of fiction. Like the original edition published by Chapman and Hall in 1855, the one acquired by Eliot and Lewes for their library did not appear under Gaskell's name. Instead, the title page announces the text as having been written by the author of *Mary Barton*, *North and South* and *Ruth*. Although the phrase 'reprinted from *Household Words*', which appeared on the title page of the 1853 edition, has been excised, there are no other substantive differences in the interior pages of the novel (Figure 3.8). Whether she was aware that the novel originated in discontinuously published papers in *Household Words* is not clear.

However, for Eliot, the inspiring aspect of *Cranford* was not its nascent plot. A journal entry dated 6 December 1857, 'How I Came to Write Fiction', provides greater illumination of the problem that Eliot had encountered in attempting to write fiction and which her reading of *Cranford* helped to solve. Undertaken a year earlier, Eliot's novel never got beyond 'an introductory chapter describing a Staffordshire village and the life of the neighbouring farm houses' because it was 'pure description' (Eliot 1998: 289). By September 1857, however, Eliot felt that she had developed a capability for wit, pathos and 'dramatic presentation' (1998c: 298–99). The letter to Gaskell suggests that *Cranford*, which she had read earlier in the spring, was at least in part responsible for this transformation.

Unlike the third-person narration of *Mary Barton*, *Cranford* relies on a narrating character to relay observed details. Although Eliot did not specify the reasons for her indebtedness to *Cranford* while working on *Scenes of Clerical Life*, Robyn R. Warhol has suggested that Eliot's interest was not in its story, or sequence of events, but in its narrative discourse, or how those events are communicated to the reader. Mary Smith and a nameless male, the homodiegetic narrators of *Cranford* and *Scenes of Clerical Life* respectively, assume cognate positions in each text and address the reader in comparable ways. In building from Warhol's premise, the subsequent sections of this chapter will show how Gaskell's rendering of detail in *Cranford* through the narrator's ironic stance is derived from *Our Village*.

Why was Eliot unable to recognise the acerbic, ironic and ambivalent elements of Mitford's text? Josephine McDonagh suggests that when Eliot decided to write what the budding novelist in her

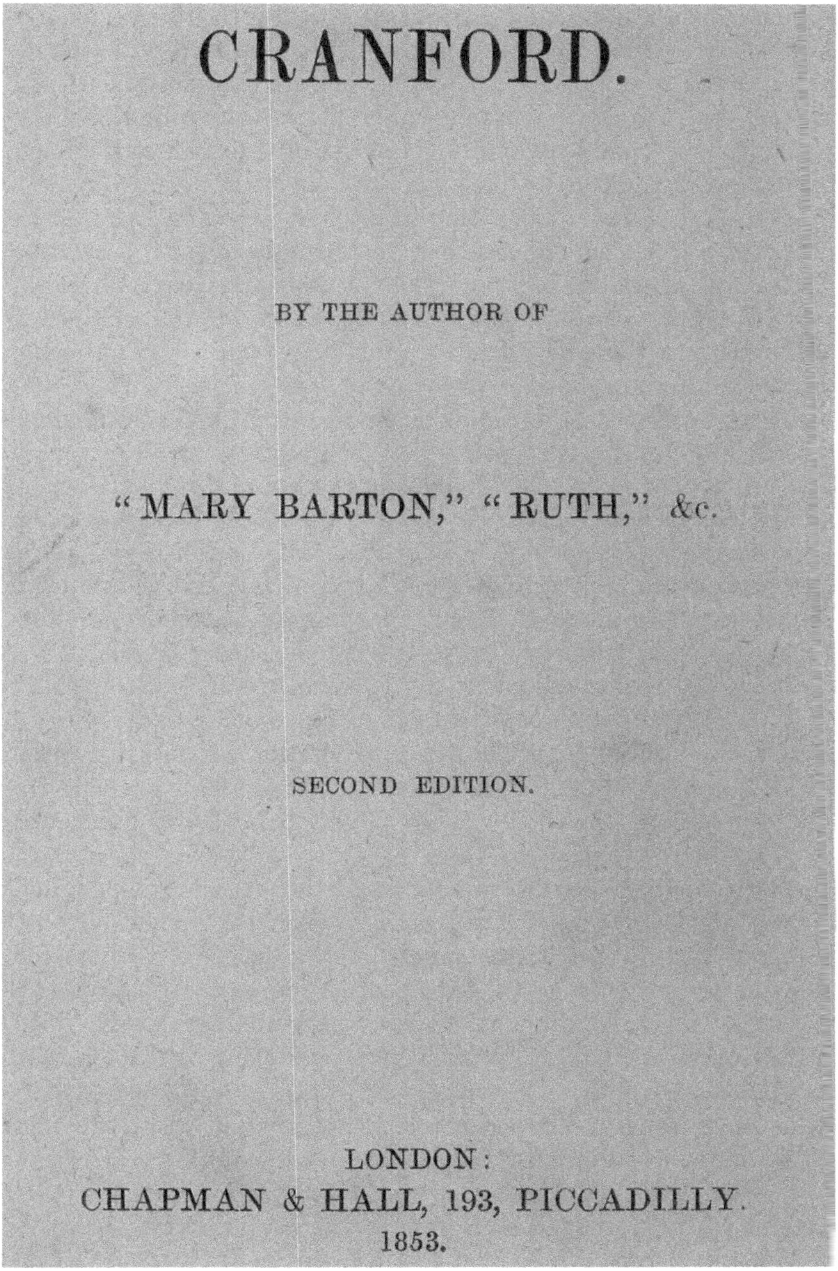

CRANFORD.

BY THE AUTHOR OF

"MARY BARTON," "RUTH," &c.

SECOND EDITION.

LONDON:
CHAPMAN & HALL, 193, PICCADILLY.
1853.

Figure 3.8 Cover page of the 1853 edition of *Cranford*. Author's copy.

journal calls a 'village story', she surely had 'Mitford's *Our Village* in mind as a successful and lucrative genre well suited to women writers' (2016: 363). This is, I think, unquestionably true. In the mid-1850s, or in other words roughly at the same time that Eliot was trying her hand at fiction, Harriet Martineau noted in her autobiography – posthumously published in 1877 – that Mitford's 'graphic description' had a significant impact on literature. She added, however, that the reader may sometimes 'weary' from the 'excess into which the practice of detail has run' (Chapman 1877: 418). The art critic John Ruskin, who was born the same year as Eliot, praised 'Merry Miss Mitford, [for] actually living in the country, actually walking in it, loving it' (1885: 17–18). These recollections by Eliot's contemporaries indicate Mitford's dominance of the genre, but they also point to descriptive non-narrativity, particularly of place, as the distinguishing characteristic of her work.

Martineau's and Ruskin's emphases on Mitford's capacity for description provide a clue to Eliot's own relationship to *Our Village*. Because Eliot struggled with 'pure detail', she would have found her powers, in modelling her earliest work of fiction on *Our Village*, stymied. Although Eliot's library included a single volume of *Our Village* when an inventory was taken after her death (Baker 1981: 93), no extant record of her impressions exists. Mitford was, in all likelihood, one of those writers for whom Eliot could only express, as she put it in her letter to Gaskell, a 'vague gratitude' for having 'charmed' her. By contrast, *Cranford* quickened her abilities as a novelist.

In other words, even though Mitford saw her interest in character and topography as fundamentally connected through her use of engaging narration, many readers of *Our Village* were attracted to – and various editions over the century increasingly drew out – her use of pictorial language to describe landscapes with which she was presumed to be familiar. By collapsing the distinction between author and narrator, which of course an engaged narration encourages, readers were increasingly unable to recognise the formal innovations of *Our Village*. As a number of writers followed in Mitford's footsteps – especially William and Mary Howitt, whose popular *The Book of the Seasons* (1831), *Sketches of Natural History* (1834) and *The Rural Life of England* (1838) were familiar to, and in some cases owned by, Eliot – and the various editions of *Our Village* that emphasised the country walk sketches proliferated, Eliot simply appraised the work differently than Gaskell.[13] What Eliot would have seen in *Cranford*, whose author she already admired, was not only a further confirmation of the genre's suitability for a woman writer, but also her innovative awakening of its untapped potential. This was, however, precisely the lesson Gaskell learned from *Our Village* when she encountered it in her youth.

Gaskell's *Our Village*

In 1821, at the age of eleven, Elizabeth Stevenson enrolled as a boarding student at Barford House, Warwickshire. The school was founded in 1810 by the Byerley sisters, the great-nieces of the potter Josiah Wedgwood, whose bequest made it possible. Although they were Anglican, the Byerleys maintained strong family ties to Unitarianism, Wedgwood's faith, which stressed the importance of educating girls as well as boys. Thus, William Stevenson, who decried the 'submissive' education girls typically received (Uglow 1999: 41), would have already been predisposed to send his daughter to Barford House even were it not for the fact that one of the Byerley sisters, Katherine, was sister-in-law to his second wife.

During the period in which Elizabeth was a pupil, Maria Byerley served as headmistress and was aided by several of her sisters. Under her superintendence, Elizabeth followed a progressive curriculum that reflected the Byerley sisters' commitment to 'Mental and Moral Culture' with 'a greater Attention to elegant accomplishments' (Chapple 1997: 239). She studied English literature, Latin, French, Italian, drawing, music, arithmetic and writing (Hubbard 2006: 9). As Jenny Uglow has noted, the Byerley sisters not only encouraged their pupils to write but also to model themselves on the foremost women writers of the day, including Felicia Hemans, Joanna Baillie, Letitia Elizabeth Landon and Mitford (1999: 38).

In 1824, the same year in which the first volume of *Our Village* appeared, the school relocated to Stratford-upon-Avon. The educational institution occupied a large eighteenth-century house with an extensive library to contain its robust holdings in English and foreign-language literature. Several of the Byerley sisters had literary inclinations. On becoming wives, Frances (Fanny), who married William Parkes in 1811, and Katherine, who wed Anthony Todd Thomson in 1820, withdrew from daily involvement in the school, but they remained regular presences. Fanny, who in 1825 published *Domestic Duties, or Instructions to Young*

Married Ladies, an influential conduct book, held parties well into the 1840s for students who were unable to return home on school breaks.[14] On her visits to the school, Katherine Thomson encouraged pupils to develop their own skills as writers.

Having published her first work in 1826, Katherine became a fairly popular novelist, anecdotal biographer and historian. With interests that spanned multiple literary fields, Thomson would have seen Mitford as a model for the professional woman writer. Indeed, Mitford's ability to work across genres distinguished her from most of the other women writers who were taught at the Byerley sisters' school. By the 1820s, Mitford was already a well-known poet and was also making her mark as a dramatist. Staged in Covent Garden in March 1823, *Julian* may not have been a critical success but nonetheless, many aspiring women writers perceived Mitford's entrance into the male-dominated theatrical world as a victory worth celebrating. Her success as a literary sketch writer was particularly pronounced: a second edition of *Our Village* was published within four months of the initial printing. Thomson, who in *The Queens of Society* refers to Mitford as 'gifted' (Wharton 1860: 148), considered her worthy of emulation.

Of all the Byerleys, Elizabeth was closest to Katherine. As sister-in-law to Elizabeth's stepmother, Katherine played a role in encouraging her budding literary aspirations long after Elizabeth attended the Byerleys' Avonbank School. In Katherine, Elizabeth could glimpse, as Jenny Uglow observes, an effective 'way in which literary production could be combined with domestic life' (Uglow 2004). On occasion, Elizabeth's literary works also nod in Katherine's direction. Gaskell famously opens *Cranford* with an ironic reference to the single women and widows of the village as warriors: 'In the first place, Cranford is in possession of the Amazons; all the holders of houses above a certain rent are women'. In *Constance: A Novel*, published in 1833, Thomson writes satirically about the 'amazons of the neighbourhood', who arrive at a country dance 'in diligent search after partners of a more permanent character than those of the dance merely' (1833: 147). Like Thomson, Gaskell's principal model in her early years was Mitford.

It is possible that Gaskell had encountered Mitford's sketches before the first volume of *Our Village* was published. There is no definitive evidence that the Byerley sisters subscribed to the

Lady's Magazine. Thomson refers to it in passing somewhat derisively in *Rosabel* (1835: 115). But by 1835, when she published her novel, the magazine's reputation had precipitously declined. In 1832 it merged with the *Lady's Monthly Museum*. Although its new name combined the titles of both periodicals, becoming known as the *Lady's Magazine and Museum of the Belles Lettres, Fine Arts, Music, Drama, Fashions, etc.*, it continued to be called the *Lady's Magazine*. If the Byerleys did subscribe to the *Lady's Magazine*, however, it would not be surprising. It was influential, as it encouraged some degree of professional authorship for women, and educational institutions for adolescent girls thus constituted a core demographic of its readership.[15]

Although I have discussed the *Lady's Magazine* at considerable length in the previous two chapters, I want to briefly underscore a few salient points that bolster the possibility of Gaskell having encountered the periodical. Occasionally characterised by critics today as little known, the *Lady's Magazine* remained eminent for much of the second series' run (1820–29). Mitford helped to shape this critical perception by referring in *Recollections of a Literary Life* to the sketches from the first volume of *Our Village* as having previously appeared in an 'obscure Journal' (Mitford 1859: viii). But this is not an objective statement of fact. It is instead a swipe against a periodical with which, as I explored in Chapter One, she had a falling out. Edward Copeland has asserted that between 1770 and 1820 'everybody' with sufficient means read the periodical. Indeed, at its zenith, one literary historian has estimated, more than 15,000 copies of the *Lady's Magazine* circulated monthly (Mayo 1962: 421n75). Although its readership had declined somewhat by the time Mitford started to contribute her *Our Village* sketches, it was certainly not 'obscure'.

For many girls and young women in the early nineteenth century, periodicals played a significant role in shaping their imaginations and inspiring them to enter the nineteenth-century literary field. In a letter dated 10 December 1840, Charlotte Brontë – a biography of whom Gaskell would publish in 1857 – expressed her regret to Hartley Coleridge that she had been born too late to contribute to the *Lady's Magazine* during the period in which it relied heavily on readers to supply its content:

> I did not exist forty of fifty years ago when the Lady's magazine was flourishing like a green bay tree – In that case I make no

doubt my aspirations after literary fame would have met with due encouragement – ... and I would have contested the palm with the Authors of Derwent Priory – of the Abbey and Ethelinda. You see Sir I have read the Lady's Magazine and know something of its contents – though I am not quite certain of the correctness of the titles I have quoted ... (Brontë 2007: 26).

Although the magazine boasted a diverse array of content, including poetry, short stories, non-fiction essays and notices of the latest fashions (with a number of accompanying plates, including several colour illustrations), its successive editors had, from the periodical's inception, been partial to serialising Gothic romances, which reflected a consciousness of the predominantly female readership. Gaskell's interest in Gothic and melodramatic tales, social satire and the literary sketch, as well as her knowledge of changing fashions, which provides some of the more humorous moments in *Cranford*, all suggest that she might have been familiar with the magazine as well.

To what extent might *Cranford* been modelled after the *Lady's Magazine*? Talia Schaffer has recently argued that *Cranford*'s fragmentariness can best be understood by attending to its original periodical context. By this, however, she does not mean that Gaskell's novel is disjointed simply because it first appeared in *Household Words*. Rather, she suggests, the text should itself be read as if it were a newspaper or a magazine (2011: 76). Building on this argument, Josephine McDonagh has suggested that it bears greater resemblance to an annual: 'a compilation of tales, with allusions to prints and fashionable commodities, in a highly sentimental ambience overshadowed by losses and bereavements which are sometimes brought about by long-distance travel, especially to India' (2018: 139). Although, as McDonagh acknowledges, the *Cranford* ladies are never depicted in possession of an annual, there are any number of indications that they would have been avid readers. Moreover, 'the annuals are evoked in indirect allusions to a style of representation, a mode of orientalism, an emphasis on prints and stylised visual images, a suffusion of emotion, [and] an economy of loss and reparation' (2018: 139). Yet much of what Schaffer and McDonagh suggest about *Cranford* and periodical culture can be attributed to the *Lady's Magazine* as well.

While periodicals including the *Gentleman's Magazine* (1731–1922) and *Blackwood's Edinburgh Magazine* (1870–1980) are referenced on several occasions in *Cranford*, the *Lady's Magazine* is never referred to directly. Miss Matty mentions to Mary Smith that the *Gentleman's Magazine* was the publication venue for one of her deceased father's poems. Samuel Johnson had the *Gentleman's Magazine* in mind when he defined magazines as a 'miscellaneous pamphlet'. Precisely because they offered a range of information, forms of entertainment and knowledge, they were intended to 'be ransacked for edification and amusement for decades or centuries to come' (Batchelor 2018: 380). Thus, Jennie Batchelor has pointed out one 'need only consult the binders' instructions printed at the back of the end-of-the-year volume of publications such as the *Lady's Magazine* to see that publishers envisaged their long-term preservation' (Batchelor 2018: 380). As Charlotte Brontë explained to Hartley Coleridge, in a letter dated 10 December 1840, she used to peruse copies that once belonged to her mother or aunt, before her father, an Anglican priest, unceremoniously burned them 'because they contained foolish love-stories' (Brontë 2007: 26). In her *Life of Charlotte Brontë*, Gaskell refers to this episode and notes the formative influence of the *Lady's Magazine* on Brontë, only six years her junior (Gaskell 1858: 108).

If Gaskell hoped that she too might have been born just slightly earlier so that she could have contributed to the *Lady's Magazine* during its heyday, she does not say. But, unlike Charlotte Brontë or George Eliot, Gaskell would have been old enough to read the magazine's entire second series. She would have found in its pages the kind of encouragement offered to aspiring woman of letters that Eliot, who lacked such a forum in her own youth, found in Gaskell's letter quoted above: a sense of fellow feeling.

In other words, although the patchwork quality of *Cranford* can be likened to a newspaper, periodical or annual, it might also be read more specifically as a kind of lady's magazine.[16] As Brontë's letter to Hartley Coleridge suggests, the periodical's influence extended well beyond its years of publication (Batchelor 2011). There was certainly something incongruous, however, in reading magazines published several decades prior, with their differences in fashions, activities and sensibilities. By the 1840s, turbans, although still occasionally worn by women, were no longer considered fashionable. Throughout the Regency period and into the 1820s, however, they were de rigueur. Thus, when Miss Matty writes to Mary Smith to ask whether turbans are in fashion and, if so, whether she might bring her one to attend the magical performance of Signor Brunoni, the narrator is placed in a difficult situation. Rather than break the news to Miss Matty that they are out of fashion, she brings the cap instead. Miss Matty responds with a rhetorical question: 'I suppose turbans have not got down to Drumble yet?' (2008: 82). The moment is funny precisely because turbans had not been routinely worn for a couple of decades. Yet within the *Lady's Magazine* they are routinely featured, discussed and illustrated. In the same chapter in which Miss Matty hopes for a turban, she also recalls an old story she had read of 'a nightingale and a musician, who strove one against the other which could produce the most admirable music, till poor Philomel dropped down dead' (2008: 92). Mitford references this same story in 'The Cowslip Ball'.[17] If Gaskell encountered the sketch in the June 1823 issue of the *Lady's Magazine*, she would have read several references to turbans and women's fashion. In the bound volume of the magazine for the year, there are nearly two dozen.

In addition to invoking fashion plates and numerous illustrations of headdresses, *Cranford* apparently nods to the frequent accounts of travel, with India regularly featured as a destination, in the *Lady's Magazine*. Miss Matty becomes a proprietor of tea, the commodity that was widely discussed in the magazine. When Miss Matty is reunited with Peter, whom she thought dead in the subcontinent, he brings her, among other gifts, an Indian muslin gown. A favourite fabric of the Cranfordians, the *Lady's Magazine* referred to muslin repeatedly in the same years in which Mitford was publishing her sketches. Gigots – last worn in England in the village of Cranford – appeared routinely in its pages too. Not coincidentally, the engraved print of Mary Russell Mitford that appeared in Chapter One (Figure 1.2), which was in wide circulation at mid-century, documents her in a wide-shouldered dress with puffed gigot sleeves. Her décolleté is modestly covered by a muslin collar at the neck and a cross-over *pelerine* or *fichu* of comparably high-quality diaphanous material. Her elaborate headdress is striking – comparable in style to those routinely featured in the *Lady's Magazine*, such as Figures 1.3 and 1.4 – but matronly.[18]

All this suggests that Gaskell may have been familiar with the original periodical context of Mitford's sketches. It is not, however, definitive evidence. As I document in Chapter One, reading Mitford's character sketches in their original periodical context makes one more alert to their satire and irony. Because these aspects of her narrative voice remain evident, albeit somewhat muted, in the biennial volumes, my argument does not depend on making the case that she first encountered them in the periodical. In the next section, I consider Mitford's influence on Gaskell's voice and her use of description.

The descriptive eye

One of Gaskell's earliest known publications, published in 1840 by William Howitt in his *Visits to Remarkable Places: Old Halls, Battle Fields, and Scenes Illustrative of Striking Passages in English History and Poetry*, is a description of a schoolgirl's visit to Clopton Hall that is part Gothic drama, part descriptive sketch. Carol Martin is surely right in her supposition that the future novelist wrote the piece as a school assignment while still a pupil of the Byerley sisters (1985: 95). Gaskell had initiated a correspondence with William and Mary Howitt in 1838 after reading an announcement of his forthcoming *Visits to Remarkable Places*. She began by thanking them for the joy she derived from the literary couple's previously published works. As the correspondence unfolded, she shared a copy of 'Clopton Hall'. Recalling a field trip to the Warwickshire estate, as Gaskell had done while a pupil at Avonbank, the narrator relates the gruesome story of Charlotte Clopton, who, assumed to have been stricken by the plague, had been unwittingly buried alive by her family.

Besides its Gothic tenor, in the vein of some sketches by Mitford, 'Clopton Hall' is richly descriptive of place. Recall Harriet Martineau's assertion that prior to Mitford and her 'new style of "graphic description"', literary works tended toward 'gorgeous or luscious generalities' (1877: 418). In 'Clopton Hall', the narrator specifies season ('we set off one beautiful autumn day'), mood ('full of delight and wonder respecting the place we were going to see') and intended destination ('Clopton Hall, about a mile from Stratford-on-Avon'). She recounts the journey ('We passed through desolate half-cultivated fields') and her initial observations on their arrival: 'we came within sight of the house – a large, heavy, compact, square brick building, of that deep, dead red almost approaching to purple'. She continues:

In front was a large formal court, with the massy pillars surmounted with two grim monsters; but the walls of the court were broken down, and the grass grew as rank and wild within the enclosure as in the raised avenue walk down which we had come. The flowers were tangled with nettles, and it was only as we approached the house that we saw the single yellow rose and the Austrian briar trained into something like order round the deep-set diamond-paned windows. We trooped into the hall, with its tesselated marble floor, hung round with strange portraits of people who had been in their graves two hundred years at least. (Gaskell 2005: 37)

In her autobiography, Mary Howitt remarks that William found Elizabeth's letter 'powerful and graphic' (1889: 28). He determined to visit the grounds and manor house for himself and was so pleased with her accuracy and evocativeness that he incorporated the passages into his *Visits to Remarkable Places* as a firsthand account by 'a fair correspondent'.

As Mary Howitt's use of the term 'graphic' suggests, the couple enjoyed Gaskell's sketch for the same reasons that they admired *Our Village*. The Howitts' own literary productions owed much to Mitford. On 27 February 1834, Mary Howitt wrote: 'Dear Miss Mitford, I rejoice in finding an occasion to address you, that I may express the very great pleasure both my husband and myself have always derived from your writing.' 'We know your "village" and all its crofts, and lanes and people', she continued, 'and we wish we had the happiness of personally knowing you' (L'Estrange 1870a: 254). Having read all five volumes of *Our Village* as they were published between 1824 and 1832, the Howitts felt as if they had themselves experienced the topography of the village and become acquainted with the individuals who populated it.

In early 1835, Mary Howitt wrote again to Mitford to express their admiration for her work. *Our Village*, which the couple had been rereading, proved particularly useful to William, who had already begun work on *The Rural Life of England*. Published in 1838, the collection of essays mourned the social and economic changes that industrialisation had wrought. In advance of exploring some of the areas that industrialisation had affected so that he could write about them for his primarily metropolitan readership, Howitt turned to Mitford. As his spouse recounts to Mitford, 'The most truly English sketches in the language are your country volumes. Well, through these volumes we have been wending this winter. We had read them before, and many of the stories were familiar to us as household words; but they have been read this time principally that William might trace out their localities, and a great additional charm has his knowledge of your part of the country given him' (L'Estrange 1870a: 259). Although *The Rural Life of England* presents farmers in idealistic terms, Howitt's principal argument is that industrialisation is pernicious, especially in its effects on the poor, and that some of the programmes allegedly designed to provide assistance to workers primarily aided manufacturers instead.

In preparing the 1840 second edition of *The Rural Life of England*, Howitt incorporated descriptive passages about Knutsford from the letters Gaskell had sent him. These passages, as Carol Martin points out, evince Gaskell's 'early interest in country folk and their tales' (1985: 96), an interest surely fired in part by Mitford's sketches. Ruskin thought Mitford distinguished herself from her contemporaries by 'finding history enough in the life of the butcher's boy, and romance enough in the story of the miller's daughter, to occupy all her mind'. Gaskell's passages are chiefly about ladies maids and servants and the peculiarities of local customs. Gaskell's attentiveness to rural practices, such as scattering grains of sand in front of homes on joyous occasions, and her capacity to explain them to an urban readership, placed her – as far as the Howitts were concerned – in the company of Mitford.

Nevertheless, Howitt did not incorporate Gaskell's passages unaltered. As Carol Martin shows in her side-by-side comparison of the passages supplied by Gaskell and those incorporated into *The Rural Life of England*, Howitt eliminated most of her first-person pronouns (1985: 98). 'Clopton Hall', for example, opens with a question to Howitt that mimicked the direct address used by Mitford's engaging narrator: 'I wonder if you know Clopton Hall, about a mile from Stratford-on-Avon. Will you allow me to tell you of a very happy day I once spent there?' (Howitt 1840: 135). In *The Rural Life of England*, however, Howitt eliminates Gaskell's use of first person. While this allows him to integrate her work more fully into his own, it also effaces one of the formal innovations that Gaskell had appropriated from Mitford.

As I noted earlier, unlike the heterodiegetic narrator in *Mary Barton* who interjects only occasionally with a first-person observation, *Cranford* is narrated from the perspective of one of its characters. By employing a homodiegetic narrator who serves as the reader's guide to the provincial village, Gaskell returns to Mitford's technique that she studied at the Byerley's school and first utilised in 'Clopton Hall'. Mary Smith is not an engaging narrator in Robyn Warhol's definition of the term because 'the narrative persona ... is not identified with the author herself' (1986: 12). Nevertheless, for much of the twentieth century, critics assumed or asserted a direct connection between Mary Smith and Gaskell.[19] In any case, Mary directly addresses the reader – 'Have you any red silk umbrellas in London?' – in the distinct conversational tone that is one of the innovative characteristics of this form of narration.

Although a character in the novel, Mary is far less fully rounded than the Cranford women she observes. Peter Keating noted long ago that while 'it would be foolish to try to argue that she is in any sense a fully developed character', Mary nevertheless 'plays an important part in establishing *Cranford*'s distinctive tone' (1976: 14). By making Mary younger than the Amazons ('two generations removed from Miss Matty and her friends') and a resident of Drumble, Gaskell can 'heighten the strangeness of Cranford's way of life by a subtle mixture of ironic distancing and affectionate concern' (1976: 15, 14). Putting aside Mary Smith's age, this stance of 'ironic distancing and affectionate concern' is comparable to Mitford's in *Our Village*. Just as Mary sympathetically deciphers the fashion, manners and practices of Cranford for the metropolitan reader with whom she is aligned, Mitford thought that she was especially qualified to tell stories about rural life to an urban readership because she occupied 'a sort of middle station between the gentry', owing to her father's bloodline, 'and the country people, almost our equals of fortune' (Mitford 1841: 67).

Thus, the narrator of Mitford's sketches and Mary Smith are positioned similarly. Mitford is an insider who revels in familiarity and playfully scorns the cosmopolitan's whirl 'half over Europe', fashioning herself as a guide to the touristic national and distinctly urban reader. Mary Smith is an outsider who nevertheless maintains special ties to Cranford. As Hilary M. Schor suggests, Mary lacks development because her real story – life with her father in Drumble – takes place outside of the narrative frame: 'we are reading her holiday self' (1992: 114). Rather than internalise the generic conventions of the travelogue, however, both Mitford and Gaskell satirised them.

Although it varied by location, touristic discourse often presents destinations as static, timeless and unchanging. As Ian Ousby contends, beginning in the eighteenth century detailed guides to rural England tended to present sites as though they were landscape engravings (1990: 158). At different times in both texts, Mitford's narrator and Mary Smith refer to their respective villages as existing in an impeccable state of preservation. In the opening sketch to the second volume of *Our Village* published in 1826, Mitford notes that her village has 'a *trick of standing still*, or remaining stationary' (Mitford 1826: 1). In chapter two of Gaskell's novel, Mary Smith remarks: 'My next visit to *Cranford* was in the summer. There had been neither *births*, *deaths*, nor marriages since I was there last.' Most critics have taken these assertions at face value. John Gross, for example, notes that it is easy to see the women as inhabiting a '*timeless* world ... the clock has stopped but *Cranford* doesn't know it'. 'The inhabitants are impressive', he continues, 'because they never suspect that they are quaint, never think of themselves as museum-pieces' (1965: 59). Of Mitford, Amanpal Garcha argues that her insistence on the timelessness of her village was also a statement of artistic aims. Mitford provided readers, he argues, with 'an explicitly *aestheticized* sense of fragmented temporality and stasis' (2009: 10). But what Mitford's narrator and Mary Smith say differs entirely from what they show.

As I demonstrated in Chapter Two, Mitford's sketches frequently depict change. Social and economic dislocations are represented by the decline of the great farmhouse as a provincial institution. Characters come and go. Lucy takes a teaching job and moves from the village. In 'Tom Cordery', the titular character, a 'friend' of the narrator who works as 'a rat-catcher, hare-finder, and broom-maker', is forced from his dilapidated abode and into the workhouse when the overseer refuses to make necessary repairs (1824a: 259). Once confined to a small apartment at the workhouse, he contracts typhus and dies. Death is a frequent presence in *Our Village*. For example, in the introduction to the third volume of Mitford's sketches, published in 1828, the narrator relays what would have been particularly shocking news to readers. The young girl who accompanies the narrator on many of her country walks along with her dog Mayflower, has died: 'Lizzy! Alas! alas! you ask for Lizzy! – Do you remember how surely at the closed gate of the flower court, or through the open door of her father's meat dwelling, we used to see the smiling rosy face, so full of life and glee; the square sturdy form, strong and active as a boy; the clear bright eyes, and red lips and shining curly hair, giving such an assurance of health and strength?' After posing further questions along similar lines to the reader, the narrator declares: 'the light hath departed; the living flower is gone; poor Lizzy is dead! Are you not sorry for poor, poor Lizzy?' (1828: 9–10).

Similarly, despite Mary Smith's claim, deaths abound in *Cranford*. Deborah Jenkyns dies early in the novel. So too does Captain Brown, the voracious reader of Charles Dickens's *Pickwick Papers* who is so engrossed in an instalment that by the time he notices a young girl on the train tracks, he can only save her, but not himself, from the oncoming locomotive. Miss Matty's reunion with Thomas Holbrook, with whom she had a failed 'love affair of long ago', is brief (2008: 23). He dies unexpectedly. Thus, it is only possible to claim, as P. D. Edwards does, that the village of Cranford is remarkable for its 'almost deathless idyllic stasis' (1988: 70) if one does not question Mary Smith's narrative.

I have already indicated the ways in which Smith's perception of age misleads critics into thinking the women are older than they in fact are. There are many other discrepancies in the text between Mary's view and – given the clues that suggest otherwise – the actual state of affairs. Mary insists, for example, that in Cranford 'no absorbing subject was ever spoken about' and that 'there was a dearth of subjects for conversation' (2008: 3). Thus, as one critic has put it, 'the Cranfordian narrative habitually waits for the story' (Croskery 1997: 206). Yet, what the sketches actually show is a community fully engaged in debates that range from their own reading practices (Samuel Johnson versus Charles Dickens) to styles of dress, conversations on theology, including the Catholic Emancipation Bill, and occultist practices (highly topical in the 1850s), and discussions of epistemology and the limits of discursive ways of knowing. '"Ah! I see; I comprehend perfectly," Miss Pole declares, pouring over her encyclopedia in the hopes of determining how Signor Brunoni will perform his tricks. "A represents the ball. Put A between B and D – no! between C and F, and turn the second joint of the third finger of your left hand over the wrist of your right H. Very clear indeed!"' (2008: 84). They also tell ghost stories, gossip about social and political matters and enthral one another with amusing absurdities, such as Miss Jenkyns's efforts to retrieve lace, 'made by the nuns abroad', that her cat has eaten, by inducing him to vomit it up (2008: 78).

Similarly, although the ladies of Cranford insist on the insularity of their village from larger social forces, itself an anachronistic notion in the 1850s, the novel is not simply one of many 'beautiful idylls'.[20] Nevertheless, a number of critics persist in taking their assertion at face value. Julia Sun-Joo Lee, for example, argues that *Cranford*, along with Gaskell's other fictional works prior to the publication of *North and South*, is strictly provincial. Lee contends that with *North and South*, however, Gaskell depicts England to be at the centre of transnational networks of trade (Lee 2010: 105). But *Cranford* reveals to readers how the village is intricately connected to the transforming demands of a global economy and, more importantly, shows us that the Cranfordians themselves are aware of this.

Thus, in response to Franco Moretti's argument that Gaskell engages in a sleight of hand – because social geography no longer 'agree[s] with the form of idyll, Gaskell must literally hibernate her village' (2005: 101) – one might observe that not only is Cranford uninsulated from the global economy but is, in fact, wholly implicated in it. Sugar, one character's 'favourite economy', was imported from the West Indies and other colonies via Liverpool, where it was refined by rival sugar manufacturers Tate and Lyle.[21] Other objects – from Indian shawls to sea-green turbans newly fashionable in France – form part of Cranford's lively consumer culture.[22] Indeed, when Miss Jenkyns opens the tea shop in her 'small dining-parlour', the rival tea-seller sends customers to her because 'the teas he kept were of the common kind, but . . . Miss Jenkyns had all the choice sorts': imported from India, Ceylon and China (2008: 144).[23] Even when Miss Jenkyns begins to participate in the marketplace, she trades in pleasures: the cup of tea for the adult and the candies for the children that are, on the one hand, immemorial English comforts and yet, on the other hand, inextricably intertwined with the economies of other places. This is a rural community segregated neither from the nation nor from the world, and whatever notions of quintessential Englishness, for which the generic form of the village sketch might be seen to stand, are at least partially undermined by the fact that the Amazons prefer Indian muslin, French turbans, handmade foreign lace, and continue to call Sam Brown 'the Signor' because 'it sounded so much better' (2008: 102).

Gaskell's fictional invocation of nineteenth-century global trade and commerce was at least partially shaped by her personal experiences. As Nancy Henry has argued, economic activity, particularly within nineteenth-century cultures of investment, had important implications for women's writing (2018: 90) 'From her earliest years', Henry writes, 'Elizabeth Gaskell was part of an extended family of businesspeople for whom global commerce was a way of life' (2018: 126). Her brother and several cousins were involved in international trade, which required them to travel the globe. Her maternal uncle, Hannah Lumb's brother, was involved in the Liverpool shipping industry, slate mining in Wales and pottery manufacturing (Chapple 1997: 170). As a young adult, Elizabeth stayed for two consecutive winters with a Unitarian family friend in Newcastle, where she would have been exposed to the coal and shipping industries (Chapple 1997: 343–57). Thus, Nancy Henry concludes, Gaskell developed a 'pragmatic, material sense of herself and her world as connected by commercial networks' (2018: 88). In writing *Cranford*, which depicts rather than evades England's global connectedness, Gaskell drew on this background.

The socially inclusive community

Gaskell also uses unreliable narration to show that the Cranfordian women are not nearly as interested in self-segregation as their repeated statements might lead us to believe. Although *Cranford* has been seen as a model female community that, in its 'man-lessness' (Edwards 1988: 79), triumphs over masculine 'reality' (Auerbach 1978: 86) and a village in which 'few males [are] allowed to reside' (Croskery 1997: 213), the statements by the Amazons about their separateness belie the fact that men remain ever-present: Captain Brown is immediately admitted into the community; Samuel Johnson and Charles Dickens provide influential and contrasting models of reading and writing; the town doctor, Mr Hoggins, marries Lady Glenmire; Peter Jenkyns returns to the village and immediately begins participating in its rituals; Thomas Holbrook is the love of Miss Matty's life and exerts a powerful hold on her both before and after his death; the grocer Mr Johnson encourages Miss Matty's tea business; Signor Brunoni, initially feared, is soon embraced when he is unmasked as Samuel Brown; and various other male figures, such as the postman and Jem, appear throughout the text.

If Robyn R. Warhol is right in her claim that Eliot's interest in *Cranford* was not in the sequence of events but in its narrative discourse, I would argue – with these examples as evidence – that the same holds true for Gaskell's fascination with *Our Village*.

Whereas Gaskell's 'Clopton Hall' demonstrates the importance of Mitford's country walk sketches to the development of her own descriptive abilities, the experiments in voice and narration in *Cranford*, also evident in her first prose work, also find their origin in Mitford's sketches. As I have contended, Mitford often employed ironic perspectives to challenge generic conventions as well as editors' attempts to fix the play of signification and homogenise the contents under the banner of a singular vision, inevitably a part of any collaborative enterprise such as a magazine. Irony is more evident in the periodical publications than in the bound volumes, where the text's didactic elements are emphasised by illustrations and paratextual framings. Mitford herself initiated this process by claiming in the preface to the 1824 edition that '[t]he following pages contain an attempt to delineate country scenery and country manners as they exist in a small village in the south of England'. By quickly qualifying this remark, however, to indicate that '[s]he has painted, as they appeared to her', the village residents' 'little frailties and their many virtues', Mitford calls attention to the unreliability of her narration (1824a: v–vi)

Gaskell puts unreliable narration to work as part of a critique of restorative nostalgia. The pastoral, as one of the principal genres of nostalgia, is often mobilised as a generator of and conduit for societal longing (Santesso 2006: 39). By the 1850s, *Our Village* was increasingly associated with this tradition. At the turn of the century, owing in part to a newly illustrated version by Hugh Thomson with an introduction by Anne Thackeray Ritchie, part of Macmillan's Cranford series, this was undoubtedly the case. 'Deep down in almost every Englishman's heart there is an inherent love for the life that is to be found in the villages of his native soil', wrote W. J. Roberts in 1904, and in an 'Englishman's library, among his treasured books – those companions of his rare leisure – there may often be found a few treating of pastoral things; among them, in a place of honour, Miss Mitford's "Our Village"' (1904: 785). Most critics have tended to view Mitford's sketches in this light. Tim Killick insists that 'Mitford's pastoral vision' provides readers with 'a sanctuary from the increasingly stultifying qualities of urban society' (2004: n.p.). 'It is not until Mary Russell Mitford's collection of tales', Sven Halse similarly asserts, 'that England acquires, for the first time since the age of innocent pastorals in the middle of the eighteenth century, an unspoiled presentation of the countryside and the village' (2008: 401).

What Gaskell recognised in Mitford's sketches, however, was the reflective quality of her nostalgia, which revealed itself in moments of humour, irony and contradiction. Instead of presenting her sketches as truth and tradition, Mitford asserts in the fifth volume of the series – in language that resonates with the first volume's preface – that she has presented the reader with 'the history, half real, half imaginary, of a half imaginary and half real little spot on the sunny side of Berkshire' (Mitford 1832a: 3). Mitford foregrounds, in other words, the ambivalence of her own longings and suggests that these feelings coexist with the critical thinking that restorative nostalgia requires one to surrender. This statement, however, does not appear in either the three-volume edition published in 1835 or the two-volume edition – with which George Eliot would have been familiar – that began appearing in the 1840s.

At mid-century, the English village was increasingly mobilised as a locus of social exclusion that stood in contrast to the city where inhabitants from diverse backgrounds intermingled. Gaskell, who at the time of writing *Cranford* had lived in Manchester for two decades, frequently longed for the Knutsford of her childhood and youth. In the city, she told Tottie Fox in a letter dated April 1850, 'we have no great external beauty either of nature or art the contemplation of which can put calm into one' (Chapple and Pollard 1966: 109). But Gaskell was also alert – as her fictional work demonstrates – to the ways in which a longing for the countryside could coexist with an awareness of its many exclusions.

Whatever backwards-looking nostalgia Gaskell may be said to have possessed was offset by the forward-looking quality of her thought. Born in 1810 to Unitarian parents, Elizabeth was raised, after the death of her mother, by a maternal aunt, Hannah Lumb, in Knutsford. Although Unitarians generally believed in political reform, religious tolerance and human equality, the chapel in which Lumb worshipped – less than thirty-five kilometres from Manchester, where the anti-slavery movement dated back decades – was particularly progressive. Lumb, who held strong abolitionist sentiments, was connected through her chapel to leading abolitionists from London, Edinburgh, Liverpool, Newcastle and Llandaff, then a small town north of Cardiff (Chapple 1997: 128–29). As Elizabeth matured, she would visit many of these cities herself.

In 1832, Elizabeth Stevenson married William Gaskell, the Unitarian Minister of Cross Street Chapel in Manchester. The chapel was, as Harold L. Platt notes, 'the fountainhead of

Manchester Liberalism [and] it exerted tremendous influence on the city and the nation for a generation' (Platt 2005: 64). Thus, as Annette B. Hopkins puts it, 'the shaping elements' of Gaskell's life all 'foster[ed] instinctive tendencies toward liberalism' (1931: 58). Motivated by a fundamental belief in human progress and individual self-development, Unitarians would form part of the backbone of the Liberal Party, when it emerged as a political force at mid-century. Before the institutionalisation of liberal politics, however, Unitarians were deeply engaged with the broader tradition of liberal thought.

Gaskell has not featured prominently, if at all, in revaluations of Victorian liberalism over the past two decades. But she was seen by many of her contemporaries as – among writers of literature – a leading proponent of its doctrines (Hopkins 1931: 57; Sanders 1996: 47). From her personal connections to notable British liberals of the period, including the Brownings, John Stuart Mill, the Liberal Member of Parliament William E. Forster and the liberal Anglican theologian F. D. Maurice, as well as her wide network on the Continent, which encompassed such personages as François Guizot, Jules Simon and Jean-Jacques Ampère, there was, observes Hopkins, 'scarcely a name in the long list of Mrs. Gaskell's acquaintances that is not distinguished among the progressives of the period' (1931: 58). Four years her senior, Mill became acquainted with Gaskell in their youth. In 1825, Gaskell's father, William Stevenson, began publishing essays in the *Westminster Review*, the London-based organ of Philosophical Radicalism founded by James Mill and to which the younger Mill also contributed.[24] By middle age, the two had a somewhat fraught relationship.[25]

Cranford was published several years before Mill's *On Liberty*, which appeared in 1859. But the two texts may be constellated through the writings and sermons of Unitarian minister William MacCall. In his *Autobiography*, Mill acknowledges his indebtedness, in formulating his own ideas about liberal individuality, to MacCall, whose *The Elements of Individualism: A Series of Lectures* (1847) circulated widely (1981: 152). As Valerie Wainright suggests, MacCall – a prominent figure in the Unitarian movement – also influenced the direction of Gaskell's thought (1994: 151). In her analysis of *North and South* (1854), Wainright contends that Gaskell's wide vision and 'pluralistic moral view' has 'significant points of contact' with Mill's later treatise, particularly its commitment to 'richly cultivated self-development and of the invigorating encounter of contending styles of life' (1994: 152).[26] Yet it is *Cranford* that opens with Mary Smith's proclamation that each of the women who inhabits the village has 'her own individuality, not to say eccentricity, pretty strongly developed' (2008: 3). To wit, Deborah Jenkyns' newspaper paths from front door to drawing-room chairs so that guests' shoes do not 'defile' her carpet; Miss Jamieson's refusal of any invitation to tea that does not include her 'ittie dog'; and Betty Barker's dressing of her cow in dark grey flannel waistcoat and drawers. But Captain Brown and Thomas Holbrook are explicitly referred to as eccentric as well.

In *The Elements of Individualism*, MacCall distinguishes between individuality and eccentricity. Those who possess a more fully developed individuality, he contends, run 'the risk of appearing singular' – as 'solitary giants'. Yet, he believed, by encouraging others to develop their individuality, 'what is extraordinary and exalted in mind and morality may one day become the inheritance of all' (1847: 131). For his part, Mill would argue that plurality of living was the answer to social conformity and individual mediocrity, which he believed to be prevalent in his era. Although Mill saw eccentricity as a tool to resist the tyranny of custom and convention, he also believed that, as humanity developed, the need for different 'experiments in living' would wane (Mill 1977c: 281).

Cranford is a town in which experiments in living abound. To Borislav Knezevic, these experiments are parasitic: 'the eccentricity of the local community is produced by its attempt to be like the national paradigm of gentility, not by its striving to be different' (2003: 76). Yet eccentricity is represented as the means by which a more inclusive ethos is generated and sustained. It is what unites the women and integrates the outsiders – from the upper-middle-class Mary Smith to the wealthy Lady Glenmire ('one who might have sat down to tea with a coronet, instead of a cap, on her head' [2008: 78]) to the Brunonis/Browns to Peter Jenkyns. It is precisely because the social etiquette of the Amazons is premised on a notion of playfulness, rather than strictly on class-based assumptions, that it proves so malleable. Although Captain Brown, 'who could speak of poverty as if it was not a disgrace', violates the ladies' social rules, those rules are quickly revised so that he becomes a member of the community: his 'opinions [become] quoted as authority' and he is 'even admitted . . . [into their various homes during] the tabooed hours before twelve' (2008: 4). Similarly, when Peter returns from India, he is immediately integrated into the various social rituals of the community. It is this ethos of playfulness that also drives the ladies' efforts to rescue Miss Matty from bankruptcy. Helping her to set up a tea shop in her home is a pleasurable pursuit that allows them to revise their supposedly strict class-based codes. 'Whereas a married woman takes her husband's rank by the strict laws of precedence', Mrs. Jamieson confidently declares, 'an unmarried woman retains the station her father occupied', and thus Miss Matty's fall into bankruptcy does not change her social rank (2008: 143). But the point of this humorous assertion, it seems to me, is not what Elizabeth Langland identifies as their 'class solidarity' (1995: 124). In fact, theirs is a class whose borders are so highly porous that specifying exactly who is included and who is excluded proves remarkably difficult. Rather, Mrs Jamieson's declaration reveals the arbitrariness of their laws and the social rules they signify. They are simply part of a collective notion of playfulness that is represented as a meaning-producing discourse within the world of the novel.

Cranford is seemingly far removed from the social and political concerns of Gaskell's industrial novels. However, her inclusive imagining of provincial society shows how the conditions of possibility for individuality – the basis of a polity as yet only an aspirational horizon in her own time – might be glimpsed in a village. Or, as MacCall might put it, what are the political means by which to secure and maintain 'Multiformity, the spontaneous and natural fruit of Humanity's Unity' (1847: 60)?

The form of ideas

Despite some obvious differences, readers and critics have – as I noted at the outset of this chapter – often likened *Cranford* to *Our Village*. Gary Kelly, who has traced the influence of *Our Village* on several Victorian writers including Gaskell, argues that Mitford's text 'helped to define ... an emergent vision of rural England as the "real" England, the essential England, but a rural England relatively free from the class conflict, mass economic hardships, and brutalising labour increasingly seen as typical of the industrial towns' (1989: 202). Yet in Chapters One and Two, I sought to show how such a conclusion can only be reached by privileging some material instantiations of *Our Village* over others. The same might be said of *Cranford*. The cheap edition of Gaskell's novel published in 1855, which Eliot read two years later while working on *Scenes of Clerical Life*, foregrounded satire and irony in ways that later illustrated editions softened. As suggested by her remarks about *Ruth*, Eliot admired Gaskell's ability to render 'graphic' and 'pretty' scenes, but she believed her own descriptive abilities in this area to be well developed. *Cranford*, which Eliot experienced as something of a revelation, is essentially a distillation of that other element of *Ruth* that Eliot found to be equally 'charming': 'sly satire'. The novel furnished Eliot with ideas for how to depict rural character as well as a form of narration suitable to the task.

Notes

1 Focusing on the poor and the working class, *Sketches by Boz* (1836) is subtitled 'Illustrative of Every-day Life and Ever-Day People'. As Dickens explained in the preface to the first edition, he hoped to furnish the reader with 'little pictures of life and manners as they really are'. He organised the sketches under four rubrics. The first, 'Our Parish', clearly alludes to its predecessor, and his treatment of the clergy as faithfully providing spiritual leadership in an urban context mirrors Mitford's representation of curates and other clerical figures in her rural village. Others, including 'Scenes', 'Characters' and 'Tales', were terms used by Mitford or used by critics to describe her work.
2 He wanted, in other words, to strike a balance between – as he told the English professor Henry Morley in a letter dated 31 October 1852 – entertaining and instructing 'the masses of readers', between the sensationalist penny weeklies, such as G. W. M. Reynolds's *Reynolds' Miscellany*, with its 'prodigious heaps of nonsense and worse than nonsense, which suffocate [readers'] better sense', and the equally inexpensive but instructive weeklies (1988: 790).
3 Her 'writing qualities', presumably the mix of serious purpose and sparkling prose, were precisely the kind that Dickens was seeking (Collin 1986: 67).
4 The focus on the everyday was, not coincidentally, part of Dickens's subtitle to *Sketches by Boz* ('Illustrative of Every-Day Life and Every-Day People'), and precisely the point of Gaskell's sketches.
5 Dickens, whose own name was conspicuously printed on each page of the magazine, insisted that all content in his magazine be unsigned. Some authors, as Deborah Wynne has pointed out, experienced this 'imposition' as a detriment to their careers. But Dickens 'remained

insensitive to the anxieties of those contributors who feared being submerged by his name' (2001: 25).

6   Critics have often characterised *Cranford* as a 'determined experiment in ethnographic narrative' (Knezevic 1998: 405). See also Schor 1992: 86.

7   Life expectancy rates of the period are enormously misleading (Clayton and Rowbotham 2008). The mortality rates for infants and children, however, were quite high, which greatly affected overall mortality rates (Charise 2020: xxii–xxiii).

8   Coral Lansbury has observed that menopausal and postmenopausal sexual desire 'has always been regarded as disgusting or a source of broad comedy'. 'The Victorians knew instinctively that an elderly woman was a figure of fun in her own right', she continues, 'but as a victim of passion she became ludicrous' (1975: 87). Yet Lansbury conflates middle and old age by using the term *elderly* to encompass both categories, whereas, I am suggesting, the novel is far more subtle in its depiction.

9   Genette refers to the frontispiece as 'a sort of more or less monumental portico entrance' in keeping with his notion of the paratext as a threshold. He does, however, develop this idea further (1982: 33)

10 As the ladies learn, however, Signor Brunoni is, in fact, the Englishman Samuel Brown. '[P]ale and feeble', with 'heavy filmy eyes', Brown transforms himself into a man of considerable power when he becomes Signor Brunoni, to whom murder and mayhem are briefly attributed during the great panic (2008: 104). Brunoni, too, plays with cultural encodings. His acts of magic, in their transformative aspects, are closely aligned to the Catholic tenet of transubstantiation, and his taking of an Italian name suggests links to Popery; the ladies themselves call him a 'Grand Turk' and 'Mussulman' and link him to a ring of French spies (2008: 87, 90). Brunoni thus stands for the exotic Other, when he is nothing more than quintessentially English.

11 See Recchio's discussion of the hesitant question about Signor Brunoni's appearance put to Miss Pole – the only Cranfordian to have seen him prior to the magical performance – by Mary Smith, and his claim that such faltering, indicative of 'self-awareness' and 'uneasiness with an apparent common-sense visual racial differentiation', 'opens a vast space for a revised definition of Englishness' (2009: 114). In his discussion of race, Julian Wolfreys has similarly argued that Gaskell's understanding of the 'heterogeneous nature' of Englishness informs all of her writings (1994: 82).

12 Thomson's illustrations have served as a touchstone for stage, film and televisual productions. For example, Mary Barnard Horne's late nineteenth-century adaptation of *Cranford* in three acts provides the following instructions: 'Costumes may be found in the edition of Cranford, illustrated by Hugh Thomson', and Miss Matty should appear as a 'delicate little old lady' (1899: 3).
13 As Baker notes, George Eliot and George Henry Lewes owned no less than 'thirty-one items' by the Howitts (1981: 25).
14 The Scottish painter Effie Gray, who enrolled in 1840, was one such student (Cooper 2010: 15).
15 In a study of eighteenth-century provincial readers, Jan Fergus has shown that male boarding schools routinely subscribed to the first series of the magazine as well (2006: 200–9).
16 On the significance of *Cranford* in Dickens's *Household Words*, see Huett 2003.
17 Angus Easson has pointed out that since the story originates with John Ford's 1628 play *The Lover's Melancholy*, discussed by Charles Lamb in his *Specimens of English Dramatic Poets*, one cannot definitely conclude that Gaskell is referencing Mitford: 'both ladies, it seems, had read their Charles Lamb and took the illustration from him' (1980: 85).

Charlotte Mitchell notes, however, that this is not the only explicit reference to *Our Village* in the text (2008: 187n63, 191n92), which thus constitutes something of a (limited) pattern.
18 In *The Life of Charlotte Brontë*, Gaskell notes that Emily and Charlotte Brontë both wore gigots as well. About the sisters, Gaskell writes, Charlotte routinely appeared in 'the womanly dress of that day of gigot sleeves and large collars', while 'Emily had taken a fancy to the fashion, ugly and preposterous even during its reign, of gigot sleeves, and persisted in wearing them long after they were "gone out"' (1858: 119, 205). She does not, however, suggest that their headwear was elaborate or, in the context of their gigots, represented a preference for muslin.
19 Miriam Allott, for example, argues that Mary Smith 'is a fictional persona for Mrs. Gaskell's youthful self, while the "Amazons" are an imaginative re-creation of the relatives and friends surrounding her beloved "Aunt Lumb"' who raised her (1960: 26).
20 John Lucas famously declared *Cranford*, along with Gaskell's *Wives and Daughters*, 'beautiful idylls' (1977: 2).

21 Tate and Lyle were rival firms until the First World War, when the sugar trade was severely disrupted and they were forced to merge (Chalmin 1990).

22 On Gaskell's engagement with 'the globalization of textile production and distribution' and 'the competitiveness of British products in the world marketplace' through an analysis of curtains and calico in *Mary Barton*, another novel often considered to be provincial, see Freedgood 2006.

23 Borislav Knezevic argues that in becoming a seller of imported tea, Miss Matty 'finds herself at one end of a world-wide system of trade whose incursion the community has dreaded all along' (2003: 99). But, as I am suggesting, there is no incursion since Cranford is already connected to global networks of consumption by the time Miss Matty opens her tea shop. On Miss Matty's negotiation of the 'conflict' between her 'moral code and that imposed by the commercial world', see Miller 1995: 91–118.

24 Sent to Knutsford after the death of her mother, and in residence at the Byerley sisters' school while her father was publishing in the *Westminster Review*, Gaskell nevertheless took an interest in his work. Limited correspondence between the two survives, but literary and intellectual production was a recurring focus of their letters (Chapple 1987: 4–5).

25 In *The Life of Charlotte Brontë*, Gaskell quotes a letter from her eponymous biographical subject that criticises Mill for an essay published in an 1851 edition of the *Westminster Review*: 'When I first read the paper I thought it was the work of a powerful minded, clear headed woman ... who longed for power and had never felt affection'. Concluding Mill was instead the author of 'The Emancipation of Women', she declared: he 'would make a hard, dry, dismal world of it; and yet he speaks admirable sense through a great portion of his article' (qtd. in Gaskell 1858: 189). The author of the essay, however, was Harriet Taylor Mill. On reading *The Life of Charlotte Brontë* a year after its publication, Mill wrote an aggrieved letter of complaint to Gaskell for printing the letter. Although Gaskell apologised for the pain she had caused, Mill responded, in a letter dated July 1859, that she had been grossly negligent in her responsibilities as an editor for publishing 'what may give just offence' (Mill 1972b: 630).

26 Wainright contends that the novel's depiction of a working-class cooperative venture established by the cotton-mill owner John Thornton – but otherwise receiving limited assistance by him,

thereby enabling the workers to become self-directing – shows that Gaskell shared Mill's belief in the social importance of individuality in opinion. The idea, after all, is Thornton's, which he reaches through inward deliberation and after divesting himself of the received opinions of his peers and mother. Once realised, the cooperative functions as a kind of experiment in living – the trials of which, Mill believed, would lead to alternative forms of social organisation.

4

Landscape-Shaped Subjectivity: George Eliot's 'Mother Tongue'

In 1902, Macmillan relaunched its celebrated *English Men of Letters* series under the general editorship of John Morley. With the release of Leslie Stephen's *George Eliot*, the publisher inaugurated its second series – which, following convention, retained the male noun as universal – with a study of a woman writer. Remarking on Eliot's turn to fiction after a number of years as an essayist, Stephen notes that her decision to write the village tales that make up *Scenes of Clerical Life* (1857) had a precedent in, among other works, Mary Russell Mitford's *Our Village* and Elizabeth Gaskell's *Cranford* (1853). For Stephen, however, this is where the comparison with her near contemporaries ended. While all three authors, he contends, wrote about the people and places they knew well, Eliot possessed 'a profoundly reflective intellect, which contemplates the little dramas performed by commonplace people as part of the wider tragi-comedy of human life; and the village communities, their thoughts and customs, as subordinate elements in the great "social organism"' (1902: 62).

Although her library included a single volume of *Our Village* at the time an inventory was taken and George Eliot surely thought of Mitford as one of the authors for whom she felt 'vague gratitude' for having 'charmed' her in the past, she records no specific impressions of her predecessor. Nevertheless, Eliot's attention to the topographical details of St Ogg's, the fictional village in *The Mill on the Floss*, bears Mitford's traces. In 'The Queen of the Meadow', which appeared in the 1827 annual the *Literary Souvenir* and was published in the third volume of *Our Village* the following year, Mitford's narrator recalls traversing a 'winding unfrequented road' that leads to 'a low, two-arched bridge, thrown across a stream of more beauty than consequence'. Just across it stands 'a small irregular dwelling, and the picturesque buildings of Hatherford Mill'. 'It was a pretty scene on a summer afternoon, was that old mill', the narrator continues, 'with its strong lights and shadows, its low-browed cottage covered with the clustering Pyracantha, and the clear brook which after dashing, and foaming, and brawling, and playing off all the airs of a mountain river, while pent up in the mill-stream, was no sooner let loose, than it subsided into its natural peaceful character, and crept quietly along the valley, meandering through the green woody meadows.' The view is so striking, the narrator acknowledges, that

> many a traveller has stayed his step to admire the old buildings of Hatherford Mill, backed by its dark orchard, especially when its accompanying figures, the jolly miller sitting before the door, pipe in mouth, and jug in hand, like one of Teniers' boors, the mealy miller's man with his white sack over his shoulders, carefully descending the out-of-door steps, and the miller's daughter, flitting about amongst her poultry, gave life and motion to the picture (1827b: 177–178).

The first chapter of *The Mill on the Floss* similarly opens with a nod to the pictorial. The narrator, in a moment of pure immediacy, avers:

> A wide plain, where the broadening Floss hurries on between its green banks to the sea, and the loving tide, rushing to meet it, checks its passage with an impetuous embrace. On this mighty tide the black ships – laden with the fresh-scented fir-planks, with rounded sacks of oil-bearing seed, or with the dark glitter of coal – are borne along to the town of St Ogg's, which shows its aged, fluted red roofs and the broad gables of its wharves between the low wooded hill and the river brink, tinging the water with a soft purple hue under the transient glance of this February sun (1998a: 7).

The wide plain appears located in the moment of observation, within the event the novel is attempting to be. Time is neutralised, because the narrator's observation takes place in a present *now* rather than in a past *then*: the Floss hurrying along between the green banks is located in 'this February sun'.

Landscape-Shaped Subjectivity: Eliot's 'Mother Tongue' 73

Initially, the relationship between the narrator, who revisits this site, and the narratee to whom the remarks are addressed is uncertain. The landscape conjures a series of recollections for the narrator, who relays them with a rapidity that matches the swift flow of the river: 'I remember those large dripping willows. I remember the stone bridge' (1998a: 7). To the extent that, as Gerald Prince argues, a depiction of a given '*narratee* emerges above all from the narrative addressed to him' (1988: 313), the novel's second paragraph starts to lessen the distinctions between the narratee, the addressee and the factual recipient. It opens: 'And this is Dorlcote Mill' (1998a: 7). The conjunction with which the sentence begins suggests the presence of a reader who is able to observe alongside the narrator.

Unlike Mitford, whose narrator – although not in 'The Queen of the Meadow' – often invites the reader to undertake a country walk with her, Eliot's narrator makes no such gesture. Nevertheless, in asking the reader to take notice of certain details of this village, one must imagine oneself as physically present at the scene the narrator describes. As the 'honest waggoner' passes by, the narrator remarks: 'See how they stretch their shoulders up the slope towards the bridge, with all the more energy because they are so near home. Look at their grand shaggy feet that seem to grasp the firm earth ...' (1998a: 8). Reminiscent of how Mitford's sketches often direct the reader's vision ('Look at the fine-flowered window blinds'), the narrator does not so much urge the narratee to observe these details because, at this precise moment, he has first noticed them. Rather, these are elements of home-grown knowledge, etched in the memory of a narrator who, like many readers, now inhabits a more urbanised environment but retains a profound tie to a rural place.

Thus, although the first paragraph gestures toward the panoramic, the references to the town's distant skyline, the situatedness of the mill and cottage on a stream surrounded by trees, and the covered wagon making its way across the bridge all indicate that the principal style is picturesque (Witemeyer 1979: 139). The cover of the third stereotyped edition of 1867 features an illustration of Dorlcote Mill precisely in this style (Figure 4.1). On the same trip in which Eliot read *Cranford* for the first time, she also saw works by Teniers, Gerard Dou and others while in Vienna and Munich with George Henry Lewes (Yeazell 2008: 96–98). Eliot shared with Mitford an interest in seventeenth-century Dutch landscape painters who she believed possessed a 'rare, precious quality of

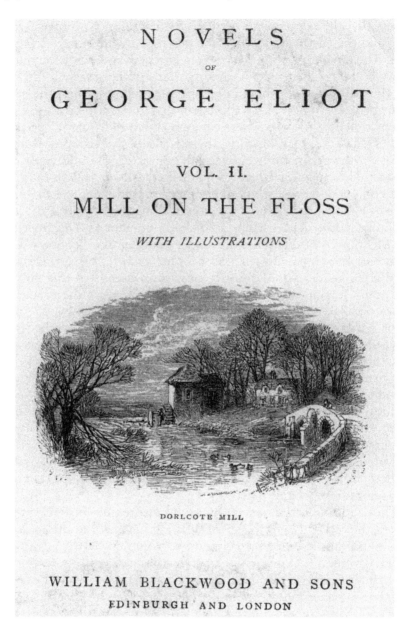

Figure 4.1 Cover of the third stereotyped edition of *The Mill on the Floss* (1867) featuring Dorlcote Mill. Illustration by E. M. W. Engraved by James Cooper. From a late nineteenth-century edition of *The Mill on the Floss* by George Eliot originally published 1860. World History Archive / Alamy Stock Photo.

Landscape-Shaped Subjectivity: Eliot's 'Mother Tongue'

truth' that led them to perceive art as 'the faithful representing of commonplace things' (Eliot 1994a: 176).

Although the end of the chapter reveals this visit to Dorlcote Mill to have been a dream, the intimate relationship between narrator and narratee remains. Just as he notices the miller's daughter, whose eyes are on the 'unresting wheel sending out its diamond jets of water', and her yapping dog, who – as Mitford would say – gives 'life and motion to the picture', the narrator begins to awaken from his nap. He exclaims:

> Ah, my arms are benumbed. I have been pressing my elbows on the arms of my chair and dreaming that I was standing on the front of Dorlcote Mill as it looked one February afternoon many years ago. Before I dozed off, I was going to tell you what Mr and Mrs Tulliver were talking about, as they sat by the bright fire in the left-hand parlour, on that very afternoon I have been dreaming of. (2008: 8–9)

Here the reader is directly addressed as the 'you' who will receive the story that is about to be relayed. Unlike the dream sequence, which undercuts the novel's realism because it insists on the reader imagining oneself standing on the stone bridge that leads to Dorlcote Mill alongside the narrator, the remainder of the novel proceeds along the lines of Gaskell's narratives in which the reader is only present at the site of reading. Yet what unites the narrator and the reader throughout the novel is their imaginatively shared relationship to the land and the social relations embedded in it.

In this chapter, I argue that Eliot's novel intervenes in debates about the affective dimension of citizenship in a liberalising polity. Drawing on thematic and formal techniques from Mitford and Gaskell, Eliot counters the emerging abstraction *nation* with everyday knowledge derived from the English provincial village. Yet Eliot is less interested in opposing the abstract to the concrete than in infusing the former with the latter. For Eliot, the provincial village functions, at its best, as an inclusive social formation in which mutual support, cooperation and shared sensory experiences of topography and milieu can form the basis for wider attachments.

The veil of pseudonymity

When William Blackwood published *The Mill on the Floss* in three volumes in 1860, the name George Eliot was already widely known to be the nom de plume of Marian Lewes. But for much of the preceding decade, she published either under the name Marian Evans – distinguishing herself in particular as a fine translator (a literary activity deemed suitable for women) – or anonymously as a reviewer and essayist whose work sometimes appeared under her name but more often without attribution. Lewes had encouraged her turn to fiction. 'From a scrap of descriptive writing she read out to him one evening at Berlin in 1855', Rosemary Ashton observes, 'he thought she might be able to write novels' (1991: 176). Yet, as I briefly considered in Chapter Three, her turn to fiction was neither inevitable nor easy.

When Evans finally set to work on 'The Sad Fortunes of the Reverend Amos Barton' in late September 1856, she had just sent off 'Silly Novels by Lady Novelists' to the *Westminster Review* a few days prior (Eliot 1998c: 63). On Evans's completion of the story in early November, George Henry Lewes acted as an intermediary between her and the publisher John Blackwood. In a letter dated 6 November 1856, Lewes indicated that he had in his possession a manuscript 'submitted to me by a friend who desired good offices with you' (Eliot 1954b: 269). Blackwood responded on 12 November to say that the 'first specimen "Amos Barton" is unquestionably very pleasant reading' and indicated an interest in seeing 'more' before he committed to publishing the short stories either in a volume or as a series in *Blackwood's Magazine* (Eliot 1954b: 272). Blackwood's hesitancy appears to have affected Evans, who – as I discussed in the preceding chapter – doubted her capacity to write fiction. As Lewes explained to Blackwood, in a letter written towards the end of November, his unnamed 'friend . . . is unusually sensitive, and unlike most writers is more anxious about *excellence* than about appearing in print' (Eliot 1954b: 276). Because the story continued to linger on his mind long after he had read it, Blackwood indicated his willingness to proceed without 'committing myself to go on with the other Tales of the series unless I approved of them' (Eliot 1954b: 275). 'The Sad Fortunes of the Reverend Amos Barton' appeared in the January and February 1857 issues of the magazine.

Although Blackwood was sure that the quality of the story portended a series, he found the continued anonymity of its writer highly peculiar. He addressed his letter of 29 December 1856 – in which he transmitted a gratis copy of the January number as well as a cheque for the story payable to Lewes – 'To the Author of Amos

Barton'. 'It gives me very great pleasure to begin the number with Amos', he writes, 'and I put him in that position because his merits will entitle him to it and also because it is a vital point to attract public attention to the *first* part of a Series, to which end being the first article of the first number of the year may contribute'. 'I have already expressed to our friend Mr. Lewes the very high opinion I entertain of Amos', he continued, 'and the expectations I have formed of the Series should his successors prove equal to him, which I fully anticipate' (Eliot 1954b: 283). Subsequent letters were sent by Blackwood to 'Amos' until Evans, in a letter dated 4 February 1857 to William Blackwood, founder of the publishing firm, gave them a name: George Eliot. She made it clear, however, that the name was a nom de plume and a means of 'preserving my incognito' (Eliot 1954b: 292). Henceforth, John Blackwood corresponded directly with the writer with payments sent to Lewes 'to hand to the mysterious George Eliot' (Eliot 1954b: 308).

Critics have proffered a variety of reasons for Evans's decision to use a male pseudonym. Certainly, as Evans had noted in 'Silly Novels by Lady Novelists', women writers who lacked talent received 'journalistic approbation' at 'the boiling pitch', while for those who evinced 'excellence, critical enthusiasm drops to the freezing point' (Eliot 1856b: 460). But by the late 1850s, a woman writer did not need to rely on a male pseudonym – as, among others, the Brontës (who used Acton, Ellis and Currer Bell) or Harriet Martineau (who wrote as V. of Norwich and Disciplus) had done – or on anonymity, as was originally the case with Gaskell, to have their work seriously considered. Because she shared a life with a married man, Evans was undoubtedly eager to preserve her privacy. Having been excommunicated by her family over her relationship with Lewes, she assumed her partner's surname and foreswore the use of Evans. 'I have renounced that name', she wrote to Bessie Rayner Parkes in a letter dated 24 September 1857, 'and do not mean to be known by it in any way' (Eliot 1954b: 384). As Rosemarie Bodenheimer has suggested, 'if George Eliot were to be unmasked, it was better that the morally dubious woman sheltered by the pseudonym be Marian Lewes than Marian Evans'. For, as Bodenheimer continues, 'Marian Evans was also the name known in Warwickshire, which had begun to recognise itself in the new stories by George Eliot; it was preferable to maintain some distance from that, as well as from the family name' (2018: 129). As for the name itself, she told John Walter Cross – the banker whom she would marry in the last year of her life – 'that George was Mr. Lewes's Christian name, and Eliot was a good, mouth-filling, easily pronounced word' (1888: 310).

Based on the generally positive responses by readers and critics to the first part of 'The Sad Fortunes of the Reverend Amos Barton', Blackwood was eager to continue the series. By February, he had read a portion of 'Mr Gilfill's Love Story', which he deemed 'bright, lifelike, and witty'. 'Many men write well and tell a story well', he explained, in a letter dated 16 February 1857, 'but few possess the art of giving individuality to their characters so happily and easily as you in both these stories' (Eliot 1954b: 297). As the story unfolded, he continued to express his 'laudations' while recommending minor alterations (Eliot 1954b: 302). 'Mr Gilfill's Love Story' ran in the magazine between March and June. As Blackwood explained in a letter dated 30 April 1857, her depiction of the countryside was particularly evocative. 'The picture reminds me strongly of the genuine English rural landscapes with which we are all familiar on canvas or in nature', he averred (Eliot 1954b: 323).

In the same month in which 'Mr Gilfill's Love Story' came to a close, however, Blackwood and Eliot began to haggle over her next story, 'Janet's Repentance', with its depiction of alcoholism and spousal abuse. Although he thought it 'exceedingly clever and some hits and descriptions of character first rate', he expresses his disappointment that it did not offer 'a pleasanter picture'. 'Surely the colours are rather harsh', he bemoans, in a letter dated 8 June 1857, 'for a sketch of English County Town life only 25 years ago'. He advises her to cut down on 'the delineation of characters', 'shorten' the first scene, and 'to *soften* your picture as much as you can' (Eliot 1954b: 344). In her response three days later, Eliot objects on the grounds of realism: the 'real town' on which her fictional setting is based 'was more vicious' than the one she depicts; a character far less 'disgusting' than the individual from whom she has taken certain features and attributes; and the depiction of 'churchmen and dissenters, with whom I am almost equally acquainted, are drawn from close observation of them in real life, and not at all from hearsay or from the descriptions of novelists' (Eliot 1954b: 347–348). Refusing to make all but '*superficial* alterations', she suggests to Blackwood that if he has any qualms about running it in the magazine 'they close the series' (Eliot 1954b: 347, 348). 'I daresay', she concludes, 'you will feel no difficulty about

Landscape-Shaped Subjectivity: Eliot's 'Mother Tongue' 179

publishing a volume containing the story of Janet's Repentance' because, unlike serialisation, the reader can apprehend its meaning and moral in a single sitting (Eliot 1954b: 348).

Although Blackwood relented, Eliot found the experience momentarily stifling. 'I am keenly alive, at once to the scruples and alarms an editor may feel', she declares, 'and to my own utter inability to write under any cramping influence' (Eliot 1954b: 348). As the assistant editor of the *Westminster Review*, Eliot was perhaps particularly attuned to the tensions between a magazine's distinct personality to which individual contributors were expected to contribute and the creative vision of individual authors. As Fionnuala Dillane has suggested, *Scenes of Clerical Life* marks less of a decisive break in Eliot's career as a journalist than critics have often assumed insofar as the 'tensions between the writer and the corporate demands of periodical production' continued to exist (2013: 103). Midway through the serialisation of 'Janet's Repentance', which ran in the July through November numbers, Eliot declared her intention to end the series. 'I am inclined to take a larger canvas', she wrote to Blackwood, in a letter dated 5 September 1857, 'and write a novel' (Eliot 1954b: 381). Writing to Blackwood on 17 October, she assured her publisher, who had praised her depiction of the Midlands landscape, that it too would 'be a country story – full of the breath of cows and the scent of hay' (Eliot 1954b: 387). To avoid any editorial interventions on his part until the story had sufficiently unfolded, however, she would not ask him 'to look at it till I have written a volume or more' (Eliot 1954b: 387).

Throughout the publication of *Scenes of Clerical Life* and into her negotiations with Blackwood over the publication of her first novel, *Adam Bede*, Evans maintained her 'incognito'. She would only reveal her identity to the publisher while he was visiting the couple at their residence in Richmond on 28 February 1858 (Eliot 1954b: 435). The three maintained the secret until circumstances necessitated otherwise. Ever since the publication of the first installment of 'The Sad Fortunes of the Reverend Amos Barton' there was considerable speculation over its author. In fact, the frenzied interest on the part of the public in identifying the author behind *Scenes of Clerical Life* was so great that Blackwood capitalised on it and rushed *Adam Bede* into press (Bodenheimer 2018: 131). It was her hope that the novel, as she professed to Blackwood in a letter dated 1 December 1858, might 'be judged quite apart from its authorship' (Eliot 1954b: 505). In addition to any qualms she may have felt about being evaluated as a woman of letters, she was also eager for her work to be seen as fiction. Just as Mitford's *Our Village* became inextricably tied to Three Mile Cross and Gaskell's *Cranford* to Knutsford, Eliot knew that her fictional world would, on being identified as its creator, be linked to her. As Lewes would later put it, after George Eliot had been unmasked, 'the object of anonymity was to get the book [*Adam Bede*] judged on its own merits, and not prejudged as the work of a woman, or of a particular woman' (1955a: 106).

Yet by not coming forward others would claim either that characters were based on them or that they had authored the works. After the publication of the first instalment of 'The Sad Fortunes of the Reverend Amos Barton', Joseph Munt Langford, Blackwood's London-based agent, wrote to the publisher to pass on a rumour he had heard that the story was based on 'the actual life of a clergyman named Gwythir'. '[H]is daughter wrote to a lady', Langford continued, 'telling her to be sure to read the story as it was their family history' (Eliot 1954b: 298). In fact, the publisher himself received a 'troublesome number' of letters expressing their conviction that the story was part of their own lived histories (Eliot 1954b: 237). In August 1857, Blackwood was contacted by one William Pitman Jones, Perpetual Curate of St Thomas, Preston, who, after reading the first two parts of 'Janet's Repentance' expressed his dismay that his deceased brother should be used as fodder. As Blackwood wrote to George Henry Lewes in a letter dated 15 August, the man 'is utterly at a loss to conceive who could have written the statements or revived what should have been buried in oblivion' (Eliot 1954b: 375). Blackwood expressed his concern that Eliot – whom he still believed to be a man – may have 'in his love of reality' founded his story on 'living characters' (Eliot 1954b: 375). Responding directly to Blackwood, Eliot insisted that the portrait of the clergyman was 'an ideal character'. 'I should consider it a fault which would cause me lasting regret', she continued in her letter of 18 August 1857, 'if I had used reality in any other than the legitimate way common to all artists who draw their materials from their observation and experience' (Eliot 1954b: 376). When in 1859 a clergyman in Lincolnshire stepped forward to claim that he knew the real author of *Scenes of Clerical Life* and that the Blackwoods had swindled him of payment for the stories, which had been sent to the publisher twelve years earlier, she and Lewes consented to lifting the veil of pseudonymity.[1]

Eliot also opted for a mode of publication that allowed her to assert greater control over her own artistic production. Mitford and Gaskell, as Eliot had done with *Scenes of Clerical Life*, often published their work in periodicals. As with *Our Village*, Mitford's other work, including *Belford Regis* (1835), *Country Stories* (1837) and *Atherton, and Other Tales* (1854) all drew on material previously published in wide variety of magazines. In addition to the Cranford papers, many of Gaskell's novels were also serialised in periodicals. Resistant to having her fiction shaped by the periodical milieu in which they might first appear, Eliot would – after Blackwood attempted to exert pressure on her to make significant alterations to 'Janet's Repentance' – only publish *Romola* in monthly magazine instalments. *Middlemarch* and *Daniel Deronda* would appear in parts publication. *The Mill on the Floss*, to which she turned her attention after the success of *Adam Bede* and the revelation of her identity, appeared in three volumes.

Novel and nation

While Eliot was writing *The Mill on the Floss* Parliament was debating a further extension of the franchise beyond the reforms introduced by the Great Reform Act of 1832. Ostensibly reducing some of the excesses of electoral corruption, the act also established in England and Wales a uniform franchise for property owners and for renters of houses in boroughs – settlements larger than a village that sent representatives to Parliament – who paid at least ten pounds per annum. The situation in the counties varied: the right to vote was extended to copyholders, freeholders (property owners), leaseholders and householders when the rental values of properties met certain thresholds and, in some instances, residence qualifications were satisfied. In any case, by weakening the aristocracy's hold on boroughs, the act was partly responsible for constructing a middle class by shaping a socio-economic stratum between the aristocracy, whose male members had the right to vote, and the working class.[2]

In the two centuries prior to the Reform Act of 1832, national subjectivity was grounded in specific property qualifications These varied between counties and boroughs. In counties those who possessed freehold property – the assessed value of which was forty shillings per annum – could vote (Stubbs 1880: 266–267). In the boroughs, voting qualifications varied widely: from those paying local assessments, known as scot and lot, to so-called burgage holders (votes attached to specific properties). Although the electorate included shopkeepers, tradesmen, yeomen and a portion of the labouring classes, political power resided almost exclusively in the gentry. Thus, until 1832, the nation was conceived largely in terms of an aggregate of freehold and landed properties.

In addition to the wide variety of voting practices between counties and boroughs, and indeed among boroughs themselves, there were debates about the definition of property as an increasing number of men who did not derive their wealth from land began to exert greater influence. But very few challenged the assumption that the right to vote should be predicated on a property qualification. Men across the political spectrum accepted John Locke's contention that the primary responsibility of government was to safeguard life, liberty and the ownership of property; hence, those who owned property believed that they were the ones who should be represented in government.[3] In Locke's theory of the social contract, individual adult men band together to overthrow an absolutist ruler. In so doing, they emerge as equals: 'The *Equality* which all Men are in, in respect of Jurisdiction or Dominion ... [originates in] that *equal Right* every Man hath, *to his Natural Freedom*, without being subjected to the Will or Authority of any other Man' (1698: 2.54). Because these men are now rendered equally free, they must decide to form a suitable system of political governance that will hold jurisdiction over them and safeguard their proprietary interests. Consenting to be governed under a political system whose end is the preservation of property, Locke's men guarantee their citizenship in the new polity.

Although propertied representation was widely accepted as a principle, it was complexly and unevenly implemented. In the seventeenth and eighteenth centuries many of those who met the property qualification were, in fact, unable to vote. The large manufacturing cities and seats of commerce, such as Birmingham, Leeds and Manchester, did not return members of parliament. Freeholders who resided there had no opportunity to select their representatives. Many boroughs were controlled by individual patrons (Porritt 1903: 309–366). A significant number of elections went uncontested (Colley 1982: 118; O'Gorman 1989: 107–112).[4]

In addition, county representation had no relationship to population size. This produced gross discrepancies in the proportion of electors to their parliamentary representative between boroughs – the smallest and most sparsely populated of which held outsized influence – and counties.

The Reform Act of 1832, therefore, introduced a number of significant alterations. With constituency changes and the redistribution of seats, the electoral map was redrawn. In England and Wales, the aforementioned uniform borough franchise was implemented for owners and renters of houses that were valued at ten pounds per annum. When a property's rental value met a specific threshold, the copyholder, freeholder, leaseholder or householder in the counties – subject in some cases to a residence qualification – was enfranchised as well. These changes ensured that the franchise was extended to a greater number of male professionals – lawyers, merchants, factory owners – in the middle classes. The oligarchic nature of the English nation was pressured by the definitional expansion of property, which permitted greater numbers of men who contributed to the national economy to formally participate in politics. While a property qualification remained an essential requirement for political representation, the definition of what counted as property was expanded from fixed to portable. The effects of the 1832 Reform Act, however, were limited: through it, only one in six adult males garnered the right to vote.

Nevertheless, the passage of the Reform Act set in motion a process of reforming and refining a sense of both what the nation was and who counted as a national subject. The rapid urbanisation of the first half of the nineteenth century led to the widespread recognition that Britain could no longer be defined as economically or demographically rural, which increased pressure on Parliament to recognise these changing conditions through a further extension of the franchise. Reform Acts put forward by the Liberals were debated in 1852, 1854 and 1860, but none garnered sufficient support to pass. Conservatives, whom John Stuart Mill would famously insult as the 'stupid party' for resisting change (1981: 277), briefly recognised during the Derby administration the direction in which the political winds were blowing. During their leadership of Parliament from 1858 to 1859, they proposed a widened franchise, which the radical John Bright derided as 'fancy franchises' as it granted the vote to groups based on education and occupation (Bright 1868: 20).

Although there was little agreement between Liberals and Conservatives on the specific ways in which the franchise might be expanded, they shared a sense that reform was inevitable. The 'radical shift in social relations' that reform was engendering and – as further changes took place – would continue to produce, as Pam Morris has argued, signified to many that 'society would have to be ordered on principles of inclusion' (2004: 3). Certainly, as intellectuals who took an active interest in the debates of their times, both Eliot and John Stuart Mill embraced inclusivity in broad terms.

Already in 1859, Eliot was beginning to imagine the contours of a socially inclusive society in the form of a village. This was a lesson she would have derived from reading *Cranford*, which – as I noted earlier – she had first taken up in 1857 and returned to the following year as she was writing *Adam Bede* (Eliot 1955a: 198–99). In a first-person address to the reader ('my good friend'), the narrator of *Adam Bede*, a novel set in the fictional village of Hayslope, asks:

> what will you do ... with your fellow-parishioner who opposes your husband in the vestry? – with your newly appointed vicar, whose style of preaching you find painfully below that of his regretted predecessor? – with the honest servant who worries your soul with her one failing? – with your neighbour, Mrs. Green, who was really kind to you in your last illness, but has said several ill-natured things about you since your convalescence? (2008: 160)

As the narrator insists, every one of these – at times 'ugly, stupid, [and] inconsistent' – individuals needs to be valued. These 'fellow-mortals', she insists, are 'as they are': 'you can neither straighten their noses, nor brighten their wit, nor rectify their dispositions'. It is 'needful', she therefore admonishes the reader, 'to tolerate, pity, and love' them (2008: 160). Just as the ladies of Cranford tolerate the improprieties of, say, Captain Brown or Lady Glenmire, and just as Mary Smith implicitly directs the reader to accept the eccentricities of her elder female companions, Eliot's narrator – in explicitly didactic terms – asks her readers to abide the shortcomings and quirks of one's neighbours.

One of the few criticisms to be levelled against Mitford's *Our Village* is that her vision of the rural community was too inclusive. Not only did she portray her 'rustic neighbours' but – as one reviewer whom I quoted earlier remarked – also adopted their 'vulgarisms' (Anon. 1825: 167). Mitford would have, perhaps, attributed this representational choice to her Radical sympathies. Similarly, Gaskell's *Cranford* features, among others, a milliner, a butcher's wife, a maid and a joiner. Her contemporaries as well as later critics understood this to be an essential element of her liberalism.[5] But of the three writers under consideration here, only George Eliot's fictional works emerge coevally with the formal transition of Whigs into Liberals.

For his own part, writing that same year, Mill notes that religious intolerance is one of the fundamental factors impeding inclusivity. 'The exclusive pretension made by a part of the truth to be the whole, must and ought to be protested against', he insists, 'and if a reactionary impulse should make the protestors unjust in their turn, this one-sidedness, like the other, may be lamented, but must be tolerated'. To the extent that Christians wanted to fashion a society in which their religion was subject to intellectual fairness by infidels, Mill continues, 'they should themselves be just to infidelity'. 'It can do truth no service to blink the fact', he concludes, 'that a large portion of the noblest and most valuable moral teaching has been the work, not only of men who did not know, but of men who knew and rejected, the Christian faith' (1977c: 257).

On the question of political inclusivity, however, Eliot and Mill differed. Radicals, like Mill, saw the measures being debated by his contemporaries as entirely too modest. The impulse to craft a socially inclusive society conflicted with a belief held by members of both parties that the franchise was 'a privilege and a responsibility, to be exercised by those who had a propertied stake in the country' (Hall 2000: 1). For the most part, while nineteenth-century Liberals and Conservatives sought to formalise principles of social inclusion, their efforts remained constricted within a Lockean framework of property ownership. The very concept of inclusiveness thus remained, paradoxically, firmly rooted in social difference. Indeed, Gladstone's proposed Reform Bill of 1866 failed in part because he could not win the support of moderate members of his own party to lower the property qualification.

At the same time, Mill took issue with the positions staked out by some of his fellow Radicals. They had been consistently campaigning for, among other reforms, the introduction of the secret ballot so that tenants would not be subject to intimidation by their landlords; the elimination of the property qualification parliaments of one to three years' duration; and a redistribution of seats that would strengthen the representation of industrial cities and commercial towns. In 1848, Richard Cobden spoke for many of his parliamentary allies when he lambasted the Russell government on the floor of the House of Commons: 'If you talk of your aristocracy and your traditions, and compel me to talk of the middle and industrious classes, I say it is to them that the glory of this country is owing. You have had your government of aristocracy and tradition; and the worst thing in this country has been its government' (Cobden 1848: 195–196). Yet Cobden was inclined to accept household suffrage – or the extension of the franchise to all male occupants of a dwelling – as the outer limit of what might be accomplished in his day.

In 1859, Mill attempted to persuade his fellow Radicals to accept a series of more significant reforms. Having retired a year earlier from the East India Company, where he occupied the second-highest position in the company's home service, Mill published three significant works in rapid succession: 'Thoughts on Parliamentary Reform', a contribution to debates over a further extension of the franchise; *On Liberty*, his encomium to the emancipating practices of free thought and individuality; and *Dissertations and Discussions*, which collected a number of essays that had previously appeared in periodicals. Mill had every indication that there would be a market for *Dissertations and Discussions*. No less eager a student of his thought than Lewes, long before he met Marian Evans, had been looking up each article individually and corresponding with Mill. 'You are certainly a conjurer, in finding out my old obscure articles', Mill wrote to him in an undated letter from the late 1840s (Mill 1963: 449).

Evidence, with varying levels of interpretability and reliability, suggests that while she was composing *The Mill on the Floss*, George Eliot became acquainted with, if not the essays themselves, the main arguments Mill was advancing. It is likely that she read *Dissertations and Discussions* when it was first published. But Eliot may well have encountered many of the essays earlier. As Lewes's correspondence with Mill suggests, readers interested in his essays would have had no difficulty in locating them. In Eliot's case, she had very easy access indeed, as she served as assistant editor of the *Westminster Review* between 1852 and 1854 and as author of the Belles Lettres column between July 1855 and January 1857. In 1851, Eliot's friend John Chapman purchased the periodical from W. E. Hickson and tasked her with writing a prospectus and assisting him as an editor. Her first draft was widely panned by associates of Chapman, including Mill, who, as former editor, worried about the periodical's drift away from its original remit as an organ of radical thought. Her subsequent effort, which appeared in 1851 as a standalone publication and, in January 1852, as a preface to the first issue under their editorship, reflects a more thorough understanding of the periodical's past. Indeed, the prospectus vowed 'to confirm and extend the influence of the Review as an instrument for the development and guidance of earnest thought on Politics, Social Philosophy, Religion, and General Literature' (Eliot 1852: n.p.). Mill continued to find aspects of the prospectus wanting. It nevertheless laid the groundwork for a publication that, during Eliot's tenure as editor, featured a variety of unorthodox viewpoints on issues of the moment, including Mill's own.

Although many contributors to the *Westminster Review* were similar to one another in the unconventional stances they took on contemporary topics, their actual positions often diverged significantly. No school of thought could encompass such distinct personages who appeared in its pages as the utilitarian James Martineau; the historian James Anthony Froude, who shocked many with the publication of his philosophical novel *The Nemesis of Faith* (1849); the Catholic theologian and former leader of the Oxford Movement John Henry Newman; and Mill. To Eliot, each was, in his own way, 'amongst the world's vanguard'. Rather than 'have a periodical to himself', the *Westminster Review* could serve as a 'common' ground, where they could 'write more openly . . than anywhere else' (Eliot 1954b: 49). As she confessed to one correspondent, however, in a letter dated 24–25 July 1852, of all the contributors to the periodical, she felt herself the 'more' intellectually inclined to Mill (Eliot 1954b: 49).

Long before the two worked together at the *Westminster Review*, Evans (as Eliot was then known) was interested in Mill's thought. As she explained in a letter to Caroline Bray dated 3 October 1851, Mill's *System of Logic* (1843), which argues that scientific, social and political problems are best resolved through empirical principles, served as a 'reference' work for her (Eliot 1954a: 363). She also eagerly read *Principles of Political Economy* when it was published in 1848. Although she had 'no consciousness' of Mill's books 'having made any marked epoch' in her life, as she explained in a letter to Elizabeth Stuart Phelps dated 13 August 1875, she nevertheless felt that both *System of Logic* and *Principles of Political Economy* were of particular 'benefit' to her. She eagerly 'studied' his other works as well (Eliot 1856: 163–164).

These other works included *On Liberty*, an 1859 edition of which was part of her library (Baker 1981: 92). As Avrom Fleischman has cautioned, we neither know all that Eliot read nor when she read the many publications mentioned in her letters, journals or other surviving documents. It is, however, safe to assume that even after her formal association with the *Westminster Review* ended in 1857, she continued to read the periodical (Fleischman 2008: 2). Her papers from the remainder of her life contain numerous references to specific issues or articles. Had she not read *On Liberty* when it was first published, or obtained a copy of 'Thoughts on Parliamentary Reform', she would have encountered extended discussions of these works in an omnibus review entitled 'Contemporary Literature', published in the April 1859 issue of the *Westminster Review*.

A common thread through *Dissertations and Discussions*, *On Liberty* and 'Thoughts on Parliamentary Reform' is Mill's interest in preserving qualitative distinctions among the opinions of people who impart them. In 'Civilization', a piece that first appeared in *The London and Westminster Review* in April 1836 just a few years after the passage of the first Reform Bill, Mill argued that the expanding franchise and emergence of commercialised societies 'in modern Europe, and especially in Great Britain' had created the conditions in which individuals were no longer solely responsible for ensuring their own survival, prosperity and security (1977a: 120–121, 129). While this development accrued many benefits, he feared that the transfer of power 'from individuals to masses' lessened the significance of 'the weight and importance of an individual' (1977a: 126). As a consequence, 'the individual is lost and becomes impotent in the crowd, and . . . individual character itself becomes relaxed and enervated' (1977a: 136). The pressing issue for modern societies, Mill asserted, is the development of 'national institutions of education, and forms of polity, calculated to invigorate the individual character' (1977a: 136). Because he believes that the best indicator of character is the capacity to form and express individuated opinions, Mill calls for the establishment of a meritocratic system that nurtures and rewards their formation

(1977a: 147).[6] For only in selecting 'doctrines for themselves' could individuals cultivate their intellect.[7]

In Mill's view, parliamentary reform was, therefore, a necessary step in creating such an environment conducive to the cultivation of individuality. He begins his pamphlet by asserting that the 'admission and exclusion' to the franchise is entirely 'capricious': 'the same description of persons are admitted in cities and parliamentary boroughs, who are excluded in all other towns and in the rural districts. Whatever qualification, or variety of qualifications, may be fixed upon, it is reasonable that they should be the same in one place as in another' (1977c: 315). Yet, Mill argues, instead of simply addressing this inconsistency and related 'evils', any attempt at reform should include an 'ideal conception of a perfect representative government, however distant, not to say doubtful, may be the hope of actually obtaining it' (1977c: 321–322). To that end, he proposes a near-universal extension of the franchise and a system of plural voting.

For Mill, the vote was a necessary component of a more expansive, and therefore inclusive, definition of citizenship. An ideal system of representation, he argues, would enable 'every grown-up human being' to participate in the management of public affairs by casting a vote (1977d: 335). Although the universalisation of the male pronoun – its extension from the specific to generic use – was common in Mill's own time, he uses the term *human being* to underscore women's inclusion in the political nation he is reimagining. Because there is no moral justification in a civilized society for rendering some the dependents of others, Mill argues, the only way to disrupt the conditions of dependency that currently exist in England is to grant everyone – with a small number of exceptions to which I will return shortly – the right to vote. In so doing, a more inclusive order can be formed. 'A person who is excluded from all participation in political business', he writes, 'is not a citizen'. Mill continues:

> He has not the feelings of a citizen. To take an active interest in politics is, in modern times, the first thing which elevates the mind to large interests and contemplations; the first step out of the narrow bounds of individual and family selfishness, the first opening in the contracted round of daily occupations. The person who in any free country takes no interest in politics, unless from having been taught that he ought not to do so, must be too ill-informed, too stupid, or too selfish, to

be interested in them; and we may rely on it that he cares as little for anything else, which does not directly concern himself or his personal connexions. Whoever is capable of feeling any common interest with his kind, or with his country, or with his city, is interested in politics; and to be interested in them, and not wish for a voice in them, is an impossibility. The possession and the exercise of political, and among others of electoral, rights, is one of the chief instruments both of moral and of intellectual training for the popular mind; and all governments must be regarded as extremely imperfect, until every one who is required to obey the laws, has a voice, or the prospect of a voice, in their enactment and administration. (1977d: 322–323)

For Mill, who recognised after his famous mental crisis that the 'cultivation of feelings' must be 'one of the cardinal points in my ethical and philosophical creed', the exercise of rational choice through the electoral process constitutes an essential means of developing attachments to one's nation (1981: 147). To the extent that an individual participates in public life, expressing one's opinion, and hence character, in spirited debates – 'one of the leading essentials of well-being' (1977c: 261) – and in casting a vote, one nurtures a feeling for the political order. This feeling for an abstraction is characterised as wider and less selfish than those bonds shared among members of a family.[8]

Eliot could not share Mill's faith in rationality and enlightened debate as the cornerstones of national community. While enlightenment, by definition, may be collective, for Eliot it does not stand to reason that individuals will necessarily feel more consciously a part of the nation simply because they have engaged in dialogue. Given her ambivalence about the extension of the franchise, she was also not inclined to see the vote as a vehicle for cultivating a feeling of citizenship. Indeed, on the question of political reform, as the tensions over the *Westminster Review* prospectus indicate, the two differed considerably. Eliot thought 'the institutions of man, no less than the products of nature, are strong and durable in proportion as they are the results of gradual development' (Eliot 1852: 3). Efficacious and lasting reforms that 'sustain such a relation to the moral and intellectual condition of the people, as to ensure their support', exemplify 'the wisdom of the time'. By contrast, Mill contended that 'changes effected rapidly & by force are often the only ones which in given circumstances would be permanent' (1972a: 53). Hence his argument for near-universal suffrage.

Landscape-Shaped Subjectivity: Eliot's 'Mother Tongue'

Yet Mill worried that until such sentiments were cultivated in the voting public, the enfranchisement of the working class would result in the tyranny of the majority. Instead of retreating from the proposition that the franchise should be widened, he proposes an educational qualification – proven ability to read, write and use basic arithmetic – that would balance the ethical imperative of expanding suffrage rights while mitigating some of the potentially deleterious consequences:

> It would do more than merely admit the best and exclude the worst of the working classes; it would do more than make an honourable distinction in favour of the educated, and create an additional motive for seeking education. It would cause the electoral suffrage to be in time regarded in a totally different light. It would make it be thought of, not as now, in the light of a possession to be used by the voter for his own interest or pleasure, but as a trust for the public good. It would stamp the exercise of the suffrage as a matter of judgment, not of inclination; as a public function, the right to which is conferred by fitness for the intelligent performance of it. (1977d: 328)

In Mill's scheme, therefore, the vote was to be held out as a right that could be obtained by those who demonstrate inchoate mental aptitude. The ability to acquire this right would serve as an incentive to develop one's faculties. As these faculties expand, one's capacity to think beyond the self and its narrow interests increases.

In advancing an educational qualification, Mill went further than even some of his fellow Radicals in Parliament who were proponents of household suffrage. For those who favoured extending the franchise but could not accept the premise that educated and uneducated voters were equal, an educational qualification proved appealing. In her letter to Charles Boner dated 9 May 1848, Mary Russell Mitford expressed her preference for such a measure. 'I myself should like an educational test', she told the poet and travel writer, 'but it will probably end in household suffrage and the ballot' (Mitford 1914: 95). But an educational qualification could be used not only to determine who would vote but also how many votes anyone person would be awarded. Of those who can read, write and utilise basic arithmetic, Mill notes: 'That all should be admitted to the franchise who can fulfil these simple requirements, is not to be expected, nor even desired, unless means were also taken to give to the higher grades of instruction additional or more influential votes' (1977d: 328).

Contending that everyone ought to have the same political right, Mill simultaneously labours to ensure that the opinions of the more highly educated, especially those who have the capacity to think beyond the self and family, are preserved. An ideal electoral system, he argues, is premised on an understanding 'that every person should have one vote, but that every well-educated person in the community should have more than one, on a scale corresponding as far as practicable to their amount of education' (1977d: 325). This system of awarding a plurality of votes to the more highly educated and intelligent would replace a property qualification. Indeed, precisely because property was an unreliable indicator of either intellect or opinion, Mill did not believe that the right to vote should be premised on it.

Distinguishing his reform proposal from others, Mill baldly asserts that not all persons have equal moral worth. 'It is the fact, that one person is *not* as good as another; and it is reversing all the rules of rational conduct, to attempt to raise a political fabric on a supposition which is at variance with fact.' To illustrate his point, Mill provides the following examples:

> [A] person who cannot read, is not as good, for the purposes of human life, as one who can. A person who can read, but cannot write or calculate, is not as good as a person who can do both. A person who can read, write, and calculate, but who knows nothing of the properties of natural objects, or of other places and countries, or of the human beings who have lived before him, or of the ideas, opinions, and practices of his fellow-creatures generally, is not so good as a person who knows these things. A person who has not, either by reading or conversation, made himself acquainted with the wisest thoughts of the wisest men, and with the great examples of a beneficent and virtuous life, is not so good as one who is familiar with these. A person who has even filled himself with this various knowledge, but has not digested it – who could give no clear and coherent account of it, and has never exercised his own mind, or derived an original thought from his own observation, experience, or reasoning, is not so good, for any human purpose, as one who has. (1977d: 323–324)

While each vote matters, the mental procedures used to formulate the opinion – of which the casting of a vote is an expression – matter more. After all, although the vote 'elevates the mind to large interests and contemplations', this is only an initial step in developing the capacity to detach oneself from 'the narrow bounds of individual and family selfishness' (1977d: 322). Those who are able to process and assimilate the knowledge they gain through education and use it to form their own individuated judgements are better fit 'for any human purpose' than those who have not. Mill proposes, therefore, to scale votes accordingly:

> If every ordinary unskilled labourer had one vote, a skilled labourer, whose occupation requires an exercised mind and a knowledge of some of the laws of external nature, ought to have two. A foreman, or superintendent of labour, whose occupation requires something more of general culture, and some moral as well as intellectual qualities, should perhaps have three. If every ordinary unskilled labourer had one vote, a skilled labourer, whose occupation requires an exercised mind and a knowledge of some of the laws of external nature, ought to have two. A foreman, or superintendent of labour, whose occupation requires something more of general culture, and some moral as well as intellectual qualities, should perhaps have three. A farmer, manufacturer, or trader, who requires a still larger range of ideas and knowledge, and the power of guiding and attending to a great number of various operations at once, should have three or four. A member of any profession requiring a long, accurate, and systematic mental cultivation, – a lawyer, a physician or surgeon, a clergyman of any denomination, a literary man, an artist, a public functionary (or, at all events, a member of every intellectual profession at the threshold of which there is a satisfactory examination test) ought to have five or six. A graduate of any university, or a person freely elected a member of any learned society, is entitled to at least as many. (1977d: 324–325)

Thus, while Mill sees the vote as essential to reorganising the political nation among inclusive lines, he rejects the possible inference that every vote ought therefore to be weighted equally. As he puts it rhetorically, 'ought every one to have an *equal* voice?'

Typically, when scholars wish to discuss Eliot's engagement with Mill's ideas, they look to her so-called political novel, *Felix Holt the Radical* (1866). As Catherine Gallagher noted long ago, 'John Stuart Mill and Matthew Arnold directly inspired George Eliot's political fiction of the 1860s' (1985: 228). From Mill, Gallagher contends, Eliot recognised the 'binding link' between her 'duty to represent politics and her role as an intellectual', whereas from Arnold she gleaned 'an even tighter bond between that duty and her role as an artist' (1985: 233). Tracing significant changes in how political and literary representation was conceived and practiced, Gallagher reads Arnold's *Culture and Anarchy* as an extension and reformulation of key themes in Mill's *Considerations on Representative Government* in order to show that the latter departs from the 'descriptive assumption' that undergirded efforts to expand the franchise. His support for a system of plural voting is an explicit denial that 'the most valuable representation is the most accurate reflection of social facts' (1985: 230). 'His proposed Parliament', she continues, 'would not correspond to any empirical social reality but would, rather, directly express, by distorting what is, that which ought to be' (1985: 231). Arnold similarly argues against a notion of the state as a simple reflection of a demographic reality: 'if England is to be saved from anarchy, if it is to deal with working-class demands for the franchise without disintegrating through intensified class conflict, the state must become the representative of something other than social facts' (1985: 235). Arnold's solution is to appeal to the *best self* of every participant in politics – an aspect of one's personality that is developed not through education, as Mill imagines it, but rather through culture.

In Gallagher's view, *Felix Holt* marks a decisive shift in Eliot's realism. Whereas Eliot's earlier works attempted to facilitate sympathetic identification with individuals through the depiction of ideal – which is to say, imaginative – characters, as she remarked to Blackwood in the controversy over *Scenes of Clerical Life*, she now accepts the responsibility of the liberal intellectual and artist to propagate a notion of the state as the embodiment of the nation's best self. To do so requires a literary form that is more than merely descriptive representation. '*Felix Holt* is the first of Eliot's novels', Gallagher writes, 'to acknowledge the contemporary political sources of this need' for an alternative.

Gallagher's influential account would consign *The Mill on the Floss* to an earlier period in Eliot's thinking about realism. Certainly, *Scenes of Clerical Life* and *Adam Bede* both sprung from the desire, as she explained to Blackwood, to teach readers that all individuals, as 'ugly, stupid, [and] inconsistent' as they are, are 'fellow-mortals' who deserve tolerance, pity and love.

Descriptive writing about provincial locales and their humble inhabitants was suitable to the task. But to view *The Mill on the Floss* in this way is to miss its engagements with contemporary political concepts and debates over the nature and meaning of national belonging. It should be seen instead as forming part of the spate of novels, ephemeral broadsides, poetry and non-fictional works of the 1860s that took up, implicitly or explicitly, the franchise question.[9] For Eliot, as the remainder of this chapter will demonstrate, national belonging has less to do, at least initially, with participating in political life than with developing affective ties. According to Terry Eagleton (1998), Daniel Cottom (1987) and Simon Dentith (1996), Eliot's emphasis on the non-political reflects her status as the quintessential bourgeois liberal humanist, who participates in ideological obfuscation by shifting material, historically specific concerns into the realm of sentimentality. Yet the cultivation of affect is, for Eliot, the single prerequisite to – and not a replacement for – expressions of national citizenship.

Theorising subjectivity

The publication of 'Thoughts on Parliamentary Reform', *On Liberty*, as well as the substantive review of these works in the *Westminster Review*, appeared at a crucial moment in Eliot's composition of *The Mill on the Floss*. She began to undertake research for the novel in January, but various interruptions prevented her from making much progress.[10] On 2 March 1859, Eliot records in her journal: 'Resumed my new novel, of which I am going to rewrite the first two chapters' (Eliot 1998c: 77). Four days later, in a letter to her publisher John Blackwood, Eliot described the novel as a 'picture of provincial life' (Eliot 1955a: 41). By 20 June, she had completed the first 110 pages, which she sent to Blackwood, who responded enthusiastically: 'I am perfectly delighted with the opening of the new story. The wealth of illustration and thought is wonderful and the lifelike minute delineation of character could not be well surpassed' (Blackwood in Eliot 1955a: 88). She would finish the first volume in October.

The following month, Eliot received the letter from Elizabeth Gaskell that I discussed in Chapter Three, which initiated the correspondence between the two writers. A rumour had reached Gaskell that *Scenes of Clerical Life* and *Adam Bede* were written by Evans under the pseudonym 'George Eliot'. She wrote to express her admiration. 'Since I heard, from authority, that you were the author of Scenes from "Clerical Life" & "Adam Bede"', Gaskell enthuses, in a letter dated 10 November 1859, 'I have read them again; and I must, once more, tell you how earnestly fully, and humbly I admire them'.[11] In an 11 November journal entry, Eliot records her satisfaction: 'Very sweet and noble of her!' (Eliot 1998c: 81). Writing to Sara Sophia Hennell, that same day, Eliot shares the news that she has received from Gaskell '[a] very beautiful letter – beautiful in feeling' (Eliot 1955a:199).

Like Gaskell and Mitford before her, Eliot certainly had her own experiences of provincial life from which to draw in penning her fiction. As has often been remarked, *The Mill on the Floss* is Eliot's most autobiographical novel. Read as a *Bildungsroman* greatly informed by Eliot's childhood in the Midlands, *The Mill on the Floss* has been critiqued for its 'persistent, mawkish nostalgia for ... the "golden gates of childhood", and a patronising facetiousness in the rendering of the petit-bourgeois Dobson sisters and their households' (Davies 1981: 258). Illustrations, such as those that included in the third stereotyped edition of 1867, have tended to skew readings in this direction (Figure 4.2). But Mitford's sketches of rural life and scenery and Gaskell's *Cranford* gave specific shape to her nostalgia for the social formation of the village. Often humorous and ironic, this nostalgia suggests both a homesickness and a sickness from being at home. Indeed, the novel combines a longing for the village's ostensibly cooperative and interdependent relations with a critical awareness of the village's limitations.

The Mill on the Floss is centrally concerned with the conflict between notions of subjectivity predicated on property ownership and the goal of social inclusion. Like Mill, whose ideal national citizen is in theory free from the constraints of property and hence class, Eliot offers a forceful critique of possessive individualism. Locating the novel a generation earlier than her own, Eliot fictionalises the debate that culminated in 1832 by pitting Jeremy Tulliver, the miller of Dorlcote Mill, who subscribes to Lockean conceptions of land tenure, against the lawyer Mr Wakem, who vaunts the power of portable property in a capitalist economy. Wakem represents a neighbour, Mr Pivart, who has been sued by Tulliver for engaging in an irrigation scheme further up the river. As Tulliver puts it, he will appeal to the legal system to enforce his 'legitimate share of water-power' and stop Pivart, 'with his dykes

Landscape-Shaped Subjectivity: Eliot's 'Mother Tongue' 97

Figure 4.2 'It was one of their happy mornings'. Illustration by Walter James Allen (active 1859–1891), engraved by James Cooper, for an undated nineteenth-century edition of *The Mill on the Floss* by George Eliot, originally published 1860. Photo 12/Alamy Stock Photo.

and erigations', from diverting water from Dorlcote Mill. But the law is not 'brought to bear o' the right side': Tulliver loses the suit and, going bankrupt in the process, loses the mill to Wakem, who assumes the mortgage (1998a: 154, 155).

Just as Jeremy possesses firm convictions about the use of rivers, which have largely been overridden by new legal paradigms, he and his wife Bessy raise their children Tom and Maggie in an environment governed by prosaic beliefs that hinder their development. In Maggie's childhood, her mother relentlessly pursues the goal of curling her daughter's hair: 'But her hair won't curl all I can do with it, and she's so franzy about having it put i' paper, and I've such work as never was to make her stand and have it pinched with th' irons.' For Mrs Tulliver, curled hair is the pre-eminent standard of beauty and 'other folks's children' do not seem to have Maggie's peculiar problem: an hour after being curled, the locks straighten.

As Mrs Tulliver sees it, her niece 'Lucy's got a row o' curls round her head, an' not a hair out o' place'. She continues: 'It seems hard as my sister Deane should have that pretty child; I'm sure Lucy takes more after me nor my own child does' (1998a: 13).

Although both children are sent to boarding school, the Tullivers hold commonplace assumptions about the purpose of female education. Mr Tulliver recognises his daughter's intellectual capacity yet remarks that its cultivation will 'fetch none the bigger price' for it on the marriage market (1998a: 12). While the novel is critical of such views, it depicts Tom's education as inadequate. His clergyman schoolmaster adheres to 'a method of instilling the Eton Grammar and Euclid into the mind of Tom Tulliver'. Tom is subject to the kind of instruction against which Mill had inveighed: rote learning of Euclid and the classics, by a man who 'believed in his method of education [as] . . . the only right way'. Thus, Tom's capacity to form 'sound opinions' through precise methods of reasoning and judging remain inchoate (1998a: 138).

Tom and Maggie's uncles and aunts, the latter all sisters of their mother, also contribute to the stultifying atmosphere in which they were raised. The actions of the Dodson sisters are animated 'by no sublime principles, no romantic visions, no active, self-renouncing faith; moved by none of those wild, uncontrollable passions which create the dark shadows of misery and crime; without that primitive, rough simplicity of wants, that hard, submissive, ill-paid toil, that childlike spelling-out of what nature has written, which gives its poetry to peasant life' (1998a: 272). The strict and resolute Mrs Glegg, much like Deborah Jenkyns in *Cranford*, presides over family affairs with an imperious air. Of Mrs Glegg, the narrator observes that she 'had both a front and a back parlour in her excellent house at St Ogg's, so that she had two points of view from which she could observe the weakness of her fellow-beings, and reinforce her thankfulness for her own exceptional strength of mind' (1998a: 119). Meanwhile, the anxious Mrs Pullet and the comparatively steady Mrs Deane are narrowly focused on their own concerns. After Jeremy Tulliver goes bankrupt and Bessy must contemplate selling her belongings, Mrs Pullet volunteers to buy her spotted tablecloths because she has 'never had so many as she wanted o' that pattern, and they sha'n't go to strangers', but declines a teapot: 'I can't do with two silver teapots, not if it *hadn't* a straight spout' (1998a: 203, 208). Mrs Deane largely declines to help out because, as her husband's career has prospered, 'the Dodson linen and plate were beginning to hold quite a subordinate position, as a mere supplement to the handsomer articles of the same kind, purchased in recent years' (1998a: 206).

After recounting the environment in which the novel's protagonists are raised, the narrator directly addresses the reader in a confidential aside. 'I share with you this sense of oppressive narrowness', she remarks, 'but it is necessary that we should feel it, if we care to understand how it acted on the lives of Tom and Maggie' (1998a: 272–273). As I noted earlier, some critics have seen the novel's depictions of the Tullivers and Dodson sisters as manifestly condescending. Simon Dentith argues that, on occasion, 'the potential comedy generated by historical distance can mutate into an uncomfortable social contempt for the world which the novel sets out to reconstruct'. Thus, the novel depicts Maggie and Tom maintaining deep ties 'to the very "oppressive narrowness" which at the same time they have to transcend' (2014: 43, 49). Certainly the narrator renders judgement in a candid and direct address to the reader: 'You could not live among such people; you are stifled for want of an outlet toward something beautiful, great, or noble; you are irritated with these dull men and women' (1998a: 272). This may seem like a moment in which the reader merely exists theoretically, as the subject of the speculative remark about one's possible responses. But the narrator's further encouragement, a bit later in the novel, that 'if you are inclined to be severe . . ., remember that the responsibility of tolerance lies with those who have the wider vision', provides instruction to the actual reader in how to respond sympathetically (1998a: 500).

This wider vision is not simply the product of historical distance. Rather, it is an aspirational horizon. For the narrator suggests that one can come to a negative conclusion about the villagers, including the Tullivers and the Dodson sisters, only by '[o]bserving these people narrowly' (1998a: 500). If one steps back, a more complicated picture comes into view. After Bessy has lost most of the household items, she is rendered somewhat listless. The narrator observes:

> Yet amidst this helpless imbecility there was a touching trait of humble, self-devoting maternity . . . . She would let Maggie do none of the work that was heaviest and most soiling to the hands, and was quite peevish when Maggie attempted to relieve her from her grate-brushing

and scouring: 'Let it alone, my dear; your hands 'ull get as hard as hard,' she would say; 'it's your mother's place to do that. I can't do the sewing – my eyes fail me.' And she would still brush and carefully tend Maggie's hair, which she had become reconciled to, in spite of its refusal to curl, now it was so long and massy. Maggie was not her pet child, and, in general, would have been much better if she had been quite different; yet the womanly heart, so bruised in its small personal desires, found a future to rest on in the life of this young thing, and the mother pleased herself with wearing out her own hands to save the hands that had so much more life in them. (1998a: 277)

Moreover, when Maggie is cast out of Dorlcote Mill by her brother Tom, after her virtue is compromised by inadvertently spending the night with Stephen Guest, her mother refuses to leave her side. Of Mrs Tulliver, the narrator avers: 'The only thing clear to her was the mother's instinct that she would go with her unhappy child' (1998a: 486).

But instead of elevating a mother's impulse to love and protect her child above other human bonds, the novel shows how it is matched by compassionate neighbourliness. After departing Dorlcote Mill, Maggie and her mother seek lodgings at the home of Bob Jakin and his family. In her childhood, Maggie had judged Bob an 'irregular character, perhaps even slightly diabolical' because of his love for snakes and bats (1998a: 47). But as they grow older, Bob, who is without a formal education, recognises Maggie's love of learning and thus the severe blow that was dealt her when the family's belongings were sold off. Motivated by the same impulse as the ladies of *Cranford*, who rally around Miss Matty after the failure of the joint-stock bank in which her funds are invested, Bob brings her an old *Keepsake*, a literary annual, as well as several issues of a lavishly illustrated periodical. The moment is worth quoting at some length in order to capture the act of kindliness:

'See here!' he said again, laying the red parcel on the others and unfolding it; 'you won't think I'm a-makin' too free, Miss, I hope, but I lighted on these books, and I thought they might make up to you a bit for them as you've lost; for I heared you speak o' pictures, – an' as for pictures, *look* here!'

The opening of the red handkerchief had disclosed a superannuated 'Keepsake' and six or seven numbers of a 'Portrait Gallery', in royal octavo; and the emphatic request to look referred to a portrait

Landscape-Shaped Subjectivity: Eliot's 'Mother Tongue' 201

of George the Fourth in all the majesty of his depressed cranium and voluminous neckcloth.

'There's all sorts o' genelmen here,' Bob went on, turning over the leaves with some excitement, 'wi' all sorts o' nones, – an' some bald an' some wi' wigs, – Parlament genelmen, I reckon. An' here,' he added, opening the 'Keepsake', – '*here's* ladies for you, some wi' curly hair and some wi' smooth, an' some a-smiling wi' their heads o' one side, an' some as if they were goin' to cry, – look here, – a-sittin' on the ground out o' door, dressed like the ladies I'n seen get out o' the carriages at the balls in th' Old Hall there. My eyes! I wonder what the chaps wear as go a-courtin' 'em! I sot up till the clock was gone twelve last night, a-lookin' at 'em, – I did, – till they stared at me out o' the pictures as if they'd know when I spoke to 'em. But, lors! I shouldn't know what to say to 'em. They'll be more fittin' company for you, Miss; and the man at the book-stall, he said they banged iverything for picturs; he said they was a fust-rate article.' (1998a: 282)

Bob's gift replaces the substantive books Maggie has lost to bankruptcy with literary annuals, which Eliot frequently derides in her fiction. But Maggie is 'deeply touched' by Bob's gesture, as the reader is cued to be as well. She initially presumes that she will need to pay him back with money that she does not have. Indeed, *The Keepsake* was, for many, prohibitively expensive. It was the first literary annual to be sold for a guinea (Harris 2015: 148), which drove up the cost of outdated copies obtained second hand. Bob rejects any such payment: 'I'd ha' gev three times the money if they'll make up to you a bit for them as was sold away from you Miss. For I'n niver forgot how you looked when you fretted about the books bein' gone' (1998a: 282–283).

This same spirit of concern for the wellbeing of Tom and Maggie motivates his attempt to help them financially as well. With few resources of his own, Bob has recently received a payment of ten sovereigns for helping to put out a fire at a nearby mill. Although he mulls what he might be able to do with those funds ('I should go about the country far an' wide, an' come round the women wi' my tongue, an' get my dinner hot at the public, – lors! it 'ud be a lovely life!' [1998: 240]), he 'resolutely' settles on sharing nine of the coins with Tom and Maggie: 'I shall p'r'aps have a chance o' dousing another fire afore long. I'm a lucky chap. So I'll thank you to take the nine suvreigns, Mr Tom, and set yoursen up with 'em somehow, if it's true as the master's broke. They mayn't go fur enough, but they'll help' (1998a: 240–241). What follows is a protracted exchange between Bob, who attempts to place the coins in Tom's hands, and the Tulliver siblings, who each reject their friends' prioritisation of their needs over his own.

Where John Ruskin praised Mitford for finding 'romance enough' in a tale of the miller's daughter, he derided Eliot's tale of the miller's children. Unlike a genre painting by Teniers, which Mitford herself evokes in her use of pictorial language and a direct reference to the Flemish Baroque artist, Ruskin considered *The Mill on the Floss* to consist of 'the sweepings out of a Pentonville omnibus' (1881: 521). His criticism is twofold. First, he contends, Eliot is entirely too interested in characters who are faulty, imperfect, off putting: their 'blotches, burrs and pimples' are made evident for all to see. Yet although Maggie's aunts and uncles fail to act as Bob Jakin does during her time of need, the narrator nevertheless encourages the reader to see them in a broader light than her characterisation of them as oppressive. Despite their individual shortcomings, they possess such traits as 'honour and rectitude', which the narrator explicitly juxtaposes with a more modern, city-based sensibility. 'Honour and rectitude', she insists, are a 'proud tradition ... which has been the salt of our provincial society' (1998a: 127).

In analogising the novel's characters to riders of an omnibus in a lower middle class London suburb, Ruskin's second (implied) criticism is that they are too modern. He had praised Mitford for living in the country and among the people. Eliot, he suggests, writes about rural figures from an anachronistic and urban perspective. But the world of the Dodsons and the Tullivers was one with which she was intimately familiar, having been raised in Nuneaton by parents who had limited resources and who counted themselves as members of the lower middle class. As the next section makes evident, Eliot was certainly interested in the relationship between the historical setting of her fiction and the modernity of its readers.

A sense of place

If Eliot is moved by such familial characteristics as honour and rectitude, she also appreciates those who possess a strong relationship to place. Focusing much of the novel on the heated dispute between Tulliver and Wakem, Eliot attempts to demonstrate that property

Landscape-Shaped Subjectivity: Eliot's 'Mother Tongue' 203

is an insufficient foundation for collective life in the modern era: it is exclusionary, divisive and non-portable – that is, it ties individuals to particular geographic localities at a time of increased mobility and thus inhibits the movement towards national and, ultimately, world community, a goal to which Eliot and many of her contemporaries were committed. St Ogg's, after all, is situated on that 'rich plain where the great river flows forever onward, and links the small pulse of the old English town with the beatings of the world's mighty heart' (1998a: 272).[12]

In the early chapters of *The Mill on the Floss*, the narrator offers a generic and non-gendered human developmental narrative of the child's relationship to the land and the individuals who people it. The first stage in this process appears to be one in which the child and its 'home-scene' are inextricably intertwined. The term *home-scene*, as used in the novel, encompasses the particular locality and the human relations that constitute one's place of birth: the physical home located in a circumscribed geographical area and the set of familial and social relations to which it is tied. Thus, the narrator reflects on

> the happiness of seeing the bright light in the parlour at home ... the happiness of passing from the cold air to the warmth and kisses and the smiles of that familiar hearth, where the pattern of the rug and the grate and the fire-irons were 'first ideas' that it was no more possible to criticize than the solidity and extension of matter. There is no sense of ease like the ease we felt in those scenes where we were born, where objects became dear to us before we had the labour of choice, and where the outer world seemed only an extension of our personality: we accepted it and loved it as we accepted our own sense of existence and our limbs. (1998a: 151)

According to this passage, the outer and inner worlds, or psychic and external reality, interact in complex ways. They are not opposed; rather, each is crucial to shaping the other. On the one hand, objects and human relations are represented as fully exterior to the self: domestic objects and human affections constitute an 'outer world'. On the other hand, domestic objects are also experienced as parts of the self: the 'pattern of the rug and the grate and the fire-irons' constitute the child's 'first ideas', or the substance of inchoate mental processes. The home-scene is considered an extension of one's own 'existence' and of one's very 'limbs' (1998a: 151).

In its fusion of past and present, and in its association of memories with particular objects, this passage manifests a strong indebtedness to William Wordsworth.[13] But the complex child psychology delineated by the novel also anticipates what psychoanalyst Nancy Chodorow has described as the projective and introjective identifications that express and create personal fantasies. Through projection and projective identification, parts of the self, such as feelings or beliefs, are put into an external other or object, whereas in introjective identification 'parts of the other [or object] can be taken away from that other and put into the self' (Chodorow 1999: 276n1). These mutually interacting modes of identification are essential to constituting individual subjectivity. Within the world of the novel, we see a similar process, although posited as universal rather than individual, whereby the child introjects aspects of the home-scene ('we accepted it [the outer world] and loved it as we accepted our own sense of existence and our limbs'). Indeed, the narrator observes, 'We could never have loved the earth so well if we had had no childhood in it' (1998a: 41). The strange syntax of this sentence suggests a childlike failure to differentiate between subject and object. In this tautological world, self and home-scene are intertwined. Because a home-scene encompasses domestic objects and familial and neighbourly relations, all are depicted as constitutive of the self. 'Every one of those keen moments' of human interrelationship lives within the child and the adult into whom the child grows (1998a: 66).

The child projects itself onto its home-scene as well. The narrator hastens to add that the landscape in which domestic objects and human affections find meaning and expression is one of the most crucial parts of a child's psychology: 'One's delight in an elderberry bush overhanging the confused leafage of a hedgerow bank', the narrator continues, is 'a more gladdening sight than the finest cistus or fuchsia spreading itself on the softest and undulating turf' if the latter are visually apprehended outside of the domestic and familiar context (1998a: 152). This, the narrator admits, might seem like an 'unjustifiable preference to a nursery-gardener, or to any of those severely regulated minds who are free from the weakness of any attachment that does not rest on the demonstrable superiority of qualities' (1998a: 152). But preference rests, the narrator insists, not on any qualities inherent in a given object but on one's own emotional investments.

Landscape-Shaped Subjectivity: Eliot's 'Mother Tongue'   205

These affective relationships to the objects that constitute one's home-scene are nurtured through the senses. Childhood, as rendered in the novel, is a positively sensual experience. Although the lit parlour mentioned in the long passage quoted earlier generates a visual gratification, touch is also emphasised: the tactile pleasures of both the heat emanating from the fireplace and the physical expressions of human warmth, the salutation of 'warmth and kisses' that evoke the emotional ideal of the familial hearth. According to the *Oxford English Dictionary*, touch is 'the exercise of the faculty of feeling upon a material object'; feeling is bound up with tactual sensation. 'Although touch is not an emotion', Ashley Montagu points out, 'its sensory elements induce those neural, glandular, muscular, and mental changes which in combination we call an emotion', and touch is thus directly linked to psychic life (1998a: 128).

In fact, the 'smiles of that familiar hearth' that greet the child on its return home are themselves signifiers of pleasure. Since the end of the eighteenth century, many had come to believe that smiles reflected the early tactual reciprocity between the child and the mother's breast. 'In the action of sucking,' Erasmus Darwin observed in the 1790s, 'the lips of the infants are closed around the nipple of the mother till he has filled his stomach, and the pleasure occasioned by the stimulus of this grateful food succeeds.' The lips, which relax on releasing themselves from the mother's nipple, 'produce the smile of pleasure: as cannot but be seen by all who are conversant with children' (1801: 1.206). The 'happiness of passing from the cold air to the warmth and kisses and the smiles of that familiar hearth', therefore, seems to evoke a very specific kind of pleasure: the state of symbiosis first experienced at the mother's breast. This oral-tactile pleasure provides the paradigm for all subsequent states of enjoyment.

As posited by the novel, other modes of sensual perception play an equal role in the child's construction of its world. The child's 'growing senses', the novel argues, are nourished in the geographic location of its home-scene by the 'familiar flowers', 'bird-notes . . . [against a] sky with its fitful brightness', and the 'furrowed and grassy fields, each with a sort of personality given to it by the capricious hedgerows' (1998a: 263, 41). The 'familiar flowers' evoke a profusion of smells, while the harmonious panoply of 'bird-notes' from sparrows, thrushes and others uttering their joyful sounds beneath a 'sky with its fitful brightness', suggest a rich auditory experience. The array of bird notes, chirping crickets and rustling leaves constitutes rural life's affective rhythm. At other times, however, the silencing of such sound is celebrated: 'The rush of the water, and the booming of the mill, bring a dreamy deafness, which seems to heighten the peacefulness of the scene. They are like a great curtain of sound, shutting one out from the world beyond' (1998a: 8). This hermetically sealed world generates a child's delight in dreamy quiet: 'the light dipping sounds of the rising fish, and the gentle rustling . . . of the willows and the reeds' (1998a: 40). As Susanne K. Langer points out, 'sound, to our ears, is diffuse, like smell' (1972: 134). Tactual and visual perceptions combine with the diffusiveness of sounds and smells to envelop the child in a range of pleasurable sensations.

The Mill on the Floss delineates an inner-object world, fashioned through projective and introjective identifications, which tells a kind of proto-story of the self. It provides an account of *Bildung* that is as much phenomenological as it is ontological – charting the movement from the love of the home-scene because it is perceived to be a *part* of the self to the love of the home-scene because one perceives it as *distinct* from the self. According to the novel, identity is redefined and reshaped through a series of 'collisions' between the 'outward and the inward' as the child becomes cognizant of its individual identity (1998a: 235). The dilemma the novel faces is how to account for the emergent self's continuing to love the home-scene once it perceives itself to be a distinct entity. What is the affective tie that will bind the child to the home-scene after the child has determined that it is separate from the landscape, the home and the set of relations that reside there? The novel resolves this dilemma by not completely demarcating the boundaries between subject and object. Indeed, the home-scene is retained within the individual long after the threshold of adulthood has been crossed: 'the sunshine and the grass in the far-off years', the narrator notes, 'still live in us', and the human relationships that are also constitutive of the home-scene leave their 'trace' as well, continuing to 'live . . . in us still' (1998a: 42, 66). The sunshine and grass of the home-scene, and the set of relations that it nourishes, continue to live on in the inner depths of one's being through memory and the feelings it generates. Thus, 'all long-known objects, even a mere window fastening or a particular door-latch, have sounds which are a sort of recognized voice to us, – a voice that will thrill and awaken, when it has been used to touch deep-lying fibres'

(1998a: 221). Although separation from the home-scene occurs on one level, conjunction is maintained on another.

In a retrospective assessment of *The Mill on the Floss*, Eliot thought that the time spent on childhood scenes constituted both the novel's greatest strength as well as a significant weakness. Writing in January 1861 to the artist François D'Albert-Durade, she notes: 'I am glad that you think there are any readers who will prefer the *Mill* to *Adam* [*Bede*]. To my feeling there is more thought and a profounder veracity in the *Mill* than in *Adam*; but *Adam* is more complete and better balanced. My love of the childhood scenes made me linger over them in an epic fashion' (Eliot 1999: 42). Eliot's stated commitment to veracity, or the capacity to perceive and convey truth, points towards the theory her novel unfolds. In the process of separation, the child begins to develop 'long memories... [of] superadded life in the life of others' (1998a: 235). As the self cannot be completely differentiated from the landscape of its home-scene, so too is it unable to differentiate itself completely from the neighbourly and familial relations that constitute this 'superadded' life. The narrator notes that an understanding of the interconnectivity of human life does not occur in the self-centredness of youth, when 'the soul is made of wants', but only at a point in life in which one has the capacity for 'long memories' (1998a: 235). This superadded life suggests a collective dimension to the self. The novel's theorisation of childhood development proposes that the self is essentially relational – a notion for which the child nursing at the mother's breast is paradigmatic.

Having established a general model of psychosocial development in which spatial and temporal experiences shape and then increasingly call attention to the self as communal, the novel then attempts to account for the way those ties are both continually reaffirmed and expressed. Because the self, according to the logic of the novel, emerges from the social and physical geography of one's home-scene, that geography, in turn, serves as the symbol for one's communal sense of self, reinforcing associative and affective ties to person and place. Landscape and human relations become metonyms for each other – the landscape standing for familial and social obligations and affections, and familial and social obligations and affections standing for the particular geographic locality of one's home-scene.

The concept of a landscape-shaped subjectivity allows Eliot to formulate an implicit critique of the gendered ontology of possessive individualism. (This was Mill's concern as well but, as I will shortly argue, Eliot sought to distinguish her vision from his.) The novel contrasts the relationship to the homescene of Mr Tulliver and his son Tom with the daughter Maggie's relationship, thereby suggesting that males transform their emotions into material property ownership while women retain their affective ties to the land. Because Maggie lacks property and is coded as incomprehensibly foreign, she is linked to other internal aliens such as the gypsies to whom she briefly flees.[14]

Dorlcote Mill has been in the Tulliver family for generations and Mr Tulliver believes in the perpetual transmission of fixed property. 'There's a story as when the mill changes hands, the river's angry', Tulliver tells one of his employees. 'I've heard my father say it many a time'. While Tulliver recognises that there is 'no telling whether there mayn't be summat in the story', the tale makes a larger claim about property inheritance: generational transmission relies on notions of naturalness, permanence and security (1998a: 263). As the holder of landed property, therefore, Tulliver feels a responsibility not just to his children but also to his forebears – the grandfather who told his stories of the family's lineage, the father who first started the malting of cereal grains on the property. When threatened with the prospect of losing the mill over a complicated legal entanglement involving a neighbour's siphoning off of river water to irrigate his own farmlands, Tulliver feels his very identity threatened: 'I should go off my head in a new place. I should be like as if I'd lost my way' (1998a: 263).

For Tulliver, property becomes indistinguishable from his sense of self. 'The strongest influence of all was the love of the old premises where he had run about when he was a boy, just as Tom had done after him', the narrator observes. When Tulliver walks across his property and 'look[s] at all the old objects', we are told, he

> felt the strain of his clinging affection for the old home as part of his life, part of himself. He couldn't bear to think of himself living on any other spot than this, where he knew the sound of every gate door, and felt that the shape and colour of every roof and weather-stain and broken hillock was good, because his growing senses had been fed on them.... Tulliver felt for this spot, where all his memories centred, and where life seemed like a familiar smooth-handled tool that the fingers clutch with loving ease. (1998a: 263)

Yet, although Tulliver retains an affective relationship to his home-scene, the novel emphasises how his emotions are tied primarily to legal ownership. His property deeds and promissory notes, kept in a tin chest that 'had belonged to his father and his father's father', are represented as the core of his self-understanding (1998a: 221).[15] The novel suggests, therefore, that for men, affective ties are conflated with possession.

At the beginning of the nineteenth century Jeremy Bentham formulated an account of property and its relationship to the emotions. One's emotions, Bentham argues, are first intertwined with property. The relationship between the owner and the thing owned is less material than it is 'metaphysical' (1931: 112). An object, in other words, never has any intrinsic value residing within it; its value as property is always based on an owner's 'conception' of that value. This is why, according to Bentham, neither one's individual relationship to property – 'to have a thing in our hands, to keep it, to make it, to sell it, to work it up into something else' (1931: 112) – nor the sum total of those various relationships adequately renders a definition of property. One's relationship to property is always intangible.

The relationship between owner and property, Bentham contends, is rooted in expectation. By definition forward-looking, expectation functions as 'a chain' that connects points on a temporal and generational plane (1931: 111). The parent who owns property can both enjoy it in the present and look forward to the pleasure the child will receive on inheriting it, and that child, too, sees his future as intertwined with the property that will one day be his. A significant but overlooked aspect to property, Bentham therefore argues, is our emotional investment in it. We come to see a portion of ourselves in the property we own or in the property that we recognise will one day be ours. In Bentham's account, the law fixes expectation; without law there would be no property. Because the law protects one's right to property, the law renders the notion of it as 'fixed and durable' and therefore transmittable to the generation that follows (1931, 110). When those expectations are destabilised, Bentham argues, a 'distinct and special evil' called 'a pain of disappointment' is experienced by the owner (1931: 112). This pain, like that experienced by Mr Tulliver when his ownership of the mill is placed in jeopardy, threatens the self's very sense of futurity.

Similarly, Tom Tulliver can be understood primarily in terms of familial legacy and obligation. His emotions are bound up with physical property and Tom's life focus becomes eradicating his father's debt and winning the mill back from the lawyer Wakem, who has acquired it. These overarching life goals are structured in terms of a generational obligation. Mr Tulliver insists that if Tom means to be his son he will promise 'never [to] forgive' Wakem and to secure, for future generations, 'th' old place' where Tom, Mr Tulliver and Mr Tulliver's father were all born (1998a: 267). Tom must master the emerging capitalist economy in order to eradicate the debt and fulfil his generational duty. Tom thus assumes his father's belief in the '*a priori* ground of family relationship and monetary obligation' (Carroll 1992: 225).

As the intermediaries between the past and future, Mr Tulliver and Tom link the generations to a common way of life. The generational transmission of property is, as Andrew Reeve points out, a way of 'tying individuals into the community through the agency of the family' (1986: 84). But Eliot is sceptical of this form of affiliation and the political rights that are conferred on the subject. To claim that emotions are tied to property is to exclude women from a theory of national citizenship, since they have no legal right to ownership. Eliot critiques property not because women lack access to it but rather because ownership perverts the original relationship to the land – represented by the non-gendered developmental narrative with which the first half of the novel is concerned – that men and women hold in common. The home-scene that figures so prominently for Maggie, therefore, is represented not so much as a compensatory mechanism, a way of affectively binding to a community from which she is barred materially, but as a kind of 'pure' tie to the landscape that is increasingly affected by processes of acculturation for both Eliot's male *and* female characters.[16]

The processes by which male characters have their affective relations to the land transformed into property ownership are shown to have disastrous consequences for the provincial community, especially as the male characters begin to disagree about the most appropriate economic base for community life. Mr Tulliver's belief in land tenure is contrasted with the perception held by Mr Deane, Mr Wakem and Stephen Guest that the town of St Ogg's must embrace a capitalist system of circulation and possession. Similarly, the dispute between Tulliver and Wakem over

Landscape-Shaped Subjectivity: Eliot's 'Mother Tongue' 211

the changing legal definition of property tears Maggie and Tom's family apart. The novel suggests that possessive individualism is inherently divisive and destructive: it engenders envy, malice and atomistic tendencies.

Possessive individualism is also represented as leading to a diminution of the senses. An ideology of proprietary subjectivity, by focusing on ownership rather than experience, deadens the human sensorium. Eliot captures this tendency in her representation of Tom's schooling:

> Tom found, to his disgust, that his new drawing-master gave him no dogs and donkeys to draw, but brooks and rustic bridges and ruins, all with a general softness of black-lead surface, indicating that nature, if anything, was rather satiny; and as Tom's feeling for the picturesque in landscape was at present quite latent . . . Mr. Tulliver, having a vague intention that Tom should be put to some business which included the drawing out of plans and maps, had complained . . . that Tom seemed to be learning nothing of that sort; whereupon that obliging adviser had suggested that Tom should have drawing-lessons. (1998a: 167)

Here Tom recoils from the idea of drawing picturesque landscapes of the type that the narrator celebrates. Instead of such borderless, intangible, emotionally evocative scenes, Tom, having developed at an early age a 'desire for mastery over . . . inferior animals' (1998a: 92), hopes to draw countable, quantifiable objects such as donkeys and dogs that can be appropriated and subjected to human domination. This preference coincides with his father's own ambitions for Tom – that he learn to draw maps and plans as a way of maintaining and extending the family property.

Since 1841, more than a decade after the period in which the novel is set, Ordnance Surveys have mapped property boundaries in the United Kingdom. Prior to this time, the country had long possessed an informal cadastral system in which land was divided into counties, shires and parishes as well as individual fields for agricultural production (Kain and Baigent 1992: 236–64). Throughout the late 1820s through the 1830s, Parliament debated various schemes that might more closely approximate the national cadastral systems on the Continent in which land, once regulated by use-rights, is converted into Euclidean space regulated by property rights and providing the boundaries of taxation. Jeremy Tulliver's ambition for his son represents the growing interest in transforming concrete landscapes into abstract representations that would enable a more efficient exploitation of property.

Like Eliot, Mill was not a proponent of possessive individualism or liberal atomism. Nevertheless, his writings leading up to the period in which Eliot was composing *The Mill on the Floss* imagined an abstracted individual – what Arnold, developing this line of thought, would term the *best self* – as the basis for political subjectivity. In contrast to the dominating tendencies associated with possessive individualism, or the abstractions of Millian liberalism, landscape-shaped subjectivity, which the novel links to authentic selfhood, is concerned with symbiosis and fusion. Eliot can be seen here as attempting to theorise what the psychoanalyst Hans Loewald calls the 'sense of and longing for nonseparateness and undifferentiation' (1980: 402). A model of human development that reaches its pinnacle in the individuated, autonomous adult, Loewald points out, has been increasingly complicated by analytic research that validates 'another striving, that for unity' (1980: 401). A century before Loewald, *The Mill on the Floss* presents a similar understanding of psychic life.

Yet the consequences of proprietary thinking are shown to corrupt even those relationships to the landscape that remain primarily affective, generating cognitive limitations by circumscribing aspiration, imagination, ideas and desire. Towards the end of the novel, Maggie explains to Stephen Guest that, because they have both committed to other relationships, they cannot pursue their mutual romantic feelings; to do so would betray the ties and obligations that constitute a home-scene. When Maggie insists that she can no longer see Stephen, the slippage between 'I' and 'we' raises the difficulty of separating self from world:

> It seems right to me sometimes that we should follow our strongest feeling; – but then, such feelings continually come across the ties that all our former life has made for us – the ties that have made others dependent on us – and would cut them in two ... I must not, cannot, seek my own happiness by sacrificing others. (1998a: 570–571)

Maggie articulates a struggle between her desire for personal satisfaction and the expectations of a community. The happiness of many (Lucy Deane and her family, Philip Wakem, the Tullivers)

Landscape-Shaped Subjectivity: Eliot's 'Mother Tongue'   213

would be sacrificed for the happiness of the few. There are, Maggie argues, shared feelings, shared memories and shared senses of duty that must take precedence over the individual. It is not enough to say that Maggie internalises these shared memories and affections, as Hao Li (2000) has claimed, for according to the developmental narrative the text establishes, they are a part of her – the residual remains of a childhood (individual) inextricably intertwined with the home-scene (collective). When Maggie refers to those 'ties that all our former life has made for us – the ties that have made others dependent on us', she is referring to the collective aspects of the self: mutual affections and obligations originally conceived as constituting a part of oneself and later understood as continuing 'to live in us' (1998a: 42).

The landscape of one's home-scene, as I have suggested, stands in a figural relation to those ties. When Stephen later takes Maggie down the Floss, her response to the changing scenery indicates a growing unease: 'She looked at the far-stretching fields – at the banks close by – and felt that they were entirely strange to her' (1998a: 464). As the boat moves down a river that opens up onto the nation and ultimately the world, Maggie recalls familiar flora and the particular constellation of memories and obligations reflected by them. The local landscape, in other words, continues to generate a sense of shared obligations and affections among those individuals who populate it. Those obligations and affections, according to the logic of the passage, must be rooted in the local.

Maggie's question to Stephen – 'If the past is not to bind us, where can duty lie?' – is the psychological equivalent of Mr Tulliver's, and indeed Tom's, belief in the material possession and generational transmission of a particular place (1998a: 475). As Lawrence Stone and Jeanne Stone explain, from the seventeenth to the nineteenth centuries there was a pervasive 'sense of moral obligation felt by most great landowners ... that they were no more than trustees for the transmission intact of their patrimony' (1986: 78). By the end of *The Mill on the Floss*, Maggie has become nothing more than the trustee of memory and local communal obligations. In her representation of Maggie, Eliot suggests that a landscape-shaped subjectivity that is rooted to the local community is an inadequate foundation for modern, mobile life. It fixes the self, like landed property, to a particular geographic spot.

The national community of readers

In *The Mill on the Floss*, Eliot can be seen to echo Mitford's and Gaskell's strategy of offering a complex representation of her village, refusing a simple substitution of the local for the national by showing how St Ogg's, although not an industrial town, is connected to the many developments taking place elsewhere in England and beyond. In addition to debates over property, the novel alludes in its first paragraph to the social transformations inexorably leading to the first Reform Act. Cargo-bearing ships, including those 'laden with . . . the dark glitter of coal', sail down the Floss to the town of St Ogg's. From this single allusion to coal, an entire chain of associations is set in motion: mechanisation of the mills spurred the iron industry, which in turn drove the coal industry. The 'black ships' transporting coal were themselves the product of the shipbuilding industry, which relied on both iron and coal. In contrast to these signifiers of modernity, linked to Guest & Co., the local mill-owning, ship-building business, are the village's 'aged, fluted red roofs and the broad gables of its wharves between the low wooded hill and the river brink, tinging the water with a soft purple hue under the transient glance of this February sun' (1998a: 7). The growth of the coal and iron industries was one of the factors that spurred changes in representation in the following decade.

As opposed to a proprietary or a rational, dialogic model of citizenship, Eliot's notion of a landscape-shaped subjectivity is posited to have preceded forms of acculturation and, therefore, as being ungendered. But she also shows how this original tie is negatively shaped by systems of property ownership: affective ties in the case of the male characters become entwined with notions of property, while in the case of females these bonds and the obligations they evoke can be experienced as tragically confining, weighing down the self much like non-portable property. However, because landscape-shaped subjectivity has a communitarian dimension that possessive individualism does not, Eliot seeks to retain its best aspects, positing it as the basis for a more inclusive notion of national belonging.

Yet it is not to Maggie that the novel asks us to turn. She does not provide an example insofar as the affections and obligations that characterise her relationship to the home-scene are shown to be incapable of expanding beyond local geography. Unlike Maggie, the narrator – a number of similarities are drawn between the narrator and Maggie – has managed to leave the rural locality and yet retain what Eliot presents as the best aspects of an original tie to the land. While initially embedded in a web of social relations rooted to a particular spot, and therefore able to achieve a 'cultivated partiality' towards it (Anderson 2001: 121), the narrator has nevertheless also obtained the necessary building blocks to expand one's sympathies beyond the local home-scene, achieving what Amanda Anderson calls 'the reflectiveness that allows one to become a "citizen of the world"' (2001: 138).

Eliot, like many thinkers of her time, was committed to a vision of the progressive history of civilisation – from the local to the national and, ultimately, to the universal human community. One influential strand in Victorian political thinking defined the universal largely in terms of the nation. That is, the nation was understood and recognised to be the most common and therefore the most universal human community yet realised.[17] The nation was a step towards ultimate universality precisely because it was the most universal of human communities to date. Eliot repeatedly returns to this idea in her works from *Middlemarch* onwards. Especially in *Daniel Deronda*, relational ties of community, in its 'highest transformation', are shown to be global, although for Eliot such a sense of world community can only be achieved after the 'character of a nationality' has been cultivated (1995: 532). In *The Mill on the Floss*, Eliot begins the task of imagining psychological and social evolution towards world community. The 'natural history of our social life', Suzanne Graver points out in her reading of Eliot's essay on W. H. Riehl, 'finds its complement in what she later called a "natural history of mind"' (1994: 33). Eliot believed, in other words, that there were 'crucial correspondences' between social and psychological development, and she sought to reconcile local attachments with the reality of urban life.

The model for this reconciliation is thus the narrator, who provides a mechanism for blurring the distinctions among the reader's experiences of the past, the characters' experiences depicted in the novel, and the experiences of the extradiegetic narrator. Perhaps not as insistent as either Mitford's or Gaskell's narrators, the narrator of *The Mill on the Floss* nevertheless repeatedly uses, as we have seen, direct address to establish an intimacy with the reader: 'we must', '[y]ou could not', 'I share with you'. This form of address is one Eliot first utilised in *Scenes of Clerical Life*, which was, as with *Cranford* and *Our Village*, initially published serially. In her first work of fiction, Eliot employs a nameless narrator – in contrast to Mary Smith in *Cranford* or the engaged narrator of Mitford's tales – to speak directly to the reader. Robyn R. Warhol has noted how in 'Amos Barton', the first of the three clerical scenes published in the January and February 1857 issues of *Blackwood's Magazine*, Eliot 'uses the conceit of the reader's presence frequently' (1986: 13). By contrast, Warhol observes, 'Mr Gilfil's Love-Story', which appeared in the March, April and May issues, only uses this conceit on two occasions. 'Janet's Repentance', which was serialised from June to October, does not use it at all. Because Eliot read *Cranford* while straining to finish 'Mr Gilfil's Love-Story', Warhol speculates that the decline in the use of this conceit is indicative of 'the influence of Eliot's having internalized the method' of Gaskell's text (1986: 13).

However, *pace* Warhol, Eliot again uses the conceit in *The Mill on the Floss*. As I noted in the opening of this chapter, the dream sequence provides an occasion to suggest the reader's presence. Another moment occurs later in the novel, when the narrator assumes the responsibility of guiding the ostensibly metropolitan reader to this site in the country:

> we must enter the town of St Ogg's, – that venerable town with the red fluted roofs and the broad warehouse gables, where the black ships unlade themselves of their burthens from the far north, and carry away, in exchange, the precious inland products, the well-crushed cheese and the soft fleeces which my refined readers have doubtless become acquainted with through the medium of the best classic pastorals. (1998a: 115)

Just as Mitford claimed to offer her readers 'a pretty picture', but proceeded to depict her village as affected by national social and economic tumult, Eliot's 'picture of provincial life', as she characterised her novel in a letter to Blackwood, acknowledges the pastoral – of which the rural idyll is associated – only to differentiate her novel from it.

In fact, the novel presents its own material form as the objective correlative of the non-gendered and egalitarian model it outlines. The novel offers itself up to the middle-class reader, through a mode of circulation and possession distinctly less pernicious than landed or liquid property, as a means to resolve the problem

Landscape-Shaped Subjectivity: Eliot's 'Mother Tongue' 217

of gender-based division through the creation of a non-gendered community of readers who are summoned by the narrator to recognise their shared ties to the land. Eliot incorporates an attenuated version of the egalitarian impulse that gives her notion of landscape-shaped subjectivity its form into the novel itself.

Both the novel and the socially inclusive model of landscape-shaped subjectivity it depicts rely on an equivalence between reading and seeing. Flora are represented in the novel as containing linguistic aspects that one can read. Like novelistic reading, the landscape generates mental images that inculcate a sense of belonging; the landscape is figured here as a 'mother tongue' for a generalisable national 'we':

> The wood I walk in on this mild May day, with the young yellow-brown foliage of the oaks between me and the blue sky, the white star-flowers and the blue-eyed speedwell and the ground of ivy at my feet – what grove of tropic palms, what strange ferns or splendid broad-petalled blossoms, could ever thrill such deep and delicate fibres within me as this home-scene? These familiar flowers, these well-remembered bird-notes, this sky with its fitful brightness, these furrowed and grassy fields, each with a sort of personality given to it by the capricious hedgerows – such things as these are the mother-tongue of our imagination, the language that is laden with all the subtle inextricable associations the fleeting hours of childhood left behind them. (1998a: 41–42)

Although this passage does not refer to a peopled scene, it suggests the power of a national landscape – juxtaposing characteristically English and therefore 'familiar' oak and ivy with the 'tropic palms' and 'strange ferns' of colonial territories – to evoke ties among those who are positioned in some relation to the land. The landscape unites a people through a shared language. At the level of the individual, language plays a crucial role in establishing subjectivity and in constituting epistemological patterns. It shapes one's structures of feeling and thinking. Here the landscape is represented as the basis of sociality itself among the members of an implied national community who are presumed to have individual but related memories of, and affective associations with, rural localities, as signified by the narrator's shift from describing specific botanical items to a more intangible evocation ('such things as these'). The novel seems to suggest that these affectionate ties to the nation rather than to the locality as home-scene can serve as the basis for a more inclusive definition of citizenship.

Although I have dwelled on how the novel registers differences in the relationship to the landscape mediated through gender, there are moments when class inequalities are noted as well. When Tom Tulliver is sent to school, he receives instruction alongside the son of the lawyer Wakem. When it comes to drawing lessons, Tom finds – in a longer passage from which I quoted earlier – much 'to his disgust, that his new drawing-master gave him no dogs and donkeys to draw, but brooks and rustic bridges and ruins, all with a general softness of black-lead surface, indicating that nature, if anything, was rather satiny; and as Tom's feeling for the picturesque in landscape was at present quite latent' (1998a: 166–167). Precisely because his relationship to the land is a form of labour, Tom must learn how to view it differently, unlike Philip Wakem who possesses a 'self-taught skill in drawing' such scenes. Tom does indeed learn 'to make an extremely fine point to his pencil, and to represent landscape with a "broad generality"'. Yet, the narrator observes, Tom continued to find such a practice and the sketches they produced 'extremely dull' (1998a: 167).

By making the novel the means through which inclusiveness might be achieved, Eliot may very well be seen to ignore the class distinctions that inhibit the kind of community she labours to create. Yet unlike lessons in landscape draftsmanship, which focus on the acquisition of skills and remained relatively inaccessible to those without adequate means, *The Mill on the Floss* circulated widely. While Eliot opposes community and capitalism in the fictional world of her novel, in her life she attempted to utilise the capitalist book trade in order to shape a readership around notions of landscape and social inclusion. Her primary readership may very well have been 'the relatively small, intellectually and socially superior audience for which most of the great nineteenth-century authors wrote' (Altick 1998: 6). After all, instead of being serialised, the novel was originally published as a three-volume octavo and priced at 31s. 6d. Nevertheless, 6,000 copies were sold within two months of publication. Cheaper editions, such as the second which sold for 12s., the third for 6s. and the fourth for 3s. 6d., and more financially accessible reprints facilitated the novelist's entry – the identity of George Eliot now widely known – 'into every kind of home' (K. Hughes 2001: 3). Unlike landed property, the novel is potentially available to anyone.

Landscape-Shaped Subjectivity: Eliot's 'Mother Tongue' 219

In the many passages outlining the developmental stages of the child, the narrator moves effortlessly between describing the shaping influences of nature and culture in order to recreate for the reader through the rhythms of language the 'sense of ease' the child feels in 'those scenes where we were born' (1998a: 151). Eliot's descriptive evocations of the rural countryside attempt to teach the reader how to become more attuned to what is figured in the novel as a kind of collective unconscious. Eliot hopes that this reawakening to what is held in common will also facilitate a fusion between, in her view, the best aspects of the traditional and supposedly collectivist community and the modern, commercial and individualistic society. This union, while not represented as achievable within the world of the novel, is still held out as a possibility for her national readership. So, too, the cultivation of civic virtues such as honour, rectitude and generosity.

In providing a non-gendered model of psychosocial development, the novel attempts, I have argued, to accomplish two goals. First, it seeks to demonstrate how relations to the land become gendered and unequal. Property ownership perverts what the novel depicts as an originating and initially egalitarian relation to the land. Second, the novel endeavours to formulate a critique of possessive individualism and to offer an alternative by suggesting that the landscape functions as a vocabulary of images – which the narrator calls a 'mother tongue' – that unites geographically dispersed readers into a national community. Such national identifications, of course, are highly problematic. The dangers inherent in Eliot's dream, indeed in any dream, of a shared language are borne out in the trajectory of Eliot's use of the landscape as an image of communion, which, in *Impressions of Theophrastus Such*, becomes highly nationalistic.[18] In it, the narrator insists on a 'birthplace of common memories and habits of mind' that provide a 'sense of special belonging' (1994b: 156).

Contextualising *The Mill on the Floss* within debates on national belonging, one can discern an initial impulse towards deploying images of communion in ways that might mitigate social exclusion. A national community defined by the mind's interaction with the (represented if not actual) landscape is, at least in theory, available to anyone. The novel thus manifests a felt urgency for theorising new geographically and spatially produced subjectivities that are based neither on proprietary and gendered considerations nor exclusively on the rational faculties of the human mind. The extent to which the relations between person and place in Eliot's novel succeed, fail, or remain insufficiently theorised reflects the magnitude and difficulty of the struggle – imagining ties to place that do not obliterate the self and that, in the process, explore other potentialities and unfulfilled promises of both community and nation.

Notes

1 See Haight's thorough account of this episode (1968: 280–94).
2 In so doing, however, the act effectively narrowed the social dimension of politics – in which the rowdy crowd made their views known to electors – by establishing the basis for a more individualised and representative political system (Vernon 1993: 1–14; O'Gorman 1989: 107–112).
3 This is a point of some debate among scholars. However, as Richard Ashcraft concedes, there is no evidence to support a contention that Locke favoured universal manhood suffrage (1992: 767–68).
4 Arguing against the notion of a passive electorate, Frank O'Gorman suggests that formal contestations took place in one quarter to one third of all elections between 1754 and 1790 (1989: 107–112). For O'Gorman, the lack of a contest does not indicate political indifference but rather deference to a local patron. 'Conversely', he argues, 'the breakdown of deferential relationships leads to election contests' (1984: 401).
5 For example, Yvonne French contends that Gaskell's 'very Liberalism embraced every suffering creature on earth'. For French, this was 'a guarantee' against the insular outlook often attributed to the novelist (1958: 140).
6 Indeed, Mill lamented the state of education in his own time, in which students are trained to accept knowledge solely on the basis of the authority of the tutor, and particularly the requirement that graduating students at the universities of Oxford and Cambridge subscribe to the thirty-nine articles of the Church of England. Although education is supposed to widen the mind, he felt that pedagogical practices as well as making the acceptance of doctrinal tenets – 'a particular set of opinions' – a prerequisite for graduation stunted the development of the intellect (1977a: 141). He contrasts the 'dull and torpid assent' to the opinions of others with the dynamism of a 'living belief' (1977c, 248, 247).
7 For Mill, the attainment of one's own individuated opinions is the very definition of character: '[A] person whose desires and impulses

Landscape-Shaped Subjectivity: Eliot's 'Mother Tongue' 221

are his own – are the expression of his own nature, as it has been developed and modified by his own culture – is said to have a character. One whose desires and impulses are not his own, has no character, no more than a steam-engine has a character' (1977c: 264).

8 Mill's belief that participation in public life helps to engender political feeling is particularly evident in *On Liberty*, in which he advocates a society made up of reasonable individuals engaging in rational discussion about the affairs of the nation.

9 Elsewhere, I constellate John Stuart Mill's speculative thought and Anthony Trollope's fiction to argue for the importance of the 1860s as a unit of literary history. See Morrison, forthcoming.

10 A journal entry for 12 January indicates that she had begun research for the novel (Eliot 1998: 76).

11 Elizabeth Gaskell to George Eliot, 10 November 1859, in Chapple and Pollard 1966: 592.

12 Because Eliot, and Victorian thinkers more generally, conceived of a historical teleology from the local to the universal human community, proprietary subjectivity could generate cognitive limitations that inhibit the attainment of wider sympathies.

13 Although a number of authors had a profound effect on George Eliot, one of her greatest intellectual debts was to Wordsworth. 'I never before met with so many of my own feelings, expressed just as I could like them', Eliot wrote in her youth, referring to a six-volume edition of his poems that she owned (Eliot 1954a: 34). He remained an abiding presence throughout her life; she and G. H. Lewes would reread his poems with 'fresh admiration for his beauties and tolerance for his faults' (qtd. in Gill 1998: 145). On the importance of Wordsworth to Eliot, see, among others, Carpenter 1986; Gill 1998; and Homans 1986.

14 I borrow and slightly modify the phrase *incomprehensibly foreign* from Jacobus (1981: 213). On Maggie's link to the gypsies, see Carroll 2003: 40–51; Helsinger 1997: 229; and Nord 2006: 101–109.

15 See Levy (2003), who provides a useful reading of this scene in terms of 'property morality'.

16 Elizabeth Helsinger has argued that we should recognise the attachment to a homescene as a turn away from the property and commercialism that define national economic life. In her account, Maggie embraces, instead, emotionally resonant home-scenes 'that she values as representations of the local affections embedded in them' (1997: 225). Helsinger contends that Maggie should be understood through her sentimental attachment to the land of her birth: 'Maggie's access

to the representational power of the home scene is offered as some compensation for the wider life – participation in (national) history – which she is denied' (1997: 229). For Helsinger, the home-scene provides Maggie with some solace for the social exclusion that she so painfully registers.

17 As H. S. Jones explains, 'Most nineteenth-century liberals, at least until the last decade or two of the century, were nationalists because they saw the nation as a step away from the particular and towards the universal' and, therefore, 'the most general and universal of actual communities' (2000: 49).

18 On the importance of such 'image[s] of communion' to national fantasy, see B. Anderson 1991: 6.

5

A Wider Horizon: Portable Interiority and Provincial Life

George Eliot's *Middlemarch* (1871–72) is not generally considered to be a political novel. That appellation is instead bestowed most often on *Felix Holt, the Radical*, with *Romola* usually not far behind. Published in fourteen monthly parts between July 1862 and August 1863 in *Cornhill Magazine*, *Romola* explores fifteenth-century Florentine republican politics through the anti-Papist reform championed by Girolamo Savonarola and the competing vision of Niccolò Machiavelli. The novel was, in George Henry Lewes's characterisation, 'flatly received by the general public though it has excited a deep enthusiasm in almost all the élite' (Haight 1968: 4, 102). This was certainly an overstatement. Stung by the criticism of *Romola*, Eliot returned to the English Midlands with *Felix Holt*. John Morley likely spoke for many in literary and intellectual circles when he insisted in a review of this later novel that, although the public holds no right to lambaste a writer for changing characters or locales, 'we may still rejoice that she has again come back to those studies of English life, so humorous, so picturesque, and so philosophical, which at once raised her into the very first rank among English novelists' (1866a: 723). Accustomed to Eliot's depictions of English rural life in *Scenes of Clerical Life*, *Adam Bede*, *The Mill on the Floss* and *Silas Marner*, reviewers and readers had simply baulked at her experiment.

Yet *Romola* and *Felix Holt* share an underlying concern. In *Romola*, Eliot attempts to think through the democratic reforms undertaken in her own time by displacing them onto a different country and an earlier era. In *Felix Holt*, which was written against the backdrop of parliamentary debates surrounding a further extension of the franchise, she explores the consequences of the Great Reform Act of 1832 on the fictional market town of Treby Magna. Harold Transome, the Tory landowner who cynically runs on a platform of reform, and his electioneering agent Matthew Jermyn are positively Machiavellian in manipulating the 'faith in the efficacy of political change' unleashed by the first Reform Act (Eliot 1871: 203).

In 1865, as she was preparing to write *Felix Holt*, Eliot re-read John Stuart Mill's *On Liberty* and *Considerations on Representative Government*, which were republished that year in inexpensive editions. In a 10 July 1865 letter to Clementia Taylor, she observed: 'I agree with you in your feeling about Mill. Some of his works have been frequently my companions of late, and I have been going through many *actions de grace* towards him.' Of Mill's decision to stand for a parliamentary seat in the 1866 general election, Eliot expressed a lack of enthusiasm: 'I am not anxious that he should be in Parliament: thinkers can do more outside than inside the House'. 'But it would have been a fine precedent, and would have made an epoch, for such a man to have been asked for and elected solely on the ground of his mental eminence. As it is, I suppose it is pretty certain that he will *not* be elected' (Eliot 1955b: 196). In the event, Mill was returned.

Although Eliot may not have accurately predicted the outcome of Mill's electoral contest, her statement about the relationship of thinkers to politics provides some insight into how she approached the craft of novel writing. Eliot is not making a bald assertion along the lines of Anthony Trollope, who claimed that – having contested and lost an election to be the Member of Parliament for Beverley – he wrote novels to express his political sentiments. In fact, as Nancy Henry has cautioned, it is quite difficult to discern Eliot's convictions from her fiction because 'her aim as an artist was to make a character's political opinions consistent with his psychology and behaviour' (2019: 170).

Because *Middlemarch* is set in roughly the same period as *Felix Holt*, I want to revisit the question of its political depth. While *Felix Holt* takes place just after the passage of the 1832 Reform Act, *Middlemarch* is set just before it. A number of critics, such as Terry Eagleton and Bernard Semmel, would assuredly disagree with me that such an inquiry is worth undertaking. In Eagleton's view, *Middlemarch* 'is an historical novel in form with little substantive historical content'. He continues: 'The Reform Bill, the railways, cholera, machine-breaking: these "real" historical forces do no more than impinge on the novel's margins' as the historical is 'displaced into ethical, and so "timeless", terms' (1998: 120). Whereas Eagleton sees such displacement as a typically liberal move, Bernard Semmel argues that Eliot stands aloof from 'English advanced liberals [who] had long bestowed [support] on French Revolutionary movements'. She is, he contends, one who generally refrained from advocating substantive political reform in England (1994: 91). Both readings – that Eliot is either too liberal or not liberal enough – raise the question of Eliot's understanding of what constitutes British national subjectivity.

In fact, Eliot considered political reform to be one of the most important changes to occur over the span of her life. She writes in her notebook that the First Reform Act produced a heightened consciousness of interdependency:

> No man now can help seeing that many of his interests are held by him in common with other men, & he can hardly even be selfish in an isolated fashion. Within lives still vigorous there have been changes such as the First Reform Bill ..., which have given a keen experimental sense that public action is also a private affair. (qtd. in Pinney 1966: 372)[1]

According to Eliot, therefore, a democratising polity – of which she saw the First Reform Act as an initial step – engenders in individuals a feeling that what takes place in the public sphere has immediate significance to them. As her narrator puts it in *Middlemarch*, 'reform' plays a 'notable part ... in developing the political consciousness' (1996: 82). Yet because, as Eliot well knew, the parliamentary act only modestly extended the franchise, she is not thereby asserting that the right to vote creates this feeling.

As I noted in the previous chapter, John Stuart Mill believed otherwise. Without the right to vote, he argued, individuals had no particular reason to see themselves as part of the social collectivity of the nation. In *Considerations on Representative Government* Mill further expands on the ideas first articulated in his pamphlet 'Thoughts on Parliamentary Reform'. By participating in enlightened debate and 'collective political action', he contends, each individual would cultivate fellow feeling and become 'consciously a member of a great community' (1977b: 469). Weighing various competing ideas and subjecting one's own 'private partialities' in such debates to the 'principles and maxims which have for their reason of existence the common good', one would become attuned to feelings 'for the general interest' (1977b: 411–412). The exercise of rational choice through the electoral process constitutes, in Mill's account, an essential means of expressing ties to the nation.

Eliot had little faith in the franchise as the basis for attachment, although she considered it to be one of its essential expressions. Instead, I will argue, she is interested in how the feeling of citizenship – that the movement towards representative government engenders ('No man now can help seeing that many of his interests are held by him in common with other men') – shapes imagination, thought and action. In *Middlemarch*, Eliot revisits her notion of the 'home-scene', which, as I argued in Chapter Four, is used by the narrator as an umbrella term to encompass the landscape, physical buildings and set of social relations located in the circumscribed geographic setting of one's birth. Instead of serving to limit the individual, however, as it does in *The Mill on the Floss*, the dynamic of exchange between mind and landscape paradoxically generates what we might call a *portable interiority* that does not require physical attachment to the local, and raises the possibility of a national interiority of affectionate ties to the nation as home-scene.[2]

Rootlessness and rootedness

John Stuart Mill, like Eliot, was interested in social feeling and its relationship to the imagination. In an essay published in the *Westminster Review* (of which Eliot, for reasons I discussed in Chapter Four, would have been well aware), Mill writes: 'The pains of others, though naturally painful to us, are not so until we have realised them by an act of imagination, implying voluntary attention' (1969a: 61). He suggests, therefore, that each individual has the capacity to feel for others, but depends on the imaginative faculty, which must be developed, in order to actualise it. In *Utilitarianism* (1863), mentioned in Eliot's *Middlemarch* notebooks as a text she read while preparing to write the novel, Mill launched a stinging critique of Jeremy Bentham over his lack of social feeling. The leading proponent of utilitarianism and a family friend who helped to raise him, Bentham was, in Mill's estimation, psychologically underdeveloped: 'the faculty by which one mind understands a mind different from itself, and throws itself into the feelings of that other mind, was denied him by his

A Wider Horizon: Portable Interiority and Provincial Life

deficiency of Imagination' (1969b: 91). Although neither Dorothea Brooke nor Edward Casaubon – the heroine of *Middlemarch* and her first husband – possess the capacity to truly understand why they both suffer in their marriage, the narrator attempts to model an approach in which her mind can access the feelings of both characters. This is especially evident when, after concentrating on Dorothea for several chapters, the narrator abruptly shifts narrative focalisation ('But why always Dorothea?' [1996: 261]). Yet despite this effort, the narrator's sympathies, and certainly the reader's, remain firmly fixed on the idealistic and ardent young woman who has made a disastrous choice of spouse.

Instead of concentrating on this aspect of the novel, which is fairly well-trod ground, in the next two sections I will consider how the feelings of social exclusion or belonging that Dorothea Brooke and her second love-interest Will Ladislaw experience produce mental representations of landscapes that are suffused with symbolic meaning. Like Will, with whom she falls in love, Dorothea is an orphan who lacks the assuredness of place that was central to Eliot's earlier novels. In these works, which take rural communities in the late eighteenth and early nineteenth centuries as their focus, home-scenes provide a kind of cognitive framework for understanding the self as part of a territorial community. Even in *Middlemarch*, the town that goes by this name is far less important a site than Tipton Grange, Mr Brooke's estate, or the fictional village of Lowick, where Dorothea's first husband resides. Yet Dorothea and Will are relative strangers to the area – born elsewhere in England, educated on the Continent and, owing to the deaths of their parents, deprived of a home-scene.

In all of Eliot's novels, a character's relationship to place reveals something essential about their moral selves. As Josephine McDonagh has argued, 'affiliation to . . . locality is a fundamental strand in their ethical make up' (2016: 356). In *Middlemarch*, a figure such as the dissipated blackmailer John Raffles is threatening, in part, because, as he notes, 'I've no particular attachment to any spot' (1996: 495). Instead of being rooted to a place, he is associated with forms of locomotion: the ship that took him on a ten-year sojourn to the United States and – on his return to England – the train. He comes and goes from the town of Middlemarch on the 'new-made railway, observing to his fellow passengers that he considered it pretty well seasoned now it had done for Huskisson'. The joke is crude. On 15 September 1830 the politician William Huskisson was accidentally killed by a train travelling from Manchester to Liverpool. As Nancy Henry points out, this expression of 'morbid humor' reflects Raffles's 'low character' (2019: 158). It also evokes another novel that takes a place for its name: *Cranford*.

Although Cranford is a village and Middlemarch a town, both novels are concerned with the effects of the newly built railways. In *Middlemarch*, the impact of the railways is particularly felt in the village of Lowick where, in one chapter, the land agent Caleb Garth surveys a parcel for possible sale. A train line is planned to run 'through Lowick parish where the cattle had hitherto grazed in a peace unbroken by astonishment'. This pits the local landowners, who seek to be paid a 'very high price ... for permission to injure mankind', and the agricultural workers who know that such a development will not benefit them (1996: 519). As the farm labourer Timothy Cooper – who, as Barbara Hardy has pointed out, is also the name of a character in Gaskell's *Cousin Phillis* (1865) – asserts, the railways will be 'good for the big folks to make money out on'. However, like many developments in his lifetime, they will leave the working man behind:

> [Such developments have] brought him neyther me-at nor be-acon, nor wage to lay by, if he didn't save it wi' clemmin' his own inside. Times ha' got wusser for him sin' I war a young un. An' so it'll be wi' the railroads. They'll on'y leave the poor mon furder behind. But them are fools as meddle, and so I told the chaps here. This is the big folks's world, this is. (1996: 526)

On this basis, the workers attack the land surveyors. Because of the agricultural depression that has taken hold throughout the south of England, the revolt of village labourers includes the breaking of threshing machines and the burning of hayricks, conditions and events that are also evoked by Mary Russell Mitford in *Our Village*.

Although these conflicts are one of several forces that lead to political reforms, Eliot's summary of the landowners' ambivalence towards the coming of the railway includes their sense that undesirable people will soon find their way into the parish. As Peter Solomon declares: 'I don't believe in any pay to make amends for bringing a lot of ruffians to trample your crops' (1996: 520). Raffles is not the sort of ruffian imagined by Solomon. He is, however, a nomad whose travels to and from the town and its surrounding parishes are facilitated by this new mode of transportation. He reeks, the narrator avers, of the 'odor of travellers' rooms in the commercial hotels of that period'. While he may purport to have 'been educated at an academy', and convinced himself of his ability 'to pass well everywhere', his scent gives the game away (1996: 388).

By the time Eliot published *Middlemarch*, the provincial community increasingly made little sense as a framework for organising individual and collective identities. Mobility had created a society in which, because of the development of the railway and the circulation of peoples within and beyond England, individuals no longer had significant ties to a particular locality as a point of origin. She thus confronts in *Middlemarch* a pressing question: is the concept of embeddedness tenable in a society comprised of individuals who lack the childhood attachments to a sense of place?

If the numerous moral failings of Raffles – including alcoholism, battery of his stepson, bribery and blackmail – are implicated in his lack of 'attachment to any spot', Dorothea Brooke and Will Ladislaw serve as his unrooted counterparts. After the death of their parents, Dorothea and her younger sister Celia become wards of their uncle Arthur Brooke. He ensures that they are educated, first by a family in England where, Mr Brooke laments, Dorothea takes to drawing architectural plans. As they look through a sketchbook, he remarks: 'you had a bad style of teaching, you know – else this is just the thing for girls – sketching, fine art and so on' (1996: 73). Second, they are sent to Lausanne where they are taught French by a Swiss family. On the completion of their studies, and before returning to England where they reside with him at his landed estate in Tipton, Mr Brooke takes them to Fribourg to 'hear the great organ' at the Cathedral of St Nicholas (1996: 61).

With his parents deceased, Will Ladislaw is looked after by his second cousin, Edward Casaubon. For Will, home is neither England nor the Continent, neither Lowick Manor, where Casaubon lives, nor Italy, where he has become affiliated with a bohemian community of expatriate German artists. Indeed, Tertius Lydgate, the young town doctor, describes Will as 'a sort of gypsy', evoking the notion of perpetual wandering and non-assimilation (1996: 410). Claiming this identity for himself, Will takes some pleasure in 'the sense of belonging to no class' (1996: 434). He enjoys ranging over what he glibly refers to as 'the entire area of Europe', which surely suggests a jocular form of cosmopolitanism (1996: 76).

While Raffles is a nomad, neither Dorothea nor Will are citizens of the world, although they are both affected by their time abroad. Nevertheless, it will be helpful to briefly turn to the burgeoning literature on Victorian cosmopolitanism that pays particular attention to Eliot's last novel, *Daniel Deronda*. In this work, the eponymous protagonist, a young English gentleman, who has read widely and travelled extensively, evinces an openness to the world: 'I want to under stand other points of view. And I want to get rid of a merely English attitude in studies' (1995: 183). When he discovers his Jewish ancestry late in the novel, he resolves to leave England altogether and devote himself 'towards restoring or perfecting . . . [the] common life' of the Jewish people (1995: 725). Thus, whereas Daniel is raised in England but leaves it to form a new community, Dorothea and Will spend much of their youth out of the country before becoming integrated into the Midlands village and town. However, despite these differences, both novels have an underlying concern with rootedness.

In the third chapter of *Daniel Deronda*, the narrator muses on the positive impact that social relations, nurtured and sustained in a particular geographical location, can have on the childhood constitution of the self. 'A human life, I think, should be well rooted in some spot of a native land', she observes, 'where it may get the love of tender kinship for the face of earth, for the labours men go forth to, for the sounds and accents that haunt it, for whatever will give that early home a familiar unmistakable difference amidst the future widening of knowledge: a spot where the definiteness of early memories may be inwrought with affection' (1995: 22). For Eliot, early communal embeddedness is what inculcates in individuals, as Amanda Anderson has shown, a 'prereflective partiality' for one's native spot of land and its inhabitants that can, in turn, serve as the affective base 'for the reflectiveness that allows one to become a "citizen of the world"' (2001: 137–138). In other words, attachments to one's family and local community during childhood are crucial stepping-stones in the individual's evolution towards membership in larger social units. This period, during which processes of embeddedness occur, enables individuals to develop the cognitive building blocks necessary for 'a higher-order self-conscious affirmation of what had been merely taken for granted: the norms of affection and solidarity that characterise familial and communal

A Wider Horizon: Portable Interiority and Provincial Life 231

bonds' (Anderson 2001: 138). Childhood rootedness thus becomes in Anderson's account the determining factor in the differing destinies of Gwendolen Harleth and Daniel Deronda. Gwendolen's lack of early rootedness, she argues, precludes 'the natural development of a prereflective partiality', and therefore leaves her without the affective foundation on which a sense of world citizenship depends. By contrast, Daniel's deep filial bonds with Sir Hugo, who raises him, and his affection for his childhood home prepare him for his later embrace of Judaism and 'the new familial and communal bonds that attend it' (1996: 137–138).

Eliot's *Middlemarch* provides reasons for thinking that the distinction between rootedness and rootlessness is not so stark. As Carolyn Lesjak has remarked, characters in Eliot's fiction who are outsiders, lacking ties to a particular community, often 'yearn for an expansive, cosmopolitan view of the world – while also desiring the rootedness of provincial life' (2021: 111). Not only do these characters desire it, but in Eliot's fiction they increasingly obtain it. While I accept Anderson's basic premise that a period of embeddedness is an essential part of what Eliot understands to be the individual's evolution from the local to the national and, ultimately, to the world community, my contention is that *Middlemarch* foregrounds the process by which individuals who have been rootless or wandering can themselves experience a period of embeddedness leading to wider communal identifications.

One aspect of Eliot's notion of embeddedness that Anderson does not discuss yet which is essential to it, given this emphasis on geographic forms of attachment, is the role of the landscape.[3] In *Middlemarch* and later in *Daniel Deronda* and *Impressions of Theophrastus Such*, Eliot approaches landscape in a manner strikingly different from her earlier works. In *Scenes of Clerical Life*, for instance, landscape is understood not as 'a medium of exchange between the human and the natural, the self and the other', as W. J. T. Mitchell has helpfully defined this term (2002: 5), but simply as metaphor: 'it is with men as with trees: if you lop off their finest branches, into which they were pouring their young life-juice, the wounds will be healed over with some rough boss, some odd excrescence; and what might have been a grand tree expanding into liberal shade, is but a whimsical misshapen trunk' (1998b: 193). As I noted in the previous chapter, *The Mill on the Floss* focuses on the development of a landscape-shaped subjectivity: a precultural psychological self with complex affective ties to the social and physical geography of one's birthplace. The narrowly focused use of rural imagery to illustrate individual progress or stunted growth in *Scenes of Clerical Life*, therefore, gives way in *The Mill on the Floss* to an understanding of the shaping power of the landscape in individual and collective – but still decidedly local – identity formation.

Rather than positing identity as largely fixed to and intelligible only within the confines of a particular geographic locality, *Middlemarch* suggests that, through a dynamic of exchange between mind and landscape,[4] one can acquire a home-scene that simultaneously prepares one for a more expansive form of affiliation: the nation. After all, the village and town are not separate from but exist within the nation, as the railways and the coming of political reform evince. As the nation is a territory of land, the central organising metaphor for bounded territorial units is that of roots. Whereas the nation is imagined as a community whose members see themselves as such regardless of whether they are actually instantiated in a geographically defined community of proximity, the nation-state is a politically, legally and geographically circumscribed area. The state becomes rooted to a particular territory, its demarcations constituted through a set of cultural, symbolic and material processes. These processes transform a generic sense of national belonging into one that is defined by geography. The rootless and the wandering disrupt this equilibrium because they call into question the semantic validity of the nation-state's organising metaphor. In this novel, I will suggest, Eliot seeks to place cultivated forms of local attachment in complementary relation to English national identifications and European cultural affiliations.

Mental expanse

In this section, I will track the role that the landscape plays in Dorothea's 'loftier' conception of life as it expands beyond Tipton Grange, past Lowick, and finally beyond the Midlands itself. As the narrator describes her, Dorothea is 'open, ardent, and not in the least self-admiring', keen 'to know the truths of life', and somewhat childlike in her innocence, particularly when it comes to 'ideas about marriage'. Her mind is 'theoretic' and concerned with 'the ends of life' (1996: 8, 26). But it is also 'oppressed' by an 'indefiniteness' of purpose, unable to conceive of life in emotionally and intellectually satisfying terms (1996: 22). Dorothea's desire for a mental framework in which her local lived experience can be understood as part of a wider context – 'some lofty conception of the world which might frankly include the parish of Tipton and her own rule of conduct there' (1996: 8) – is much like the 'young hopefulness of immediate good' that characterises political reform efforts (1996: 782).

Dorothea's own interest in reform has been shaped by her time in Switzerland. Under the tutelage of one Monsieur Liret, a Vaudois clergyman, Dorothea studies the history of the Waldenses. A French religious sect that formed in the Middle Ages and during the sixteenth-century Protestant revolution challenged the authority of the Roman Catholic pope, the Waldenses committed themselves to the simple principle of earnestly doing good to others. When Dorothea returns to live at her uncle's landed estate, she notices the dilapidated state of the cottages in which Mr Brooke's tenant farmers live. As she tells her uncle, there is a family of nine whose residence is a single 'sitting room and one bedroom hardly larger than this table!' There is another family, she argues, who live in 'the back kitchen' of a 'tumble-down farmhouse', while leaving 'the other rooms to the rats!' (1996: 365).

Inspirited by her religious studies and convictions, Dorothea begins to sketch drawings for renovating the cottages on the estate. 'I shall think I am a great architect', she says to her sister playfully, 'if I have not got incompatible stairs and fireplaces' (1996: 14). While Celia dismisses her sister's efforts as a 'favourite *fad*', Sir James Chettam, a neighbour of Mr Brooke's, is intrigued but nevertheless thinks it folly to expend money on cottages whose tenants 'can never pay rent to make it answer' (1996: 34, 29). But Dorothea, in attempting to persuade her uncle of the scheme's value, argues that 'it is better to spend money in finding out how men can make the most of the land which supports them all, than in keeping dogs and horses only to gallop over it'. She continues: 'It is not a sin to make yourself poor in performing experiments for the good of all' (1996: 16). In making this claim about social reform, Dorothea is simultaneously emphasising its political dimension. Because men like Mr Brooke have failed to address the needs of labourers, she argues, the wealthy 'deserve to be beaten out of our beautiful houses with a scourge of small cords – all of us who let tenants live in such sties as we see round us' (1996: 29). In fact, the narrator avers, one of the tenant farmers, Dagley, who lives in the tumble-down farmhouse, is increasingly receptive to 'muddy political talk, a stimulant dangerously disturbing to his farming conservatism, which consisted in holding that whatever is, is bad, and any change is likely to be worse' (1996: 370).

Through Dorothea's commitment to cottage reform, the novel directs the reader's attention to contemporaneous nostalgic attachments to an idyllic countryside. In an exchange with her uncle, Dorothea objects to the pictures of country life that adorn his walls. 'I used to come from the village with all that dirt and coarse ugliness like a pain within me', she frustratingly laments, 'and the simpering pictures in the drawing-room seemed to me like a wicked attempt to find delight in what is false, while we don't mind how hard the truth is for the neighbours outside our walls' (1996: 365). While Mr Brooke's pictures are never described in detail, the narrator criticises the pastoral mode in painting and prose that represents the countryside of the late 1820s and early 1830s as idyllic. When uncle and niece arrive at Mr Dagley's home to investigate a poaching incident, the narrator observes:

> It is true that an observer, under that softening influence of the fine arts which makes other people's hardships picturesque, might have been delighted with this homestead called Freeman's End: the old house had dormer-windows in the dark red roof, two of the chimneys were choked with ivy, the large porch was blocked up with bundles of sticks, and half the windows were closed with grey worm-eaten shutters about which the jasmine-boughs grew in wild luxuriance; the mouldering garden wall with hollyhocks peeping over it was a perfect study of highly mingled subdued colour, and there was an aged goat . . . lying against the open back-kitchen door. The mossy thatch of the cow-shed, the broken grey barn-doors, the pauper labourers in ragged breeches who had nearly finished unloading a wagon of corn into the barn ready for early thrashing; the scanty dairy of cows being tethered for milking and leaving one half of the shed in brown emptiness; the very pigs and white ducks seeming to wander about the uneven neglected yard as if in low spirits from feeding on a too meagre quality of rinsings, – all these objects under the quiet light of a sky marbled with high clouds would have made a sort of picture which we have all paused over as a 'charming bit', touching other sensibilities than those which are stirred by the depression of the agricultural interest, with the sad lack of farming capital, as seen constantly in the newspapers of that time. But these troublesome associations

were just now strongly present to Mr Brooke, and spoiled the scene for him. (1996: 369)

All of the elements for a picturesque 'scene' are here: the dark-red – presumably pitched – roof, the roof dormer with its window, the ivy-covered chimney, the rural workers and animals, and the quiet light that is soft and subdued. It is only 'a sort of picture', however, because Mr Brooke recognises the condition of the house and the surrounding milieu to be implicated in the widespread economic depression that undermines the stability and harmony associated with the picturesque.

There is no reason to think that Eliot had *Our Village* specifically in mind when she wrote this passage. But, as I noted in the last chapter, Mitford dominated literary depictions of rural life well into the latter half of the century. Although it is impossible to know with certainty the exact edition Eliot read, there is a fairly narrow range of possibilities. Her library contained 'a single vol. ed.' (Baker 1981: 93). Because there were no single-volume editions until 1870, it is likely that this was one volume of a pair. Regularly published in two volumes by Henry G. Bohn between 1843 and 1856, these editions were bound in dark green sumptuously embossed cloth with gilt spine title and include the same eighteen woodcut illustrations by George Baxter – to which I refer in Chapter Two – that had been commissioned by George Whittaker for the new three-volume edition of *Our Village* in 1835. In Bohn's edition, the sketches were reordered, with some clustered according to theme. The first volume, for example, contains all of the 'Walks in the Country' sketches, even though they initially appeared in four of the five original biennial volumes. Whereas Whittaker's edition contained no more than a few illustrations in any one volume, the publication of the sketches in two volumes meant, of course a higher concentration of illustrations in each.

By mid-century, a new edition of Mitford's most famous work had created its own audiences and meanings. As I have earlier indicated, Mitford often lapsed into pictorial language when describing her village and its surrounding milieu. In 'Wheat-Hoeing', her narrator declares: 'How fine a view of the little parsonage we have from hence, between those arching elms, which enclose it like a picture in a frame!' (1828: 107). Remarking on a yew-tree, an adjacent pond, and 'a clump of horse-chestnuts over-hanging some low weather-stained buildings' in 'A New Married Couple', the narrator observes that the 'assemblage of objects ... would tempt the pencil of a landscape-painter' (1828: 30–31). In Bohn's new edition, which substantially altered the reader's experience, such terminology seems to reinforce the notion of the volumes as cultural objects of aesthetic rather than use value that overwhelmingly emphasise the pastoral and idyllic qualities of Mitford's village.

To become the pre-eminent novelist of rural life, Eliot had to displace Mitford, who continued to dominate the market. In order to do so, she drew on techniques she learned from Gaskell. In Chapter Three, I noted that when Eliot was beginning to develop her craft she turned to Gaskell as, among her contemporaries, a remarkably effective writer in having characters reveal themselves through dialogue or narratorial description. Eliot's use of this technique is particularly evident in *The Mill on the Floss* and *Middlemarch*. In the former novel, Mrs Pullet evinces her superficiality in an exchange over the prospect of her cousin's impending death, which will pre-empt her wearing of a newly purchased bonnet because she will have to don mourning wear. In the latter work, Solomon Featherstone sees an opportunity to profit from the construction of railway tracks near his property. To drive up the asking price, 'he set about acting ... in a thoroughly diplomatic manner by stimulating suspicion' among residents in the small hamlet of Frick, who, the narrator avers, '[i]n the absence of any precise idea as to what railways were', took a position decidedly against them (1996: 520). Without explicit depictions of Solomon as a gossip, unlike those with Mrs Cadwallader, *Middlemarch* nevertheless suggests his centrality to whispering campaigns, such as when his sister remarks that 'everybody says ... how unsteady young [Fred] Vincy is, and has been forever gambling at billiards'. 'My brother Solomon', she continues, 'tells me it's the talk up and down in Middlemarch' (1996: 98).

Yet, as I also previously noted, Eliot believed that Gaskell lacked a capacity for conveying 'the half tints of real life', which, unlike 'sharp contrasts', could engender sympathy. Those sharp contrasts stem in part from Gaskell's use of irony – a device that Mitford had modelled for her but in whose hands was more cutting than tender. *Our Village* may have charmed Eliot too, but she would have seen it – based on the edition available to her – as falling well short of what she saw as the moral and social imperative of realism. As she writes in her essay on the German sociologist

A Wider Horizon: Portable Interiority and Provincial Life 237

Wilhelm Riehl's 'The Natural History of German Life' (1856), published in the July 1856 issue of the *Westminster Review*:

> Art is the nearest thing to life; it is a mode of amplifying experience and extending our contact with our fellow-men beyond the bounds of our personal lot. All the more sacred is the task of the artist when he undertakes to paint the life of the People. Falsification here is far more pernicious than in the more artificial aspects of life. It is not so very serious that we should have false ideas about evanescent fashions – about the manners and conversations of beaux and duchesses; but it *is* serious that our sympathy with the perennial joys and struggles, the toil, the tragedy, and the humour in the life of our more heavily-laden fellow-men, should be perverted, and turned towards a false object instead of the true one. (1883: 145)

Much more so than the biennial volumes published between 1824 and 1832 or the three-volume edition of 1835, Bohn's edition actualises a potential understanding latent in the text of rural life and scenery as already a painting or picture. Eliot would have seen this as a violation of her sacrosanct principle in representing rural life.

Publishers are, of course, cognizant that bibliographic codes shape the reader. As Pierre Macherey contends, 'readers are made by what makes the book' (1978: 70). Thus, Bohn's two-volume *Our Village* cannot be considered in isolation from the kinds of readers it sought to call into being. Just as Mr Brooke must bracket the 'depression of the agricultural interest, with the sad lack of farming capital, as seen constantly in the newspapers' in order to enjoy the picturesque scenes decorating his walls (1996: 370), Mitford's *Our Village* – a portion of which was written in the same span of time in which Eliot often set her novels – would have seemed, in this new instantiation, oddly discordant. Of course, sketches such as 'Violeting', 'A Great Farm-House' and 'The Incendiary' are all included. But whatever power these sketches had to unsettle readers encountering them in their original periodical context, and to a lesser extent the early bound volumes, dissipates in this edition.

Thus, Dorothea's rejection of Mr Brooke's pictures is also a refusal of the neglectful social relations that make such picturesque scenes possible. While Mitford's narrator in 'Violeting' insists that she has 'no power to remove or alleviate' the poverty she confronts, Dorothea attempts to take matters into her own hands.

Indeed, although she briefly frames her argument in revolutionary terms that resonate with local incidents of machine-breaking and rick-burning, asserting as I noted earlier that the wealthy 'deserve to be beaten out of our beautiful houses with a scourge of small cords', Dorothea's aims are utopian. If she can only convince James Chettam to build model cottages on his property, Dorothea believes, local landowners will perhaps follow suit and 'it would be as if the spirit of Oberlin had passed over the parishes to make the life of poverty beautiful!' 'Life in cottages might be happier than ours', she concludes, 'if they were real houses fit for human beings from whom we expect duties and affections' (1996: 29).

The point of cottage reform is not simply to achieve harmony between the landed interests and labouring classes. Rather, it is to undertake a civic action to improve one's community. This action necessitates imagining oneself and others as belonging to the same social unit. One might argue that Dorothea's unidirectional phraseology ('from whom we expect duties and affections') indicates her adherence to a deferential and paternalistic social model. But this moment cannot be separated from others in the novel, which I will discuss in the pages that follow, depicting her attempt to think of, and Will Ladislaw's efforts to bring into being, a social realm in which everyone has inherent duties and affections as members of a polity.

This vision, which Eliot endorses, is evident in the cover illustration of the novel's original publication. Between December 1871 and December 1872, *Middlemarch* appeared in eight paperback instalments, each with a sage green cover. The novel's title, covered in vines, is prominently displayed on the cover. Just below the title and in a smaller typeface is the author's name, which appears above a sphere-shaped vignette of a country scene. Printed underneath the illustration, and surrounded by foliage on both sides, is the name of the respective 'book', and the only difference to occur among the different parts: 'Miss Brooke', 'Old and Young', 'Waiting for Death', 'Three Love Problems', 'The Dead Hand', 'The Widow and the Wife', 'Two Temptations' and 'Sunset and Sunrise'. The publisher's name, William Blackwood and Sons, appeared at the bottom of the cover along with its two principal locations: Edinburgh and London.

As George Eliot's unofficial agent, George Henry Lewes had initially proposed a publication schedule in which each book would appear at two-month intervals. Writing to John Blackwood

A Wider Horizon: Portable Interiority and Provincial Life 239

on 7 May 1871, Lewes suggested that the novel appear 'in *half-volume parts* either at intervals of one, or as I think better, two months.... Considering how slowly the public mind is brought into motion, this spreading of the publication over 16 months would be a decided advantage to the sale – especially as each part would contain as much as one ought to read at a time.' To persuade Blackwood to adopt this scheme, Lewes suggested that the publisher might use this innovative format to bypass Mudie's and other circulating libraries and sell directly to readers. 'If in a stiff paper cover – attractive but not bookstallish – (I have one in my eye) this part ['Miss Brooke'] ought to seduce purchasers, especially if Mudie were scant on supplies', he writes. 'It would be enough to furnish the town with talk for some time' (Eliot 1955c: 146). After the first four books appeared, however, Lewes suggested that the publication schedule be altered to take advantage of the Christmas market. As a result, the last two books appeared monthly.

In addition to the format of the novel's publication, Lewes took an active interest – as he had with Eliot's other works – in its promotion. On 7 September 1871, Lewes wrote to Blackwood and suggested that he advertise the novel in Maga, as the venerable *Blackwood's Edinburgh Magazine* was known, beginning in the October number (Eliot 1955c: 184). Several days later, on 11 September, he again wrote to Blackwood, this time to suggest the wording for a promotional spot in a different periodical. 'I think paragraph in Athenaeum should simply say "A new story of English Provincial Life by George Eliot will be published by Messrs. Blackwood in December"' (Eliot 1955c: 185). He continued to involve himself in discussions about how the novel could most effectively be promoted and sold in the months leading up to the first part's appearance.

Although Lewes took the lead in business matters, Eliot was keenly interested in all aspects of publication, including sales figures, geographical circulation and the translation of her novels into other languages. One facet of *Middlemarch* to which she was particularly alert was the physical appearance of the original parts. Although Blackwood's Edinburgh manager, George Simpson, was responsible for commissioning a design, Eliot played a role in selecting the wrapper's green colour, having contemplated yellow, lilac mauve and an ochre (Haight 1968: 436). Having found herself 'charmed' by the illustrations that appeared in the cheap editions of her novels, Eliot hoped that one 'representing a manor house or bit of town with steeple and gables' might be added to the cover (Eliot 1955c: 192). Lewes duly conveyed the request to Blackwood, who immediately acceded. The publishing house secured Myles Birket Foster, who had worked as an illustrator for *Punch* magazine and the *Illustrated London News*, to produce a rural scene (Figure 5.1). Eliot's friend Barbara Bodichon thought the choices were dreadful. Although she reckoned the colour was not 'bad', she detested the font, design and illustration. 'I do not like the cover at all, it is not artistic enough', she complained, 'much better have nothing on the cover than that riggle and landscape' (qtd. in Haight: 1968, 436). But Lewes, Eliot and Blackwood were satisfied, and Birket Foster's vignette of a romanticised townscape with Dorothea and her St Bernard in the foreground would grace the cover of the cheap edition of 1874 (Figure 5.2).

The cover that so offended Bodichon aligns *Middlemarch* with the tradition of writing about rural character and scenery inaugurated by Mitford. The vignette's foreground is dominated by woodland, including bushes and the stump of a tree that has been cut and felled. In the distance are three buildings of unequal height, which suggest both undulating terrain and economic disparity. One structure is recognisably a church. Another is a manor house. The third, a humbler abode, is perhaps a labourer's cottage. As for the actual setting, the illustration is indistinct.[5] Heather Miner suggests it is a picturesque scene that shows 'a cottage nestled among rolling hills and agricultural figures' (2012: 195). To make this argument, however, she must bracket the other two buildings, which would surely complicate the primacy of place her reading gives to the cottage. To my mind, Eliot was attracted to the image because it encapsulated for her the notion of constitutive duties and affections in a locality. The vignette need not have depicted the fictional town because, as I will shortly explain, the novel is ultimately interested in the generic rather than the specific.

Although the illustration is not a direct representation of any locality in the novel, the foreground is reminiscent of the bordering wood to which Dorothea retreats early in the novel. Having interacted with Casaubon on several occasions, Dorothea is immediately enamoured by his significant accomplishment – the research notes for his *Key to All Mythologies* 'already made a formidable range of volumes' – and imminent greatness: 'the crowning task would be to condense these voluminous still-accumulating results and bring them, like the earlier vintage of Hippocratic books, to

A Wider Horizon: Portable Interiority and Provincial Life   241

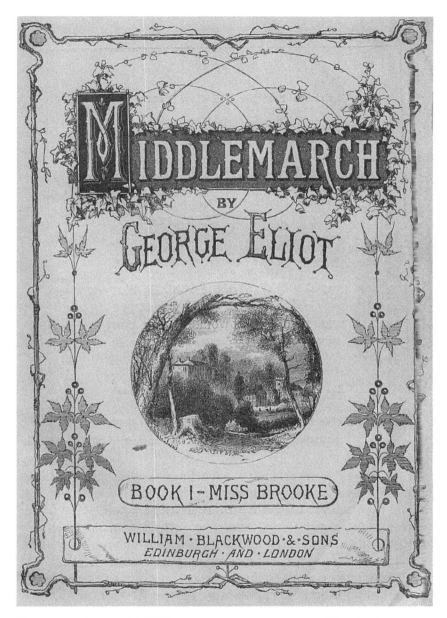

Figure 5.1 Cover of Middlemarch (1871–72 parts publication). Illustration by Myles Birket Foster. Engraved by C. Jeens. George Eliot *Middlemarch: A Study of Provincial Life*. Edinburgh and London: William Blackwood & Sons, 1871. In Parts. Courtesy of the Armstrong Browning Library, Baylor University.

Figure 5.2 Cover vignette of *Middlemarch*, cheap edition, 1874. Illustration by Myles Birket Foster. Classic Collection 3/Alamy Stock Photo.

fit a little shelf' (1996: 22–23). She finds herself quickly ruminating on the possibility of a life together. 'Here was something beyond the shallows of ladies' school literature: here was a living Bossuet', the narrator says, referring to the seventeenth-century French theologian, ventriloquising Dorothea's thought process, 'whose work would reconcile complete knowledge with devoted piety; here was a modern Augustine who united the glories of doctor and saint' (1996: 23). Because she sees Casaubon's knowledge as vast, Dorothea pedestalises him as a great teacher – as one artist sought to capture in 1888 (Seguin 1888) (Figure 5.3). Dorothea also perceives him to treat her as 'a fellow-student', although the narrator is quick to explain that this is simply because Casaubon does not have 'two styles of talking at his command' (1996: 23).

A Wider Horizon: Portable Interiority and Provincial Life 243

Figure 5.3 Illustration of Casaubon and Dorothea by an unknown artist, 1888. The Reading Room/Alamy Stock Photo.

Thus, soon after one of their visits together, Dorothea sets out to be alone with her thoughts. On that 'beautiful breezy autumn day', she reflects on the possibility of marrying Casaubon:

> [She] hurried along the shrubbery and across the park that she might wander [alone] through the bordering wood .... There had risen before her the girl's vision of a possible future for herself to which she looked forward with trembling hope, and she wanted to wander on in that visionary future without interruption. (1996: 25)

Dorothea's retreat into the woods allegorises her own retreat into herself. But the scene is not simply metaphorical. The walk in the woods is both the setting and the means of self-discovery. In contrast to many scenes in Eliot's earlier novels in which a walk in the woods generates childhood recollections, this scene shows the landscape stimulating fantasies of the future. Significantly, the woods lead away from Tipton Grange and toward Casaubon's manor house at Lowick – the site of the future about which she fantasises. Dorothea's longing to stay 'without interruption' in the woods that lay between Tipton Grange and Casaubon's home is not simply a desire to remain in a physical space. Rather, the passage suggests that Dorothea wishes to stay in that 'visionary future' where her lofty conceptions about the world and her place in it are realised.

Much has been made of Dorothea's literal nearsightedness and her figurative blindness, of which this scene would seem to be yet another example. In Anna K. Nardo's reading, 'Eliot exposes the blindness that leads Dorothea to marry a reflection of her own longings in order, she believes, to attain far-reaching knowledge' (2003: 93–94). Bernard Paris notes that in characterising Dorothea's ideas about marriage as 'childlike', the narrator seems to attribute 'inexperience or immaturity' to the novel's protagonist (2003: 34). Rather, Paris contends, Dorothea's fantasies about Casaubon, which cloud her ability to see clearly, 'reflect ... compensatory needs' because of the limitations imposed on women (2003: 34). But emphasising Dorothea's blindness obscures the essential insight of her youthful fantasies: that marriage might be something more than 'the niceties of the *trousseau*, [and] the pattern of plate' (2003: 22), and that it might closely approximate equality. She does not, therefore, experience the woods as confining or blocking vision. In fact, quite the opposite: they represent an avenue, enabling an imaginative view of Lowick as that place towards which Dorothea's future seems to 'open'.

One might argue that this kind of vision is simply a different form of blindness. Dorothea appears to prefer imaginative ideals to concrete reality by yearning for some 'lofty conception of the world' (1996: 8). It would be easy to read the word *lofty* as dismissive, except that in the context of Dorothea's life at Tipton Grange, and later at Lowick, both her uncle and her husband are shown to lack any capacity for imaginative vision and are unable to imagine social change. Indeed, as the narrator avers, Casaubon 'did not care about building cottages, and diverted the talk to the extremely narrow accommodation which was to be had in the dwellings of the ancient Egyptians as if to check a too high standard'. In such a context a 'lofty conception of the world' would almost be an imperative.

Before she discovers this aspect of her husband's personality, Dorothea convinces herself that marriage represents the possibility

A Wider Horizon: Portable Interiority and Provincial Life 245

of giving shape to the 'indefiniteness' of her life by providing a specific focus that accords with her lofty conceptions: becoming the helpmate to a man of increasingly national prominence. Comparing her future husband to John Milton, the theologian Richard Hooker and the religious writer Blaise Pascal, Dorothea notes that 'the use I should like to make of my life would be to help some one who did great works' (1996: 342). Casaubon's pamphlet on the 'Catholic Question' virtually guarantees him a position as Bishop in the Church of England if the Wellington government remains in power. Dorothea believes that, in helping Casaubon in his work, she will assume responsibilities of importance far beyond those consigned to women by nineteenth-century gender ideology: 'Fine art, poetry, that kind of thing, elevates a nation', as Mr Brooke explains women's ideal contributions (1996: 365–366). At this point in the novel Dorothea imagines her own subjectivity through Casaubon. He would be 'a guide who would take her along the grandest path', help her to 'see the truth by the same light as great men' of national consequence and, in so doing, assist her in realising her own vision of 'a grand life here – now – in England' (1996: 27).

Even as the interactions of her mind with the rural topography stimulate fantasies about the future, Dorothea finds that this same dynamic enables her to register the conflict between her inner world and the external world that constitutes her lived reality. As her marriage to Casaubon wears on, Dorothea finds 'the large vistas and wide fresh air' that she imagined within her husband's mind have become, instead, 'anterooms and winding passages' (1996: 183), a metaphor for the confining narrowness of his thinking. It becomes clear to Dorothea that her fantasy of the compensating 'large vistas and wide fresh air' of her husband's mind will remain unfulfilled. The repeated scenes of Dorothea's gazing from her boudoir window, on the lime trees with their far-reaching shadows in the autumn months and the bleak, snow-covered landscape in winter, suggest that, for her, the promised vistas – a future that will open out towards Lowick, towards the realms of knowledge with which she associated Lowick, and towards the actions that such knowledge might inspire – have become distinctly unpromising. 'Her blooming full-pulsed youth stood there in a moral imprisonment which made itself one with the chill, colourless, narrowed landscape', the narrator remarks. The openness of the landscape turns, instead, to shadows and dreariness.

Dorothea's imaginative vision becomes blocked when she discovers that the avenue she has chosen does not lead to new realms and that the prospect before her (figuratively and literally) is bleakly repetitious. This prospect of bleak repetition differs strikingly from Eliot's depictions of repetition in her early novels, and especially in *The Mill on the Floss*, in which the narrator asks, 'What novelty is worth that sweet monotony where everything is known, and *loved* because it is known?' (1998a: 94). For Dorothea, monotony is a source of revulsion. She equates it with circumscription, confinement and even death: 'what was fresh to her mind was worn out' to Casaubon's, the narrator observes, 'and such capacity of thought and feeling as had ever been stimulated in him by the general life of mankind had long shrunk to a sort of dried preparation, a lifeless embalmment of knowledge' (1996: 184).

Having earlier imagined her own existence through Casaubon, with him serving as a 'guide . . . along the grandest path', Dorothea begins to imagine over the course of the novel a distinct existence for herself within a larger web of social relations:

> She opened her curtains, and looked out towards the bit of road that lay in view, with fields beyond outside the entrance-gates. On the road there was a man with a bundle on his back and a woman carrying her baby; in the field she could see figures moving – perhaps the shepherd with his dog. Far off in the bending sky was the pearly light; and she felt the largeness of the world and the manifold wakings of men to labour and endurance. She was a part of that involuntary, palpitating life, and could neither look out on it from her luxurious shelter as a mere spectator, nor hide her eyes in selfish complaining. (1996: 741)

How are we to read the novel's reference to an 'involuntary, palpitating life'? An important aspect of this rural scene is its lack of geographic or human particularity. It is, instead, iconic. The entrance gates establish a foreground, the road and field a middle distance, and the 'bending sky' a background. There is no particular focal point for interest. Instead, focus is dispersed across the landscape and the human activities that take place within it. Indeed, the 'man with a bundle on his back and a woman carrying her baby' are figures that do not fix the gaze; they are inseparable and not distinct from the landscape, with its 'bit of road' and 'bending sky'. Neither the landscape nor the human activities are the focus; both work together to produce Dorothea's sense of 'the

A Wider Horizon: Portable Interiority and Provincial Life 247

largeness of the world' and her feelings of collective attachment. Dorothea does not notice anything in the landscape – say, Lowick Church – that would fix its meaning as definitively local. The scene is dehistoricised and delocalised. It is, in other words, much like the spherical vignette that appears on the covers of the original eight parts.

Of course, on one level Dorothea *is* looking out of her window, so the scene must be a familiar one. But the lack of specificity suggests that Dorothea's response to the rural scene is not a sense of shared obligations to and memories of a particular locality and the individuals who people it; rather, the scene generates an enlarged conception of human interiority not premised on a specifically fixed locale. After all, the figures in the landscape are not immediately recognisable as individuals whom she knows – '*perhaps* the shepherd with his dog' (emphasis mine). Moreover, the stress on movement in this rural scene points away from the local towards a wider horizon. The 'man with a bundle on his back' and the 'woman carrying her baby' are both walking down a 'bit of road', and the term *bending sky*, too, evokes motion – winding or meandering or twisting toward that 'pearly light' in the distance.

Juxtaposing Dorothea at her window with the passage from *The Mill on the Floss* discussed in the preceding chapter demonstrates a shift in Eliot's thinking about landscape and its relationship to interiority. When Stephen Guest takes Maggie Tulliver down the Floss – a river that 'links the small pulse of the old English town with the beatings of the world's mighty heart' – Maggie's responses to the shifting scenery indicate a growing unease: 'She looked at the far-stretching fields – at the banks close by – and felt that they were entirely strange to her' (1998a: 464). The changing views as they sail further away remind Maggie not just of the landscape of her home-scenes but of the particular constellation of memories and obligations rooted there. They call to mind those 'ties that have made others dependent on us' (1998a: 449). Even as their boat moves down a river that opens onto the nation and ultimately the world, Maggie's own currents pull her away from the nation and back towards her local home-scene. The landscape thus generates a sense of shared obligations and affections among the individuals who populate a home-scene, but those obligations and affections, according to the logic of the passage, must be rooted in the local.

For Dorothea, however, the interiority generated by the rural scene on which she fixes her attention is abstract. It is not dependent, as it was in *The Mill on the Floss*, on familiar terrain and the set of social or familial relations they might evoke; the mind draws on the landscape for its figures of thinking but does not require the specificity of a particular landscape. This abstract interiority, detached from the geographically fixed, points to a conception of the self that is not strictly tied to the local. That we might see this new conception of the self as explicitly national – a prerequisite to the international sympathies that Eliot's own readership was cultivating – is suggested by several moments in the novel. I wish to focus on three: Dorothea's honeymoon in Rome and the novel's prelude and finale, both of which are concerned with questions of national belonging.

The evocation of a painting in the scene of Dorothea at her window echoes an earlier moment in the novel when she and Will, having crossed paths in the Italian capital, discuss art. Dorothea, who has been spending her days in the art museums of Rome while Casaubon conducts research at the Vatican, recounts her experiences to Will. 'At first when I enter a room where the walls are covered with frescoes, or with rare pictures, I feel a kind of awe', she explains to Will. 'I feel myself in the presence of some higher life than my own. But when I begin to examine the pictures one by one, the life goes out of them' (1996: 193). The paintings, taken together, evoke a sense of the universal, inspiring a 'kind of awe', but the particular, without the context of the universal, appears lifeless. Yet the novel *does* valorise the particular as a means of gaining access to the universal. Dorothea's remark to Will that 'most of our lives would look much uglier and more bungling than the pictures, if they could be put on the wall' is reversed by the narrative when Dorothea looks outside her bedroom window and gains a sense of a wider existence of which she is a part (1996: 206). What Dorothea comes to recognise in this moment, the novel suggests, is that the universal is, in fact, realised through the particular.[6]

But there is an added significance to this scene at the window. While Eliot was writing *Middlemarch*, John Ruskin was giving a series of lectures on art at Oxford University. As these lectures unfolded throughout 1870, Ruskin argued for a distinctively English way of viewing art. In turn, when 'trained by surrounding art', he insisted, one could view a natural scene differently: 'Landscape can only be enjoyed by cultivated persons; and it is only by music, literature, and painting, that cultivation can be given' (1905: 36). Because Ruskin defined English viewing as a 'form of disciplined freedom', in which the aesthetic experience of a landscape is a mode of 'physical and mental self-control', as Elizabeth Helsinger argues, in conception it was limited to 'English-bred Protestant males' (1994b: 126, 129, 139). Women and the working class were included in Ruskin's vision but as classed and gendered beings, 'different and unequally national subjects' (Helsinger 1994b: 139).

Born in the same year and sharing similar interests in the moral purpose of art, likely shaped by their comparable evangelical upbringings, Eliot knew Ruskin's work well. In the June 1854 issue of the *Leader*, for which George Henry Lewes served as the literary editor, she published a laudatory review of his *Lectures on Architecture and Painting*. Just before she began to write fiction, she published an equally admiring essay on volume three of his *Modern Painters* in the April 1856 issue of the *Westminster Review*. In recognition of Ruskin's importance to her intellectual and artistic development, Eliot arranged for a copy of *Scenes of Clerical Life* to be sent to him when it was published in January 1858. Although she took little interest in his political views, she continued to follow his thinking in art, including reports of his lectures and new publications, until her death in 1880.[7]

Despite Eliot's admiration for Ruskin, *Middlemarch* includes an incipient critique of the gendered limits of Ruskin's national subjects. Elizabeth Helsinger has focused on one aspect of the 'second-class citizenship he offers women in a nation of art viewers' (1994b: 138). Because women are too often, for Ruskin, objects of aesthetic representation, they are limited in their capacity to be viewing – and therefore national – subjects. Helsinger attends to the famous scene in Rome where Adolf Naumann, Will Ladislaw's bohemian friend and artist, attempts to undertake a painting of Dorothea. Ladislaw objects on the grounds that a woman is not 'a mere coloured superficies'. Thus, Helsinger points out, both Dorothea and Ladislaw ultimately turn their backs on Italian art: the former finding the 'deep impressions' too perplexing and the latter because it lacks the 'movement and tone' that gives life to representation.

But Eliot – who, as I documented in the previous chapter, was attempting to think through the possibility of the landscape as the ground for social inclusivity – emphasises a different commonality between Dorothea and Will as well. While in Italy, surrounded by sculptures and painting, they are both depicted as longing for the countryside of the English Midlands. I will return to the novel's characterisation of Will's relationship to the Midlands in the next section. Here, I want to highlight Dorothea's, of whom the narrator observes, 'She did not really see the streak of sunlight on the floor more than she saw the statues: she was inwardly seeing the light of years to come in her own home and over the English fields and elms and hedge-bordered highroads; and feeling that the way in which they might be filled with joyful devotedness was not so clear to her as it had been' (1996: 190). Finding herself excluded from the research Casaubon is undertaking, Dorothea begins to question the role she might play in transforming those voluminous notes into a manuscript on their return to Lowick. Nevertheless, she conceptualises her duties and responsibilities against the backdrop of a national landscape ('English fields and elms and hedge-bordered highroads' [1996: 190]).

Dorothea's sense of being part of an 'involuntary, palpitating life' while standing at her window is also linked implicitly and explicitly to Saint Theresa, who goes forth into the world, the narrator tells us, with a 'coherent social faith' and a heart 'beating to a national idea' (1996: 3). Thus the prologue suggests that the expanded definition of Dorothea's rural home-scene is like Saint Theresa's 'national idea', which refers to the affective dimension of a collectively shared belief in Catholicism. Like Eliot's attempt in *The Mill on the Floss* to fuse urban and rural values in order 'to create the moral sanctions offered in the past by religion', as Suzanne Graver remarks (1994: 15), what Eliot seems to be getting at here is that Saint Theresa's national idea, emptied of its religious but not national content, can serve as the basis for a shared inner moral life in English Protestant culture. A national idea, like an 'involuntary, palpitating life', suggests that it is pre-political. It also suggests a kind of gliding back and forth, if we superimpose the terms of Saint Theresa's Catholicism onto Eliot's notion of the many layers of collectivity between the local (the parish), the regional (the diocese) and the national – that which is imagined in common with other believers within a bounded territory beyond the local and the regional – as distinct but related categories of experience.

While Saint Theresa achieves an epic life, Dorothea does not. As Nancy Paxton notes, 'Dorothea's "grand woman's frame", her powerful and "theoretic" mind, and her large ambitions for a life of "intensity and greatness" all show that she possesses the physical and intellectual capacities which will allow her to partake

A Wider Horizon: Portable Interiority and Provincial Life

fully in the "common fund of ideas"' (1991: 181). Her attempts to work on pressing social issues – improving the living conditions of the working poor and the access to, and quality of, healthcare – certainly suggest that her heart increasingly beats to a national idea as well. Yet the contrast between Saint Theresa and Dorothea serves to highlight Eliot's perception that the former accomplished her goals because citizenship within her time was premised on an inward sense of an 'idea' that was then given broad latitude for social expression.

Landscape and metamorphosis

The novel's account of the interaction between Dorothea's mind and the countryside is initially used to draw attention to her aspirations for a life beyond Tipton Grange. Over time, these aspirations, always juxtaposed with landscape description, become wider and increasingly national in scope. Yet unlike Will, Dorothea has no effective means of realising her ambitions given the narrow and gendered construction of nineteenth-century political citizenship. While Dorothea experiences a period of embeddedness that equips her with the necessary capabilities to become involved in national affairs, such as through her projects to improve the living conditions of the poor, she nevertheless remains unable to channel her aspirations for service into any meaningful activity beyond the duties associated with the domestic sphere. Dorothea's acquired home-scene enables her to think beyond her immediately lived experience. Yet, as the novel repeatedly highlights, she lacks the direct means of expression available to Will. His acquired roots serve as the affective foundation that enable him to assume increasing political responsibilities and ultimately to leave the provincial village and town for service to the nation.

Will's social marginalisation is multi-layered. His Anglo mother 'betrayed' the family by marrying someone devoid of property, and his father is ethnically Polish. As one of the town residents exclaims, 'our mercurial Ladislaw has a queer genealogy!' In fact, while his temperament is unpredictable, Will's very appearance is also mutable:

> The first impression on seeing Will was one of sunny brightness, which added to the uncertainty of his changing expression. Surely, his very features changed their form, his jaw looked sometimes large and

sometimes small; and the little ripple in his nose was a preparation for metamorphosis. When he turned his head quickly his hair seemed to shake out light, and some persons thought they saw decided genius in this coruscation. Mr. Casaubon, on the contrary, stood rayless. (1996: 196)

Of course, the comparison between Casaubon and Ladislaw is striking. Where Casaubon is associated with unlit interiors, a mind comprised of 'anterooms and winding passages which seemed to lead nowither' (1996: 183), the younger cousin is linked to the life-giving properties and transformative effects of the sun. But the emphasis in this passage is on Will's fluctuating appearance, which matches his professional formlessness and peripatetic itinerary.

New to Middlemarch and its surrounding villages, and therefore a stranger, Will is greeted by residents with a combination of bemusement and suspicion comparable to the reception of outsiders in *Cranford*. Rather than confine himself to an enclave of similarly positioned individuals, Will's 'sense of belonging to no class' motivates his frequent tendency 'to ramble about among the poor people', which strikes many as considerably odd (1996: 435). Will, the narrator recounts, frequently takes

> little hatless boys with their galligaskins much worn and scant shirting to hang out, little girls who tossed their hair out of their eyes to look at him, and guardian brothers at the mature age of seven ... on gypsy excursions to Halsell Wood at nutting-time, and since the cold weather had set in he had taken them on a clear day to gather sticks for a bonfire in the hollow of a hillside, where he drew out a small feast of gingerbread for them, and improvised a Punch-and-Judy drama with some private home-made puppets (1996: 435).

His flouting of other social conventions, such as laying down on the carpets at 'houses where he got friendly' while conversing with their inhabitants was occasionally discovered by callers 'for whom such an irregularity was likely to confirm the notions of his dangerously mixed blood and general laxity' (1996: 435).

As I noted earlier, the epithet *gypsy* is frequently bestowed on him by Lydgate. It is also used by many other acquaintances and neighbours. In fact, for them, such behavioural oddities can only be explained in biological terms: the circulation of 'cursed alien blood, Jew, Corsican, or Gypsy' within him (1996: 676).

One of the ways his gypsyhood manifests itself is in his 'anomalous course', as Casaubon puts it, of studying at a university in the German city of Heidelberg. 'On leaving Rugby he declined to go to an English university, where I would gladly have placed him' (1996: 74), Casaubon laments, in referring to the renowned public school that prepared pupils for entrance to Oxford or Cambridge and provided them with a foundation for entering one of the highly educated professions. In fact, even after his studies are complete, Will refuses to enter the legal and medical fields or take holy orders and become a clergyman. Instead, after a brief return to England, Will decides 'to go abroad again, without any special object'. He refuses to fix on any more precise destination than 'the entire area of Europe' in search of 'what he calls culture, preparation for he knows not what', Casaubon says derisively to Dorothea and Mr Brooke (1996: 76, 74). Mr Brooke tries to cast a positive spin on this decision: 'He has a thirst for travelling; perhaps he may turn out a Bruce or a Mungo Park', referring, respectively, to the Scottish travel writer and explorer. But Casaubon dismisses such perpetual wandering as motivated by vague desires rather than clear intentionality: 'No, he has no bent towards exploration, or the enlargement of our geognosis' (1996: 75).

Although one should not necessarily put too much stock in Casaubon's derisive remarks, the novel itself is at pains to point out Will's mobility. His identity is characterised not only by a lack of fixed address but also by an unclear career trajectory. For much of the novel, Will is depicted as idle, an amateur artist and an intellectual dilettante who relies on Casaubon's financial support. Much to his cousin's dismay, Will seems to evince an 'aversion' to the medical, legal or clerical 'callings by a dislike to steady application' (1996: 75). Moreover, Will's antipathy towards these professions, the narrator suggests, stems from an oversized estimation of his own greatness. As the narrator sardonically opines of Will, 'Genius, he held, is necessarily intolerant of fetters: on the one hand, it must have the utmost play for its spontaneity; on the other, it may confidently await those messages from the universe which summon it to its peculiar work, only placing itself in an attitude of receptivity towards all sublime chances' (1996: 76). Thus, where Casaubon would characterise Will as stationary, his younger cousin sees committing to a profession as an impediment to motion. In fact, although Casaubon lectures him on the necessity of 'patience' and 'the toil of years preparatory' to any significant accomplishment, Will recognises in his cousin's own life a 'pitiable' example 'of long incubation producing no chick' (1996: 75, 77).

Of course, Eliot does not condemn mobility itself. Dorothea experiences Casaubon's manor house – described as 'a virtual tomb' (1996: 446), with all the feelings of claustrophobia that such a phrase invokes – as highly confining. Equally for Dorothea, as well as Will, life in the provincial community is at times both narrow and oppressive. Eliot follows in the footsteps of Mitford and Gaskell in depicting the centrality of gossip to village life. In 'Lucy', which appeared in the first volume of *Our Village*, the narrator declares of her favourite servant: 'She had another qualification for village society – she was an incomparable gossip, had a rare genius for picking up news, and great liberality in its diffusion' (Mitford 1824a: 60). There is no sense of self-conscious irony on the part of the narrator, who has already declared that she takes pleasure in residing in a location 'where we know every one, are known to every one, interested in every one' (Mitford 1824a: 1). The gossip that circulates in *Cranford*, characterised as 'piece[s] of intelligence', is generally harmless (2008: 76), but in *Mary Barton*, the other work of fiction that had a formative influence on Eliot, its effects on the eponymous protagonist are deleterious.

In *Middlemarch*, gossip has an effect on a number of different characters. If 'this world ... [is] apparently a huge whispering-gallery', as the narrator puts it, the provincial community is a microcosm (1996: 386). Revelations about individuals or relationships are, once articulated or discovered, 'soon to be loudly spoken of' (1996: 675). The nexus of gossip is Mrs Cadwallader who, as the wife of the rector of Tipton, is well-positioned to gain salacious information. Regaling others who 'would have felt a sad lack of conversation but for the stories about what ... [she] said and did', Mrs Cadwallader 'gave neighbourliness to both rank and religion, and mitigated the bitterness of uncommuted tithe' (1996: 48). At one point in the novel, her chatter about Ladislaw, while professing that, of course, she hopes 'all bad tales about anybody may be false', unsettles the budding romance of Dorothea and Will (1996: 590). If, as Josephine McDonagh argues, '*Middlemarch* is a novel about gossip, and the ways in which circulating stories both falsify realities and derail intended outcomes' (2016: 364), Will and Dorothea's ultimate departure at the end of the novel seems a necessity for their psychic and emotional development.

A Wider Horizon: Portable Interiority and Provincial Life 255

Yet the novel does suggest that identity would be inherently meaningless without roots to people and place, which is different from saying that identity makes sense only in the confines of a particular place. By integrating Will into a community to which he has no childhood attachments, landscape plays a crucial role in the process of his metamorphosis from continental wanderer to active participant in the local community to a figure involved in regional and national issues – his views on which are defined by his wider European perspective. Indeed, Will's predilection for landscape, which mirrors Dorothea's, is established during the same period in Rome: 'One fine morning a young man whose hair was not immoderately long, but abundant and curly, and who was otherwise English in his equipment, had just turned his back on the Belvedere Torso in the Vatican and was looking out on the magnificent view of the mountains from the adjoining round vestibule' (1996: 176). Unlike Naumann, who revels in the art on display, Will is gazing out the window and deriving visual pleasure from the vista before him. As Elizabeth Helsinger observes, this act of looking towards the mountains rather than 'the statues, [is] a quite Ruskinian sign of his Englishness' (1994b: 138). Despite his seemingly aimless travels and conscious refusal to identify with his nationality, therefore, Will is figured as essentially, if inchoately, English.

When he returns to England, the novel subtly traces the ways in which he increasingly draws on the landscape for his figures of thinking and, in so doing, becomes rooted to the provincial community. Setting out for Lowick Church in the hope of seeing Dorothea at Sunday service, 'Will walked to Lowick as if he had been on the way to Paradise, crossing Halsell Common and skirting the wood, where the sunlight fell broadly under the budding boughs, bringing out the beauties of moss and lichen, and fresh green growths piercing the brown. Everything seemed', the narrator continues, 'to approve of his going to Lowick Church' (1996: 442). While Will walks across Halsell Common – open ground that one may traverse in reaching Lowick – his mind blurs the distinctions between himself and the landscape. Finding in nature confirmation of his own mental state, Will comes to embody the countryside's beauty, appearing as 'an incarnation of the spring' (1996: 443). This scene could very well be read as what Ruskin calls the 'pathetic fallacy' – the 'falseness of all our impressions of external things' when we seek in nature a response to our internal emotions (Ruskin 1901: 165). Eliot had singled out the concept in her review of the third volume of *Modern Painters* for particular consideration, where she notes that the 'pleasure we derive from this fallacy is legitimate when the passion from which it originates is strong' (1856a: 631). Presumably the same could be said of pain: Will's walk to Lowick parallels the moment Dorothea looks out the window at 'the chill, colourless, narrowed landscape' and senses her 'blooming full-pulsed youth' merging with it. Yet as he approaches the church, Will's relationship to the landscape deepens as he sings a 'ready-made melody': 'The thought that one may think me dear, / The place where one was known' (1996: 443). These lines encapsulate the sense of rootedness, at once both social and geographic, that is essential to Eliot's conception of the self and which resonates with her notion of the home-scene.

Will's growing sense of connection with others in Middlemarch begins to widen and become increasingly national as his narrow sympathies, focused solely on Dorothea's marital plight, expand to include a variety of sufferings that, he imagines, can be redressed through political reform. In addition to arranging 'gypsy excursions' and bonfires with children who have been raised in impoverished households, Will frequently accompanies Miss Noble, the elderly aunt of a local vicar, on her visits to the poor. With meagre resources herself, Miss Noble pilfers small items of food when she is at her nephew's home and collects them in a small basket that she always carries on her arm. 'Will became a favourite ... with little Miss Noble', the narrator observes, 'whom it was one of his oddities to escort when he met her in the street with her little basket, giving her his arm in the eyes of the town, and insisting on going with her to pay some call where she distributed her small filchings from her own share of sweet things' (1996: 435). The recipients of her beneficence, the narrator remarks, are the children of the friends she has made among the poor, 'fostering and petting all needy creatures being so spontaneous a delight to her' (1996: 158). Because Will possesses a distinct 'attitude of receptivity' that makes him keenly responsive to those around him (1996: 76), it is only a matter of time before he begins – as Dorothea had with her model cottage drawings – to imagine more far-reaching solutions to their plight.

When Mr Brooke decides to contest a parliamentary seat as a proponent of reform, he identifies Will as a natural ally. Writing to offer him a job as a journalist at the *Pioneer*, Mr Brooke notes that 'they could find a great many things to do together' in this 'period of peculiar growth' with 'the political horizon expanding'

A Wider Horizon: Portable Interiority and Provincial Life 257

(1996: 274). In discussing his plans with Casaubon, Mr Brooke provides this character assessment of Will:

> 'He seems to me a kind of Shelley, you know,' Mr. Brooke took an opportunity of saying, for the gratification of Mr. Casaubon. 'I don't mean as to anything objectionable – laxities or atheism, or anything of that kind, you know – Ladislaw's sentiments in every way I am sure are good – indeed, we were talking a great deal together last night. But he has the same sort of enthusiasm for liberty, freedom, emancipation – a fine thing under guidance – under guidance, you know. I think I shall be able to put him on the right tack; and I am the more pleased because he is a relation of yours, Casaubon.' (1996: 337–338)

For all of his protean qualities and characteristics, Will maintains throughout the novel a set of political opinions that do not waiver. As Mr Brooke learns in the conversation that occurred the previous evening, to which the reader does not have access, Will espouses views that go far beyond Mr Brooke's tepid commitment to reform.

Thus, although Mr Brooke provides Will with a rationale for – as well as the means of staying near – Dorothea, it is wide of the mark to conclude that he formulates his political opinions in an arbitrary way. The point is not, I think, that, as Amanda Anderson argues, 'he falls into the role of journalist for the cause of reform only because he wishes to stay in Middlemarch near Dorothea and is willing to work for the wayward Mr Brooke' (2016: 70). Rather, unlike Dorothea's reformist aspirations, Will's can find definitive shape in the form of employment, which lays the foundation for a career. By contrast, Dorothea is able to draw cottages that create positive and uplifting effects for its inhabitants. She is also able to generate enthusiasm in others for her plans. However, it is ultimately men who realise her dream and, therefore, accrue the consequent accolades.[8] The zeal Dorothea possesses for reform (to borrow a phrase from the prelude) is 'ill-matched with the meanness of opportunity' afforded women in the period (1996: 3).

It is true, of course, that prior to Mr Brooke's offer of employment to Will, Casaubon's young cousin is vocationally adrift. But it is Mr Brooke himself who recognises that the expanding political horizon opens up new opportunities for someone like Will. In fact, after further reflection, Mr Brooke remarks that Will is 'a sort of Burke with a leaven of Shelley' (1996: 469). The combination – to which I will return in greater detail later – may seem curious: Shelley believed in the ideals that motivated the French Revolution and often championed the people, while Edmund Burke denounced the French Revolution and extolled the virtues of tradition, hierarchy and property. By linking Shelley and Burke in his conception of Will, Mr Brooke makes clear that he is not simply attempting to underscore Will's defiance and acute responsiveness to his surroundings.[9] Through the comparison, he is also suggesting that Will has the capacity to be a national figure, whose 'enthusiasm for liberty, freedom, emancipation' is in dialogue with those held by England's European neighbours (1996: 337–338). As he says to Will on one occasion, 'I can't help wishing somebody had a pocket-borough to give you, Ladislaw' (1996: 432).

To Mr Brooke, Will's enthusiasm wants guidance, which he intends to provide by successfully persuading the young man to work for him as a journalist at his recently acquired newspaper. With the burgage-holders of Middlemarch wary of reform, Mr Brooke believes that Will's capability of 'putting ideas into form' – particularly essential given that Mr Brooke's own thought processes roam 'the globe', 'from China to Peru' – will help the newspaper 'clear the pathway for a new candidate' (1996: 474, 283). Long before he had purchased it, the *Pioneer* had established itself as a leading voice of progress, taking for itself a motto from Charles James Fox, the influential Member of Parliament on such matters as religious toleration and individual freedom, whom Mary Russell Mitford so admired. Although the newspaper's readership had fallen over its championing of the Catholic Relief Act of 1829, which eliminated the ban on Roman Catholics becoming Members of Parliament, Mr Brooke believes that with the election of Charles Grey as prime minister in 1830 and the introduction of John Russell's Reform Bill in 1831, the time is ripe for a resurgence. Mr Brooke believes that he and Will can build on the publication's legacy to make 'a new thing of opinion here' (1996: 431).

Just as it does with Dorothea, the novel outlines the role that the local landscape plays in cultivating partiality for a figure who does not possess indigenous affective ties to the provincial community. In order for Will to play a role in making 'a new thing of opinion here', after all, he must become invested in the place. One aspect of his growing attachment is the small pleasures the landscape affords. 'I told Mr. Brooke not to call for me', Will explains to Dorothea after finishing one of his visits to Casaubon's residence. 'I would rather walk the five miles. I shall strike across Halsell Common, and see

A Wider Horizon: Portable Interiority and Provincial Life 259

the gleams on the wet grass. I like that' (1996: 346). These pleasures are shown increasingly to replace those he once derived from wandering: he develops 'the gamut of joy in landscape' that, the narrator tells us, is peculiar to 'midland-bred souls' (1996: 96). Over the course of the novel, the town of Middlemarch and its neighbouring village increasingly become Will's 'familiar little world', made up initially of his relationship to Dorothea and later of the journalistic and political activities and associations that have begun to mould his professional aspirations (1996: 753). He commits himself 'to leave off wandering', as Dorothea insists to Casaubon, becoming tied instead to the notion of Middlemarch as a home-scene (1996: 210). Because he has no other affective ties to people or place, when Mr Brooke offers him the opportunity to work for the newspaper he has just purchased, Will tells Dorothea, 'I would rather stay in this part of the country than go away. I belong to nobody anywhere else' (1996: 345). Will's emotional attachment to Dorothea becomes intertwined with his business relationship to Mr Brooke and his own pleasures in the countryside.

The problem when it comes to working with Mr Brooke, of course, is that Dorothea's uncle lacks political conviction. When he is first introduced to the reader Mr Brooke is described as 'a man nearly sixty, of acquiescent temper, miscellaneous opinions, and uncertain vote'. His 'conclusions', the narrator continues, 'were as difficult to predict as the weather' (1996: 8). Even after he decides to contest the election, Mr Brooke cannot settle on a definite opinion about reform: 'Only I want to keep myself independent about Reform, you know; I don't want to go too far. I want to ... work at Negro Emancipation, Criminal Law – that kind of thing'. 'But of course', he adds, 'I should support Grey' (1996: 283). Because Will recognises that the coming election, which was triggered by the fall of Grey's government in April 1831, is a crucial moment for the reform effort, he goads him into re-evaluating his position:

> 'If you go in for the principle of Reform, you must be prepared to take what the situation offers,' said Will. 'If everybody pulled for his own bit against everybody else, the whole question would go to tatters.'
>
> 'Yes, yes, I agree with you – I quite take that point of view. I should put it in that light. I should support Grey, you know. But I don't want to change the balance of the constitution, and I don't think Grey would.'

'But that is what the country wants,' said Will. 'Else there would be no meaning in political unions or any other movement that knows what it's about. It wants to have a House of Commons which is not weighted with nominees of the landed class, but with representatives of the other interests. And as to contending for a reform short of that, it is like asking for a bit of an avalanche which has already begun to thunder.'

'That is fine, Ladislaw: that is the way to put it. Write that down, now. We must begin to get documents about the feeling of the country, as well as the machine-breaking and general distress.' (1996: 431–432)

Although Will hopes to fashion Dorothea's uncle into an admittedly imperfect standard-bearer of progressive ideas and causes, Mr Brooke lacks an intrinsic commitment to them. After his catastrophic appearance before the weavers and tanners of Middlemarch, who grow so restless with his rambling, incoherent speech that they begin pelting him with eggs, Mr Brooke withdraws from the electoral contest and sells the *Pioneer*. Unlike Will, the new owners have much more modest intentions for its editorial content.

One's national identity, the novel seems to suggest, must be developed within the dynamics of the local town, which is itself situated in the larger context of the region. In helping Mr Brooke's election campaign, Will takes up a regional question: how will distinct provincial localities represent themselves to the nation? According to Will, borough representation must 'not [be] weighted with nominees of the landed class, but with representatives of the other interests' (1996: 432). 'The only conscience we can trust to', he insists, 'is the massive sense of wrong in a class, and the best wisdom that will work is the wisdom of balancing claims' (1996: 437–438). He argues for a more representative system that includes the interests of labourers from Middlemarch and surrounding areas, whose plight he has witnessed first hand, and he also calls attention to the social good that might be generated through the clash of different class-based opinions and observations. Therefore, in 'place of dilettanteism', he begins 'thoroughly to like the work' of 'meditating on the needs of the English people' or 'criticising English statesmanship' by becoming involved in regional politics and Mr Brooke's campaign (1996: 433).

With his career at the *Pioneer* effectively over, Will contemplates his next move. In fact, in his exchange with Mr Brooke, Will

A Wider Horizon: Portable Interiority and Provincial Life 261

reveals himself to be a radical. In a leading article in the *Trumpet*, a rival Tory-leaning newspaper, Will is branded 'an energumen' who, in 'speechify[ing] by the hour against institutions "which had existed when he was in his cradle"', conceals 'the poverty of knowledge' on which his opinions are based 'in the brilliancy of fireworks' (1996: 434). When an associate of the newspaper's editor inquires about the meaning of the word energumen, he replies: 'Oh, a term that came up in the French Revolution' (1996: 435). Although the first Reform Act produced only very modest changes, there was widespread belief at the time that the measure would fundamentally alter England's existing political institutions and social arrangements. Thus, Mr Brooke refers to charging the 'balance' of the constitution and Mrs Cadwallader to its 'overturn[ing]' (1996: 432, 63). A historical counterpart to these fictional characters, John Wilson Croker, the long-time Secretary of the Admiralty, sketched what he saw as the consequences of reform in a letter to Walter Scott dated 5 April 1831: 'No King, no Lords, no inequalities in the social system; all will be levelled to the plane of the petty shopkeepers and small farmers; this, perhaps, not without bloodshed, but certainly by confiscations and persecutions' (Croker 1885: 2, 113). Croker resigned from Parliament in 1832 when the bill passed.

Although Mr Brooke has failed to advance the cause of reform, Will recognises through his experience at the *Pioneer* that there are other means to promote change. By undertaking 'political writing, political speaking, [which] would get a higher value now [that] public life was going to be wider and more national', Will senses that his exertions need not be confined to their specific locality. He also recognises that by contributing to this 'wider and more national' effort, he would grow in prominence and, therefore, 'not seem to be asking Dorothea to step down to him' when he proposes marriage (1996: 477).

Because Will is often discussed as a flawed romantic partner for Dorothea, the compatibility of their political views often goes unremarked. Like Will, Dorothea takes an active interest in the lives of the poor. On one occasion, instead of condescending to a farm labourer, she actively engages with him on an issue of importance to him. She stops 'to talk to old Master Bunney who was putting in some garden-seeds', the narrator remarks, 'and discoursed wisely with that rural sage about the crops that would make the most return on a perch of ground, and the result of sixty years' experience as to soils – namely, that if your soil was pretty mellow it would do, but if there came wet, wet, wet to make it all of a mummy, why then . . .' (1996: 737). In addition, her own views tend towards radicalism. While she believes that the wealthy 'deserve to be beaten out of our beautiful houses with a scourge of small cords' so long as their tenants suffer, she also questions 'why land should be entailed' when it enables a clear 'wrong': disinheritance because of gender and class biases. The narrator asks: 'Was inheritance a question of liking or of responsibility? All the energy of Dorothea's nature went on the side of responsibility – the fulfilment of claims founded on our own deeds, such as marriage and parentage' (1996: 349).

The foundation of her relationship with Will, therefore, is a shared vision of reform. This provides at least a partial explanation for the narrator's observation that the two 'were bound to each other by a love stronger than any impulses which could have marred it' (1996: 782). Because Will believes that political measures can cure social ills, he contests a seat and is 'returned to Parliament, by a constituency who paid his expenses'. Thus, the narrator notes in the finale, 'Dorothea could have liked nothing better, since wrongs existed than that her husband should be in the thick of a struggle against them, and that she should give him wifely help' (1996: 782–783). He takes up his parliamentary work in earnest at a time 'when reforms were begun with a young hopefulness of immediate good which', the narrator bemoans, 'has been much checked in our days'. The implication, of course, is that any excitement one may have felt immediately following the passage of the first Reform Act had – in the years following the enactment of the 1867 Reform Act – dissipated.

There were any number of reasons to be cynical depending on one's own view of reform. For some, the need for a second reform bill underscored the limitations of the first. Although the 1867 Reform Act extended the franchise to every male adult householder in the boroughs and to any male paying ten or more pounds for rooms, the legislation continued to rely on a property qualification. It also did not resolve significant exclusions in the countryside. Those who advocated universal suffrage, of course, saw the legislation as woefully inadequate. As Member of Parliament for Westminster, taking his seat in the general election of 1865, John Stuart Mill blasted the bill: 'this is not a democratic measure'. 'It neither deserves that praise, nor, if honourable members will have it so', he continued, 'that reproach' (Mill 1988: 61). Mill advocated a quasi-universal suffrage that included women and the vast majority of the working class. His argument was based on a vociferous objection to any property qualification. As he explained in *Considerations on Representative Government*, the 'accident' of property ownership had 'so much more to do than merit with enabling men to rise in the world' (Mill 1977b: 474). Having made the case in his amendment for altering the language of the bill from *man* to *person*, as he had years earlier in his pamphlet, 'Thoughts on Parliamentary Reform', Mill perhaps found the measure that did pass especially galling.

Of course, Eliot never aligned herself with the women's suffrage movement nor did she lend her voice to the campaign for extending the vote to working-class men. In a letter dated 30 May 1867, Eliot explained to the women's rights activist Clementia Taylor – who had beseeched her to publicly support Mill's amendment to the reform bill enfranchising women on the same basis as men – that she shared the underlying impulse:

> I do sympathise with you most emphatically in the desire to see women socially elevated – educated equally with men, and secured as far as possible along with every other breathing creature from suffering the exercise of any unrighteous power. That is a broader ground of sympathy than agreement as to the amount, and kind, of result that may be hoped for from a particular measure. (Eliot 1955b: 366)

Although Eliot goes on to express her 'hope' that 'much good' might follow the airing of 'women's claims' in Parliament, she declines to offer an endorsement. Sceptical that any 'particular measure' could bring about tangible changes, Eliot prefers – as her remarks about Mill's possible election suggest ('thinkers can do more outside than inside the House') – to shape the world by acting on her readers.

The 'Representation of the People Act' of 1832 set in motion a range of subsequent improvements to which the novel alludes, including the abolition of slavery, improvement of working conditions in mines and factories, further extension of rights to religious minorities and continued modernisation of Britain's political system and institutions. Yet *Middlemarch* indicts the reform culture it unleashed for the lack of educational opportunities and social positions it made available to women.[10] As I argued in the previous section, the novel shows Dorothea's capacities for sympathy and aspiration expanding to become wider and potentially national, while simultaneously noting the confinement and circumscribed actions that her life – her moving from Tipton to Lowick and then becoming the wife of a politician – brings. 'Many who knew her', the narrator observes, 'thought it a pity that so substantive and rare a creature should have been absorbed into the life of another . . . . But no one stated exactly what else that was in her power she ought rather to have done'. This absorption, in which she finds herself known in certain circles only 'as a wife and mother' (1996: 783), is already alluded to by the scene in which Dorothea stands at her window: although the image on which she gazes suggests mobility rather than fixity, the 'man with a bundle on his back' and the 'woman carrying her baby' emphasise a fundamentally gendered distinction between them.

For women, Eliot seems to be suggesting, the possibilities for national expression are decidedly narrow. Thus, Dorothea's role is to provide 'wifely help' to Will, who, as 'an ardent public man', is able to pursue the kinds of social changes that animate them both (1996: 782). One might, therefore, conclude that Eliot is not arguing that Dorothea's actions should be more limited than her capacity for affect or imaginative vision. Rather Eliot continues throughout the novel to point out that they are limited, leaving it to the reader to decide whether this is wasteful. At the same time, she also urges readers to appreciate what Dorothea is able to accomplish in the circumscribed domestic, but no longer local, setting of her life.

Of universal manhood suffrage, Eliot was similarly equivocal. If *Felix Holt* can be seen as representative of her thoughts on the matter, then Eliot believed that the debate over the franchise was a spectacular distraction from pressing economic and social problems that would not be solved simply because more people could cast a vote. This view has often been used as evidence of her essential conservatism. Certainly, it was not a label from which she shied away. As she explained to Clifford Allbutt in a letter of August 1868, 'the bent of my mind is conservative rather than destructive' (Eliot 1955b: 472). But Eliot's underlying point in *Felix Holt* is that a franchise based on the arbitrary figure of ten pounds does nothing to eradicate poverty, illiteracy or ignorance. Following the passage of the 1867 Reform Bill, John Blackwood, her Tory publisher, suggested, in a letter dated 7 November 1867, that she

A Wider Horizon: Portable Interiority and Provincial Life 265

write an 'address to the Working Men on their new responsibilities' (Eliot 1955b: 395). She does not appear to have been enthusiastic about the idea. In her reply two days later, she thanks him for the offer: 'Felix Holt is immensely tempted by your suggestion, but George Eliot is severely admonished by his domestic critic not to scatter his energies' (Eliot 1955b: 397). Blackwood, however, made the 'repeated request', and she finally relented (Eliot 1998c: 131). In his 'Address to Working Men', which appeared in the January 1868 issue of *Blackwood's Magazine*, Felix Holt proclaims that 'No political institution will alter the nature of Ignorance, or hinder it from producing vice and misery' (Eliot 1868, 8). While the issue was at the printers, Blackwood wrote to Eliot, in a letter dated 28 December, to thank her for doing this 'personal favour' for him (Eliot 1955b: 411). While this essay is often used as an interpretive tool for understanding the politics of *Felix Holt*, it is important to keep in mind the pressure that Blackwood exerted on her. As Nancy Henry points out, 'She felt under obligation to him for gracefully taking her back after her defection to George Smith for the publication of *Romola* in 1863' (2019: 162).

In fact, attempting to discern Eliot's political views from the 'Address to the Working Men' obscures significant differences between the two novels. Where the character of Felix Holt espouses a view that, in Raymond Williams's assessment, would make him 'a very convenient ally of the opponents of reform' (1966: 105), in *Middlemarch* it is Lydgate who, in a debate with Will about whether political measures can cure social ills, expresses a comparable opinion: 'You go against rottenness, and there is nothing more thoroughly rotten than making people believe that society can be cured by a political hocus-pocus' (1996: 437). One element of that charlatanism, Lydgate contends, is having aristocrats put themselves forward as champions of the people: 'That is the way with you political writers, Ladislaw – crying up a measure as if it were a universal cure, and crying up men who are a part of the very disease that wants curing' (1996: 437). But Will points out that the 'cure must begin somewhere', and that reformers cannot wait to 'find immaculate men to work with'. After deriding the notion ('Wait for wisdom and conscience in public agents – fiddlestick!'), Will declares: 'The only conscience we can trust to is the massive sense of wrong in a class, and the best wisdom that will work is the wisdom of balancing claims. That's my text – which side is injured? I support the man who supports their claims; not the virtuous upholder of the wrong' (1996: 437–438). This is, as Henry Staten points out, precisely the 'pragmatic argument' put forward by the trades-union man in *Felix Holt* to counter the eponymous character's anti-political views: 'the workers should support a "liberal aristocrat" if he will serve their ends' (2000: 994). Thus, Will's disagreement with Lydgate, which results, as the latter concedes, in a 'checkmate', can also be read as a rejoinder to Felix Holt.

If we accept, for argument's sake, that Eliot aligned herself with Felix Holt in 1866 and Will Ladislaw in 1871–72, what caused this change of perspective? In June 1866, the *Saturday Review* published John Morley's fulsome review of *Felix Holt* to which I referred at the outset of this chapter. Although the review was unsigned, George Henry Lewes and George Eliot soon learned that its author was Morley, with whom Lewes had occasionally interacted at the *Leader*. Two months later, Morley published an omnibus review of Eliot's fiction in *Macmillan's Magazine*. 'It is not the assiduous cultivation of a style, as such' he contended, in speaking of her prose, 'but the cultivation of the intellect and feelings, which produces good writing' (1866b: 279). Soon after reading the essay, Lewes and Evans began inviting Morley to dine at their home 'pretty frequently' (Hirst 1927: 41).

In his late twenties and no longer able to believe in the divinity of Christ, Morley was searching for a substitute belief system. While at Oxford, where he graduated in 1859 with a degree in Classical Moderations, Morley had encountered the work of John Stuart Mill and was known to have practically memorised *On Liberty*, which was published during his final term (Hirst 1927: 1, 22). Having acquired his religious beliefs from his parents, which were reinforced at the schools to which they had sent him, Morley concluded on reading *On Liberty* that his faith was not – what Mill would call – a living belief, or a profoundly held conviction that animates one's being (Morrison 2018b: 23–26). Elsewhere, I have explored the complicated dynamics of the intergenerational friendship Morley, who was then in his late twenties, developed with Lewes and Eliot, who were forty-nine and forty-seven respectively. The three bonded over an intense interest in the positivist philosophy of Auguste Comte (Morrison 2021b).

Their intellectual camaraderie was so pronounced that when Lewes decided to step down as editor of the *Fortnightly Review*, with which he and Eliot had been involved since its inception a year earlier, he handpicked Morley to succeed him. On 22 November

A Wider Horizon: Portable Interiority and Provincial Life 267

1866, Eliot wrote to her friend Sara Sophia Hennell about Lewes's decision to hand over the reins: 'His successor in the editorship is Mr. John Morley, a very accomplished man, and I hope he will be able to keep up the Review in the same spirit' (1955b: 315). Between February and July 1867, Morley published a four-part series of essays on Edmund Burke (1867a–d). These formed the basis of his *Edmund Burke: A Historical Study*, published towards the end of the year (1867e).[11]

For Morley, who was increasingly finding himself drawn to the Radicalism of Mill, Burke may have seemed to some an odd choice. The Whig grandee at one point in his career, Morley acknowledges, 'assumed an attitude identical with that of the least liberal and enlightened people among ourselves' by framing the principle of religious toleration that he propagated as a battle of godliness against atheism (1867e: 37). But a thorough understanding of Burke's thought, Morley contends, reveals him to be one who embraced 'conformity to general utility' as the foundational principle of good government. Because the French Revolution – despite its 'thousand errors of detail, some of them the worst and grossest that the history of politics has to show' – was 'the most gigantic effort that has ever been made to establish' the 'criterion of general happiness . . . firmly and permanently in political affairs', Morley argues that Burke was far 'nearer to the best, most vital, and most durable part of the Revolution than he knew, and than his successors have supposed' (1867e: 310).

Emphasising his antagonism towards the monarchy, support of the American Revolution and his restoration of the idea that Parliament serve all people, Burke is, in Morley's hands, leavened with a bit of Shelley. As he would later put it more succinctly, what he learned from Burke, who revered social and political institutions for the wisdom they acquired over time, is that 'nations have the best chance of escaping a catastrophe . . . [when they] find a way of opening the most liberal career to the aspirations of the present, without too rudely breaking with all the traditions of the past' (Morley 1907: 154). To Eliot, who feared that reforms might unravel the fabric of continuity emblematised by the provincial village, this version of Burke propagated by her friend and fellow liberal intellectual would have surely resonated.

Critics have generally panned Will. One of the few exceptions has been Raymond Williams, who argued a number of years ago that:

Ladislaw is a free man in the way the others are not; a free mind with free emotions; a man who is wholly responsive. He isn't tied by property, which he can reject in a principled way ... Coming from 'nowhere', belonging 'nowhere', he is able to move, to relate and so to grow in ways that the others are not . . . . This is George Eliot thinking beyond, feeling beyond, the restrictions and the limitations she has so finely recorded; thinking into mobility not as dislocating but as liberating; with some anxiety, certainly ... but following a thread to the future. (1970: 93)

Although I generally agree, I would add an emendation and a qualification. First the emendation: although the narrator expresses a degree of cynicism about political reform, Eliot nevertheless depicts Will, in contrast to Mr Brooke, as a laudatory aspirant for Parliament. When John Stuart Mill decried a property qualification as the basis for either the right to vote or to hold elected office, he insisted in *Considerations on Representative Government*, a text Eliot knew well, that the 'accident' of ownership had 'so much more to do than merit with enabling men to rise in the world' (1977b: 474). By establishing himself as a writer and journalist and using that as the basis for launching his political career, Will is depicted as being able to rise in the world through merit – in Williams's terms, 'a free mind with free emotions' – rather than owing his seat in Parliament to either birth or connections (1970: 93).

But Will, as I have attempted to show, does not belong nowhere. For Eliot, rootless or wandering characters embody modernity's instability; their lack of geographic attachment and ideational grounding render the whole notion of individual and national identity unintelligible to her. In her depiction of Will, Eliot is clearly rejecting the 'antinational cosmopolitanism' (Semmel 1994: 143) that was increasingly taking hold among some intellectuals and aligns herself with an influential strand in Victorian political thinking that defined the universal largely in terms of the nation.[12] That is, the nation was understood and recognised to be the most inclusive human community yet realised. The nation was a step towards ultimate universality precisely because it was the most universal of social formations to date.[13] Eliot repeatedly returns to this idea in her works from *Middlemarch* forward. In *Daniel Deronda*, relational ties of community, in its 'highest transformation', are shown to be global, but such a sense of world community can only be achieved after 'the character of a nationality' has

A Wider Horizon: Portable Interiority and Provincial Life 269

been cultivated (1995: 535).[14] The affective foundation that Will has acquired in Middlemarch, shaped by his interactions with the local topography and expressed through his socio-political activities, equips him with what Eliot imagines to be a necessary building block for the expanding collective units of which he becomes a part. Thus, his involvement in local and regional politics is an expression of his emergent partiality for this geographic area.

Unlike the pre-reflective nature of indigenous attachments to a provincial locality foregrounded in *The Mill on the Floss*, *Middlemarch* refigures the landscape as something that can be read for symbolic meaning and thus can include rootless and wandering figures such as Dorothea and Will. After all, collectivities defined by the mind's interaction with the landscape are, at least in theory, available to anyone.[15] The novel reflects Eliot's interest in conceptualising how mobile individuals might become attached to local sites yet also develop the capacity to rise above immediately lived experience and to embrace wider ties and a larger communal existence. Home-scenes in this novel, therefore, are posited as relational rather than territorial.[16] They are a way of thinking and feeling about one's place within increasingly larger abstract social units.

Thus, Dorothea and Will become attached to the provincial community as they draw their figures of thought from the landscape. But they also increasingly register in moments of communion with nature an awareness of their place not only in provincial life but also their embeddedness in more complex formations. Having acquired the foundational affections and obligations of a home-scene, Dorothea and Will are equipped with what Eliot imagines to be a set of fundamental and portable social skills – in her lexicon, sympathy, temperance and the duties that follow from a sense of obligation to and bonds with others.[17] *Middlemarch* offers a way of imagining a liberal polity that, for Eliot, closely resembles, in its best aspects, provincial life.

Notes

1. The other significant occurrence Eliot mentions is 'the better understanding of disease' (qtd. in Pinney 1966: 372). She represents both political and medical reform, of course, in *Middlemarch*.
2. The concept of 'portable interiority' contributes to the growing interest in landscape as imaginatively moveable. See, for example, Matthew Ingleby and Matthew Kerr who argue in another context

that the seaside in the nineteenth century was increasingly rendered 'portable, transportable and available' (2018: 7).
3. Other works on Victorian cosmopolitanism have stimulated my thinking, even though I do not engage them directly here. On 'partial cosmopolitanism', which does not capture the fraught relation between attachment and detachment that interests me, see Appiah 2006. On the dangerous tensions seen by some novelists between provincialism and cosmopolitanism without the mediating term of the nation, see Buzard 2005.
4. Kate Flint has noted how, in *Middlemarch*, 'the world of things and the life of the mind' are inseparable (2006: 85). However, Flint's interest is in material objects rather than landscape.
5. Thus, Linda K. Hughes has referred to it as depicting 'a country town' rather than, say, a clear representation of the town of Middlemarch (2005: 163).
6. As Carolyn Lesjak puts it, 'Eliot's thinking and her novels move by necessity from the small and measurable to the large and potentially limitless; from foreground to background, matter to knowledge and symbol to meaning – all subject to history' (2021: 89).
7. Ruskin delivered his scathing assessment of *The Mill on the Floss*, which I briefly discussed in the previous chapter, a year later.
8. The new cottages are built on James Chettam's estate, Freshitt. Caleb Garth oversees the effort.
9. For George Levine, the repeated references to Will as Shelleyan are intended to highlight his 'rebelliousness and sensibility' (1983: 298).
10. Laura Green has argued that the depictions of Dorothea Brooke, Rosamond Vincy and Mary Garth 'can be read as responses to the plans for women's higher education that Eliot's reforming feminist friends, such as Barbara Bodichon and Emily Davies, were beginning to instigate in the 1860s' (2001: 71).
11. Morley published a second work for the English Men of Letter series, *Burke*, in 1879.
12. As scholars ranging from A. Anderson (2001) to Cheah (1998) have shown, transnationalism in the nineteenth century was not something that would necessarily follow nationalism but already coexisted with it.
13. H. S. Jones explains: 'Most nineteenth-century liberals, at least until the last decade or two of the century, were nationalists because they saw the nation as a step away from the particular and towards the universal', regarding the nation as 'the most general and universal of actual communities' (2000: 49).

A Wider Horizon: Portable Interiority and Provincial Life 271

14 Like many of her time, Eliot saw the nation as a necessary stage in human social and political development. Since the realisation of the nation was understood to be an essential phase in the gradual process toward universal human community, the inculcation of a sense of local attachment, which is narrativised in *Middlemarch*, was the necessary first step in developing gradually wider ties. While acknowledging the reality of transnational ties in many of her novels, Eliot seems to be insisting, in her representation of Will and Dorothea, on the need for individuals to follow a developmental trajectory that mirrors her teleological understanding of human history.

15 While Will and Dorothea *are* rootless and wandering, one might argue that it does not necessarily follow that they stand for all those who are rootless and wandering, including the gypsies on whom Eliot draws in her depiction of Will. To the extent that this model is inclusive, one could conclude, it is only within acceptable class boundaries. Indeed, that Raffles – a rootless wanderer from the lower classes – never becomes integrated into a community suggests that there are limits to Eliot's project. Yet, although she does seem to restrict her account, the *process* that she describes is not class specific.

16 See Graver (1994) for a discussion of the shift in Eliot's thinking from territorial-based models of community to relational ones.

17 But the novel also suggests that under the regime of an 'imperfect social state' and one of its primary apparatuses, the institution of marriage, women may, like men, acquire the affective foundations necessary to participate in larger social units and yet, because society deprives them of meaningful channels for expression, continue to be thwarted in their efforts to lead 'a grand life here – now – in England' (Eliot 1996: 784, 27).

Conclusion

George Eliot's *Felix Holt, the Radical* (1866) opens with a coachman and a traveller passing through districts of the English Midlands by stagecoach. Seated on the box next to the coachman, the 'happy outside passenger' revels in the driver's stories of 'English labours in town and country' and in his detailed knowledge of the landscape. The narrator notes that as the traveller's journey unfolds, he passes from 'one phase of English life to another': from 'a village dingy with coal-dust, noisy with the shaking of looms', quickly followed by 'a parish all of fields, high hedges, and deep rutted lanes', to a 'manufacturing town, the scenes of riots and trades-union meetings', and within 'ten minutes' to a 'neighbourhood of the town' whose inhabitants care nothing for politics (1871: 10). It would be 'easy', the narrator avers, for the 'traveller to conceive that town and country had no pulse in common' (1871: 10). But should Eliot's readers?

Reflecting on this scene, Raymond Williams once remarked that the introduction to *Felix Holt* engages in a mystification. In comparison to the 'busy scenes of the shuttle and the wheel, of the roaring furnace, of the shaft and the pulley', to say nothing of the violence of rioters in the manufacturing regions, the peacefulness of the countryside – with its 'low gray sky' that seems to effect 'an unchanging stillness as if Time itself were pausing' – would be experienced by the traveller as a welcome relief (Eliot 1871: 10). Because the journey takes place thirty-five years before the novel was written, Williams suggests that Eliot – who directs the reader to view the Midlands through the eyes of the traveller (Williams 1973: 178) – engenders in readers a nostalgia for the past.

Yet throughout the novel, Eliot, in fact, shows that both town and country are fundamentally interconnected and share the same 'pulse'. In *Our Village*, Mitford's narrator insists that her village had 'a trick of standing still, of remaining stationary, unchanged and unimproved in this most changeable and improving world' (Mitford 1826a: 1). The narrative itself, however, reveals not only changes but significant changes. Similarly, in Gaskell's *Cranford*, Mary Smith's statement that nothing has happened between her visits to the village from the industrial town of Drumble may conjure in one's mind a timeless world. But her narrative, too, documents all sorts of change.

Although Mitford, Gaskell and Eliot have been frequently incorporated into mobilisations of restorative nostalgia, I have highlighted moments of ironic disjunction in which the coexistence of 'longing and critical thinking' (Boym 2001: 50), absent in restorative efforts to reconstruct what has been lost, is registered. In so doing, I have sought to recover the reflective tendencies evident in the fiction of all three writers. Contending that one element of provincial fiction by Mitford, Gaskell and Eliot is the reflective quality of their nostalgia, I have traced a chain of influence in which Gaskell adopts several techniques characteristic of Mitford's sketches in addition to ironic disjunction, including direct address and descriptive detail, that Eliot picks up and adapts for her realist novels.

Why might an argument about influence matter? In showing the impact that Mitford had on Gaskell, and through Gaskell on Eliot, I have attempted to foreground the significance of a writer who remains understudied today. Mitford was widely credited by her contemporaries as having invented the mode of descriptive writing in which Gaskell and Eliot are often said to have excelled. I have also endeavoured to highlight Mitford's and Gaskell's importance to Eliot's realist novels, as well as to her liberalism. If one solely focuses on the intellectual contexts of a novel such as *Middlemarch* (examining, say, its engagements with the evolutionary thought of Charles Darwin and Herbert Spencer or the social and political criticism of Matthew Arnold), one can miss the way in which it is part of a tradition of women's writing inherited from Mitford and Gaskell. Given Eliot's statements about women writers, her political position on female suffrage, and her profoundly European intellectual and philosophical roots, one might assume that the novelist herself occluded these connections to Gaskell and Mitford.[1] But perhaps that responsibility rests instead with Virginia Woolf.

In *A Room of One's Own*, Woolf recalls pondering the phrase *women and fiction* soon after being asked to give an address on the topic at the University of Cambridge. One way of approaching the subject, she remarks, in a gently sardonic tone, is to enumerate the many influential writers of the modern period who were women:

> When you asked me to speak about women and fiction I sat down on the banks of a river and began to wonder what the words meant. They might mean simply a few remarks about Fanny Burney; a few more about Jane Austen; a tribute to the Brontës and a sketch of Haworth Parsonage under snow; some witticisms if possible about Miss Mitford; a respectful allusion to George Eliot; a reference to Mrs Gaskell and one would have done. But at second sight the words seemed not so simple. (1929: 3)

Of course, Woolf eschews this 'simple' approach. But her implicit valorisation of Eliot over Mitford and Gaskell is elsewhere made far more explicit. In *Flush*, Woolf characterises Mitford as a hack who, driven by the need for 'money', 'scarcely knew what tragedy to spin, what annual to edit'. Mitford's output, Woolf concludes, was of marginal literary value (1933: 22). Gaskell fares somewhat better. While Woolf praises aspects of Gaskell's social problem novels, she finds *Cranford* wanting: 'Too great a refinement gives "Cranford" that prettiness which is the weakest thing about it, making it, superficially at least, the favourite copy for gentle writers who have hired rooms over the village post-office' (1984: 144). The problem with Gaskell, in Woolf's estimation, is that she is a 'sympathetic amateur' who lacks both 'cleverness' and wit (1984: 142, 143). This inhibits Gaskell's ability to produce compelling characters. Additionally, by 'adding detail after detail' in a 'profuse impersonal way', Gaskell reveals an incapacity 'to concentrate' on what might truly matter in her depiction of reality: 'What we want to be there is the brain and the view of life; the autumnal woods, the history of the whale fishery, and the decline of stage coaching we omit entirely' (1984: 142).

By contrast, Woolf sees George Eliot's fiction as a significant literary and intellectual achievement. Many of Eliot's contemporaries lauded her as one of the great English novelists.

Conclusion 275

Indeed, the artist Frederic Burton convinced Eliot to sit for a portrait by him in 1864, when he considered her to be at the height of her powers as a fiction writer, and to allow him to exhibit it in the Royal Academy of Arts (Figure 6.1). But by the 1870s, many critics felt that she had produced her best work prior to *Romola* (1863): *Scenes of Clerical Life* (1857), *Adam Bede* (1859), *The Mill on the Floss* (1860) and *Silas Marner* (1861) were generally assumed to be superior to her later novelistic efforts. As Leslie Stephen asserted in his volume on Eliot in Macmillan's *English Men of Letters* series: '*Middlemarch* seems to fall short of the great masterpieces', while *Daniel Deronda* evidences a decline in Eliot's 'imaginative sense', with her characters 'becoming symbols of principle, and composed of more moonshine than solid flesh and blood' (1902: 184, 191). In *The Common Reader*, Woolf demurs: 'It is not that her power diminishes, for, to our thinking, it is at its highest in the mature *Middlemarch*, the magnificent book which with all its imperfections is one of the few English

Figure 6.1 George Eliot. Chalk portrait by Sir Frederic William Burton, 1865. © National Portrait Gallery, London.

novels written for grown-up people' (1948: 213). Rejecting her father's stance, Woolf's essay spurred Eliot's rehabilitation in the twentieth century.

Woolf does not discuss at length what she sees as the distinguishing features of Eliot's fiction. But – largely sidestepping the descriptive elements in Eliot's work – she does point to Eliot's capacity to create character. Unlike Gaskell, of whose novels, Woolf claims, one remembers the fictional world but not the people who populate it, Eliot has a striking ability to depict a range of figures: 'fools and failures, mothers and children, dogs and flourishing midland fields, farmers, sagacious or fuddled over their ale, horse-dealers, inn-keepers, curates and carpenters' (1948: 213). Because Eliot emphasises 'the everyday lot' of individuals, 'the homespun of ordinary joys and sorrows', the reader might at times feel 'now bored, now sympathetic' (1948: 210, 211). But as Eliot takes the reader on a 'ramble' through her villages, one is always engaged with the characters: they are 'flesh and blood and we move among them' (1948: 212, 211). Although, as I have argued, Eliot's developing craft as a novelist was shaped by Mitford's literary sketches and Gaskell's Cranford papers, Woolf attributes this capacity for character to what Eliot's predominantly male critics would characterise as her 'not strongly feminine' mind. While Eliot found herself charmed by Mitford and Gaskell, Woolf would insist that Eliot herself was not 'charming' (as this term was associated with conventional femininity). As an unequivocal feminist, Woolf never assumed a 'masculine narrative persona' (Booth 1992: 15). But she would not have eschewed the appellation *charmless*, which was – in the hands, or rather mouths, of male critics – a synonym for learned. Yet the Eliot whom Woolf admires would not, perhaps, have been quite the same writer had she not been preceded by Mitford and Gaskell.

Note

1 On points of contact between Eliot's fiction and European fiction writers, particularly Honoré de Balzac, see Rignall 2011. On Eliot and Schiller, see Guth 2003.

Bibliography

Addison, C. (1988), 'Gender and Genre in Mary Russell Mitford's *Christina*', *English Studies in Africa* 41.2: pp. 1–21.
Allott, M. (1960), *Elizabeth Gaskell*, London: Longmans.
Altick, R. D. (1998), *The English Common Reader: A Social History of the Mass Reading Public, 1800–1900*, Chicago: University of Chicago Press.
Anderson, A. (2001), *The Powers of Distance: Cosmopolitanism and the Cultivation of Detachment*, Princeton: Princeton University Press.
——. (2016), *Bleak Liberalism*, Chicago: University of Chicago Press.
Anderson, B. R. (1991), *Imagined Communities: Reflections on the Origin and Spread of Nationalism*, London: Verso.
Anon. (1810), [Review of Mary Russell Mitford's *Poems*], *Quarterly Review* 4.8: 514–18.
——. (1811), Review, *Literary Panorama* 10 (London): p. 844.
——. (1823a), 'Manners', *Lady's Magazine* (March): pp. 150–52.
——. (1823b), Review of *Julian*, *London Literary Gazette* (22 March : pp. 177–78.
——. (1823c), 'Theatrical Examiner', *Examiner* (23 March): p. 203.
——. (1823d), 'Theatricals', *John Bull* (23 March): pp. 94–95.
——. (1823e), 'The Winter Evening's Fire-Side: A Rhapsody.' *Lady's Magazine* (January): pp. 40–42.
——. (1823f), 'On the Folly and Wickedness of Having a Long Nose' *Lady's Magazine* (April): pp. 226–29.
——. (1823g), 'The Village Bells', *Lady's Magazine* (1823): pp. 81–83.
——. (1825), 'Our Village: Sketches of Rural Character and Scenery', *Quarterly Review* 31 (December 1824 and March 1825): pp. 166–74.
——. (1850), 'Biographical Sketch of Mary Russell Mitford', in

M. R. Mitford, *The Works of Mary Russell Mitford, Prose and Verse.* Philadelphia: Crissy and Markley, pp. 3–4.
——. (1853). 'Miscellaneous Reviews.' *Gentleman's Magazine* (July–December): pp. 493–94.
——. (1854), 'Mary Russell Mitford', *Hogg's Instructor* 3: pp. 301–08.
——. (1873). 'Preface', in M. R. Mitford, *Our Village: Tales*, London: Ward, Lock.
——. (1881), 'Biographical Preface', in M. R. Mitford, *Village Tales and Sketches*, Edinburgh: Nimmo, pp. 5–8.
——. (1915), *Catalogue of Books in the Children's Department of the Carnegie Library of Pittsburgh*, Vol. 1, Pittsburgh: Carnegie Library.
Appiah, K. A. (2006), *Cosmopolitanism: Ethics in a World of Strangers*, New York: Norton.
Arnheim, R. (1988), *The Power of the Center: A Study of Composition in the Visual Arts*, Berkeley: University of California Press.
Arnold, G. W. (1912), *A Mother's List of Books for Children*, Chicago: McClurg.
Arnold, M. (1960–77), *The Complete Prose Works of Matthew Arnold*, ed. R. H. Super, 11 vols, Ann Arbor: University of Michigan Press.
——. (1965) [1869], *Culture and Anarchy* in MA 1960–77, vol. 5, pp. 85–230.
——. (1968) [1873], 'Preface [to *Literature and Dogma*, 1st edn]', In MA 1960–77, vol. 6, pp. 147–51.
——. (1968b) [1873], *Literature and Dogma*, in MA 1960–77, vol. 6, pp. 139–411.
——. (1972) [1876], 'Bishop Butler and the zeit-geist', in MA 1960–77, vol. 8, pp. 11–62.
Ashcraft, R. (1992), 'The Radical Dimension of Locke's Political Thought: A Dialogic Essay on Some Problems of Interpretation', *History of Political Thought* 13: pp. 759–68.
Ashton, R. (1991), *G. H. Lewes: A Life*, Clarendon: Oxford University Press.
Aslet, C. (2010), *Villages of Britain: The Five Hundred Villages That Made the Countryside*, London: Bloomsbury.
Astin, M. [1930], *Mary Russell Mitford: Her Circle and Her Books*, London: Douglas.
Auerbach, N. (1978), *Communities of Women: An Idea in Fiction*, Cambridge: Harvard University Press.
Baker, W. (1981), *The Libraries of George Eliot and George Henry Lewes*, Victoria: ELS.

Balston, T. (1934), 'English Book Illustrations, 1880–1900', in J. Carter (ed), *New Paths in Book Collecting: Essays by Various Hands*, London: Constable, pp. 163–90.
Barthes, R. (1972), *Mythologies*, trans. A. Lavers, New York: Hill.
Batchelor, J. (2018), "'[T]o Cherish Female Ingenuity, and to Conduce Female Improvement": The Birth of the Woman's Magazine', in J. Batchelor and M. N. Powell (eds), *Women's Periodicals and Print Culture in Britain, 1690s–1820s*, Edinburgh: Edinburgh University Press, pp. 377–92.
——. (2011), '"Connections, which are of service... in a more advanced age": "The Lady's Magazine," Community, and Women's Literary Histories', *Tulsa Studies in Women's Literature* 30 (2): pp. 245–67.
Bentham, J. (1931), *The Theory of Legislation*, New York: Brace.
Bermingham, A. (1989), *Landscape and Ideology: The English Rustic Tradition, 1740–1860*, Berkeley: University of California Press.
Beshero-Bondar, E. (2009), 'Romancing the Pacific Isles before Byron: Music, Sex, and Death in Mitford's *Christina*', *ELH* 76 (2): pp. 276–308.
Bevir, M. (2001), 'The Long Nineteenth Century in Intellectual History.' *Journal of Victorian Culture* 6 (2): pp. 313–35.
Bloom, H. (1997), *The Anxiety of Influence: A Theory of Poetry*, New York: Oxford.
Bodenheimer, R. (2018), *The Real Life of Mary Ann Evans: George Eliot, Her Letters and Fiction*, Ithaca: Cornell University Press.
Bolton, C. (2016), *Writing the Empire: Robert Southey and Romantic Colonialism*, London: Routledge.
Booth, A. (2016), *Homes and Haunts: Touring Writers' Shrines and Countries*, Oxford: Oxford University Press.
——. (1992), *Greatness Engendered: George Eliot and Virginia Woolf*, Cornell: Cornell University Press.
Boym, S. (2001), *The Future of Nostalgia*, New York: Basic.
Brake, L. (1994), *Subjugated Knowledges: Journalism, Gender and Literature in the Nineteenth Century*, New York: New York University Press.
——. (1995), 'The 'Wicked Westminster', the *Fortnightly*, and Walter Pater's *Renaissance*', in J. O. Jordan and R. L. Patten (eds), *Literature in the Marketplace: Nineteenth-Century British Publishing and Reading Practices*, Cambridge: Cambridge University Press, pp. 289–305.
Bright, J. (1868), *Speeches of John Bright, Esq., M.P. ...*, London: Hamilton.

Brontë, C. (2007) [1840], 'To Hartley Coleridge' in M. Smith, *Selected Letters of Charlotte Brontë*. Oxford: Oxford University Press, pp. 25–28.
Brooks, P. (1985), *Reading for the Plot: Design and Intention in Narrative*, Cambridge, MA: Harvard University Press.
Brown, W. (1995), *States of Injury: Power and Freedom in Late Modernity*. Princeton: Princeton University Press.
Butt, J., and K. Tillotson (2013), *Dickens at Work*, London: Methuen.
Buzard, J. (2005), *Disorienting Fiction: The Autoethnographic Work of Nineteenth-Century British Novels*, Princeton: Princeton University Press.
Byerley, Alison (1999), 'Effortless Art: The Sketch in Nineteenth-Century Painting and Literature', *Criticism* 41 (3): pp. 349–64.
Carpenter, M. W. (1986), *George Eliot and the Landscape of Time: Narrative Form and Protestant Apocalyptic History*, Chapel Hill: University of North Carolina Press.
Carroll, A. (2003), *Dark Smiles: Race and Desire in George Eliot*, Athens: Ohio University Press.
Carroll, D. (1992), *George Eliot and the Conflict of Interpretations*, Cambridge: Cambridge University Press.
Chalmin, P. (1990), *The Making of a Sugar Giant: Tate & Lyle, 1859–1989*, New York: Routledge.
Chapple, J. (1997), *Elizabeth Gaskell: The Early Years*, Manchester: Manchester University Press.
Chapple, J. A. V. (1987), 'William Stevenson and Elizabeth Gaskell', *Gaskell Journal* 1: pp. 1–9.
Chapple, J. A. V., and A. Pollard (eds) (1966), *The Letters of Mrs. Gaskell*, Manchester: Manchester University Press.
Chapman, M. W. (1877), *Harriet Martineau's Autobiography with Memorials*, vol. 1., London: Smith & Elder.
Charise, A. (2020), *The Aesthetics of Senescence: Aging, Population, and the Nineteenth-Century British Novel*, Albany: SUNY Press.
Chartier, R. (1994), *The Order of Books: Readers, Authors, and Libraries in Europe between the Fourteenth and Eighteenth Centuries*, trans. L. G. Cochrane, Cambridge: Polity.
Chase, K. (2009), *The Victorians and Old Age*, New York: Oxford University Press.
Cheah, P. (1998), 'Given Culture: Rethinking Cosmopolitical Freedom in Transnationalism', in P. Cheah and B. Robbins (eds), *Cosmopolitics: Thinking and Feeling Beyond the Nation*. Minneapolis: University of Minnesota Press, pp. 290–328.

Chodorow, N. J. (1999), *The Power of Feelings*, New Haven: Yale University Press.

Clayton, J. and E. Rothstein (1991), 'Figures in the Corpus: Theories of Influence and Intertextuality', in J. Clayton and E. Rothstein (eds), *Influence and Intertextuality in Literary History*, Madison: University of Wisconsin Press, pp. 3–36.

Clayton, P. and J. Rowbotham (2008), 'An unsuitable and degraded diet? Part One: Public Health Lessons from the Mid-Victorian Working Class Diet', *Journal of the Royal Society of Medicine* 101 (6): pp. 282–89.

Cobden, R. (1848), *Hansard's Parliamentary Debates*, third Series, vol. c, London: Hansard.

Colby, R. B. (1995), *Some Appointed Work to Do: Women and Vocation in the Fiction of Elizabeth Gaskell*, Westport: Greenwood.

Collin, D. (1986), 'The Composition and Publication of Elizabeth Gaskell's *Cranford*', *Bulletin of the John Ryland Library* 69 (1): pp. 59–95.

Coles, W. A. (1956), *The Correspondence of Mary Russell Mitford and Thomas Noon Talfourd (1821–25)*, Harvard University thesis, HU 90.7129.10.

——. (1959), 'Magazine and Other Contributions by Mary Russell Mitford and Thomas Noon Talfourd', *Studies in Bibliography* 12: pp. 218–26.

——. (1957), 'Mary Russell Mitford: The Inauguration of a Literary Career', *Journal of the John Rylands Library* 40: pp. 33–46.

Colley, L. (1982), *In Defiance of Oligarchy: The Tory Party, 1714–60*, London: Cambridge University Press.

'Contemporary Literature' (1859), *Westminster Review* (April): pp. 311–50.

Cooper, S. F. (2010), *Effie: The Passionate Lives of Effie Gray, John Ruskin, and John Everett Millais*, New York: St Martin's Press.

Copeland, E. (1995), *Women Writing about Money: Women's Fiction in England, 1790–1820*, Cambridge: Cambridge University Press.

Cottom, D. (1987), *Social Figures: George Eliot, Social History, and Literary Representation*, Minneapolis: University of Minnesota Press.

Craver, H. W. (1915), *Illustrated Editions of Children's Books: A Selected List*, Pittsburgh: Carnegie Library.

Croker, J. W. (1885), *The Croker Papers: The Correspondence and Diaries of the Late Right Honourable John Wilson Croker . . .* , ed. L. J. Jennings, vol. 2, London: Murray.

Croskery, M. Case. (1997), 'Mothers without Children, Unity without

Plot: Cranford's Radical Charm', *Nineteenth-Century Literature* 52. (2): 198–220.
Cross, J. (1888), *George Eliot's Life as Related in Her Letters and Journals*, vol 1., New York: Harper.
Cutmore, J. (2008), *Contributors to the Quarterly Review: A History, 1809–25*, London: Pickering and Chatto.
D'Albertis, D. (2007), 'The Life and Letters of E. C. Gaskell', in J. L. Matus (ed), *Cambridge Companion to Elizabeth Gaskell*, Cambridge: Cambridge University Press, pp. 10–26.
Dames, N. (2001), *Amnesiac Selves: Nostalgia, Forgetting, and British Fiction, 1810–1870*, New York: Oxford University Press.
Darwin, E. (1801), *Zoonomia, or the Laws of Organic Life*, 4 vols., London: Johnson.
Davies, T. (1981), 'Education, Ideology, and Literature' in T. Bennett, G. Martin, C. Mercer, and J. Woollacott *Culture, Ideology, and Social Process*, London: Batsford, pp. 251–60.
Dentith, S. (1986), *George Eliot*, Atlantic Highlands. NJ: Humanities.
Dentith, S. (2014), *Nineteenth-Century British Literature Then and Now: Reading with Hindsight*, Farnham: Ashgate.
Derrida, J. (2021), *Writing and Difference*, Chicago: University of Chicago Press.
Dibdin, T. F. (1836). *Reminiscences of a Literary Life . . . vol. 2*. London.
[Dickens, C.] (1850), 'A Preliminary Word.' Household Words 1 (30 March), 1–2.
Dickens, C. (1981), *The Letters of Charles Dickens*, vol. 5: 1847–1849, ed. by G. and K. J. Fielding, Oxford: Clarendon.
——. (1988), *The Letters of Charles Dickens*, Vol. 6: 1850–1852, ed. by G. Storey, K. Tillotson, and N. Burgis, Oxford: Clarendon.
Dillane, F. (2013), *Before George Eliot: Marian Evans and the Periodical Press*, Cambridge: Cambridge University Press.
Donkin, E. (1995), *Getting into the Act: Women Playwrights in London, 1776–1829*, London: Routledge.
Donovan, J. (1983), *New England Local Color Literature: A Women's Tradition*, New York: Ungar.
Duncan, I. (2002), 'The Provincial or Regional Novel', in P. Brantlinger and W. B. Thesing (eds), *A Companion to the Victorian Novel*, Oxford: Blackwell, pp. 318–35.
Dyce, A. (1825), *Specimens of British Poetesses*, London: Rodd.
Eagleton, T. (1998), *Criticism and Ideology: A Study in Marxist Literary Theory*, London: Verso.

Easley, A. (2004), *First-Person Anonymous: Women Writers and Victorian Print Media, 1830–1870*, Burlington, VT: Ashgate.
Easson, A. (2016) [1979], *Elizabeth Gaskell*, Abingdon: Routledge.
——. (1980). 'The Musician and the Nightingale: Charles Lamb and the Elizabethan Drama', *Charles Lamb Bulletin* (January): pp. 85–9.
Edwards, P. D. (1988), *Idyllic Realism from Mary Russell Mitford to Hardy*. London: Macmillan.
Eliot, G. (1999), *The Letters of George Henry Lewes*, vol. 3, ed. by W. Baker, Victoria: ELS editions.
——. (1998a), *The Mill on the Floss*, London: Oxford University Press.
——. (1998b), *Scenes of Clerical Life*, London: Penguin.
——. (1998c), *The Journals of George Eliot*, ed. by M. Harris and J. Johnston. Cambridge: Cambridge University Press.
——. (1996), *Middlemarch*, Oxford: Oxford University Press.
——. (1995), *Daniel Deronda*, London: Penguin.
——. (1994a), *Adam Bede*, London: Penguin.
——. (1994b) [1879], *Impressions of Theophrastus Such*, ed. by Nancy Henry, Iowa: University of Iowa Press.
——. (1954–1986), *The George Eliot Letters*, ed. G. Haight, 9 vols, New Haven: Yale University Press.
——. (1954a), *The George Eliot Letters: Vol. I, 1836–1851*, in GE 1954–1986.
——. (1954b), *The George Eliot Letters: Vol. II, 1852–1858*, in GE 1954–1986.
——. (1955a), *The George Eliot Letters: Vol. III, 1859–1861*, in GE 1954–1986.
——. (1955b), *The George Eliot Letters: Vol. IV, 1862–1868*, in GE 1954–1986.
——. (1955c), *The George Eliot Letters: Vol. V, 1869–1873*, in GE 1954–1986.
——. (1956), *The George Eliot Letters: Vol. VI, 1874–1877*, in GE 1954–1986.
——. (1978), *The George Eliot Letters: Vol. IX, 1871–1881*, in GE 1954–1986.
——. (1909), *Tom and Maggie Tulliver*, London: Thomas Nelson.
——. (1883), 'Natural History of German Life' in *The Essays of George Eliot*, ed. by N. Sheppard, New York: Funk, pp. 141–77.
——. (1871), *Felix Holt, The Radical*, New York: Harper.
——. (1868), 'An Address to the Working Men, by Felix Holt', *Blackwood's Edinburgh Magazine*: pp. 1–12.

[Eliot, G.]. (1856a), [Rev. of Modern Painters, Vol. 3], *Westminster Review* (January and April): pp. 625–33.

——.1856b, 'Silly Novels by Lady Novelists', *Westminster Review* (October): pp. 442–61.

Eliot, G. (1852), 'Prospectus of the Westminster and Foreign Quarterly Review', *Westminster Review* (January): pp. iii–vi.

Felmingham, M. (1998), *The Illustrated Gift Book, 1880–1930*, Aldershot: Scolar Press.

Fergus, J. (2006), *Provincial Readers in Eighteenth-Century England*, Oxford: Oxford University Press.

Fleischman, A. (2008), 'George Eliot's Reading: A Chronological List', *George Eliot – George Henry Lewes Studies 54/55* (September): pp. 1–106.

Flint, K. (2006), 'The Materiality of Middlemarch' in K. Chase (ed), *Middlemarch in the 21st Century*, Oxford: Oxford University Press, pp. 65–86.

——. (1995), *Elizabeth Gaskell*, Devon: Northcote House.

Freedgood, E. (2006), *The Ideas in Things: Fugitive Meaning in the Victorian Novel*, Chicago: University of Chicago Press.

French, Y. (1958), 'Elizabeth Cleghorn Gaskell' in R. C. Rathburn and M. Steinmann, Jr., *From Jane Austen to Joseph Conrad: Essays Collected in the Memory of James T. Hillhouse*, Minneapolis: University of Minnesota Press, pp. 133–45.

Friedman, S. S. (1991), 'Weavings: Intertextuality and the (Re)Birth of the Author' in j. ay Clayton and E. Rothstein, *Influence and Intertextuality in Literary History*, Madison: University of Wisconsin Press, pp. 146–80.

Gallagher, C. (1995), *Nobody's Story: The Vanishing Acts of Women Writers in the Marketplace*, Berkeley: University of California Press.

——. (1985), *The Industrial Reformation of English Fiction: Social Discourse and Narrative Form, 1832–1867*, Chicago: University of Chicago Press.

Garcha, A. (2009), *From Sketch to Novel: The Development of Victorian Fiction*. Cambridge: Cambridge University Press.

Garrett, M. (2004), 'Mitford, Mary Russell (1787–1855)', in H. C. G. Matthew and Brian Harrison (eds), *Oxford Dictionary of National Biography*, Oxford: Oxford University Press. Available at http://www.oxforddnb.com/view/article/18859 (last accessed 4 December 2020).

Gaskell, E. (2008), *Cranford*, Oxford: Oxford University Press.

——. (2006), *Mary Barton*, Oxford: Oxford University Press.

——. (2005), 'Clopton Hall', in J. Shattock (ed), *Works of Elizabeth Gaskell: Journalism, Early Fiction, and Personal Writings*, London: Routledge, pp. 37–42.
——. (1858), *The Life of Charlotte Brontë*, New York: Appleton.
Genette, G. (1987), *Paratexts: Thresholds of Interpretation*, trans. by J. E. Lewin, Cambridge: Cambridge University Press.
——. (1982), *Figures of Literary Discourse*, trans. by A. Sheridan. New York: Columbia University Press.
——. (1980), *Narrative Discourse: An Essay in Method*, trans. by J. E. Lewin. Ithaca: Cornell University Press.
Gifford, T. (2020), *Pastoral*, London: Routledge.
Gill, S. (1998), *Wordsworth and the Victorians*, Oxford: Clarendon.
Graver, S. (1994), *George Eliot and Community: A Study in Social Theory and Fictional Form*, Berkeley: University of California Press.
Green, L. (2001), *Educating Women: Cultural Conflict and Victorian Literature*, Athens: Ohio University Press.
Gross, J. (1965), 'Mrs. Gaskell' in I. Watt (ed), *The Novelist as Innovator*, London: BBC Books, pp. 49–63.
Guth, D. (2003), *George Eliot and Schiller: Intertextuality and Cross-Cultural Discourse*, Surrey: Ashgate.
Hadley, E. (2010), *Living Liberalism: Practical Citizenship in Mid-Victorian Britain*, Chicago: University of Chicago Press.
Haight, G. (1968), *George Eliot: A Biography*, London: Penguin.
Hall, C., K. McClelland, and J. Rendall (2000), 'Introduction' in C. Hall, K. McClelland, and J. Rendall, *Defining the Victorian Nation: Class, Race, Gender and the Reform Act of 1867*, Cambridge: Cambridge University Press, pp. 1–70
Hall, S. C. (1826). 'Preface', *Amulet; or Christian and Literary Remembrancer*, London: Baynes, pp. v–viii.
Halse, S. (2008). 'The Literary Idyll in Germany, England, and Scandanavia, 1770–1848', in G. Gillespie, M. Engel, and B. Dieterle *Romantic Prose Fiction*, Amsterdam: Benjamins, pp. 383–411
[Hamilton, Jr., S]. (1823), 'Address', *Lady's Magazine* (January): pp. 1–2.
Hardy, B. (2015), 'Elizabeth Gaskell in Middlemarch: Timothy Cooper, The Judgement of Solomon, and the Woman at the Window', *George Eliot Review* 46: pp. 16–20.
Harris, K. D. 2015. *Forget Me Not: The Rise of the British Literary Annual, 1823–1835*. Athens: Ohio University Press.
Heath, K. (2009), *Aging by the Book: The Emergence of Midlife in Victorian Britain*. Albany: SUNY Press.

Helsinger, E. K. (1997), *Rural Scenes and National Representation: Britain, 1815–1850*, Princeton, NJ: Princeton University Press.

Helsinger, E. K. (1994a), 'Turner and the Representation of England' in W. J. T. Mitchell (ed), *Landscape and Power*. Chicago: University of Chicago Press, pp. 103–25.

——. (1994b), 'Ruskin and the Politics of Viewing: Constructing National Subjects', *Nineteenth-Century Contexts 18*: pp. 125–46.

Henry, N. (2019) 'George Eliot and Politics', G. Levine and N. Henry (eds), *The Cambridge Companion to George Eliot*, Cambridge: Cambridge University Press, pp. 155–174.

——. (2018), *Women, Literature, and Finance in Victorian Britain: Cultures of Investment*, Cham: Palgrave Macmillan.

——. (2002), *George Eliot and the British Empire*, Cambridge: Cambridge University Press.

Hill, C. (1920), *Mary Russell Mitford and Her Surroundings*, London: Lane.

Hirst, F. W. (1927), *Early Life and Letters of John Morley*, vol. 1, London: Macmillan.

Homans, M. (1986), *Bearing the Word: Language and Female Experience in Nineteenth-Century Women's Writing*, Chicago: University of Chicago Press.

Hopkins, A. B. (1952), *Elizabeth Gaskell: Her Life and Work*, London: Lehman.

——. (1931), 'Liberalism in the Social Teachings of Mrs. Gaskell', *Social Service Review* 5 (1): pp. 57–73.

Horn, P. (1980), *The Rural World, 1780–1850: Social Change in the English Countryside*, London: Hutchinson.

Horne, M. B. (1899, *The Ladies of Cranford: A Sketch of English Village Life Fifty Years Ago*, Boston: Baker.

Howitt, M. (1889), *Autobiography*, vol. 2., London: Isbister.

Howitt, W. (1840), *Visits to Remarkable Places*. . . . London: Longman, Orme, Brown et al.

Hubbard, S. (2006), *Writers in Warwickshire*, Warwick: Cosimo.

Huett, L. (2003), 'Commodity and Collectivity: *Cranford* in the context of *Household Words*', *The Gaskell Society Journal* 17: 34–49.

Hughes, K. (2001), *George Eliot: The Last Victorian*, New York: Cooper Square Press.

Hughes, L. K. (2014), 'SIDEWAYS!: Navigating the Material(ity) of Print Culture.' *Victorian Periodicals Review* 47 (1): pp. 1–30.

——. (2005), 'Constructing Fictions of Authorship', *Victorian Periodicals Review* 38.2: pp. 158–79.

Hughes, L. K, and M. Lund. 1995. 'Textual/Sexual Pleasure and Serial Publication.' in Jordan and Patten, pp. 143–64.
Hunter, S. (1984), *Victorian Idyllic Fiction: Pastoral Strategies*, London: Macmillan.
Ingleby, M. and M. Kerr (2018), 'Introduction' in M. Ingleby and M. Kerr, *Coastal Cultures of the Long Nineteenth Century*, Edinburgh: Edinburgh University Press, pp. 1–28.
Ives, M. (1995), 'A Bibliographical Approach to Victorian Publishing', in Jordan and Patten, pp. 269–88.
Johnson, S. (1756), *A Dictionary of the English Language*, 2nd edition, London: J. Knapton et al.
Jones, H. S. (2000), *Victorian Political Thought*, New York: St. Martin's.
Jones, S. (1989), *Hazlitt: A Life: From Winterslow to Frith Street*. Oxford: Clarendon Press.
Jordan, J. O., and R. L. Patten (eds) (1995), *Literature in the Marketplace: Nineteenth-Century British Publishing and Reading Practice*, Cambridge: Cambridge University Press.
Kain, R. J. P. and E. Baigent (1992), *The Cadastral Map in the Service of the State: A History of Property Mapping*, Chicago: University of Chicago Press.
Keating, P. (1976), 'Introduction', in P. Keating (ed), *Cranford/Cousin Phillis* by Elizabeth Gaskell. London: Penguin.
Keith, W. J. (1974), *The Rural Tradition: A Study of the Non-Fiction Prose Writers of the English Countryside*, Toronto: University of Toronto Press.
Kelly, G. (1989), *English Fiction of the Romantic Period 1789–1830*, London and New York: Longman Group UK.
Kemble, F. A. (1875), 'Old Woman's Gossip, III', *Atlantic Monthly* 36, Boston: Houghton, pp. 444–59.
Killick, T. (2004), 'Mary Russell Mitford and the Topography of Short Fiction', Journal of the Short Story in English 43 [online edition], http://journals.openedition.org/jsse/396
King, A. (2019), *The Divine in the Commonplace: Reverent Natural History and the Novel in Britain*, Cambridge: Cambridge University Press.
Knezevic, B. (1998), 'An Ethnography of the Provincial: The Social Geography of Gentility in Elizabeth Gaskell's *Cranford*', *Victorian Studies* 41 (3): pp. 400–26.
——. (2003), *Figures of Finance Capitalism: Writing, Class, and Capital in the Age of Dickens*, New York: Routledge.

Kooistra, L. J. (2002), *Christina Rossetti and Illustration: A Publishing History*. Athens: Ohio University Press.

——. (2011), *Poetry, Pictures, and Popular Publishing: The Illustrated Gift Book and Victorian Visual Culture, 1855–1875*, Athens: Ohio University Press.

Koustinoudi, A. (2012), *The Split Subject of Narration in Elizabeth Gaskell's First Person Fiction*, Lanham: Lexington Books.

Kristeva, J. (1986), 'The System and the Speaking Subject', in Toril Moi (ed), *The Kristeva Reader*, Oxford: Basil Blackwell, pp. 89–136.

Landor, W. S. (1876), 'To Mary Russell Mitford', in *The Works and Life of Walter Savage Landor*, vol. 8., London: Chapman and Hall, p. 301.

Landry, D. (2001), *The Invention of the Countryside: Hunting, Walking, and Ecology in English Literature, 1671–1831*, Houndmills: Palgrave.

Langer, S. K. (1972), *Mind: An Essay on Human Feeling*, vol. 2., Baltimore: Johns Hopkins University Press.

Langland, E. (1995), *Nobody's Angels: Middle-Class Women and Domestic Ideology in Victorian Culture*, Ithaca: Cornell University Press.

Lansbury, C. (1975), *Elizabeth Gaskell: The Novel of Social Crisis*, London: Elek.

——. (1984), *Elizabeth Gaskell*, Twayne.

Ledbetter, K. (1996), "BeGemmed and BeAmuletted': Tennyson and Those 'Vapid' Gift Books', *Victorian Poetry* 24 (2): 235–45.

Lee, J. Sun-Joo, (2010), *The American Slave Narrative and the Victorian Novel*. New York: Oxford University Press.

Lesjak, C. (2021), *The Afterlife of Enclosure: British Realism, Character, and the Commons*. Stanford: Stanford University Press.

Levine, G. (1983), *The Realistic Imagination: English Fiction from Frankenstein to Lady Chatterley*, Chicago: University of Chicago Press.

Levy, E. P. (2003), 'Property Morality in *The Mill on the Floss*', *Victorian Institute Journal* 31: pp. 173–86.

Lewes, G. H. (1852), 'The Lady Novelists', *Westminster Review* (July): pp. 129–41.

Li, H. (2000), *Memory and History in George Eliot: Transfiguring the Past*, New York: St. Martin's.

Livesy, R. (2016), *Writing the Stage Coach Nation: Locality on the Move in Nineteenth-Century British Literature*, Oxford: Oxford University Press.

Locke, J. (1698), *Two Treatises of Government*, London.

Loewald, H. (1980), 'The Waning of the Oedipus Complex', *Papers on Psychoanalysis*, New Haven: Yale University Press, pp. 384–404.

Lootens, T. (2017), *The Political Poetess: Victorian Femininity, Race, and the Legacy of Separate Spheres*, Princeton: Princeton University Press.

Lucas, J. (1977), *The Literature of Change: Studies in the Nineteenth-Century Provincial Novel*, Brighton: Harvester.

Lynch, D. (2000), 'Homes and Haunts: Austen's and Mitford's English Idylls.' *PMLA* 115: pp. 1103–08.

MacCall, W. (1847), *The Elements of Individualism: A Series of Lectures*. London: John Chapman.

Macleod, J. and P. Denney. (2018), 'Liberalism, Literature, and the Emotions in the Long Nineteenth Century', *Occasion* 11: 1–20.

Magruder, J. (1895), *Child-Sketches from George Eliot: Glimpses at the Boys and Girls in the Romances of the Great Novelist*, Boston: Lothrop.

Malfait, O. (2010), 'Domestic Humour in Elizabeth Gaskell's Cranford', in S. Jung, *Elizabeth Gaskell: Victorian Culture and the Art of Fiction*, Gent: Academia, pp. 71–82.

Martin, C. (1985), 'Elizabeth Gaskell's Contributions to the Works of William Howitt', *Nineteenth-Century Fiction* 40 (1) (June): pp. 94–100.

Mathieson, C. (2015), *Mobility in the Victorian Novel: Placing the Nation*, Basingstoke: Palgrave.

Maxwell, R. (2002), 'Introduction' in R. Maxwell, *The Victorian Illustrated Book*, Virginia: University Press of Virginia, pp. xxi–xxx.

Mayo, R. D. (1962), *The English Novel in the Magazines, 1740–1815*, London: Oxford University Press.

McDonagh, J. (2018), 'Women Writers and the Provincial Novel', in L. Hartley (ed), *The History of British Women's Writing, 1830–1880*, London: Palgrave, pp. 125–42.

——. (2016), 'Imagining Locality and Affiliation: George Eliot's Villages', in A. Anderson and H. E. Shaw, *A Companion to George Eliot*, Malden: Wiley, pp. 353–69.

——. (2013), 'Rethinking Provincialism in Mid-Nineteenth-Century Fiction: *Our Village* to *Villette*', *Victorian Studies* 55 (3): pp. 399–424.

——. (2012), 'Place, Region, and Migration', in J. Kucich and J. B. Taylor (eds), *The Nineteenth-Century Novel, 1820–1880*, Oxford: Oxford University Press, pp. 361–76.

McLean, R. (1972), *Victorian Book Design and Colour Printing*, 2nd ed., Berkeley: University of California Press.

Mill, J. S. (1963–91), *The Collected Works of John Stuart Mill*, ed. J. M. Robson, 33 vols, Toronto: University of Toronto Press.

——. (1988), 'Representation of the People [2], 13 April 1866', in *Public and Parliamentary Speeches Part I, November 1850–November 1868*, ed. J. M. Robson and B. L. Kinzer, pp. 58–68.

——. (1981) [1873], *Autobiography*, in *Autobiography and Literary Essays*, JSM 1963–91, vol. 1, ed. J. M. Robson and J. Stillinger, pp. 1–290.

——. (1977a) [1836], 'Civilization', in *Essays on Politics and Society [Part 1]*, JSM 1963–91, vol. 18, ed. J. M. Robson, pp. 116–47.

——. (1977b) [1861], *Considerations on Representative Government*, in *Essays on Politics and Society [Part 2]*, JSM 1963–91, vol. 19, ed. J. M. Robson, pp. 371–577.

——. (1977c) [1859], *On Liberty*, in *Essays on Politics and Society [Part 1]*, JSM 1963–91, vol. 18, ed. J. M. Robson, pp. 212–310.

——. (1977d [1861]), 'Thoughts on Parliamentary Reform', in *Essays on Politics and Society [Part 2]*, JSM 1963–91, vol. 19, ed. by J. M. Robson, pp. 311–40.

——. (1972a) [1851], 'To John Chapman', in *The Later Letters of John Stuart Mill, 1849–1873*, JSM 1963–91, vol. 14, ed. F.E. Mineka and D. N. Lindley, p. 53.

——. (1972b) [1859], 'To Elizabeth Cleghorn Gaskell', in *The Later Letters of John Stuart Mill, 1849–1873*, JSM 1963–91, vol. 14, ed. F.E. Mineka and D. N. Lindley, pp. 629–30.

——. (1969a) 'Sedgick's Discourse', in *Essays on Ethics, Religion and Society*, JSM 1963–91, vol. 10, ed. J. M. Robson, pp. 33–74.

——. (1969b) 'Utilitarianism', in *Essays on Ethics, Religion and Society*, JSM 1963–91, vol. 10, ed. J. M. Robson, pp. 203–60.

——. (1963), 'To George Henry Lewes', in *The Earlier Letters of John Stuart Mill: 1812–1848 [Part 2]*, JSM 1963–91, vol. 13, ed. F. E. Mineka.

Miller, A. (1995), *Novels Behind Glass: Commodity, Culture, and Victorian Narrative*, Cambridge: Cambridge University Press.

Miner, H. (2012), 'Reforming Spaces: The Architectural Imaginary of *Middlemarch*', *Victorian Review* 38.1: pp. 193–209.

Mingay, G. E. (1998), *Rural Life in Victorian England*, Phoenix Mill, U.K.: Sutton.

Mitchell, C. (2008), 'Explanatory Notes', in E. Gaskell, *Cranford*, Oxford: Oxford University Press.

Mitchell, W. J. T. (2002), 'Imperial Landscape', in W. J. T. Mitchell (ed), *Landscape and Power*, Chicago: University of Chicago Press, pp. 5–34.

Bibliography 291

[Mitford, J. and W. Gifford] (1810), 'Mary Russell Mitford's *Poems*', *Quarterly Review* 4 (August and November): pp. 514–18.

Mitford, M. R. (undated), letter to Thomas Noon Talfourd, [1822 or 1823], Harvard University Houghton Library, MS Eng 1339, volume 2.

——. (1810), *Poems*. London: Valpy.

——. (1811a), 'Beauty, an Ode', *Lady's Magazine* [June].

——. (1811b), 'Blanch', *Lady's Magazine* (July).

——. (1811c), *Christina, The Maid of the South Seas*, London: Valpy.

[Mitford, M. R.]. (1812a), 'Another—The Storm', *Lady's Magazine* [February]: p. 86.

——. (1812b), 'Love-Sick Maid', *Lady's Magazine* [Jan.]: pp. 39–40.

Mitford, M. R. (1812c), *Watlington Hill; a Poem*, London: Valpy.

——. (1813), *Narrative Poems on the Female Character, in the Various Relations of Human Life . . .*, London: F. C. and J. Rivington.

——. (1814), 'Solitude', *Lady's Magazine* [January]: p. 41.

——. (1815a). 'Coursing', *Lady's Magazine* [May]: p. 236.

——. (1815b), 'The Hermit', *Lady's Magazine* [Supplement for the year]: p. 622.

——. (1818), letter to William Elford, 1 November 1818, Mitford MSS. correspondence, vol. 3, Reading Central Library.

——. (1821a). 'On Letters and Letter-Writers', *New Monthly Magazine and Literary Journal* 2 (August): pp. 142–46.

——. (1821b), letter to Thomas Noon Talfourd, 9 March 1821, Harvard University Houghton Library, MS Eng 1339, volume 1.

——. (1821c), letter to Thomas Noon Talfourd, 16 March 1821, Harvard University Houghton Library, MS Eng 1339, volume 1.

——. (1821d), letter to Thomas Noon Talfourd, 24 March 1821, Harvard University Houghton Library, MS Eng 1339, volume 1.

——. (1821e), letter to Thomas Noon Talfourd, 9 June 1821, Harvard University Houghton Library, MS Eng 1339, volume 1.

——. (1822a), letter to Thomas Noon Talfourd, 31 March 1822, Harvard University Houghton Library, MS Eng 1339, volume 1.

——. (1822b), letter to Thomas Noon Talfourd, [summer?] 1822, Harvard University Houghton Library, MS Eng 1339, volume 1.

——. (1822c), 'Lucy', *Lady's Magazine* (September): pp. 478–83.

——. (1822d), letter to Thomas Noon Talfourd, 20 November 1822, Harvard University Houghton Library, MS Eng 1339, volume 2.

——. (1822e), letter to Thomas Noon Talfourd, undated November, Harvard University Houghton Library, MS Eng 1339, volume 2.

——. (1822d), 'Our Village', *Lady's Magazine* (December): pp. 645–50.

——. (1823a), letter to Thomas Noon Talfourd, [undated] 1823, Harvard University Houghton Library, MS Eng 1339, volume 2.
——. (1823b), 'Hannah', *Lady's Magazine* (January): pp. 25–28.
——. (1823c), 'The Talking Lady', *Lady's Magazine* (January): pp. 16–18.
——. (1823d), 'A Great Farm-House', *Lady's Magazine* (February): pp. 102–05.
——. (1823e), 'Walks in the Country, No. III, Violeting', *Lady's Magazine* (April): pp. 229–31.
——. (1823f), letter to Thomas Noon Talfourd, [?] April 1823, Harvard University Houghton Library, MS Eng 1339, volume 2.
——. (1823g), letter to Thomas Noon Talfourd, 24 April 1823, Harvard University Houghton Library, MS Eng 1339, volume 2.
——. (1823h), 'Bramley Maying', *Lady's Magazine* (May): pp. 280–83.
——. (1823i), letter to Thomas Noon Talfourd, 17 May 1823, Harvard University Houghton Library, MS Eng 1339, volume 2.
——. .(1823j), 'Ellen', *Lady's Magazine* (September): pp. 489–94.
——. (1823k), 'A Country Cricket Match', *Lady's Magazine* (July): pp. 386–90.
——. (1824a), *Our Village: Sketches of Rural Life and Scenery*, London: Whittaker.
——. (1824b), 'Lucy Re-visited', *Lady's Magazine* (August): pp. 399–404.
——. (1824c), letter to Thomas Noon Talfourd, [12?] April 1824, Harvard University Houghton Library, MS Eng 1339, volume 2.
——. (1824d), letter to Thomas Noon Talfourd, 17 May 1824, Harvard University Houghton Library, MS Eng 1339, volume 2.
——. (1824e), letter to Thomas Noon Talfourd, 6 June 1824, Harvard University Houghton Library, MS Eng 1339, volume 2.
——. (1824f), letter to Thomas Noon Talfourd, 23 September 1824, Harvard University Houghton Library, MS Eng 1339, volume 2.
——. (1824g), letter to Thomas Noon Talfourd, [undated] 1824, Harvard University Houghton Library, MS Eng 1339, volume 1.
——. (1824h) letter to Thomas Noon Talfourd, [undated] 1824, Harvard University Houghton Library, MS Eng 1339, volume 1.
——. (1826a), *Our Village: Sketches of Rural Character and Scenery*, London: Whittaker.
——. (1826b) [1825], 'The Vicar's Maid: A Village Story', *Amulet; or Christian and Literary Remembrancer*, London: Baynes, pp. 130–46.
——. (1827a) [1826], 'The Chalk-Pit. (A True Story)', *Amulet; or Christian and Literary Remembrancer*, London: Baynes, pp. 145–53.
——. (1827b) [1826]. 'The Queen of the Meadow', in A. A. Watts (ed), *Literary Souvenir*, London: Longman, pp. 177–88.

——. (1828), *Our Village: Country Stories, Scenes, and Characters*, London: Whittaker.

——. (1832a), *Our Village*, London: Whittaker.

——. (1832b) [1831], 'The Incendiary: A Country Tale', *Friendship's Offering*, London: Smith, Elder, & Co, pp. 1–17.

——. (1841), 'Hop-Gathering', *Findens' Tableaux: The Iris of Prose, Poetry, and Art*, London: Black and Armstrong, pp. 63–69.

——. (1842), letter to Elizabeth Barrett Browning, 4 May 1842, in M. B. Raymond and M. R. Sullivan (eds), *The Letters of Elizabeth Barrett Browning to Mary Russell Mitford, 1836–1854*. 3 vols. [Waco]: Armstrong Browning Library of Baylor University, 1983.

——. (1854), *The Dramatic Works of Mary Russell Mitford*, vol. 1., London: Hurst and Blackett.

——. (1870a), *The Life of Mary Russell Mitford: Related in a Selection of Her Letters to Her Friends*, vol. 1, ed. A. G. L'Estrange, London: Bentley.

——. (1870b), *The Life of Mary Russell Mitford: Related in a Selection of Her Letters to Her Friends*, vol. 2, ed. A. G. L'Estrange, London: Bentley.

——. (1870c), *The Life of Mary Russell Mitford: Related in a Selection of Her Letters to Her Friends*, vol. 3, ed. A. G. L'Estrange, London: Bentley.

——. (1870d), *The Life of Mary Russell Mitford: Told by Herself in Letters to Her Friends*, Vol. 1, ed. H. Chorley, New York: Harper.

——. (1870e), *The Life of Mary Russell Mitford: Told by Herself in Letters to Her Friends*, Vol. 2, ed. H. Chorley, New York: Harper.

——. (1859), *Recollections of a Literary Life . . . .*, London: Bentley.

——. (1880), *Children of the Village*, London: Routledge.

——. (1884), *Our Village: Country Pictures and Tales*, London: Blackwood.

——. (1893), *Our Village*, London: Macmillan.

——. (1909), *Sketches of English Life and Character*, Edinburgh: T. N. Foulis, 1909.

——. (1914), in E. Lee (ed), *Mary Russell Miford Correspondence with Charles Boner & John Ruskin*, London: Fisher Unwin.

——. (1928), *Sketches of English Life and Character*, London: John Lane, 1909.

——. (1986), *Our Village*, New York: Prentice.

——. (1987), *Our Village*, New York: Penguin.

Montagu, A. (1986), *Touching: The Human Significance of the Skin*, New York: Harper.

Moretti, F. (2005), *Graphs, Maps, Trees: Abstract Models for a Literary History*, London: Verso.
Morley, J. (1867a), 'Edmund Burke (Part I)', *Fortnightly Review* (February): pp. 129–45.
——. (1867b), 'Edmund Burke (Part II)', *Fortnightly Review* (March): pp. 303–18.
——. (1867c), 'Edmund Burke (Part III)', *Fortnightly Review* (April): pp. 420–35.
——. (1867d), 'Edmund Burke (Part IV)', *Fortnightly Review* (July): pp. 47–61.
——. (1867e), *Edmund Burke: A Historical Study*, London: Macmillan.
[Morley, J]. (1866a), 'Felix Holt, the Radical', *Saturday Review* (June): pp. 722–24.
Morley, J. (1866b), 'George Eliot's Novels', *Macmillan's Magazine* (August): pp. 272–79.
——. (1879), *Burke*, London: Macmillan.
——. (1907), *Studies in Literature*, London: Macmillan.
Morris, P. (2004), *Imagining Inclusive Society in Nineteenth-Century Novels: The Code of Sincerity in the Public Sphere*, Baltimore: Johns Hopkins University Press.
Morrison, K. A. (Forthcoming), 'Reimagining Society: Mill, Trollope, and the Expanding Electorate', in P. Gilbert (ed), *Nineteenth-Century Literature in Transition: The 1860s*, Cambridge: Cambridge University Press.
——. (2021a), '"Darling, Darling Little Flushie": Elizabeth Barrett Browning's Dog Love', in K. A. Morrison (ed), *Victorian Pets and Poetry*, London: Routledge, pp. 89–110.
——. (2021b), 'A "Less than Enthusiastic" Friendship: John Morley, George Eliot, and George Henry Lewes', *English* 70 (268): pp. 66–86.
——. (2018a), *Victorian Liberalism and Material Culture: Synergies of Thought and Place*, Edinburgh: Edinburgh University Press.
——. (2018b), *A Micro-History of Victorian Liberal Parenting: John Morley's 'Discreet Indifference'*, Cham: Palgrave.
——. (2015), 'Modulating Narrative Voice: Mary Russell Mitford's Sketches of Rural Character', *Women's Writing* 22 (4): pp. 505–24.
——. (2012), 'Mary Russell Mitford', in F. Burwick, N. M. Goslee, and D. Long Hoeveler (eds), *The Encyclopedia of Romantic Literature*, 3 vols., Malden, MA: Blackwell, pp. 865–69.
——. (2011), 'Cultural Embeddedness, Gendered Exclusions: The Symbolic Landscapes of Middlemarch', *Victorians Institute Journal* 39: pp. 317–35.

——. (2008a), 'Foregrounding Nationalism: Mary Russell Mitford's *Our Village* and the Effects of Publication Context', *European Romantic Review* 19 (3): pp. 275–87.

——. (2008b). '"The Mother Tongue of Our Imagination': George Eliot, Landscape-Shaped Subjectivity, and the Possibility of Social Inclusion', *Victorian Review: An Interdisciplinary Journal of Victorian Studies* 34 (1): pp. 83–100.

Nardo, A. K. (2003), *George Eliot's Dialogue with John Milton*, Columbia: University of Missouri Press.

Newton, K. M. (2005), 'Revisions of Scott, Austen, and Dickens in Daniel Deronda', *Dickens Studies Annual* 35: 241–66.

Nord, D. E. (2006), *Gypsies and the British Imagination, 1807–1930*, New York: Columbia University Press.

O'Gorman, F. (1984), 'Electoral Deference in 'Unreformed' England: 1760–1832', *The Journal of Modern History* 56 (3): pp. 391–429.

——. (1989), *Voters, Patrons, and Parties: The Unreformed Electoral System of Hanoverian England, 1734–1832*, Oxford: Clarendon Press.

Onslow, B. (2000), *Women of the Press in Nineteenth-Century Britain*, New York: St. Martin's.

Ousby, I. (1990), *The Englishman's England: Taste, Travel and the Rise of Tourism*, Cambridge: Cambridge University Press.

Parker, M. (2000), *Literary Magazines and British Romanticism*, Cambridge: Cambridge University Press.

Parkinson, S. (1888), *Scenes from 'George Eliot' Country*, Leeds: Richard Jackson.

Paris, B. J. (2003), *Rereading George Eliot: Changing Responses to Her Experiments in Life*, Albany: SUNY Press.

Parry, J. P. (1993), *The Rise and Fall of Liberal Government in Victorian Britain*, New Haven: Yale University Press.

Patten, R. L. (1978), *Charles Dickens and His Publishers*, Oxford: Oxford University Press.

——. (2006), 'Publishing in Parts' in J. Bowen and R. L. Patten, *Palgrave Advances in Charles Dickens Studies*, Houndmills: Palgrave, 2006, pp. 11–47.

——. (1996), 'When Is a Book Not a Book? *Oliver Twist* in Context', *Biblion: The Bulletin of the New York Public Library* 4 (2): pp. 35–62.

——. (2003), 'From House to Square to Street: Narrative Traversals', in H. Michie and R. R. Thomas, *Nineteenth-Century Geographies: The Transformation of Space from the Victorian Age to the American Century*, New Brunswick, N.J.: Rutgers University Press.

Paxton, N. L. (1991), *George Eliot and Herbert Spencer: Feminism, Evolutionism, and the Reconstruction of Gender*, Princeton: Princeton University Press.

Pearson, J. (1996), '"Books, My Greatest Joy": Constructing the Female Reader in *The Lady's Magazine*', *Women's Writing* 3 (1): pp. 3–15.

Pearson, R. (2000), *W. M. Thackeray and the Mediated Text: Writing for Periodicals in the Mid-Nineteenth Century*, Burlington, VT: Ashgate.

Peterson, L. H. (2009), *Becoming a Woman of Letters: Myths of Authorship and Facts of the Victorian Market*, Princeton, NJ: Princeton University Press.

Pinney, T. (1966), 'More Leaves from George Eliot's Notebook.' *The Huntington Library Quarterly* 29: pp. 353–76.

Platt, H. L. (2005), *Shock Cities: The Environmental Transformation and Reform of Manchester and Chicago*. Chicago: University of Chicago Press.

Plotz, J. (2008), *Portable Property: Victorian Culture on the Move*, Princeton: Princeton University Press.

———. (2018), *Semi-Detached: The Aesthetics of Virtual Experience since Dickens*, Princeton: Princeton University Press.

Porritt, E. (1903), *The Unreformed House of Commons. Vol. 1: England and Wales*, Cambridge: Cambridge University Press.

Prince, G. (1988), 'Introduction to the Study of the Narratee', in M. J. Hoffman and P. D. Murphy (eds), *Essentials of the Theory of Fiction*, Durham, NC: Duke University Press, pp. 213–33.

[Pringle, T.] (1823), 'Friendship's Offering, or the Annual Remembrancer; a Christmas Present, or a New Year's Gift, for 1824', *Lady's Magazine* 4 (November): pp. 655–56.

Ray, G. Norton (1976), *The Illustrator and the Book in England from 1790 to 1914*, New York: Dover.

Recchio, T. (2009), *Elizabeth Gaskell's Cranford: A Publishing History*, Farnham: Ashgate.

Redding, C. (1858), *Fifty Years' Recollections . . .*, vol. 2, London: Skeet.

Reedpen, P. [C. F. Adderley] (1834), *Our Town; or Rough Sketches of Characters, Manners, &c.* Vol. 1, London: Bentley.

Reeve, A. (1986), *Property*, Basingstoke, UK: Macmillan.

Rhys, E. (1891), 'Introduction', in M. R. Mitford, *Our Village*, London: Scott, pp. vii–xvii

Rignall, J. (2011), *George Eliot, European Novelist*, Farnham: Ashgate.

Ritchie, A. T. (1893), Introduction to M. R. Mitford, *Our Village*. London: Macmillan.

Roberts, W. J. (1904), '"Our Village": A Little Pilgrimage to Miss

Mitford's Country', *The Book Monthly*, edited by James Milne. (October 1903–September 1904): pp. 785–89. London: Simpkin et al.

Room, A. (1988), *Dictionary of Pseudonyms*, 3rd edition, Jefferson: McFarland.

Ruskin, J. (1885), *On the Old Road: A Collection of Miscellaneous Pamphlets* . . . , London: George Allen.

——. (1881), 'Fiction—Fair and Foul', *Nineteenth Century* 10 (October): pp. 941–62.

——. (1901), *Modern Painters III*, London: Allen.

——. (1905), *Lectures on Art and Aratra Pentelici* in E. T. Cook and A. Wedderburn, *The Works of John Ruskin*, vol. 20, London: Allen.

Russo, M. (1999), 'Aging and the Scandal of Anachronism', in K. Woodward, *Figuring Age: Women, Bodies, Generations*, Bloomington: Indiana University Press, pp. 20–33.

Saglia, D. (2000), *Poetic Castles in Spain*, Amsterdam: Rodopi.

Sanders, A. (1996), 'A Crisis of Liberalism in *North and South*', *Gaskell Journal* 10: 42–52.

Santesso, A. (2006), *A Careful Longing: The Poetics and Politics of Nostalgia*, Newark: University of Delaware Press.

Schaffer, T. (2011), *Novel Craft: Victorian Domestic Handicraft and Nineteenth-Century Fiction*, New York: Oxford University Press.

Schellenberg, B. A. (2005), *The Professionalization of Women Writers in Eighteenth-Century Britain*, Cambridge: Cambridge University Press.

Schor, H. M. (1992), *Scheherezade in the Marketplace: Elizabeth Gaskell and the Victorian Novel*, Oxford: Oxford University Press.

Scott-James, A. (1987), 'Introduction', in M. R. Mitford, *Our Village: Sketches of Rural Character and Scenery*, Harmondsworth: Penguin, pp. vii–xvi.

Semmel, B. (1994), *George Eliot and the Politics of National Inheritance*, New York: Oxford University Press.

Sha, R. C. (1998), *The Visual and Verbal Sketch in British Romanticism*. Philadelphia: University of Pennsylvania Press.

Siskin, C. (1998), *The Work of Writing: Literature and Social Change in Britain, 1700–1830*, Baltimore: Johns Hopkins University Press.

Staten, H. (2000), 'Is Middlemarch Ahistorical?', *PMLA* 115.5, pp. 991–1005.

Staves, S. (2006), *Literary History of Women's Writing in Britain, 1660–1789*. Cambridge: Cambridge University Press.

Seguin, L. G. (1888), *Illustration for Scenes and Characters from the Works of George Eliot, a Series of Illustrations by Eminent Artists*. London: Strahan.

Stephen, L. (1902), *George Eliot*, London: Macmillan.
Stone, L., and J. Stone (1986), *An Open Elite?*, New York: Oxford University Press.
Stubbs, W. (1880), *The Constitutional History of England: In Its Origin and Development*, vol. 3, Oxford: Clarendon Press.
Suarez, M. F. (2009), 'Introduction', in M. F. Suarez, S. J., and M. L. Turner, *The Cambridge History of the Book in Britain: Vol. V, 1695–1830*, Cambridge: Cambridge University Press, pp. 1–35
Talfourd, T. N. (1821), letter to Mary Russell Mitford, 27 December 1821. University of Manchester John Rylands Library, GB 133 Eng MSS 665–67.
Tattle, M. (1823), 'Paris Chit-Chat.' *Lady's Magazine* (January): pp. 13–15.
Thomas, D. W. (2004), *Cultivating Victorians: Liberal Culture and the Aesthetic*. Philadelphia: University of Pennsylvania Press.
Thomson, Mrs. A. T. (1833), *Constance: A Novel*, vol. 1, London: Bentley.
——. (1835), *Rosabel: A Novel*, vol. 1, London: Longman.
Uglow, J. (2010), *Elizabeth Gaskell: A Habit of Stories*, London: Faber and Faber.
——. (2004), 'Gaskell (née Stevenson, Elizabeth Cleghorn (1810–1865)', in H. C. G. Matthew and B. Harrison, *Oxford Dictionary of National Biography*, Oxford: Oxford University Press. 5 May 2020. https://www.oxforddnb.com/view/10.1093/ref:odnb/9780198614128.001.0001/odnb-9780198614128-e-10434
Verdon, N. (2009), 'Child Work in Agriculture in Britain', in H. D. Hindman (ed), *The World of Child Labor: An Historical and Regional Survey*, London: Sharpe, pp. 558–62.
Vernon, J. (1993), *Politics and the People: A Study in English Political Culture, c. 1815–1867*, Cambridge: Cambridge University Press.
Wainright, V. (1994), 'Discovering Autonomy and Authenticity in *North and South*: Elizabeth Gaskell, John Stuart Mill, and the Liberal Ethic', *Clio* 23 (2): 149–65.
Walsh, W. S. (1898), *Curiosities of Popular Customs...*, London: Lippincott.
Warhol, R. (2005), 'Neonarrative, or How to Render the Unnarratable in Realist Fiction and Contemporary Film', in J. Phelan and P. J. Rabinowitz, *A Companion to Narrative Theory*, Oxford: Blackwell Publishing, pp. 220–35.
——. (1989), *Gendered Interventions: Narrative Discourse in the Victorian Novel*, New Brunswick: Rutgers University Press.

——. (1986), 'Letters and Novels 'One Woman Wrote to Another': George Eliot's Responses to Elizabeth Gaskell', *Victorian Newsletter* 70: pp. 8–14.
Watson, V. (1949), *Mary Russell Mitford*, London, Evans Brothers.
Wharton, G. and P. [pseud.] (1860), *The Queens of Society*, New York: Harper.
Williams, R. (1966), *Culture and Society 1780–1950*, New York: Harper and Row.
——. (1970), *The English Novel from Dickens to Lawrence*, New York: Oxford University Press.
——. (1973), *The Country and the City*, New York: Oxford University Press.
Williams, W. S. (2014), *George Eliot, Poetess*, London: Routledge.
Witemeyer, H. (1979), *Landscape and the Beholder in George Eliot's Works*, New Haven: Yale University Press.
Wolfreys, J. (1994), *Being English: Narratives, Idioms, and Performances of National Identity from Coleridge to Trollope*, Albany: SUNY Press.
Woolf, V. (1929), *A Room of One's Own*, Orlando: Harvest.
——. (1933), *Flush: A Biography*, New York: Harcourt, Brace, and Company.
——. (1948), *The Common Reader*, London: The Hogarth Press.
——. (1984), in Michèle Barrett (ed), *Women and Writing*, Ontario: Quadrant.
Wright, P. (1986), *On Living in an Old Country*, New York: Verso.
Yeazell, R. B. (2008), *Art of the Everyday: Dutch Painting and the Realist Novel*. Princeton: Princeton University Press.

Index

Ackermann, Rudolph, *Forget Me Not*, 81, 102, 120n9
Allbutt, Clifford, 264
Ampère, Jean-Jacques, 163
Amulet; or Christian and Literary Remembrancer, 102, 104, 106, 120nn9,10
Anniversary, 120n9
anonymous publishing, 49, 68, 123
Arnold, Matthew, 25, 193–4, 212, 273
  Culture and Anarchy, 194
Austen, Jane, 54, 84, 85, 274
Avonbank School, 10, 148, 153; *see also* Barford House

Baillie, Joanna, 36, 147
Balzac, Honoré de, 276
Barford House, Warwickshire, 147; *see also* Avonbank School
Barrett, Browning, Elizabeth, 54, 112, 163
Baxter, George, 117, 235
Behn, Aphra, 35
Bentham, Jeremy, 226
  and one's emotional investment in property, 209
Bijou, 120
Bildungsroman (*The Mill on the Floss* as), 196, 206
Blackwood's Edinburgh Magazine, 150, 239

Blackwood's Magazine, 74n14, 123, 176, 216, 265
Blackwood, John, 176, 177–81, 194, 195, 238–40, 264–5
Blackwood, William, 139, 175, 177
Bodichon, Barbara, 240, 270n9
Bohn, Henry G., 32, 34, 126, 235–7
Boner, Charles, 191
Bright, John, 183
Brontë, Charlotte, 139, 149, 151, 168n18
Browne, Hablot, 29n7
Browning, Robert, 163
Burke, Edmund, 257, 258, 267
Burney, Frances (Fanny), 35, 274
Burton, Frederic, 275
Byerley, Frances (Fanny), 149
  Domestic Duties, or Instructions to Young Married Ladies, 147
Byerley, Katherine, 147, 148, 149
Byerley, Maria, 147, 149
Byron, George Gordon, Lord, 38

Cameo, 120n9
Campbell, Thomas, 41, 43, 44, 48
Captain Swing riots, 111, 118
chaplain of the British Embassy at Constantinople, 'Some Account of the Chaldaean Christians', 104
Chapman, John, 186–7
Christmas, 103, 239
Christmas books, 7

300

Index

Clare, John, 44
Cobbett, William, 37, 98
  Political Register, 37
Cobden, Richard, 186
Colburn, Henry, 42–3, 74n14
Coleridge, Hartley, 149, 151
Comic Offering, 120n9
Comte, Auguste, 266
Coote, John, 39
Cornhill Magazine, 223
Cowper, William, 54
Croker, John Wilson, 261
Cross, John Walter, 177
Cruikshank, George, 93, 29n7

D'Albert-Durade, François, 207
Darwin, Charles, 273
Darwin, Erasmus, 205
Davies, Emily, 270n10
Defoe, Daniel, 85
Derby administration, 120n11, 183
Dibdin, Thomas Frognall, 46
Dickens, Charles, 8, 9, 16, 29n7, 51, 132, 160
  and Gaskell, 123–4
  Household Words, 1, 51, 122, 123, 124, 128, 144, 150
  The Pickwick Papers, 158
  Sketches by Boz, 122, 166nn1,4
  'Sketches of London', 122
Dou, Gerard, 173
Du Maurier, George, 139
Dyce, Alexander, 39–40
  Specimens of British Poetesses, 39

Eagleton, Terry, 195, 224–5
Edgeworth, Maria, 35
Elford, William, 38, 43, 45, 46, 54, 56, 57, 60, 61, 62, 63, 64, 65, 67, 112, 113, 114
  encouraged by Mitford to market her work, 100
Eliot, George
  ambivalence about extending franchise, 190
  and feeling of citizenship as shaping imagination, thought, and action, 226
  and inclusive social formation of English provincial village, 175
  and publisher John Blackwood, 176, 177–81, 195, 238–40, 264–5
  as assistant editor of *Westminster Review*, 179, 186, 188
  awareness of longing for rural community, 15
  debt to *Cranford*, 143–6
  debt to Wordsworth, 221n13
  desire for rootedness of provincial life in her fiction, 231, 256, 268
  familiarity with Mill's works, 186–8, 224, 226, 268
  influenced by Arnold and Mill, 194
  influenced by Gaskell, 141–3
  knowledge of and admiration for Ruskin, 249, 255–6
  knowledge of Bohn's edition of *Our Village*, 126, 235–6
  landscape in her fiction, 231–2, 246–8, 249, 255–6, 258–9, 269
  liberalism of, 2, 15, 24, 25–6, 27, 195, 225, 273
  on universal manhood suffrage, 264–5
  posthumous illustrated extracts from her work, 22
  reads 1855 edition of *Cranford* in 1857, 139, 144, 165–6
  rejects 'antinational cosmopolitanism', 268
  uses Gaskell's narratorial technique, 236
Eliot, George, works by
  Adam Bede, 15, 28n1, 139, 140, 141, 142, 143, 179, 180, 181, 184, 194, 195, 196, 223, 275
  Daniel Deronda, 181, 215, 268, 275: concern with rootedness of, 230–1
  Felix Holt, the Radical, 193–4, 223–4, 264–6, 272–3
  'How I Came to Write Fiction', 144
  Impressions of Theophrastus Such, 219, 231

Eliot, George, works by (cont.)
    'Janet's Repentance', 139, 178, 179, 180, 181, 216
    Middlemarch: A Study of Provincial Life, 4, 15, 20, 27, 181, 215, 223–69, 271n14, 273, 275: and national identity, 260–1, 271n14; and *portable interiority*, 28, 226; book cover illustration of, 240; concern with rootedness in, 230–1, 268; gossip in, 254; 'home-scenes' in, 226, 227, 232, 247, 251, 256, 259, 269; iconic rural scene in, 246–7; impact of railways in, 228–9; indictment of reform culture of, 263; landscape in, 255–6, 258–9, 269; nostalgic attachments to idyllic countryside in, 234; publication schedule of, 238–9
    The Mill on the Floss, 15, 20, 27, 28, 171–3, 175, 181, 186, 194–220, 223, 226, 236, 246, 247, 250, 269, 275: as critique of possessive individualism, 196–7, 208, 211–12, 214, 219; critique of property in, 210–11; evolution towards world community in, 215; 'home-scenes' in, 203–7, 213; landscape-shaped subjectivity in, 207–8, 213, 214, 217, 219, 231–2; and national landscape, 217–18, 248; non-gendered model of psychosocial development of, 219; primary readership of, 218
    'Mr Gilfill's Love Story', 178, 216
    Romola, 181, 223, 265, 275
    'The Sad Fortunes of the Reverend Amos Barton', 28n1, 139, 176, 178, 179, 180, 216
    Scenes of a Clerical Life, 15, 20, 139, 141, 142, 143, 144, 166, 171, 179, 181, 195, 196, 215, 223, 231, 232, 249, 275: controversy over authorship of, 180, 194
    Silas Marner, 20, 28, 223, 275

'Silly Novels by Lady Novelists', 139–40, 176, 177
Evening Chronicle, 122
Examiner, 61

Finden's Tableaux, 120n9
Friendship's Offering, 81, 102, 110, 120n9
Ford, John, *The Lover's Melancholy*, 168n17
Forster, John, 51, 123
Forster, William E., 17, 163
Foster, Myles Birket, 240
Fortnightly Review, 266
Fox, James, 37
Fox, Tottie, 162
franchise, 27, 181–4, 185–6, 188–91, 194, 195, 223, 225, 226, 262, 264
    Mill's educational qualification for, 191–3
    see also suffrage
Froude, James Anthony, *The Nemesis of Faith*, 187

Gaskell, Elizabeth
    affinities with Mill, 169n26
    as inventor of 'engaging narration', 12
    awareness of longing for countryside of, 162
    evocation of nineteenth-century global trade and commerce in, 158–60
    knowledge of *Lady's Magazine*, 149
    liberalism of, 163, 185, 220n5
    Mitford as early model for, 148
Gaskell, Elizabeth, works by
    'Clopton Hall', 10, 153, 155–6, 161
    Cousin Phillis, 228
    Cranford: age of principal characters in, 127–35; and possibilities for individuality, 165; as modelled after *Lady's Magazine*, 150–2; as representative of Gaskell's Englishness, 23; debt to Mitford

of, 10–11, 13, 26–7, 124–5,
    161, 165; influence on Eliot of,
    143–6; thematic of death in, 158;
    unreliable narration in, 160–1
  The Life of Charlotte Brontë, 151,
    168n18, 169n25
  *Mary Barton: A Tale of Manchester
    Life*, 11, 12, 15, 123, 140,
    141–3, 144, 155, 169n22, 254
  North and South, 144, 159, 163
  'Our Society at Cranford', 124
  Ruth, 11, 12, 140–1, 143, 144, 166
  Wives and Daughters, 28, 168n20
Gaskell, Florence, 126
Gaskell, Julia, 126
Gaskell, William, 126, 162
Gem, 120
Genette, Gérard, 30, 73n2, 74n17,
    167n9
  and matalepsis, 11
  and paratexts, 50–1, 74n16, 131,
    167n9
  Figures of Literary Discourse, 30
  *Paratexts: Thresholds of
    Interpretation*, 50
Gentleman's Magazine, 150–1
George Routledge and Sons (Toy
    Books series), 18
  Children of the Village, 18
Gifford, William, 36, 73n6
Gladstone, William, 185
Guizot, François, 163

Hall, Samuel Carter, 104
Hamilton, Samuel, Jr, 47–8, 49, 50,
    63–5, 81
  financial improprieties of, 63–4
Harness, William, 83, 98, 102
Harrison, Henrietta, 114
Haydon, Benjamin Robert, 42, 57, 83
Hazlitt, William, 8, 43, 56–7, 58, 127
  Characters of Shakespeare's Plays,
    56
  *Lectures on the English Comic
    Writers*, 56
  Lectures on the English Poets, 56
  'On the Modern Poets', 56
  'Table Talk', 43, 57

Heath, Charles, 64–5, 68–9, 70 101
Hemans, Felicia, 39, 104, 147
Hennell, Sara Sophia, 196, 267
Hickson, W. E., 187
Holfland, Barbara, 101
Hooker, Richard, 245
Howitt, Mary, 154
Howitt's Journal, 123
Howitt, William, 154–5
  The Rural Life of England, 10, 146,
    154–5
  Visits to Remarkable Places, 10,
    153–4
Howitt, William and Mary, 153, 154
  The Book of the Seasons, 10, 146
  The Boy's Country Book, 10
  debt to Mitford's *Our Village*
    volumes, 154
  *Homes and Haunts of English
    Authors*, 10
  Sketches of Natural History, 10,
    146
  The Tear-Book of the Country, 10
Huskisson, William 228

illustrated books, 'boom in', 16–17
Illustrated London News, 240
Irving, Washington, 60
  Old Christmas, 17
  Sketch Book, 86

John Bull, 61
Johnson, Samuel, 151, 158, 160
Jones, William Pitman, 180

The Keepsake, 200–1
Kemble, Charles, 46, 61
Knutsford, Cheshire (Gaskell's
    village), 20, 127, 155, 162,
    169n24, 180

Lady's Magazine
  and Mitford's 'interactive
    convergences' with, 51, 58–9
  as model for *Cranford*, 150–2
  content of, 49
  domestic ideology of, 59
  frequent travel accounts in, 89, 152

Lady's Magazine (cont.)
   Mitford's reliable income from, 48
   merges with *Lady's Monthly Museum*, 149
   monthly circulation of, 149
   paratexts of, 50
   readership and cost of, 40–1
   selection of articles from, 82
   thematic of death in, 92
   see also Mitford, Mary Russell
Lady's Magazine and Museum of the Belles Lettres, etc., 73n11, 149
Lamb, Caroline, 35
Lamb, Charles, 8, 41, 57, 71, 105
   Specimens of English Dramatic Poets, 168n17
Landon, Letitia Elizabeth, 35, 104, 147
Landor, Walter Savage, influenced by Mitford, 8–9
Langford, Joseph Munt, 180
Leader, 249, 266
legislation
   Catholic Emancipation Bill, 158
   Catholic Relief Act (1829), 258
   Education Act (1870), 17
   enclosure acts, 93–4
   Reform Bill (1831), 258
   Reform Bill (1866), 185
   Reform Act (1832), 78, 113, 118, 181, 183, 214, 224, 261, 262, 263
   Reform Act (1867), 262, 264
Lennox, Charlotte, 35
Lewes, George Henry, 28n2, 139, 144, 168n13, 173, 176, 177–8, 180, 181, 223, 228, 249
   as admirer of Mill, 186
   friendship with John Morley, 266–7
   on Jane Austen, 85
   promotes *Middlemarch*, 239–40
liberalism (nineteenth-century), roots and characteristics of, 24–5
literary annuals, 7, 8, 16, 29n6, 31, 44, 76, 99, 100, 102–4, 111, 118, 201
   contents and topics of, 81, 103
   Mitford's publications in, 120n9

Literary Panorama, 35
Literary Souvenir, 120n9, 171
Locke, John, 182, 185, 196, 220n3
The London and Westminster Review, 188
London Literary Gazette, 61
London Magazine, 42, 57
Lumb, Hannah, 160, 162

MacCall, William, 163–4, 165
   The Elements of Individualism: A Series of Lectures, 163, 164
Machiavelli, Niccolò, 223
Macmillan
   Cranford series, 17, 22, 23
   English Men of Letters series, 171, 275
Macmillan's Magazine, 266
Macready, William Charles, 45–6, 61–2
Manley, Delarivier, 35
Martineau, Harriett, 8, 9, 10, 60, 139, 146, 153, 177, 187
   on Mitford's 'graphic description', 77
Maurice, F. D., 163
Maying (season of), 87–8, 124
Mill, Harriet Taylor, 169n25
Mill, James, 163
Mill, John Stuart
   complaint against Gaskell, 169n25
   critique of Bentham, 226–7
   critique of 1867 Reform Bill, 262–3
   educational rather than property qualification, 191–3
   ideas about liberal individuality of, 163, 189
   on contemporary pedagogical practices, 220n6
   on franchise: 189–90, 226
   on religious intolerance, 185
   sociopolitical views of, 185–6, 188–9, 262–3
Mill, John Stuart, works by
   Autobiography, 163
   'Civilization', 188
   Considerations on Representative

Index 305

Government, 194, 224, 225, 263, 268
Dissertations and Discussions, 186, 188
On Liberty, 163, 186, 188, 195, 221n8, 224, 266
Principles of Political Economy, 187–8
System of Logic, 187–8
'Thoughts on Parliamentary Reform', 186, 188, 195, 225, 283
Utilitarianism, 226
Milton, John, 106, 245
Mitford, George, 34, 35, 36, 38, 64–5
financial woes of, 41
Mitford, Mary Russell
admiration for Hazlitt, 56–7
admiration for Lamb, 57, 105
and the condition of agricultural labourers, 98
and literary annuals, 102–4, 120n9
and William Macready, 45–6, 61–2
as 'poetess', 39–40
as 'tour guide' for urbanites, 85–6
breaks with *Lady's Magazine*, 70, 101
country walks of, 76–9, 84–5
financial difficulties of, 65–6, 101–2
narrative voice of, 8, 33–4, 60, 71, 76
on Jane Austen and William Cowper, 54
political views of, 112–14
reflective nostalgia of, 89–99, 118
rhetorical style of, 53
Mitford, Mary Russell, works by
'Another – The Storm', 39
Atherton, and Other Tales, 181
'Beauty: An Ode', 39
Belford Regis, 181
'Blanch', 39, 40
'Boarding School Recollections. No. I. The French Teacher', 47
'Boarding School Recollections. No. II. My School Fellows', 47
'Boarding School Recollections. No. III. The English Teacher', 47
'Bramley Maying', 85, 86–8

'The Chalk-Pit (A True Story)', 104, 106–10
Charles I: An Historical Tragedy in Five Acts, 74n13, 116
Christina, the Maid of the South Seas, 38, 39, 40
'Claudia's Dream', 47
'A Country Cricket Match', 55
'Coursing', 39
'The Cowslip Ball', 152
Dramatic Works of Mary Russell Mitford, 38
'Ellen', 55, 85
'Field Flowers', 43
Fiesco, 45
Foscari, 46
Gaston de Blondeville, 74n13
'A Great Farm-House', 59–60, 71, 85, 90, 120n7, 237
'Hannah', 60, 64
'The Hermit', 39
'The Incendiary: A Country Tale', 110–11, 237
Inez de Castro, 74n13
Julian, 61–3, 64, 65, 67, 70, 148
'Love-Sick Maid', 39
'Lucy', 47, 52–3, 64, 71, 81, 84, 85, 110, 111, 157, 198, 254
Narrative Poems on the Female Character, 39
'A New Married Couple', 235
'On a Bust of Fox', 37
'On Maria's Winning the Cup', 37
'On the Comedies of Thomas May', 43
Otto of Wittlesbach, 74n13
'Our Village', 20, 43, 46–7, 55, 6–, 84–6, 111, 117
Our Village: as respectable morality, 17; criticised as too inclusive, 184–5; marketing of, 116–17; modelling mechanism of, 72; read by Gaskell, 125–7; thematic of death in, 157–8; volumes of as objects of display, 117
Our Village: Country Stories, Scenes and Characters, 8, 31, 181

Mitford, Mary Russell, works by (*cont.*)
  Our Village: Sketches of Rural Character and Scenery, 8, 19, 31, 119n2
  'A Parting Glance at Our Village', 111, 118
  Poems, 38, 40, 49, 50, 62, 70: reception of, 35–8
  'The Queen of the Meadow', 171–3
  Recollections of a Literary Life, 70, 149
  Rienzi, 74n13, 116
  Sadak and Kalasrade, 74n13
  sketches: as less restorative than reflective, 92; bound-volume formats of, 71, 111–12, 115, 117–18; cultural nationalism of, 78, 80; discursive play of, 54; genesis of, 43; illustrations of as invitations to restorative nostalgia, 118; influence on Eliot, 16; influence on Gaskell, 26–7, 124–5; marketing of, 17–19; nostalgia of and longing in, 19; origins of, 26, 31; paratextual reframing of, 71–2, 111, 116; publishing success of, 31–2; remuneration for, 43–4, 47–8, 83
  Sketches of English Character and Scenery, 19
  'Solitude', 39
  'The Talking Lady', 47, 57–9, 60, 71, 115
  'To G. L. Wardle, Esq. on the Death of His Child', 36
  'Tom Cordery', 85, 157
  'The Vicar's Maid: A Village Story', 104–5
  'Walks in the Country: The First Primrose', 85
  'Walks in the Country: Frost and Thaw', 85
  'Walks in the Country: Violeting', 18, 85, 93–8, 98, 237
  Watlington Hill, 39
  'Wheat-Hoeing', 235

Morley, John, 171, 223
  admiration for Mill, 266
  Edmund Burke: A Historical Study, 267
  friendship and affinities with Eliot and Lewes, 266–7

Napoleonic Wars, 83
narration
  engaging narration (Robyn R. Warhol), 12
  extradiegetic narrators, 215
  heterodiegetic narrators, 12, 155
  homodiegetic narrators, 12, 14, 144, 155–7
  metalepsis (Gérard Genette), 11
  the *paranarratable* (Robyn R. Warhol), 103
Newman, John Henry, 187
New Monthly Magazine, 31, 42, 43, 44
Nuneaton, Warwickshire (Eliot's village), 20

'On the Folly and Wickedness of Having a Long Nose' (anonymous), 92
Opie, Amelia, 81

Palmer, Charles Fyshe, 114
'Paris Chit-Chat' (anonymous), 55
Parkes, Bessie Rayner, 177
Parkes, William, 147
Pascal, Blaise, 245
Peel, Robert, 120n11
periodicals and the periodical market, and opportunities for women writers, 7, 41–2, 49
Phelps, Elizabeth Stuart, 118
Pledge of Friendship, 120n9
Poetical Register, 39
political parties
  Conservatives, 120n11, 183, 184, 185
  Liberals, 120n11, 163, 183, 184, 185
  Radicals, 36, 37, 62, 112, 113, 114, 120n11, 185, 186, 191, 267

Tories, 38, 112, 114, 120, 224, 261, 264
Whigs, 36, 62, 112–13, 114, 121, 185, 267
Political Register, 37, 98
Portico Library (Manchester), 125
Pringle, Thomas, 81, 82, 83
  Friendship's Offering, 81
provincial fiction, 3–4
  and earnestly engaged narrators, 24
  as aligned to women's writing, 6
  as a means to imagine the nation, 5
  eludes geographic knowability, 5
  voice as intrinsic element of, 26
Punch, 240

Quarterly Review, 35, 36, 37, 39, 50, 53, 62, 68, 114, 115

Redding, Cyrus, 44, 48, 102
religion
  Catholicism, 158, 167, 187, 233, 245, 250, 258
  Protestantism, 233, 249, 250
Remembrance, 120n9
restorative nostalgia, 1, 15, 23, 92, 97, 118, 161, 162, 273
Reynolds, G. W. M., 166
  Reynolds' Miscellany, 166n2
Richardson, Samuel, 56
Richmond, George, 135
Riehl, Wilhelm, 215
  'The Natural History of German Life', 237
Ritchie, Ann Thackeray, 16, 98, 131, 161
Roberts, W. J., 161
Robinson and Roberts, 49
Rogers, Samuel, 41
Rowden, Frances, 35, 45
Ruskin, John, 100, 146, 202, 255
  harshly critiques *The Mill on the Floss*, 202, 270n7
  Lectures on Architecture and Painting, 249
  Modern Painters, 249, 256
  on the enjoyment of landscape, 248–9
Russell, John, 186, 258

Saint Theresa, 250–1
Savonarola, Girolamo, 223
Scott, Sir Walter, 41
serialised novels in the Victorian period, 30–1
Shelley, Percy Bysshe, 257–8, 267, 270n9
Sheridan, Richard Brinsley, 112
Sherwood, Mary Martha, 'What is the World', 104
Simon, Jules, 163
sketch writing (nineteenth century), 9–10, 31
  as stylistically distinctive, 33
Smith, George, 265
Smith, Horace, 43
Simpson, George, 239
Spencer, Herbert, 273
Statesman, 113
Stephen, Leslie, 275
  George Eliot, 171
Stevenson, Elizabeth, 162
Stevenson, John, 126
Stevenson, William, 147, 163
suffrage, 114, 186, 190, 191, 220n3, 262–3, 264, 273; *see also* franchise

Talfourd, Thomas Noon, 44, 54, 63, 64, 66, 69, 70, 99, 101, 102, 114
  negotiates on behalf of Mitford, 42–3, 45–7
Taylor, Clementia, 224, 263
Teniers, David, 172, 173, 202
Thackeray, William, 16
Thelwall, John, 101–2
  Panoramic Miscellany, 101
Thomson, Anthony Todd, 147
Thomson, Katherine, 148
  Constance: A Novel, 148
  The Queens of Society, 148
  Rosabel, 149
Thomson, Hugh, 17, 96, 112, 131, 138, 161, 168n12

Thomson, Hugh (*cont.*)
  and comic deprecation of illustrations to *Cranford*, 131–6
  and notions of racial otherness in illustrations to *Cranford*, 136
  and 'process line block' reproduction, 20, 29n9
  shapes *Cranford* into a chronicle of racial characteristics, 137–8
Three Mile Cross, Berkshire (Mitford's village), 4, 20, 31, 35, 41, 43, 57, 71, 83, 116, 180
  portrayed as 'exotic' or foreign location, 89
Tobin, John, 45
  The Honey Moon, 45, 74n12
Trollope, Anthony, 221n9, 224
Trollope, Frances, 8

Valpy, Abraham John, 35, 38, 46, 120n7
  Museum, 46, 120n7
Valpy, Richard, 35
'The Village Bells' (anonymous), 89, 90, 91, 92, 93, 98

Walker, C. E., *Wallace*, 45
Wardle, Gwyllym Lloyd, 36
Ward, Lock and Company (Lily Series), 17–18

Wedgwood, Josiah, 147
Westminster Review, 163, 169nn24,25, 176, 179, 186, 190, 195, 226, 237, 249
  'Contemporary Literature' (omnibus review), 188
  contributors to, 187
Wheble, John, 39
White, Gilbert, 84, 85, 119n6
  The Natural History and Antiquities of Selbourne, 85
Whittaker, George B., 16, 31–2, 67, 101, 115, 117, 118, 121n12, 235
  markets collected volumes of *Our Village*, 115–17
  organises Mitford's sketches for publication, 66
William Blackwood and Sons (Education Series), *Our Village: Country Pictures and Tales*, 18
Williams, Raymond, 265, 267–8, 272
Winter's Wreath, 120n9
Woolf, Virginia
  The Common Reader, 275
  Flush, 274
  on *Cranford*, 274
  on *Middlemarch*, 275–6
  A Room of One's Own, 274
Wordsworth, William, 107, 204, 221n13